ting Parlor. For The Right Hon.ble The Earl of Bective.

Adelphi Dec.r 2.d 1775.

The Irish Georgian Society

A CELEBRATION

The Irish Georgian Society wishes to acknowledge a great debt of gratitude to Marion Cashman for overseeing and coordinating the production of this volume.

Copyright © The Irish Georgian Society
Published by the Irish Georgian Society, 2008.
Irish Georgian Society
74 Merrion Square, Dublin 2, Ireland.

Edited by The Lilliput Press
Designed and produced by Anne Brady
and Kevin Dunne at Vermillion, Dublin
www.vermilliondesign.com
Printed by Nicholson & Bass, Belfast

ISBN 978-0-9545691-2-9

All rights reserved. No part of this publication may be reproduced, stored in a retrieval system or transmitted in any form or by any means electronic, photocopying, recording or otherwise without prior written permission from the publisher.

Images on endpapers:

Robert Adam's original drawings, now part of the Paul Mellon Collection at the Yale Center for British Art.

Inside front cover: Headfort, Kells, Co. Meath, the Eating Parlour – section showing elevation of chimney wall.

Inside back cover: Headfort, Kells, Co. Meath, the Eating Parlour – section showing ceiling plan.

Images on the following pages:

Left page: Leixlip Castle, Co. Kildare, the library.

Right page: Dedication surround: design taken from a map by John Senex, 1720.

Following left page: Castletown, Co. Kildare, the Wonderful Barn.

MADE IN IRELAND

Photographic Credits

The Hon. Desmond Guinness, whose albums over a fifty-year period have been the source of most of the photographs in the book.
Alessandro Albrizzi
Alfred Beit Foundation
Don Allen
Tim Beddow
Anne Brady
Butler Family Foundation
Donough Cahill
Carter, Birr, Co. Offaly
Marion Cashman
Cork Examiner
Country Life
David Davison
Department of Environment, Heritage and Local Government
Stephen Farrell
Desmond FitzGerald, the Knight of Glin
Gandon Press
Getty Images, Slim Aarons
David Griffin
Mariga Guinness
Marina Guinness
Garry Heatherly
Emmeline Henderson
Holiday Magazine, Slim Aarons
Horst P. Horst, Art + Commerce
Hugh Doran collection, Irish Architectural Archive
The Illustrated London News
The Interior Archive Ltd
Irish Architectural Archive
Irish Georgian Society
The Irish Press
The Irish Times
Fionn McCann
Christopher Moore
Jacqueline O'Brien
Office of Public Works
John Redmill
William Ryan
Nick Sheaff
Christopher Simon Sykes
David Synnott
The Sunday Express
Sunday Independent
Nicholas Thompson

The Irish Georgian Society

A CELEBRATION

W.V.09

*To Dennis,
with best wishes,
Robert O'Byrne*

ROBERT O'BYRNE

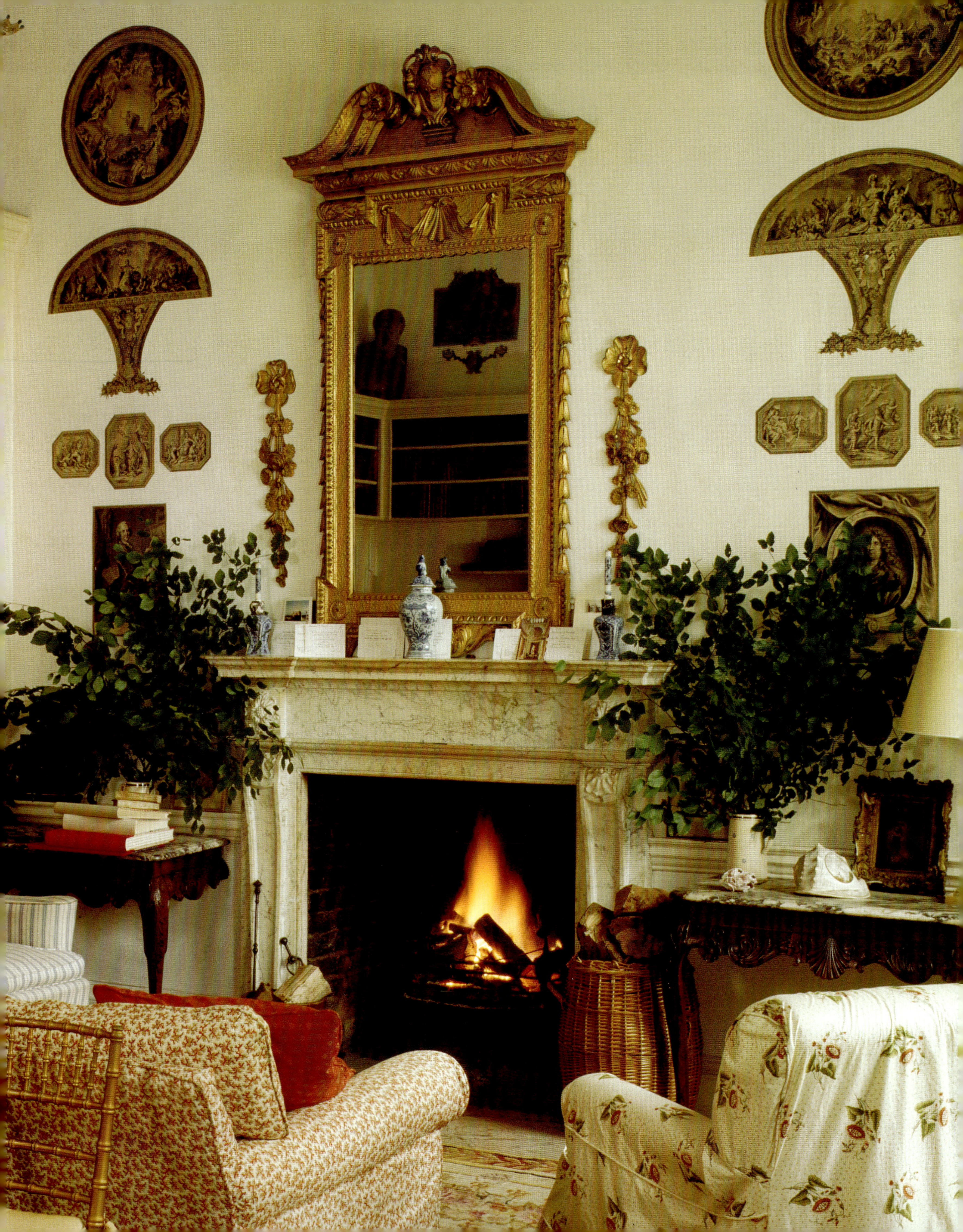

For Desmond Guinness
and his late wife, Mariga,
who founded the Irish Georgian
Society in 1958.

And for all the members,
volunteers and patrons
who supported the Society
over the last fifty years.

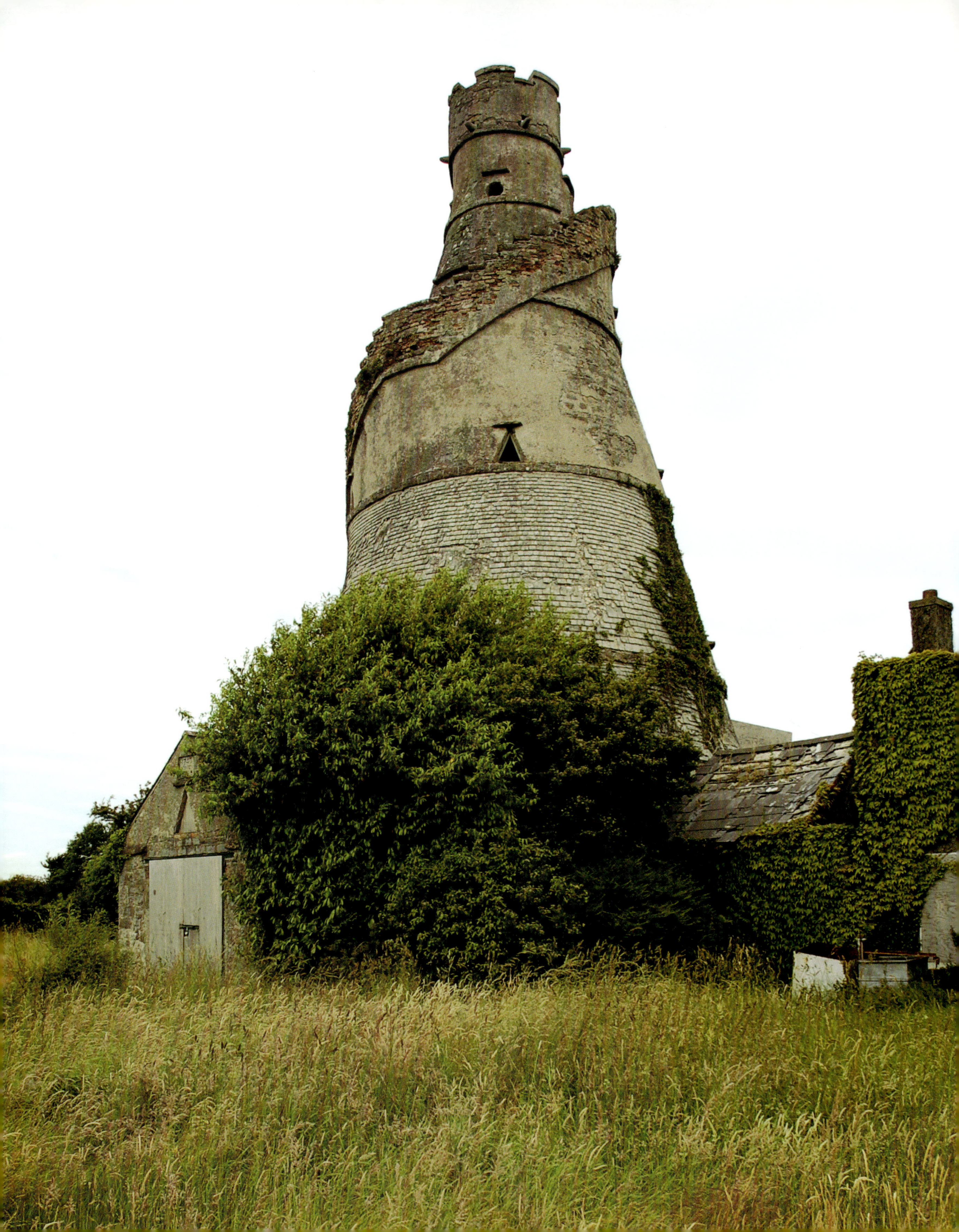

CONTENTS

Patrons	X
Sponsors	XII
Foreword *by Mary McAleese, President of Ireland*	XVI
Author's Note and Acknowledgments	XVIII

Chapter 1 Introduction — arrival of Desmond and Mariga Guinness in Ireland — conditions in the country in the 1950s — lack of interest in architectural conservation — the origins of the Irish Georgian Society
Panels: early members, Liam Miller and the Dolmen Press — 2

2 Desmond and Mariga Guinness at Leixlip Castle — early days of the Irish Georgian Society — original members and activities — the *Bulletin* — touring at home and abroad — the Georgian cricket matches
Panels: overseas tours and Georgian cricket — 16

3 The Society begins active conservation work — saving the Conolly Folly — Dromana Gateway and Fiddown Chapel — the first volunteer workers — Riverstown House
Panels: the Conolly Folly and Riverstown House — 34

4 Georgian Dublin at risk — public indifference or hostility towards eighteenth-century architecture — the fight to save Lower Fitzwilliam Street — the Tailors' Hall — St Catherine's Church
Panels: the Tailors' Hall and the kindness of donors — 46

5 Challenges faced by country house owners — Castletown is sold to speculators — Castletown is bought by Desmond Guinness — the house is restored and opened to the public — the establishment of HITHA — Festival of Music in Great Irish Houses
Panels: Castletown House and the Castletown Balls — 62

Chapter	6	Rampant destruction of Georgian Dublin ∽ the Hume Street debacle ∽ Molesworth Street redeveloped ∽ Mountjoy Square ∽ the fight to preserve the square ∽ opposition to the Society and its work *Panels: Henrietta Street and Mountjoy Square*	84
	7	The Society's work around the country ∽ Skiddy's Almshouses in Cork ∽ Robertstown and its Festa ∽ Longfield ∽ Roundwood ∽ Brian Molloy ∽ Damer House *Panels: volunteers and Brian Molloy*	104
	8	Desmond Guinness starts travelling to the United States ∽ Joseph Ryle and the Irish Georgian Society Inc. ∽ early American Chapters ∽ ongoing American support ∽ the Society's indebtedness to the United States ∽ Irish regional Chapters ∽ the London Chapter ∽ its vigorous programme of activity and fund-raising ∽ *Panels: the Birr, Limerick and Cork Chapters*	120
	9	Ongoing problems for Irish country houses ∽ the threat to their survival ∽ houses sold and contents lost ∽ Doneraile Court and its restoration ∽ Ledwithstown ∽ the Swiss Cottage *Panels: the St Legers of Doneraile and the Swiss Cottage, Cahir*	146
	10	Renewal as the Society marks its quarter-century ∽ grants to restoration projects throughout the country ∽ gains and losses ∽ Strokestown ∽ Frescati House ∽ Drogheda Grammar School *Panels: Mariga Guinness and the Thatched Cottage, Freshford*	162
	11	Heritage Council established ∽ Knight of Glin becomes Society's president ∽ *Vanishing Country Houses of Ireland* ∽ *The Irish Country House* film ∽ seminars on Irish art and architecture *Panels: scholars and scholarships and more tours*	174

Chapter	12	Urban redevelopment and its drawbacks — the Society's conferences on urban conservation — Traditional Building Skills exhibitions — National Gallery of Ireland and George's Quay: two vulnerable sites — the Society marks its fortieth anniversary *Panels:* Irish Architectural and Decorative Studies *and* 20 *Lower Dominick Street*	188
	13	The 2000 Planning and Development Act — Ireland's economic boom: the advantages and disadvantages to architectural heritage — the Society begins monitoring planning applications — further grants and support — the Irish Heritage Trust *Panels: Headfort and the* YIGs	204
	14	Changes in Ireland over the past fifty years — what has been achieved, saved and learnt — what remains to be done — the Society in the next fifty years — work still to be done	220

Select Bibliography 232

Appendices
    I. Irish Georgian Society Board, Chapters, Committees and Staff 234

    II. Funding of Heritage and Conservation Activities 235

Index 239

PATRONS

James Adam and Sons

Lady Ashtown

Galen and Tess Bales

Rory and Siobhan Brady

Gerard and Fidelma Browne

William and Laura Burlington

Marion Cashman and Adrian Masterson

Edward Lee Cave

John Coote

Cork Chapter of the Irish Georgian Society

Edmund Corrigan

Anne Crookshank

Dallas Chapter of the Irish Georgian Society

Sir David Davies

Lady Davis-Goff

Polly Devlin Garnett

Marie Donnelly

The Dowager Duchess of Devonshire

Electricity Supply Board

Desmond FitzGerald, Knight of Glin

Paula Fogarty and Craig Tiggleman

Samuel H. and Carol McGroarty Frazier

Sheila O'Malley Fuchs and Joseph Fuchs

J. Paul Getty Charity Trust

Hon. Desmond Guinness

Mr and Mrs Robert C. Guinness

Hon. Rory Guinness

Timothy Gwyn-Jones

Judith P. Hadlock

May Hannon

William B. Hart

Noel Heavey

Patrick Horsbrugh

Miranda, Countess of Iveagh

Michael and Pepper Jackson

Paul and Chris Johnston

Lawrence Kent-Sweeney

Liz King and Paul Farrell

John Kirkpatrick

Fred and Kay Krehbiel

Jacquelynne P. Lanham

Lauchentilly Charitable Foundation

Anne Madden le Brocquy

Louis le Brocquy

Samantha Leslie

Annette Lester

Henry S. Lynn

Dermot and Camilla McAleese

Johnnie McCoy

Paul McGuinness

Margaret McGuire

Marcus and Michelle McQuiston

Mr and Mrs J.R. Martin Jr

Esmé Mitchell Trust

Christopher Moore

Pat Murray

Martin and Carmel Naughton

Michael Neagle

Kevin B. Nowlan

Consuelo O'Connor

Nigel O'Flaherty

Cormac and Moira O'Malley

Rose Marie O'Neill

Chantal O'Sullivan

Thomas and Valerie Pakenham

Donald Perry

John J. and Mary Agnes Quinn

Cav. John Redmill and Desmond Barry

John and Sonia Rogers

John Ronan

Dr and Mrs Stephen W.J. Seager

Candida N. Smith and Carroll J. Cavanagh

Diarmuid Teevan

Tom and Anne Tormey

David Treacy

Maribeth and Ellen Welsh

SPONSORS

The Duke of Abercorn
Tom and Mary Alexander
The Aliaga-Kelly Family
Darina Allen
Myrtle Allen
Nöel and Caroline Annesley
Bruce Arnold
Daphne Bailey
Ballymore Properties
Viscount and Viscountess Bangor
Beltrim Charitable Trust
Viscountess Boyd
Sarah Bradford
Michael and Isabel Briggs
Sir Francis Brooke
Mary Bryan
John Bryson
Daniel Caffrey
Oliver Caffrey

Daniel Calley
John Cantwell
Charles and Eithne Carroll
Henry Channon
Hugh Charlton
Harold Clarke
Mr and Mrs Marcus Clements
Edward Clive
Alec Cobbe
Alfred Cochrane
Sir Marc Cochrane
Patricia Coleman
Dolores Collins
Ann Corcoran
Sandra Coughlan
John Cowdy
Brian Coyle
Rose Mary Craig
Noel and Deirdre Cromer

SPONSORS

H. Beck Crothers II

Cecily Cunningham

Ambassador and Mrs Walter J. Curley

Grattan de Courcy-Wheeler

Richard Deeble

Curt DiCamillo

Simon Dickinson

Val and Helen Dillon

Anne Dillon Carrigan

Martin Drury

The Marchioness of Dufferin and Ava

Mairead Dunlevy

Viscount Dunluce

The Earl of Dunraven

June Eiffe

Liam Farrell

Barbara FitzGerald

Pauline Fitzpatrick

Wilhelm Franke

Michael Frayne

Geraldine Gahan

Sean Galvin

The Georgian Group

Viscount Gormanston

The Earl of Gowrie

Anita Green

David Griffin

Hon. Erskine and Louise Guinness

Hon. Finn and Mary Guinness

Hon. Jasper and Camilla Guinness

Hon. Kieran Guinness

Penelope Guinness and Teresa Cuthbertson

Hon. Sebastian and Peggy Guinness

Tony Hand

Mr and Mrs E. Harris

J. Healy and Dr R. Manning

Carmencita Hederman

Tom and Mirabel Helme

SPONSORS

Emmeline Henderson

Catherine Hesketh

Kelland Homes

Éamonn and Anne Hurley

Colette Jordan

Lawrence and Linda Kelly

Michael Keohan

David Ker

Lady Rose Lauritzen

Richard John Leonard

Rolf Loeber

Charles Lysaght

James P. McDonnell

Harry McDowell

Ivor McElveen

Revd Thomas McGlynn

R.T. McHenry

Andrew and Orla McKeon

Dr Edward McParland

David Maher and the Hon. Sarah Lawson-Maher

Dr A. Marcus

Markland Holdings Ltd

Elizabeth Mayes

Hugo and Elaine Merry

David and Martha Mlinaric

N.J. Molloy

William Montgomery

Cynthia B. Moran

John and Alexandra Morley

Adrian Moroney

Lord Moyne

Elizabeth Murphy

Kate Nagle

Henry Nelson

Damian O'Brien

Maeve O'Connor

Revd Sean O'Doherty

James O'Donoghue

Colm and Janet O'Reilly

Mafra O'Reilly

Andrew and Delyth Parkes

Sally Phipps

Letitia Pollard

Aileen Power

Sean Rafferty

Peter Rankin

Brian Redmond

Ann Reihill

John P. Reihill

Dermot Rice

Nicholas Robinson

The Earl of Rosse

Lord Rossmore

Olga Rowe

Gordon St George Mark

Allen Sanginas-Krause

Nicholas Sheaff

Desiree Shortt

George Stacpoole

June Stuart

Glascott and Adrienne Symes

David Synnott

Eleanor Ticher

Dyanne Connelly Tosi

Hugh Weir

Brian White

Martin Williams and Gillian Darby

David Willis

Primrose Wilson CBE

Mr and Mrs George F. Wintersteen

Michael Wood

Richard Wood

Princess Josephine zu Löwenstein

FOREWORD

It is with great pleasure that I congratulate the Irish Georgian Society on the fiftieth anniversary of its establishment. Ireland's heritage of art and architecture is justly famed throughout the world; though small in size, our island is blessed by the many fine edifices erected by our forebears. Among our principal glories are the many eighteenth-century houses and public buildings found throughout the country. The vision of the Hon. Desmond Guinness and his late first wife Mariga in founding an organization to celebrate this unique cultural legacy is commendable.

At the time of the Society's establishment, in the straitened 1950s, Ireland lacked both today's resources and more widespread appreciation of eighteenth-century architecture. Thanks to the Irish Georgian Society's pioneering work, and history's onward march, attitudes have changed and we have grown proud of our architectural heritage, represented in buildings such as Castletown House, County Kildare, each one a showcase of Irish craftsmanship at its best. These buildings are also important tourist attractions and the Society has done much useful work in developing this aspect of our tourism industry. Visitors to Ireland reap the benefits of fifty years of committed work by the Society, preserving and restoring distinguished monuments from the past including Damer House in Roscrea, Roundwood in County Laois and the Tailors' Hall in central Dublin.

None of the Society's work in saving these and many other buildings could have taken place without the support of its members. Ireland has a long and honourable tradition of voluntary help in the community and the Irish Georgian Society's endeavours owe a great deal to the time and labour invested by successive generations of its members since 1958. It is heartening to find that the spirit of volunteerism that gave birth to the Society fifty years ago continues to flourish today.

Help received from overseas benefactors has been highly fundamental to ensuring the Society's success. For a long time Ireland could provide the manpower but not the funds needed to help the Society's work. Thanks to the outstanding generosity of donors from Britain and especially the United States, the Society was able to undertake many large-scale projects, which would otherwise have been beyond its means. Aid from the Society's United States membership remains enormously important. Their generosity is immortalized in the heritage they have helped to preserve. We are indebted to them all.

Over five decades, the Irish Georgian Society has provided a fine example of the extraordinary lasting effect that a small but committed organization can have. I am delighted to salute its work, and hope that it will long continue to flourish, and with it, Ireland's beautiful Georgian heritage.

Mary McAleese
UACHTARÁN NA HÉIREANN *President of Ireland*
21 May 2008

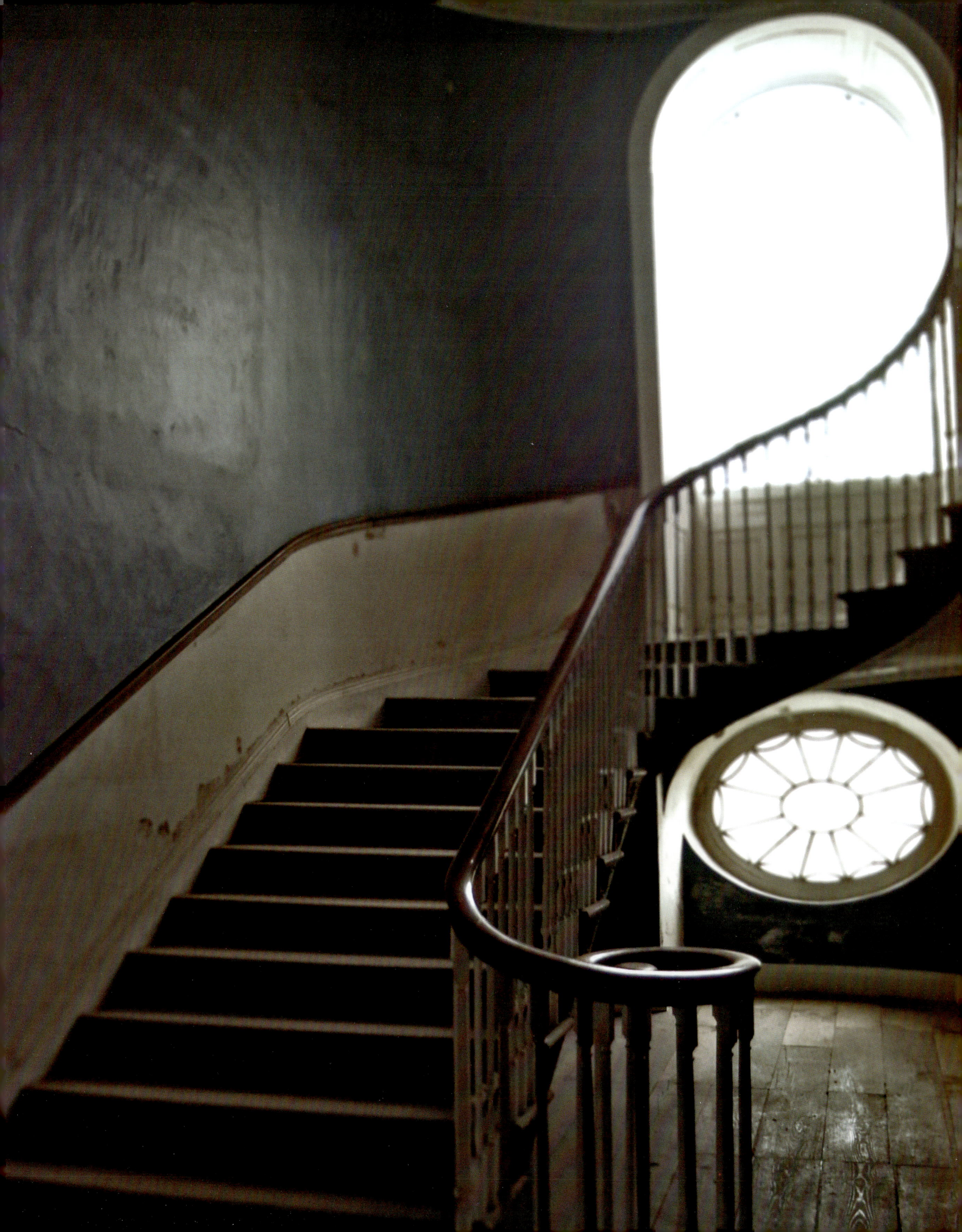

AUTHOR'S NOTE

This book could have been twice its present length. Indeed, it might now be so had not Marion Cashman (who deserves credit for overseeing the whole venture) insisted that everyone involved stick to previously agreed deadlines. This meant limits had to be set with regard to the amount of material consulted and included. As it is, the finished work runs to at least a third longer than was originally planned; even allowing for restrictions of time and space, there was just so much to say.

Nevertheless as author I'm conscious of how much had to be left out. For example, an entire book could – and perhaps one day will – be written about the Irish Georgian Society's happy relationship with its American supporters. Likewise the London Chapter's contribution deserves more space than it has perforce received. In fact, the same point could be made about almost every project in which the Society has been involved over the past fifty years, as well as every group and individual who has offered support and help over the same period. A voluntary organization such as this one is heavily reliant upon its members, all of whom have in one way or another ensured that the present anniversary could be reached. Many of those members have been mentioned in the text but probably not as many as ought to be the case. However, omission should not be taken to indicate lack of appreciation; anybody involved with the Society in whatever capacity has been important to its history and deserves its gratitude. All being well, in a further fifty years another history of the Irish Georgian Society can be written to celebrate its centenary and then some of this book's omissions will be made good.

In the meantime, my sincere apologies for any untoward absences; these were certainly not intentional. And many thanks to those who provided assistance and support during the present work's research and writing.

Previous page: Doneraile Court, Co. Cork, staircase.
Opposite: Letter of 22 July 1957, from the Hon. Desmond Guinness, *The Irish Times*, 23 July 1957.

AUTHOR'S ACKNOWLEDGMENTS

I should particularly like to thank the following: all the staff of the Irish Georgian Society (Donough Cahill, Emmeline Henderson, Aoife Kavanagh, Doreen McNamara, Marjorie Malcolm); Charles Aliaga-Kelly; Arthur Bassett; Fiona Bourke; Mary Bryan; John and Rose Bryson; Kevin Byrne; Michael and Aileen Casey; Marion Cashman; Carroll Cavanagh; Julian Charlton; Alfred Cochrane; Dr Maurice Craig; Rose Mary Craig; Professor Anne Crookshank; Amanda Douglas; the staff of Dublin City Library and Archive; Audrey Emerson; Laurence and Mary Feeney; Dr Jane Fenlon; Desmond FitzGerald, the Knight of Glin; David Fleming; Paula Fogarty; Carol McGroarty Frazier; David Griffin and the staff of the Irish Architectural Archive; Penelope Guinness; Kevin Hurley; Robert Jennings; John Joyce; Fred Krehbiel; William Laffan; Ursula Lee; Ian Lumley; Matt McNulty; Dr Edward McParland; Marjorie Malcolm; Gordon St George Mark; John Molloy; Arthur Montgomery; Christopher Moore; Professor Kevin B. Nowlan; Damian O'Brien; Cormac O'Carroll; John O'Connell; Brian and Consuelo O'Connor; Elizabeth O'Kelly; Cormac and Moira O'Malley; Carina O'Neill; Rose Marie O'Neill; Thomas and Valerie Pakenham; Ronald Porter; Arthur Prager; John Redmill; George Stacpoole; David Synnott; Nicholas Thompson; Peter Verity; Maribeth Welsh; Jeremy Williams; Richard Wood; and above all the Hon. Desmond Guinness.

Robert O'Byrne, 2008

GEORGIAN DUBLIN

Sir,—As the Georgian Society seems to have lapsed, has anyone any objection to my restarting it? Our aims are to bring the photographic records up to date, publish further volumes of the Georgian Society's books, and fight for the preservation of what is left of Georgian architecture in Ireland.—Yours, etc.,

DESMOND GUINNESS

Carton, Maynooth,
Co. Kildare. July 22nd, 1957.

Introduction ~ arrival of Desmond and Mariga Guinness in Ireland ~ conditions in the country in the 1950s ~ lack of interest in architectural conservation ~ the origins of the Irish Georgian Society ~ Panels: early members, Liam Miller and the Dolmen Press

CHAPTER

1

Sir, – As the Georgian Society seems to have lapsed, has anyone any objection to my restarting it? Our aims are to bring the photographic records up to date, publish further volumes of the Georgian Society's books, and fight for the preservation of what is left of Georgian architecture in Ireland.

Yours, etc.
Desmond Guinness,
Carton, Maynooth, Co. Kildare.

This polite enquiry appeared in *The Irish Times* on 23 July 1957. Presumably nobody raised any objections to the proposal because six months later, on the afternoon of 26 February 1958 more than 100 people accepted an invitation to tea at Carton, County Kildare, then home to the Hon. Desmond Guinness and his wife Mariga. The couple used the occasion to make an announcement: they now intended to re-establish the Irish Georgian Society. According to a brief report carried in the following day's *Irish Press*, the new organization's function would be

> to awaken an interest in Ireland's heritage of Georgian architecture; to investigate reports of Georgian buildings in danger of demolition or decay and, where necessary, to campaign for their preservation; to arrange expeditions to buildings of interest; and to continue the work of the old Georgian Society in recording Georgian architectural features and later publish a book listing houses as yet unknown to the public.

CHAPTER I

Hon. Desmond Guinness and his wife Mariga at Luttrellstown Castle, Co. Dublin, 1964.

All these tasks, and many more besides, have been undertaken by the Irish Georgian Society over the past fifty years.

There was no reason why the Guinnesses, private individuals married just a few years and with two young children, should have taken on the role of guardians of Ireland's Georgian heritage. Born in London in September 1931, Desmond Guinness was the son of Bryan Guinness, later second Lord Moyne, and the Hon. Diana Mitford. It was while studying at Oxford that he met his future wife. A year younger than her husband, Hermione Marie-Gabrielle von Urach – universally known as Mariga – had also been born in London, the daughter of a Scottish mother and a German father, Prince Albrecht von Urach, a member of a junior branch of the royal house of Wurttemberg. Desmond and Mariga were married in June 1954 and initially lived near Cirencester so that he could study agriculture at the college. 'I determined to be a farmer because I didn't want to go into an office,' he says, although in a 1971 interview with *The Daily Telegraph* he admitted, 'somehow milking cows doesn't thrill me the way it thrills some people'.

Nevertheless, having finished his time at Cirencester, he and Mariga decided to move to Ireland in search of a house and farm. Prior to their marriage, she had only visited Ireland once, spending a week in County Cork with the family of future historian Mark Bence-Jones and arriving still clad in the dress she had worn to a ball in London the previous night. She then stayed with Desmond for Horse Show week. He, on

CHAPTER I

Carton demesne, Co. Kildare.

the other hand, was familiar with Ireland where his ancestor Arthur Guinness had established a highly lucrative brewery in the eighteenth century. With his father Bryan he had spent many holidays at Knockmaroon, the family home just beyond Dublin's Phoenix Park. Meanwhile, after the end of the Second World War his mother and her second husband, Sir Oswald Mosley, lived first at Clonfert Palace in County Galway and, after this was badly damaged by fire in 1954, at Ileclash, County Cork.

It was, therefore, quite understandable that Desmond and Mariga Guinness should think of settling in Ireland, especially since both land and houses were so cheap at the time. The 1950s was a spectacularly bad decade for the Irish state, which had achieved independence from Great Britain barely thirty years earlier. Lack of employment opportunities meant that, between 1951 and 1961, some 400,000 Irishmen and women were forced to emigrate from their native country; in 1957, the year before the Irish Georgian Society was founded, 54,000 citizens left Ireland and another 78,000 were registered as unemployed. Both these figures established regrettable records, as did the statistic that four out of every five children born in the 1930s would emigrate in the 1950s. By the close of the decade, Ireland was the only country in the western world where the total volume of goods and services consumed had fallen rather than risen.

Under these circumstances, it is no wonder that land was relatively inexpensive and so too were large historic houses. Studies such as Dr Terence Dooley's 2001 book, *The Decline of the Big House in Ireland*, have shown that while many important properties were destroyed during the War of Independence and Civil War in the early 1920s, even more were subsequently abandoned or pulled down by owners who lacked the funds to pay for the buildings' maintenance or the crippling rates on land and

Above: Monument to Lady Anne Dawson by Joseph Wilton, 1774, in the Dartrey Mausoleum, Co. Monaghan.

Left: Dartrey Mausoleum, Co. Monaghan.

buildings. Unlike Britain, Ireland possessed no National Trust prepared to assume responsibility for these houses and estates and at the same time the cash-strapped Irish government had neither the funds nor the inclination to offer assistance of any kind. Some families clung on to their homes even as they became progressively more dilapidated; in his *Twilight of the Ascendancy*, Mark Bence-Jones tells of Miss Dorothea O'Neill Daunt who typically managed to remain in Kilcascan Castle, County Cork, by gradually disposing of the contents until one day she announced, 'I've sold out my drawing room.' Penury forced other house owners to abandon the struggle. Cynthia O'Connor's article on the dispersal of country-house collections in Volume XXXV of the Irish Georgian Society *Bulletin*, chronicles a number of sales such as that held over five days at Charleville Forest, County Offaly, in November 1948 when a set of five views of the demesne by William Ashford went for £18; in 1991 two of the set reappeared on the market and were sold at Christie's in London for £120,000 and £100,000 respectively.

Rates were payable on any domestic building with a roof; accordingly the removal of slates became a common phenomenon. An iniquitous tax system meant the highest rates were charged in poor counties like Leitrim, which had few inhabitants and poor land, and the lowest in more densely populated areas such as Kildare and Meath. Some of Ireland's finest houses were lost in the 1950s, among them Lismore, County Cavan (attributed to Edward Lovett Pearce); Mrs Delany's former home, Delville, in County Dublin; Mespil House in central Dublin; Dunsandle, County Galway; Dromore Castle, County Limerick; Tudenham, County Westmeath; and French Park, County Roscommon. The fate of two houses during this period is typical. Dartrey in County Monaghan was a vast Elizabethan Revival mansion built in 1846 for Richard Dawson, later first Earl of Dartrey. Just over a century later his descendant, Lady

CHAPTER I

Dartrey estate, Co. Monaghan, stables.

Edith Windham, having already disposed of Dartrey's superlative contents in 1937, arranged to have the building demolished. From this she made a profit of £3000 – less than one-tenth of what it had cost to construct Dartrey a hundred years before. (In 1961 the Irish Georgian Society undertook repairs to the Dawson Mausoleum, an important eighteenth-century funerary monument on the Dartrey estate, and a decade later the Society provided additional funds, and a voluntary workforce, for its preservation and for the restoration of the estate's stables dating from *circa* 1760. Nevertheless, the Dawson Mausoleum still remains at risk from vandalism. At the time of writing, after years of neglect the Dawson Mausoleum is the subject of an ongoing conservation programme by a local heritage group.)

Similarly, not long after the Society was established, novelist Elizabeth Bowen finally abandoned the struggle to hold on to her eighteenth-century family home Bowen's Court, County Cork, since inheriting the place in 1930. She sold it to a local man, Cornelius O'Keefe, in the belief that he and his own family would inhabit and look after the house. A mere year later, the artist Derek Hill – who wrote a poignant appreciation of the house in Volume IV of the Irish Georgian Society *Bulletin* – went to paint a picture of Bowen's Court for its former owner and found the roof already removed; within months the whole site had been cleared. It was, as Elizabeth Bowen gallantly noted, a clean end, leaving the land 'more as it was ... with no house there'.

Losses of this kind provoked little, if any, protest or regret. Most of the Irish population had other, more immediate concerns than what happened to properties with which they felt no great affinity; in the popular mind, historic houses were associated with the old regime. Official organizations were equally unconcerned. The Land Commission, a statutory body charged with breaking up old estates and distributing land to farmers in small parcels, was at best apathetic when it came to historic monuments. In 1946 the commission offered for sale Hazlewood, a large Palladian house in County Sligo, built in 1731 to the designs of Richard Castle, on condition that the new owner demolish the building, remove all materials and level the site. (Curiously, Hazlewood somehow survived this threat and there are currently plans for its restoration.)

Only very occasionally was the Land Commission subject to public criticism, such as the outcry in 1957 following news of its intention to demolish Shanbally Castle in County Tipperary, the largest and finest house in Ireland designed by John Nash. Writing in the *Cork Examiner*, Professor Denis Gwynn condemned the commission's behaviour as an 'act of vandalism' and asked, 'What conceivable justification can there be for incurring the great expense of demolishing this unique Irish mansion?' But it was to no avail; shortly afterwards, Shanbally's roof was removed while its cut stone was gradually broken into smaller pieces for use in road building. Justifiably, when Desmond Guinness reviewed the activities of the Land Commission in Volume XXXI of the Society's *Bulletin*, he was caustic, especially about the commission's treatment of historic properties. 'The buildings were emptied and left shuttered for years,' he wrote. 'The trees were cut, the garden went wild and no longer gave any employment. In terms of national investment it was a waste. The house would be advertised for sale, through the means of a five-line advertisement on the back page of the local paper, to ensure that no-one except the demolition men could possibly be misguided enough to buy it.'

Not every house, of course, was necessarily condemned to destruction. As Mark Bence-Jones has also noted, some of them, such as Curraghmore in County Waterford and Dunsany Castle in County Meath, continued to be kept up by the latest generation of families who had lived in these houses for centuries. At Birr Castle, County Offaly, the Earl and Countess of Rosse enhanced their already magnificent gardens and the Hon. Mrs Plunket lived in palatial splendour at Luttrellstown, County Dublin. There were even a few new arrivals prepared to take on the responsibility of looking after an historic property, most notably Sir Alfred Beit who with his wife Clementine bought Russborough, County Wicklow, in 1952 and filled it with their outstanding collection of pictures and furniture.

But these examples were the exception rather than the norm and when Desmond and Mariga Guinness arrived in Ireland in 1956, plenty of places had already gone the same way as Shanbally Castle and Dartrey, or seemed destined to do so before long. The couple were able to rent one of the country's finest houses, Carton, ancestral home of the FitzGeralds, Dukes of Leinster, who had been obliged to sell the estate in 1949 when it was bought by the second Lord Brocket who mainly lived in England. From this base, the Guinnesses made forays around the island looking for somewhere to buy. As Desmond Guinness told *The World of Hibernia* in spring 2000, 'So many places were for sale, but everywhere cracks were papered over and dry rot seemed to be a national epidemic.' Chief among the couple's preferred options was Kilshannig, County Cork, designed in the 1760s by Davis Ducart and decorated with superlative stuccowork in the principle rooms by the Lafranchini brothers. This might have been bought except that a new road to Cork city was planned to cut through the estate. They also considered Bellamont Forest, County Cavan, a perfect Palladian villa designed by Sir Edward Lovett Pearce around 1730; this was being offered with some seventy acres for £3500.

But eventually Desmond and Mariga settled on a house close to Dublin, Leixlip Castle, which dates back to the middle ages and is sited on a rock at the point where the river Rye flows into the Liffey. It proved to be an apt choice because the

Top: Portrait of Sir Alfred and Lady Beit in front of Russborough, Co. Wicklow, by Edward McGuire.

Bottom: Kilshannig, Co. Cork, designed in the 1760s by Davis Ducart.

2 Kildare Place, Dublin, during demolition in 1957. Designed by Richard Castle and executed after his death in 1751 by John Ensor.

village of Leixlip was where Arthur Guinness, founder of the family business, had taken on his own brewery in 1755. Twenty-four years before that date the castle had been bought by William Conolly, nephew and heir to Speaker Conolly, the builder of nearby Castletown House, which, from 1968, would become headquarters of the Irish Georgian Society. Initially, however, the Guinnesses were reluctant to commit themselves to Leixlip; according to Desmond they thought the castle 'the most hideous thing we'd ever seen', its exterior 'somewhat ungainly with windows of different shapes and sizes and ugly downpipes'. Only gradually did they came to appreciate that behind its ungainliness and subfusc decoration lay fine eighteenth-century interiors. In late 1957 they purchased Leixlip Castle and 180 adjacent acres for £15,500.

Inspecting so many properties during their search for a home over the preceding two years achieved a couple of unexpected results: it refined Desmond and Mariga's already intuitive aesthetic sensibilities, and it made them acutely aware of just how many eighteenth- and nineteenth-century buildings around Ireland were suffering such acute neglect that they were liable soon to be lost for good. However, it was the demolition of Georgian buildings in Dublin rather than the disappearance of a country house that inspired the couple to establish the Irish Georgian Society. On their visits to the capital from 1956 onwards, they had seen Dublin Corporation workers clearing away magnificent mansions on Lower Dominick Street and Hardwicke Place and replacing them with blocks of local authority flats. (Tragically, when the Irish Georgian Society enquired in September 1959 whether any record had been made of the demolished Dominick Street houses, they were informed by an officer of the city authority that only two exterior photographs of the street were taken while the buildings were being pulled down in June 1957.) Most of these old properties had long ago deteriorated into squalid tenements; their loss, though unwelcome, was comprehensible.

Shanbally Castle, Co. Tipperary. Garden front during demolition, *c.*1957.

But in July 1957 the government authorized the demolition of two eighteenth-century houses on Kildare Place, only a matter of yards from the Dáil in Leinster House. No. 2 Kildare Place had been designed by Richard Castle and executed after his death in 1751 by John Ensor; its neighbour was of a slightly later date. Both houses were in excellent condition and there was no reason for their destruction other than an unwillingness on the part of the state to maintain them. As a correspondent wrote in the *Irish Architect and Contractor*: 'In the year 1957 when financial stringency decrees that 50,000 of our people must leave in order that our balance of payments be preserved, our Government allows the wilful destruction of forty thousand pounds of Irish public property, which, from a point of view of history and tradition, is priceless.'

Desmond Guinness remembers that the first he knew of the Kildare Place demolitions was on coming out of the adjacent Shelbourne Hotel and seeing workmen on the roofs removing slates. In July 1957 he wrote a letter of protest to the editor of *The Irish Times* and proposed that rather than being destroyed the houses should be preserved and used to display properly the neighbouring National Museum's fine collection of eighteenth-century furniture, which at the time was squeezed into a couple of rooms and 'stacked as though in a saleroom for lack of space'. An editorial in the same edition concurred with his suggestion and decried the official 'barbarous decision to destroy the two handsome houses'. And in his 'Cruiskeen Lawn' column in the same newspaper, Myles na gCopaleen asked whether the clearance of Kildare Place meant 'that there is no regard by the State to what may be called the nation's soul'? A petition was sent to the taoiseach, Éamon de Valera, and there was further agitation in the press but all to no purpose. In August 1957 the houses were taken down and an ugly grey brick wall erected in their place; half a century later it is there still.

This piece of wanton government-sanctioned devastation prompted the Guinnesses to establish an organization that would champion Ireland's built heritage since the state was clearly unwilling to do so. Presciently, in his letter to *The Irish Times* about Kildare Place, Desmond suggested that 'If the opposition to this vandalism

CHAPTER I

Sir John Pentland Mahaffy's house,
38 North Great George's Street, Dublin 1,
2007. Restored by Desiree Shortt.

would only unite in some Society for the preservation of Georgian Dublin, a well co-ordinated effort might produce results next time,' before going on to say that he would 'be glad to hear from anyone interested in forming such a group'. That someone turned out to be he and Mariga, as the couple announced at their Carton tea party in February 1958.

It should be pointed out that the Guinnesses were not entirely alone in their anxiety over the future of Ireland's heritage. As the dismay of Professor Gwynn over the demolition of Shanbally Castle had indicated, at least a few Irish citizens shared their concerns. And some of them had come together more than ten years before the foundation of the Irish Georgian Society to establish a voluntary body that would campaign for 'The Protection of Places of Interest and Beauty in Ireland'. Formed in September 1946, An Taisce (from an Irish term of endearment approximating to the English 'my treasure') was given by its founders the subtitle, 'The National Trust for Ireland'. Indeed, like its British equivalent, An Taisce was initially much concerned with the natural environment; among its founding organizations were the Dublin Naturalists' Field Club, the Geographical Society of Ireland and the Irish Society for the Protection of Birds. So while the preservation of historic buildings was – and remains – of importance, this has never been the group's only interest. As was stated in a book published to commemorate its fiftieth anniversary, An Taisce is an environmental organization with interests that extend 'from the natural heritage of land, air, water, animal and plant life to the made heritage of buildings and gardens'.

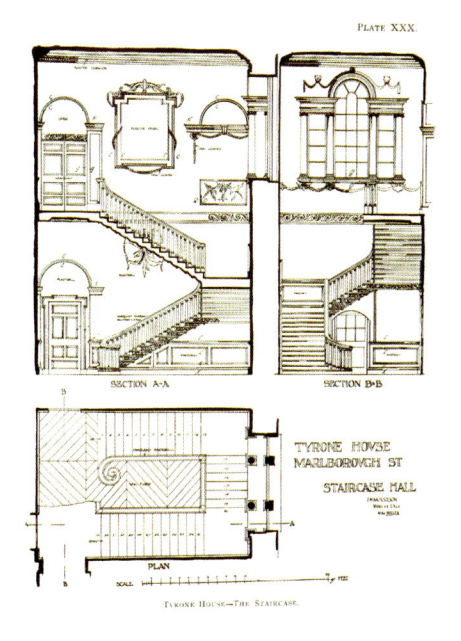

On the other hand, the Irish Georgian Society's founders envisaged their organization as having an altogether more specific brief. Its constitution, published at the beginning of 1959, states that the Society's objective is 'to encourage an interest in and the preservation of distinguished examples of architecture and the allied arts in Ireland'. Inspiration for this mission came from the earlier Georgian Society, which had been founded half a century before. Its driving force was the Revd John Pentland Mahaffy, a classical scholar who became provost of Trinity College, Dublin, in 1914. Irascible and witty – when quizzed by an advocate of women's rights on the difference between the two sexes, he responded, 'I can't conceive' – Mahaffy also had a keen interest in Georgian architecture; from 1865 onwards he lived at 38 North Great George's Street, built in 1785 by stuccodore Charles Thorp. (After Mahaffy's death in 1919 this house gradually deteriorated into tenement flats until bought in 1975 and then slowly restored by long-time Irish Georgian Society member Desiree Shortt.)

As envisaged by Mahaffy and his fellow enthusiasts – including Desmond Guinness's great-grandfather, Lord Iveagh, who was an honorary vice-president – the Georgian Society established in 1908 had a specific purpose: 'To inspect and note the eighteenth century (or Georgian) architectural and decorative work which remains in Dublin, and to record such work by means of sketches, measured drawings, and photographs.' The results were published in a series of five volumes that appeared between 1909 and 1913, the last of them dealing with country houses in Ireland. But as Desmond Guinness noted when the first society's work was reissued in 1969, it 'was not dedicated to preservation', nor did it actively campaign for the preservation

The Georgian Society Records.

Left: Tyrone House: the staircase hall. Vol. III, Georgian Society Records.

Middle: 53 Merrion Square: doorway. Vol. III, Georgian Society Records.

Right: 58 Mountjoy Square: staircase. Vol. I, Georgian Society Records.

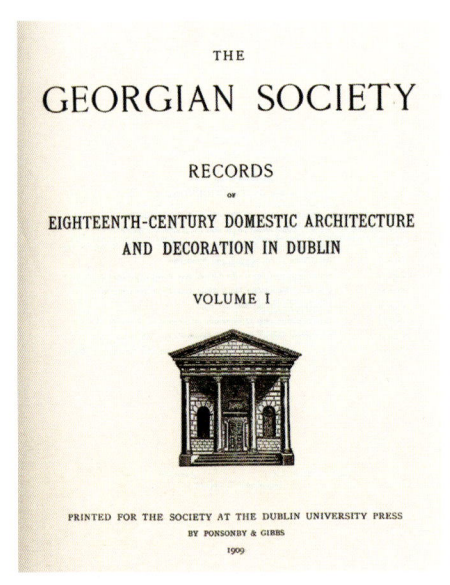

The Georgian Society Records, Vol. 1.

of historic buildings. In fact, the preface to Volume One had sadly observed that most of eighteenth-century Dublin's 'monuments of a brilliant Society are doomed to decay and disappearance'.

It was precisely to prevent the realization of this gloomy scenario that a new Irish Georgian Society was created fifty years after the original. Desmond and Mariga Guinness had become familiar with the earlier organization's publications 'through people like Lady Dunsany who had a set of the volumes and we'd pored over them'. But from the start they intended to go further than had their predecessors. 'We wanted to change the government's attitude to places like Lower Dominick Street,' Desmond recalls. 'Obviously we were very happy for the slum residents to be re-housed, but we pointed out that these and others were unique buildings, each one different from its neighbours. Of course we were right. Had they been preserved, they'd each be worth at least €1 million by now.' In other words, the Irish Georgian Society was a lobby group from the start, working to encourage wider appreciation of eighteenth-century architecture and thereby ensure it did not suffer 'decay and disappearance'.

But the organization also intended to play a direct role in ensuring the preservation of the national heritage. According to its original constitution, while the Society sought regular members who would pay an annual subscription of £1, it also looked for larger contributions of £25 towards the creation of a trustee fund. The latter would be used to gain by purchase or otherwise buildings, furniture and land 'considered by the trustees to be worthy of acquisition' on account of their architectural and artistic merit or their amenity value. If no one else was prepared to save 'distinguished examples of architecture' in Ireland, then the Irish Georgian Society would do so.

That intention was clearly stated on the day the new Society was officially launched, Friday, 21 February 1958, a date chosen because it was precisely fifty years since the original Georgian Society had been established. At a press conference in Dublin, the Guinnesses outlined the purpose of their organization, announced they already had some 200 members (and would have double that number before the end of the year) and sought help in building up a trustee fund so that they could 'buy and equip a genuine Georgian house for headquarters'. Desmond was to be president of the Society and Mariga joint honorary secretary (along with architect Percy LeClerc, Inspector of National Monuments at the Office of Public Works). The occasion was reported in the following day's newspapers, with *The Irish Press* explaining that, according to Desmond, 'many fine buildings were being lost because there was no organization to fight for their protection'. In 'An Irishman's Diary' in *The Irish Times*, 'Quidnunc' included Mariga's retort to an enquiry about the chilliness of old houses. 'It's quite simple,' she said, 'one just piles on more jerseys – and anyway, you get used to it soon.' Desmond, meanwhile, was quoted as giving reassurances that the government and the state tourism agency, Bord Fáilte, were 'becoming Georgian-minded at last – though they prefer to use the term "18th century"'.

'No matter what they call themselves,' concluded Quidnunc, 'if they save the remaining Georgian relics in Ireland, nobody is likely to complain.' Unfortunately it wasn't long before this prediction would prove to be somewhat inaccurate.

EARLY MEMBERS

Within a year of being established, the Irish Georgian Society could claim more than 400 members 'living in all parts of the world, of whom about 60 are students'. Many of those who first joined the Society were friends of Desmond and Mariga Guinness and had been invited to the Carton tea party in February 1958, owners of historic houses such as the Shirleys of Lough Fea in County Monaghan, Lord Altamont of Westport House, County Mayo, and Lady Rosemary FitzGerald of Borris House, County Carlow. But this was not universally the case. 'In the early days,' Ursula Lee recalls, 'there were an awful lot of oldish ladies from around the Wellington Road area of Dublin. They'd be members of the RDS and that sort of thing.' In addition, the Gate Theatre's founders, Hilton Edwards and Micheál Mac Liammóir, were early supporters of the Society, as was historian Maurice O'Connell (a great-great-grandson of Daniel O'Connell whose correspondence he edited and published in eight volumes). So too was the modernist Irish architect Michael Scott, who would later prove an invaluable ally in the battle to save Dublin's Mountjoy Square.

Athlone-based writer John Broderick, whose first novel *The Pilgrimage* would be published to acclaim in 1961, was another of the Society's original members. He soon found himself drawn into a discussion about establishing a branch of the Society in his native Athlone but responded in a style familiar to anyone who has read his fiction, 'I have never quite been able to believe that faith can move mountains,' and suggested Desmond Guinness should come to the County Westmeath town and lecture there on the merits of Georgian architecture to members of a local arts club.

But the publicity won by the Society meant members of the general public were soon attracted to its cause. A letter written to the organization in February 1958 by Francis Mooney of 221 North Circular Road, Dublin, enclosed a postal order covering the £1 membership fee. 'I am very interested in all Georgian houses especially those of historic interest,' Mr Mooney remarked. 'I shall also get as many of my friends interested in this Society as I can as I think it a wonderful idea.' Indeed, members frequently begat members by spreading the word and encouraging their acquaintances to join the Society. Lydia Prescott, a White-Russian general's widow who lived in Donnybrook, Dublin, was especially good at winning support during those early years. In June 1959 she wrote to Mariga Guinness with the information that 'I have got you a new member, a very nice Mrs D. Batchen, and also her daughter of 17 who is a student at Trinity so will be the 5/- member.' Likewise Sybil le Brocquy, mother of artist Louis le Brocquy, diligently persuaded anyone of her circle who could be convinced to join the Society and regularly sent their names to Desmond Guinness. A typical letter, written by Pauline Cunningham of Ballsbridge, Dublin, in August 1959, requests that a membership form be posted to a friend of hers, Mrs Kenneth Davies of Killoughter House, County Wicklow, who wished to support the organization. Mrs Davies' son, Sir David Davies, today sits on the Irish Georgian Society's committee of management and has been instrumental in the founding of the new Irish Heritage Trust. Finally, it should be noted that some of the early members could make unusual requests. 'A large membership does bring its problems with it,' Desmond Guinness remarked in one of the Society's *Bulletin*s, 'and we receive the strangest enquiries. On one day in February, for instance, we were asked to value some furniture for a member in Limerick (photos enclosed), and to provide hunt ball escorts for the seventeen-year-old daughters of two members in South Carolina (no photos).'

Borris House, Co. Carlow, home of Lady Rosemary FitzGerald in 1958.

13

LIAM MILLER AND THE DOLMEN PRESS

Liam Miller, founder of the Dolmen Press.

The most distinguished printer and publisher of his era, Liam Miller was born in County Laois in 1924 and trained as an architect, working for a number of practices in London and Dublin during the 1940s and 1950s. Helped by his wife Josephine, he began printing from home in 1951, teaching himself the necessary skills and using only a hand press. He soon developed a reputation for the outstanding quality of his craftsmanship and under the Dolmen Press imprint was responsible for publishing superbly designed volumes by many of Ireland's finest writers including Austin Clarke, Thomas Kinsella, Richard Murphy, Samuel Beckett and John Montague. A 1969 Dolmen Press edition of *The Táin*, translated from the Irish by Kinsella, and with illustrations on almost every page by Louis le Brocquy, is widely considered to have been his outstanding achievement. A man of wide learning and many interests, Miller was unfortunately never an astute businessman and relied on commercial printing jobs to keep the Dolmen Press solvent.

Desmond Guinness remembers that the first time he came across Liam Miller's work was in 1957 when the Music Association of Ireland held a concert to mark the centenary of the organ in Carton's saloon, the programmes for this occasion having been designed and printed by the Dolmen Press. On the establishment of the Irish Georgian Society the following year (by which time Liam Miller had moved his operation into premises on Upper Mount Street), the Dolmen Press was given responsibility for producing the new organization's *Bulletin*. 'More than that,' Desmond Guinness wrote forty years later, Liam Miller 'laid out the title page, helped to word the membership form and generally encouraged us in this leap into the dark.' The Dolmen Press continued to print all the Society's material for the next five years. Liam Miller set each letter in the old manner of printing, with illustrations clustered together on art paper instead of being interwoven with the text. This was not an altogether satisfactory arrangement and so in 1963 the Society began working with a printer with offset litho, permitting text and pictures to appear on the same pages.

Without question the early image of the Irish Georgian Society as an organization dedicated to encouraging greater appreciation of fine design was improved by Liam Miller's contribution. In a celebration of the Dolmen Press published in 2001, Jarlath Hayes commented that Miller's 'typography was pellucid ... by his own alchemy, he achieved a new grace and a civilized assurance which was fresh and original in the face of the degraded typography and wooden pages of the day'. Those first *Bulletin*s, posters and programmes of the Irish Georgian Society, printed on carefully selected paper and featuring images adapted from eighteenth-century engravings, remain as beautiful today as they were half a century ago. It is immediately apparent that typeface and layout have been carefully harmonized. Each item produced for the society was subtly different from the others but displayed the same consistently high standards. And if the finished work carried an occasional error in spelling or punctuation, somehow this only added to the appeal.

The Dolmen Press continued in operation until the time of Liam Miller's death in 1987. Many of its publications, including those for the Irish Georgian Society, are now highly prized by collectors.

Cover of a 1961 IGS *Bulletin*. Design adapted from an eighteenth-century engraving of a baroque fountain.

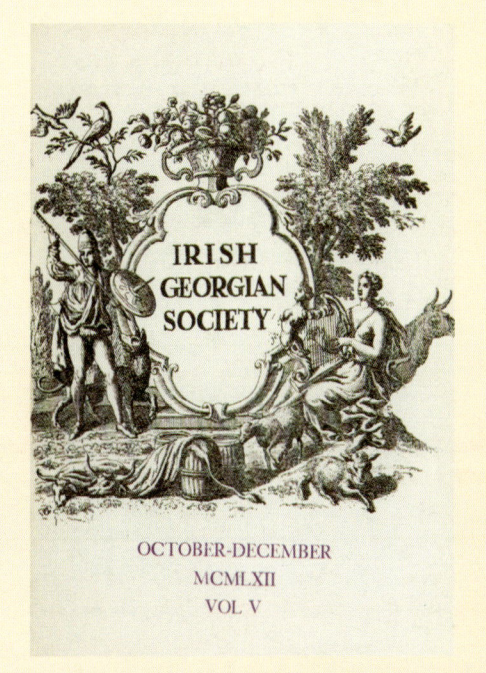

Top: Cover of a 1958 IGS *Bulletin*. Design taken from a vignette engraving on Noble and Keenan's map of Co. Kildare, 1752, of the Conolly Folly, built in 1740.

Bottom: Cover of MCMLXII (1962) IGS *Bulletin*. Design taken from a map of Ireland by John Senex, 1720.

Desmond and Mariga Guinness at Leixlip Castle ~ early days of the Irish Georgian Society – original members and activities ~ the Bulletin ~ touring at home and abroad ~ the Georgian cricket matches ~ Panels: overseas tours and Georgian cricket

CHAPTER

2

Opposite (left to right): Hon. Desmond Guinness with his son Patrick and daughter Marina, Leixlip Castle, Co. Kildare, 1962.

On 1 March 1958, Desmond and Mariga Guinness, together with their two children Patrick and Marina, took possession of Leixlip Castle, which for the next decade acted as both family home and headquarters of the fledgling Irish Georgian Society. A vast amount of work needed to be done to the building; the main bedroom had previously been used for storing oats and baths were found in surrounding fields where they had served as feeding troughs. Much of the restoration and redecoration was undertaken by the Guinnesses themselves; it turned out to be excellent training for similar work they would undertake on behalf of the Society in the years ahead. And the need to acquire furniture meant they haunted auction rooms and house sales, thereby honing their taste still further. It was a slow task, observed Valentine Lawford in the November 1964 edition of American *Vogue*, since Desmond and Mariga, 'rather than be satisfied even temporarily with the second-best, are patiently picking up whatever they take a liking to in other great houses doomed to destruction, or at local sales'.

But the eventual result was universally applauded. As Christopher Gibbs wrote in *The Daily Telegraph* after Mariga Guinness's death, at Leixlip 'the boldness and vigour of Irish decoration, combining rustic strength and 18th-century elegance, brought fresh life to empty rooms. Huge canvases in carved frames of shabby gilding; fireplaces where fossils sprawled against mouldings; great consoles where eagles' beaks held garlands of black mahogany – all were garnished with Chinese pots, marble busts and sparkling Irish silver'. In *The Inspiration of the Past*, published in 1985, John Cornforth

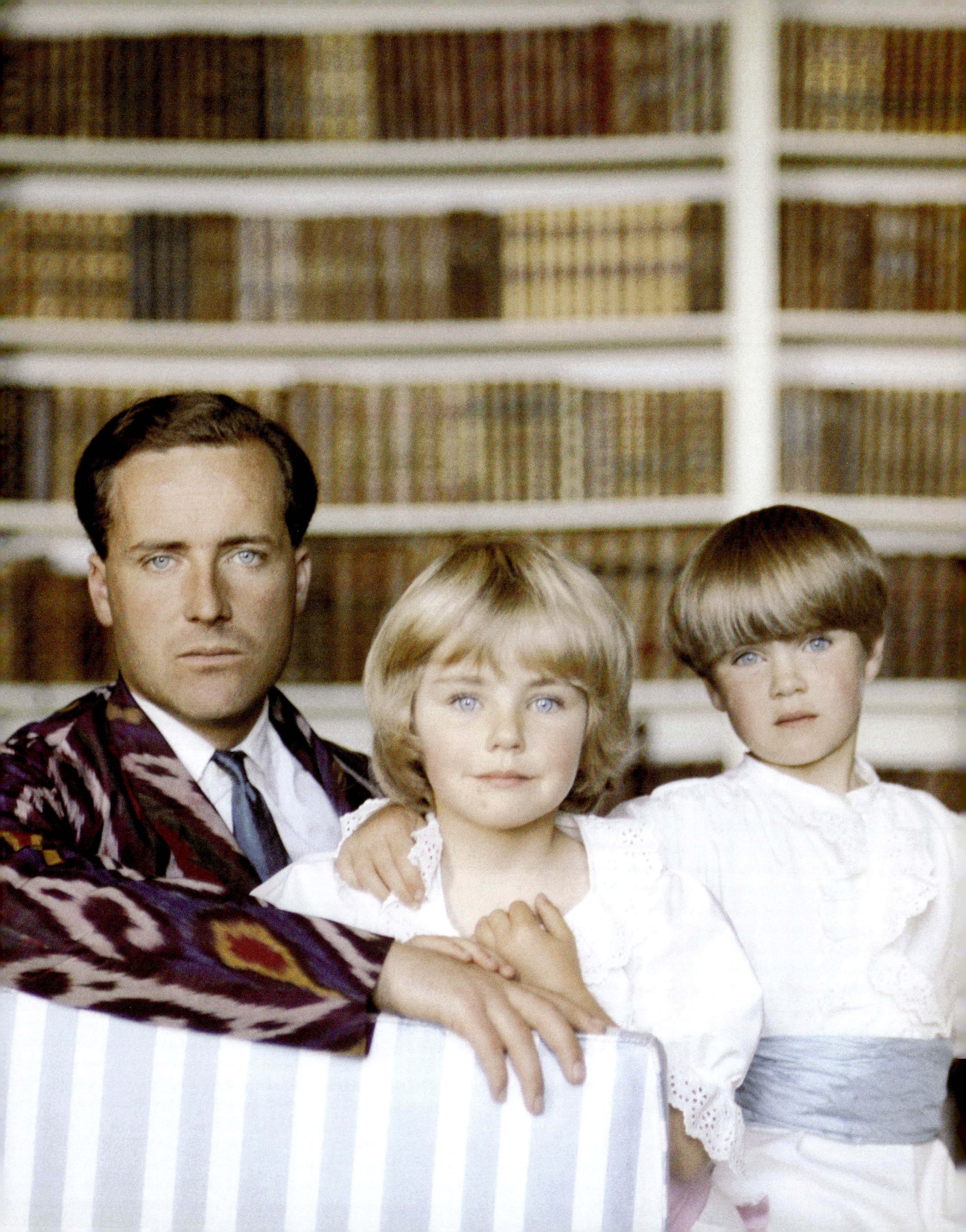

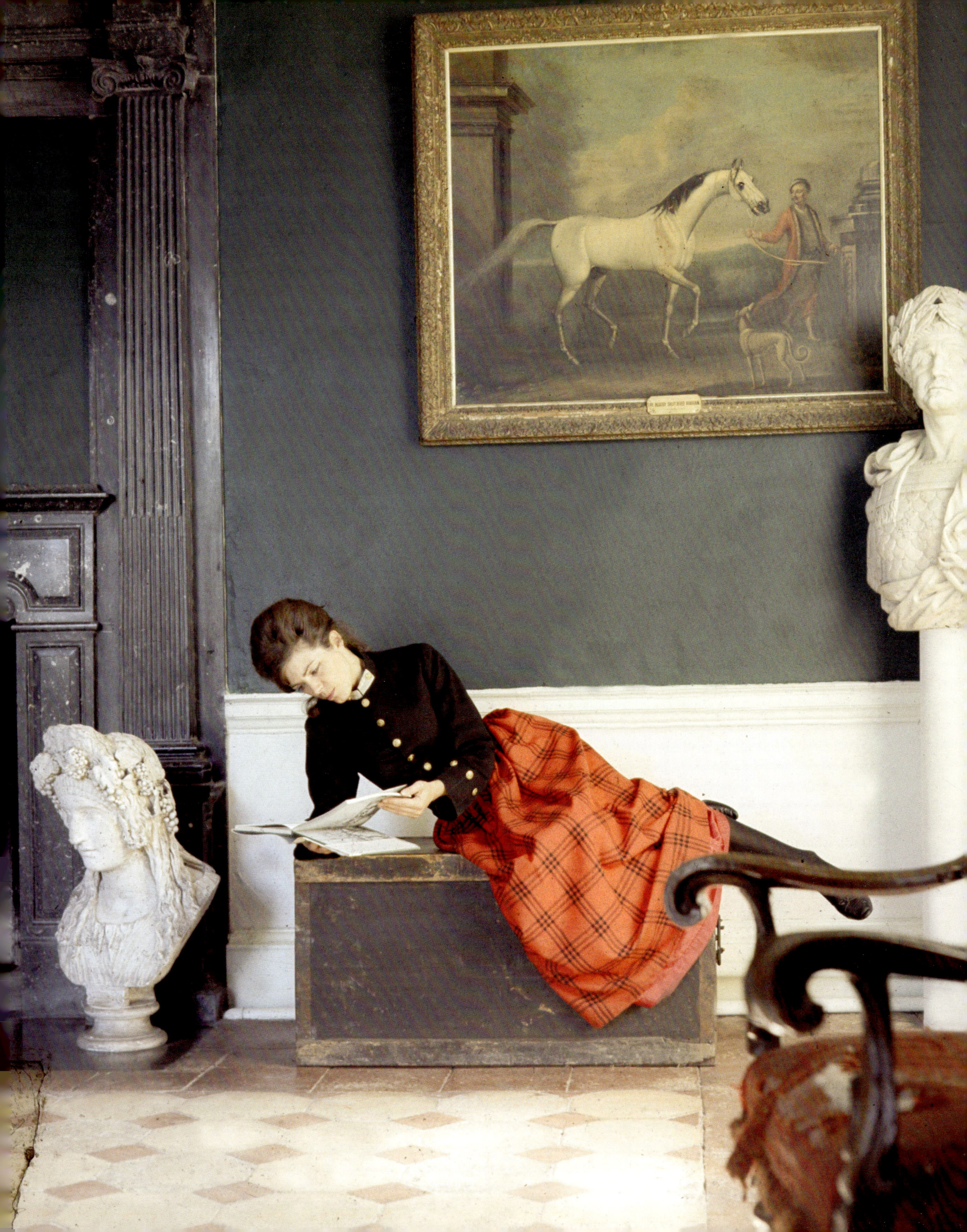

commented on Mariga's 'rare gift for composing objects and rooms in a stimulating way and combining unlikely, and occasionally unpromising objects to create memorable effects', and described the Guinness home as 'the key country house in the British Isles in the late 1950s and 1960s'.

There can be no doubt that the decoration of Leixlip was enormously influential in reviving an interest in Georgian interiors, especially within Ireland where owners of even the most beautiful eighteenth-century properties rarely showed much interest in their ornamentation. Desmond Guinness tells the story of an individual who, when quizzed about a particular piece of furniture in his possession, merely replied that it was 'of the period'. Leixlip demonstrated that historic houses need not be austere or bleak but on the contrary, with sufficient imagination and even on a modest budget, could be made extremely comfortable and attractive. Over the next ten years the castle was much photographed, most notably by Horst for *Vogue's Book of Houses, Gardens, People*; published in 1968 which included one memorable image of Mariga elegantly reclining across an antique army officer's trunk in the entrance hall at Leixlip.

Leixlip Castle, Co. Kildare, boathouse and church. Aquatint by Jonathan Fisher, April 1792.

The wide dissemination of these images meant the couple's decorative flair became well known at home and abroad. But it also achieved widespread renown because the Guinnesses were so consistently sociable. Young, good-looking, highly personable and, in an era of near-universal poverty, relatively affluent, Desmond and Mariga soon developed a wide circle of friends who were regularly entertained at Leixlip where the front door was never locked – although sometimes it was kept shut by means of a stick jammed against the top step. Distinguishing between private events and those held in support of the Irish Georgian Society was difficult at the time and is no easier fifty years later. 'In its early years,' remembers David Synnott, 'the IGS flourished not only because of the quality of its administration and the extensive social contacts of Desmond and Mariga, which conjured up a steady flow of scholarly and distinguished lecturers, but also very markedly because of the unbounded hospitality at Leixlip Castle.' During his own visit to the house, Valentine Lawford wrote that a 'typical summer Sunday brought, among others, two of Long Island's more awe-inspiring hostesses, the literary editor of a London newspaper, a County Kildare baronet, and two young men who were practising for a top-hatted, costumed cricket match'. No wonder Desmond was heard to murmur drily, 'Here it always seems to be this weekend or the next.'

Professor Anne Crookshank remembers,

> the most important thing about the Guinnesses was that for the first time I met every sort of person invited because they were interested in Irish art and architecture. There were every sort and kind of social class, from Mariga's princely background through Desmond's family to ordinary folk doing ordinary jobs who had probably never been a guest in a big house before. Cross old ladies, difficult young ones, learned old gentlemen: all combined and chatted together.

But thanks to the character of its founders, one of the Irish Georgian Society's most consistent characteristics has been sociability; many early members joined simply

Opposite: Mariga Guinness in the hall at Leixlip Castle, Co. Kildare, photographed by Horst P. Horst for the 1968 *Vogue's Book of Houses, Gardens, People* by Valentine Lawford.

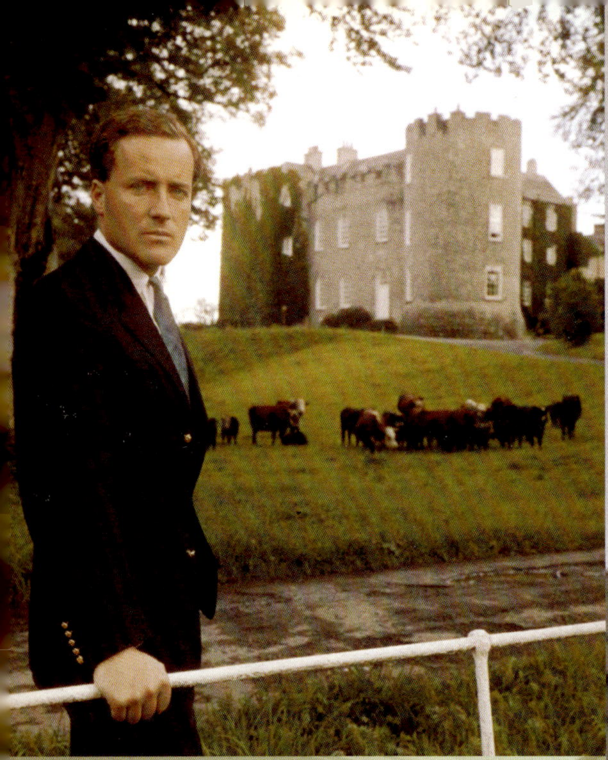
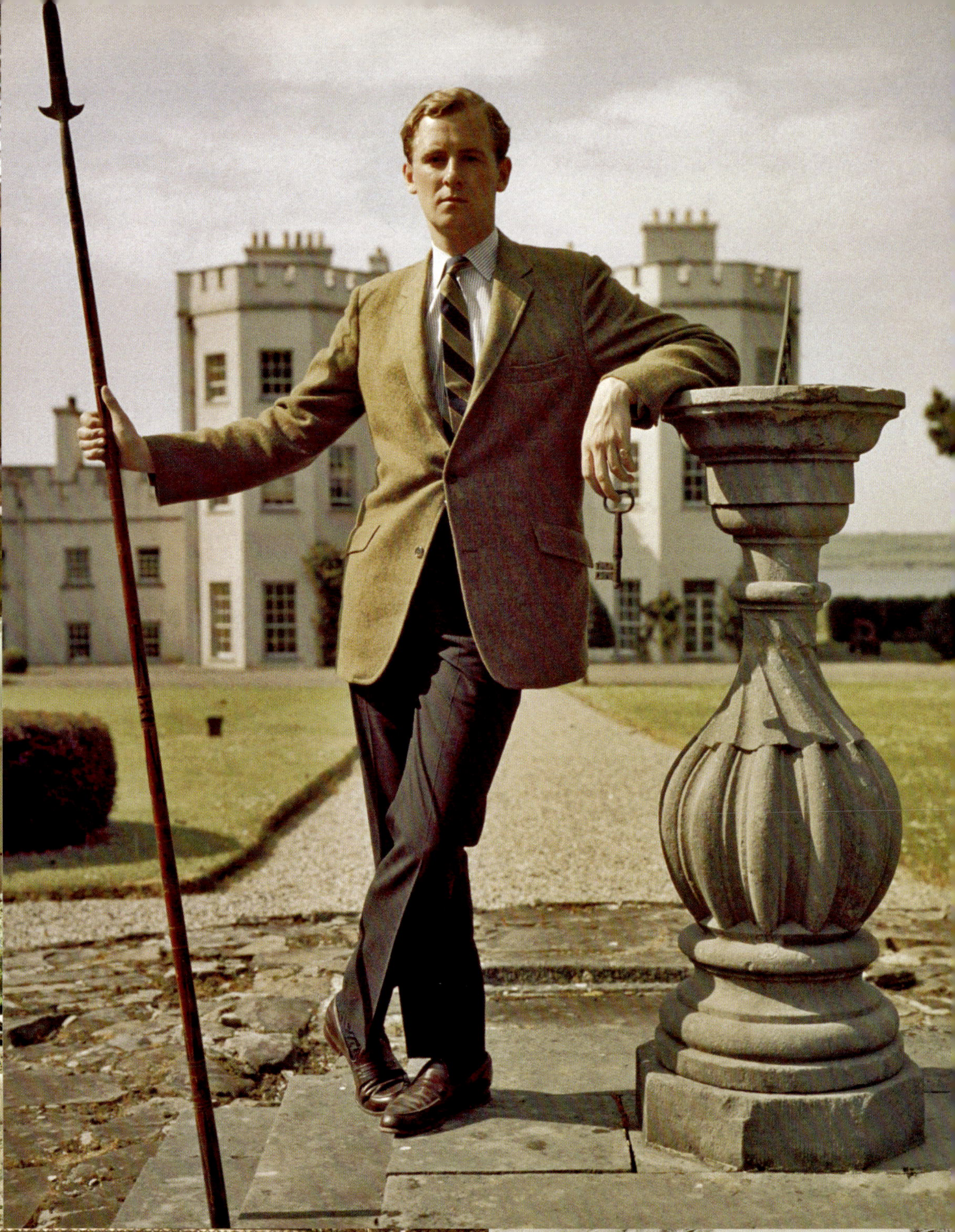
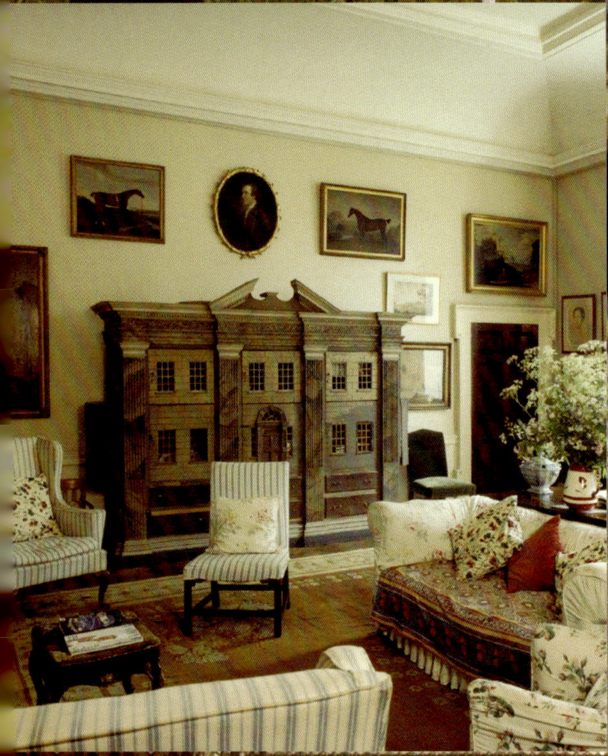
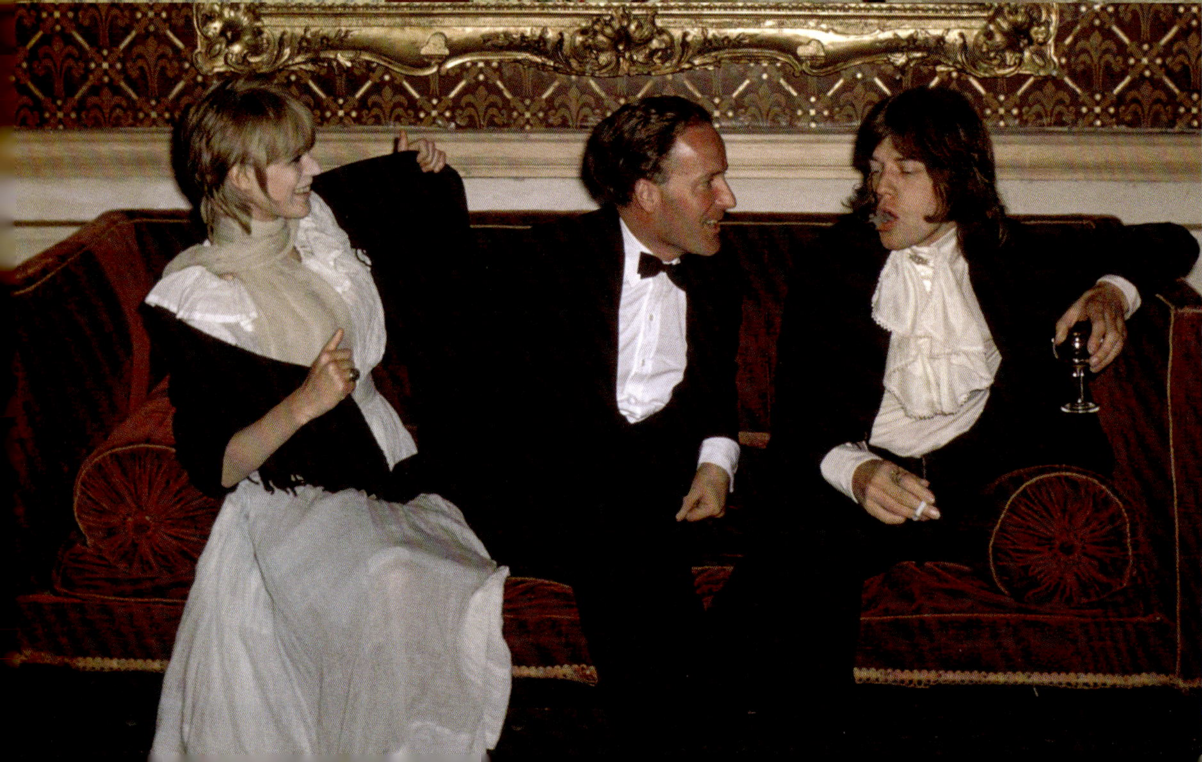
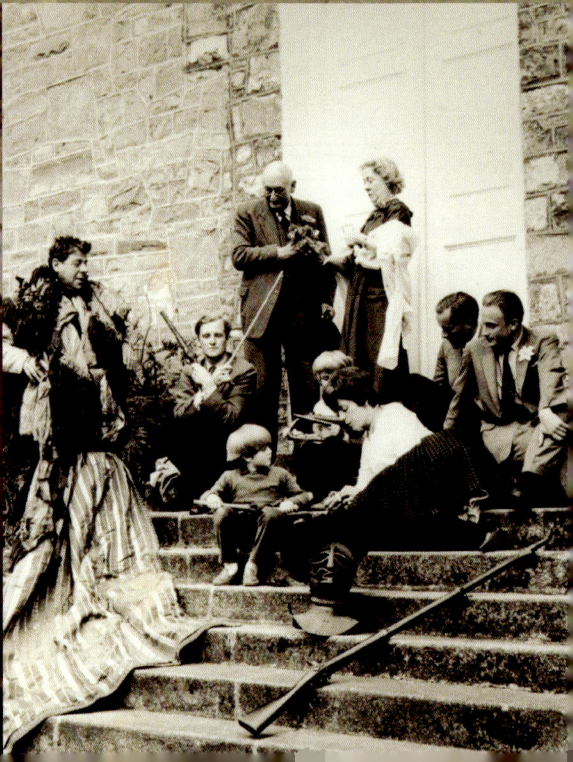

CHAPTER 2

OPPOSITE:

Top left: Hon. Desmond Guinness, Leixlip Castle, Co. Kildare, 1961.

Middle left: The Newbridge Dolls House at Leixlip Castle, Co. Kildare.

Bottom left (left to right): Marianne Faithfull, Hon. Desmond Guinness and Mick Jagger at Castletown, Co. Kildare, 1968.

Top right: Desmond FitzGerald, Knight of Glin, Glin Castle, Co. Limerick, 1963.

Bottom right (anticlockwise from left): Rex Beaumont, Desmond FitzGerald, Knight of Glin; Colonel Charles Howard Bury of Belvedere, Co. Westmeath; Christabel, Lady Aberconway; Hon. Desmond Guinness; John Semple; Mariga Guinness, on the steps of Leixlip Castle, Co. Kildare, 1960.

ABOVE:

Left to right: Lady Elizabeth More O'Ferrall, Prof. R.B. McDowell, Mrs Audrey King, Hon. Hugh O'Neill, Mariga Guinness, Adrienne Ring, Roderick More O'Ferrall, Desmond FitzGerald, Talitha Pol, at Leixlip Castle, Co. Kildare, 1960.

CHAPTER 2

Maurice Craig (left) and Desmond FitzGerald, Knight of Glin, at Glin Castle, Co. Limerick.

because they knew Desmond and Mariga, and had been invited to their home. Naturally the original committee was principally composed of friends of the couple, among them Lord Talbot de Malahide (who was the Society's first vice-president), Sir Alfred Beit, Lady Dunsany, the Knight of Glin and Sir George Mahon. Both then and later the presence of so many members of what would, at the time, have been considered the old Ascendancy class inevitably led to accusations of elitism and exclusivity.

In fact the Guinnesses were entirely egalitarian and the Society's full committee represented a reasonable cross section of Irish life including Daithí Hanly (who resigned on being appointed Dublin City Architect); genealogist Eoin O'Mahony; Edwin Bryson whose family had a long-established linen business in Northern Ireland; Edgar Deale, a philanthropic Dublin businessman (and composer) who would later lead the Society's fight against the destruction of sixteen houses on Lower Fitzwilliam Street; John Wylie whose father was a well-known judge; R.B.D. French, a lecturer in the English Department of Trinity College, Dublin; Máire Bhreathnach, a civil servant in the Department of Finance; and Dr Michael Magan, an anaesthetist who was destined to meet his future wife Croine on one of the Irish Georgian Society's tours.

Despite these diverse backgrounds, one attribute the inaugural committee shared with all other members of the new Society was their interest in Ireland's Georgian heritage and a concern for its conservation. And while many of them knew a certain amount on the subject, they were always happy to learn more. Hence another feature of the Society from the start: its regular programme of lectures and talks. In October 1958, for example, the Earl of Antrim spoke at Dublin's old City Assembly Rooms on South William Street about the National Trust's work in Northern Ireland. The following year Maurice Craig lectured on eighteenth-century Irish architecture, Eoin O'Mahony on Henrietta Street and Dean Robert Wyse Jackson of Cashel on Dean Swift.

These occasions attracted large audiences and helped to generate publicity for the Society. When future British Poet Laureate John Betjeman (who had spent some years in Dublin during the Second World War) was invited to speak about Victorian architecture at Newman House in February 1961, he drew a capacity crowd, *The Irish Times* noting that 'the Hon. Mrs Guinness and her corps of indefatigable helpers inserted enough extra chairs to get any Dublin theatre closed down for ever'. There were so many fashionable, well-dressed attendees at this event that 'the difficult insertion into the crowd of a couple of thoroughbreds would have turned the whole affair into a race meeting'. Other speakers that same year included Sir Shane Leslie on Mrs FitzHerbert and George IV, Dr Patrick Logan on Dublin doctors in the eighteenth century, the Earl of Rosse on Russian architecture and museums (his son, the present Earl, would write on the building of St Petersburg for Volume VIII of the Society's *Bulletin*) and Eoin O'Mahony (an inveterate public speaker) on the Rotunda Hospital's Assembly Rooms.

Talks on a similarly diverse range of topics but of a consistently high standard continue to be part of the Society's annual programme. Richard Wood remembers accompanying Mariga and Marina Guinness to a lecture on Irish eighteenth-century

Above: Exterior of Leixlip Castle, Co. Kildare.
Left: Leixlip Castle, Co. Kildare, entrance hall.

wallpapers and fabrics given by Mrs Ada Leask (widow of one of the original Irish Georgian Society members, Harold Leask, and 'a terrifying woman', according to Maurice Craig). At the conclusion of her talk, she faced the audience with hands on hips and demanded to know whether there were any questions. Only one person was brave enough to quiz her: the Knight of Glin, who asked, says Mr Wood, 'a most perceptive question'. Mrs Leask's response, on the other hand, was to draw her tiny frame up to its full height, stare at the Knight with open hostility and remark, 'I don't know who you are' – which was unlikely to have been the case – 'and I don't know who you *think* you are.' No further questions were asked.

Alongside these lectures, there were also exhibitions arranged or hosted by the Society, the very first looking at Georgian architecture in Northern Ireland. This was held in the Russell Hotel, St Stephen's Green, in early May 1958 to mark a visit to the Republic by some sixty members of Britain's Georgian Group whose chairman was the Earl of Rosse. In June 1959, during what would prove a seminal visit to Dublin by members of the Society of Architectural Historians of America, the Society co-sponsored an exhibition at the Municipal Gallery in Parnell Square focussing on W.B. Yeats's association with that institution. Five years later, in conjunction with the late Dr James White (then curator of the self-same Municipal Gallery) Professor Anne Crookshank, who at the time worked at the Ulster Museum in Belfast, and the Knight of Glin, the Irish Georgian Society arranged a ground-breaking exhibition, 'Irish Houses and Landscapes'. Featuring eighty-seven pictures of Irish topographical interest the show opened in Belfast on 27 June and in Dublin on 2 August, and was visited by over 20,000 people. Anne Crookshank recalls that at the time much less was known about Irish art than is now the case and

> we didn't really believe that there were two Thomas Roberts, brothers, and we had never heard of Jeremiah Hodges Mulcahy who signed the picture of Glin

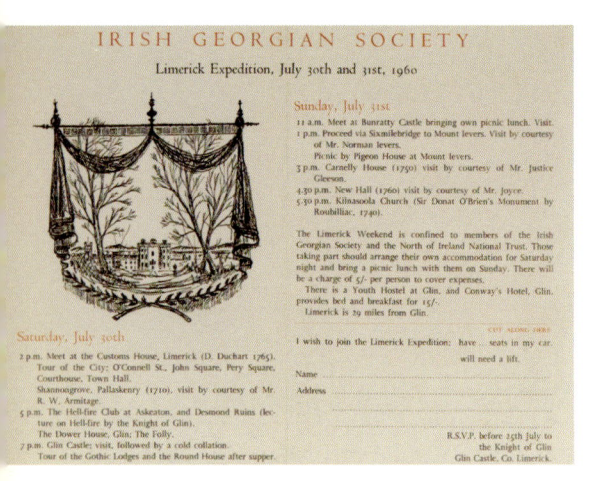

Above: IGS 1960 tour pamphlet to Limerick and Clare, designed by Desmond FitzGerald, Knight of Glin.

Right: Glin Castle, Co. Limerick. Home of Desmond FitzGerald, Knight of Glin.

Castle which Desmond had cleaned for the exhibition …This exhibition certainly inspired us both to look into who did what in Ireland though new names still turn up and all we have done in nearly forty years is to give a sort of beginning.

Soon after its establishment the Society also began helping to preserve significant buildings by raising money for this purpose. In November 1959, it held a reception at 8–10 Henrietta Street 'in aid of the repairs to these beautiful houses occupied by the Sisters of Charity of Saint Vincent de Paul'. One of the nuns, Sister Anthony, had written to Desmond Guinness the previous month, saying she had 'tried every avenue to get some money to mend our roof, but without success … You are my last and only hope – I have no funds nor committee to help me. Not only would you be doing a most charitable and noble work, but our famous house would owe its very existence to you.' Fortunately the buildings still stand and have undergone extensive restoration in recent years.

Information on these and other matters was provided to the Society's members through its *Bulletin*, the first issue of which was published to coincide with the launch of the organization. Superbly designed and printed by Liam Miller, for forty years the *Bulletin* not only served as a vehicle for news of the Irish Georgian Society's activities but also carried features on a variety of relevant topics written by academics and enthusiastic amateurs alike.

In its first issue, for instance, Maurice Craig wrote 'A Note on Courthouses' and the widow of genealogist and heraldic expert Thomas Sadleir – who had been a stalwart of the original Georgian Society – offered a piece by her late husband, 'Industry at Celbridge'. In later *Bulletins* that same year the Marquess of Sligo considered the imminent demolition of his family home, Westport House, County Mayo, designed by Richard Castle and with interiors by James Wyatt. Despite his observations that the building was in 'excellent condition' and had low maintenance costs, he wrote that it 'will in any case not be pulled down until next year so there is still time for a solution to be found'. An equally gloomy note was struck by Lady Rosemary FitzGerald in her 'Valediction to Borris House', County Carlow, which 'will soon be empty and roofless'. Fortunately, both authors' fears proved unfounded, and Westport and Borris remain standing. (In August 1960 the Irish Georgian Society organized a ball and preview of couturier Sybil Connolly's forthcoming autumn/winter collection at Westport in aid of the house; tickets were priced at two guineas each, including supper.) But while Westport was saved, other properties continued to be lost as novelist and playwright Molly Keane noted in her melancholic piece, 'Death of a House', also published in the *Bulletin*'s first year, with the property in question 'dismantled, gutted and bereft of all dignity, the torn paper on its walls lolled in the soft evening air like idiots' tongues'.

Looking back over a complete set of the Society's *Bulletin*, what strikes a reader is the range of subjects and writers it attracted. In 1959 the Knight of Glin wrote about his family home, Glin Castle (and illustrated the piece with a charming line drawing of the house), a year later William Dillon discussed the Tailors' Hall in Dublin, which was soon to become the focus of so much attention from the Society. Indeed this was true of many other architecturally important structures, whether the Conolly Folly or Riverstown House. Topics ranged from a discourse on the nineteenth-century architect, Patrick Byrne (responsible for some of the capital's earliest post-emancipation Catholic churches), to the Hon. Mrs Oliver Colthurst's analysis, 'The Problems of House Opening', in which she asked those considering the option of allowing members of the public into their homes, 'Did you realise that you will have to provide lavatories?' and warned them that they should 'be prepared for an unending demand for cups of tea and soft drinks'.

Many specialists also contributed to the *Bulletin*, Kurt Ticher writing about three Huguenot goldsmiths in Dublin in the early 1700s, Edward Malins on Mrs Delany and landscaping in Ireland, and Maurice Craig on Sir Edward Lovett Pearce. Over the years, regular contributors included Dr Edward McParland, Ada Longfield, Michael Wynne and Cynthia O'Connor as well as Desmond Guinness, who not only wrote on different aspects of eighteenth-century Ireland but also kept members of the Society informed of its various activities and campaigns through the *Bulletin* until a separate newsletter for this purpose was created in autumn 1983. Although the *Bulletin* initially appeared four times a year, by 1961 – when the Society had started to be a more actively campaigning organization and there were therefore greater demands on the editor's time – this had dropped to three per annum and by the early 1980s it was an annual publication. In 1998 the *Bulletin* was superseded by a new yearly volume, *Irish Architectural and Decorative Studies*, which has since provided an admirable outlet for authoritative primary research material on Irish topics that would otherwise lack a suitable outlet. The full forty years of *Bulletin*s, many of which had become exceedingly rare, were scanned onto disc in 2005 and made available by the Irish Georgian Society.

There was always a proselytizing element to the character of the *Bulletin*, especially when it came to consideration of buildings at risk. Already in the first year of existence,

Glin Castle, Co. Limerick, entrance hall.

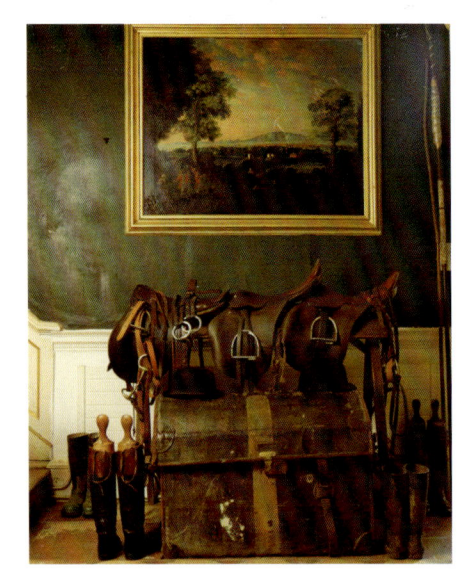

Top: Leixlip Castle, four-poster bed.

Bottom: Leixlip Castle, saddles.

for example, the Irish Georgian Society used its own publication to express concern for the fate of Vernon Mount, County Cork. Dating from the 1780s and described as a 'charming cottage-palace' thanks to wonderful painted interiors, the house and surrounding wooded park of thirty acres had been put on the market by its owners for £3500. A note to Desmond Guinness in early November 1958 from the auctioneers handling the sale commented, 'We believe that those who are interested require it for demolition purposes. This we believe to be a crime.' Given Vernon Mount's vulnerable proximity to Cork city, the Society was worried lest the property would fall into the wrong hands. 'Can some member please find a buyer for this house and save it from the demolishers?' wrote Desmond Guinness in the *Bulletin* and many similar appeals regarding Vernon Mount would be made in the years that followed. (It is still a major cause of concern for the Society today.)

Vernon Mount was not the only house looking for a new owner. In spring 1961, for instance, the *Bulletin* warned that the mid-eighteenth-century Browne's Hill outside Carlow town was due for imminent demolition unless a buyer could be found; the house on just five acres (the Land Commission having taken and distributed all the rest) was being offered for £2500. Somehow it survived after being bought by a local travel agent and converted into flats, albeit with the loss of its magnificent triumphal arch gateway (this was later re-erected at the entrance to Lyons, County Kildare).

If the *Bulletin* helped raise awareness of and interest in Irish Georgian architecture, so too did the tours to interesting country houses that quickly became part of the Society's programme of events. The first such visit, in April 1958, was to the late-eighteenth-century Charleville, County Wicklow, which, after lying empty for twelve years, in 1941 had been bought and restored by Donald and Mary Davies who established a clothing factory in the property's stable yard. Other outings soon followed and it was not long before a procession of cars led by the Guinnesses and carrying members of the Irish Georgian Society could regularly be spotted careering about the countryside. In late July 1960, for example, there was a two-day excursion to Counties Limerick and Clare co-ordinated by the Knight of Glin (who compiled an elegant notebook for the occasion), with participants each charged five shillings to visit places like Mount Ievers, Carnelly House, New Hall and Glin Castle. The schedule was often packed. A one-day outing to County Westmeath in July 1961 (cost five shillings per member) began at Ballinlough Castle, continued via the ruins of Killua to Mullingar Cathedral, followed by a picnic lunch at the ruins of Tudenham Park, before the cavalcade called into Belvedere House, Kilbixy Church and Ballynagall and finally arrived for what must have been very welcome drinks at Pakenham Hall (now Tullynally).

Richard Wood remembers many such trips from his early days with the Society when there was much zeal to rescue endangered buildings. 'I thought this was a marvellous idea, for two reasons. We would be helping to support "The Cause", and it would enable us to penetrate beyond great gateways to explore what lay inside with an excuse that contained at least the shadow of plausibility. Literally, exciting avenues were opening to us.' In those early days, when the road network was more imperfect than is now the case and motor ownership far less widespread, it was quite normal for sections of the group to get lost and never reach the intended destination. 'We used to go miles and miles to see someone's house,' remembers Ursula Lee who joined the Society at the very beginning. 'Some of us would get stopped at traffic lights and then one lot would go one way, and the rest off in another.' Owners of houses of potential interest could find themselves effectively, if amiably, invaded without any prior notice.

Mariga Guinness in particular soon became known for her unflagging determination to gain admission even into houses from which the public was always excluded. One owner awoke in bed to hear her in the corridor outside describing his home to members of the Society and it was said that only the Countess of Granard at Castle Forbes, County Longford, stubbornly refused to permit her across the threshold. Jeremy Williams tells of an occasion when Mariga brought a group to see Newbridge, County Dublin, now open to the public but then occupied by the distinctly unwelcoming Tommy Cobbe who demanded to know why these unannounced visitors wished to see his home. 'It is so pretty,' explained Mariga before unhelpfully adding, 'you are also.' As she and her party hastened to their cars, Mr Cobbe reached for his shotgun.

An abiding trait of trips undertaken by the Society and its members was that they included lunchtime picnics, for which Mariga Guinness had a lifelong fondness and on which she often announced her intention to write a book. Everyone was meant to contribute something to the meal, usually taken in the shadow of some gaunt ruin and regularly eaten sitting on damp grass in a persistent drizzle. But even in the gloomiest weather conditions, warmth was provided both by the stimulating company and conversation and, just as importantly, by the consumption of alcohol (again, this was an era when the drink-driving laws were more lax than is the case today). According to David Synnott, on their travels about the country Desmond and Mariga

> developed the habit of bringing large quantities of vin rosé with them, and of creating a party more or less wherever they went. 'Vin rosé,' said Mariga quite truthfully, 'nourishes the Georgian Society.' I remember seeing Patrick and Marina, then quite small, rolling a huge container of vin rosé which they had been asked to bring from the car and which was too big for them to carry.

The same drink also sustained members of the Irish Georgian Society on their initial tours outside the country, as a report on the organization's visit to York in May 1963 makes plain. 'Mr Guinness had an extraordinary stock of large stone jars which accompanied us on all our journeys,' wrote the anonymous author of this document. 'What was in those jars? No, it wasn't stout or beer, it was wine ... The jars had priority on the bus, next place to the driver and at lunchtime when the bus stopped, down they came with us and during the meal our glasses were filled and refilled again if need be.' Overseas touring began in June 1960 when a group of twenty-seven, including seven Americans, spent a week exploring Edinburgh and its environs 'packed full of excursions and social events which were duly and faithfully carried out'. The trip set the tone for those to follow over the coming decades, with lots of opportunities to see

Tour of Edinburgh led by the Hon. Desmond Guinness in June 1960. First foreign tour, Temperance Hotel.

houses not usually open to the public, including Hopetown, Kinross and Thirlestane Castle, the last of these then home to the dowager Countess of Lauderdale whose daughter was married to Lord Carew and living in Castletown, which in just a few years' time would become the Irish Georgian Society's headquarters.

But just as important were the parties to which the group was invited; as one participant, the Dublin psychiatrist Dr Melisande Zlotover, later wrote, 'The hospitality we received in Edinburgh town and country from our various hosts was most heartening. It transformed our tour into a veritable festival and gave us something worthwhile to remember.' It also established a precedent and from then on the Irish Georgian Society's overseas tours were popular as much for their convivial as their cultural dimension.

More overtly social in purpose were the cricket matches that also made their debut during the organization's first year. The initial match took place on the afternoon of Saturday, 16 August 1958 at Furness, County Kildare, a house dating from around 1740, which was then owned by Major Pierce Synnott (and is now home to Desmond and Mariga Guinness's son Patrick and his family). In typical fashion, the card inviting members to this event advised that 'Tea should be brought along.' The game came about as follows: Major Synnott's teenage son David (then a student at Ampleforth College in Yorkshire, he wrote an account on Georgian aviation published in Volume 1 of the Society's *Bulletin*) enjoyed a game of cricket even though, 'I played so badly that the school 2nd eleven would not have me, much less the 1st eleven.'

Despite this handicap, he and his father mustered together one team and challenged Desmond Guinness to do likewise; among the day's players were author Ulick O'Connor, the Indian ambassador and the butler from a neighbouring house, Forenaughts. The agreement was that the game would be played according to the first published laws of cricket dating from 1744, an example of which David Synnott found in the library at Ampleforth and arranged to have thirty copies printed. The principal differences from the current laws were as follows: each wicket consisted of two stumps twenty-two inches high and six inches apart; all hits had to be run out, regardless of whether they passed the boundary ropes or not; there was no lbw; the over consisted of four balls; the bowling was underarm; the bats, specially made, were large, weighing about four pounds each, and without splices; and no protection such as pads or gloves was permitted.

Correctly judging that it would be well-nigh impossible to find three-cornered Georgian hats for twenty-two players, David Synnott suggested the use of top hats, which cricketers usually wore for a period in the nineteenth century, and so these came into ordinary use for the game. Lord Carew and Peter Jury acted as umpires, the latter wearing an enormous scarlet affair on his head which, it transpired, was the inside of a hatbox made to contain a top hat. About 100 members of the Society turned up to support the match, played on a section of Furness's back lawn, roughly mown for the occasion and with a cord of twine serving as a boundary rope. After an afternoon of glorious play on almost the only dry day that summer, the Furness team won by a single run. But while this event, and many others like it, were undoubtedly great fun, in the years to come they were not allowed to distract the Irish Georgian Society from more serious tasks.

Opposite: Leixlip Castle, Co. Kildare, Gothic window, dining room, *c.*1740.

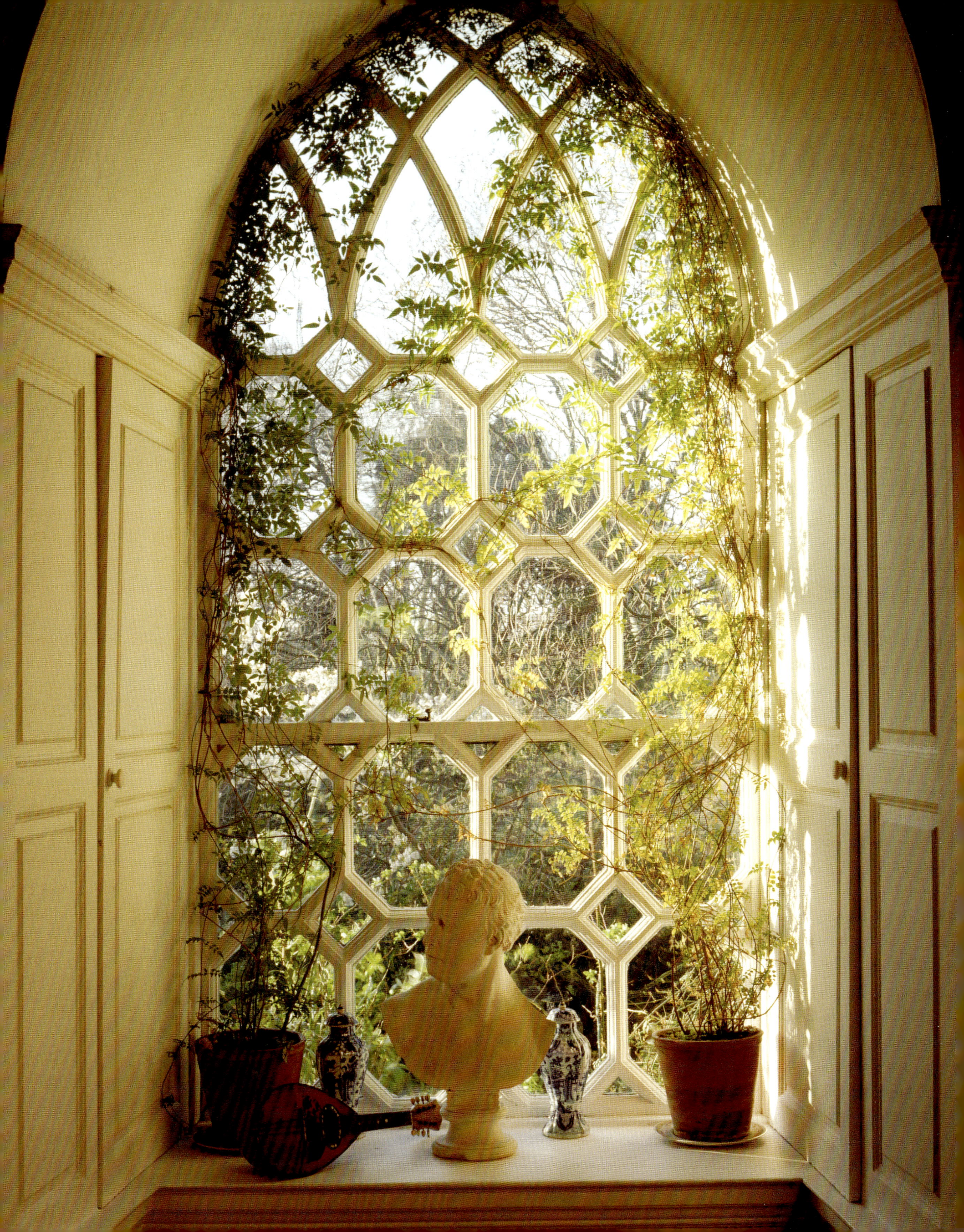

THE IRISH GEORGIAN SOCIETY VENTURES OVERSEAS

Three-week tour of India led by Mariga Guinness, 1970. *Left to right:* Greg McCambridge, Mary McGrath, Natasha Allen, Hubert Corrigan, Dr M.P. Bruce, Myrtle Allen, Mariga Guinness, Elizabeth O'Kelly, Anne Yeats, Mrs Vigors, Mrs E. McCabe, Mrs Bracegirdle, Anne Fennely, Hugh O'Neill.

After a first overseas tour to Edinburgh and environs in June 1960, three years passed before the Irish Georgian Society took a group abroad again, this time to York city and county. From then on, visits to places outside Ireland gradually became an essential and highly popular feature of the organization. In the first years, both Desmond and Mariga Guinness prepared the itinerary and accompanied the group, but as more and more of his time was taken up lecturing and fund-raising on behalf of the Society in the United States, she assumed responsibility. It is clear that Mariga was a conscientious, if somewhat erratic, tour guide and many participants in these early trips recall their feast-or-famine character; it was quite normal to dine in magnificent private surroundings and then go to bed in the cheapest, most unappealing hotel.

Mariga and Desmond Guinness's unrivalled network of social connections throughout Europe helped to ensure access to many houses that would otherwise have remained closed to members of the Society had they tried to gain admission on their own. Brian and Consuelo O'Connor remember that when viewing Badminton House, one member of the group was only interested in finding out how much land its owner possessed; 'about 35,000 acres', the Duke of Beaufort eventually conceded after persistent questioning on the subject. Prior to this tour, Mariga sought help from a friend, the Hon. John Jolliffe with whom she visited many houses. Prior to the tour he was besieged with letters asking such questions as 'Where is Bowood near? What is Castle Combe? Name of the shut house with rather unfriendly people near Dyrham? Name of Gothick nonsense near Bristol? Do you think Longleat and Stourhead might be possible on the same morning?' And on another occasion: 'Should one *buy* knives, for picnics, or does one borrow them somewhere?'

As a rule, Mariga would undertake a preparatory trip, sometimes bringing one or two friends with her. In September 1964, for example, accompanied by John Jolliffe, Elizabeth O'Kelly and designer David Vicary, she went to Leningrad (now called St Petersburg once more) in anticipation of the Irish Georgian Society tour of that city the following year. Participants, who paid £175 for first-class travel including a ticket to see the Bolshoi Ballet in Moscow, were warned that in Russia, 'Soap and W.C. paper are provided but are of mediocre quality' and were advised, 'Chocolate is very expensive. Bring this, bubble gum and biro pens for children in streets.' But regardless of preparation, the trip itself took some unexpected turns. Alfred Cochrane, who as a teenager barely out of school was by far the youngest member of the 39-strong group, remembers that when they went to see Tsarskoe Selo not all of the former Tsarist palace had yet been restored following its assault by the German army during the Second World War. Nothing daunted, Mariga reached inside her capacious fur muff, produced a wire-cutter and proceeded to make an opening in the chain fence so she and her party could inspect those parts of the building closed to the public. 'By the time the curator found us, he was so impressed that we were shown everything.'

Naturally this story was not included in the rather dry account of the tour she wrote for the Society's *Bulletin* later that winter, nor in the lecture she subsequently delivered to members back in Dublin. At the end of her talk, remembers Thomas Pakenham, questions were invited from the audience, one of whom complained that all the slides had shown buildings and angrily demanded to know where were the people of Leningrad. 'Well,' said Mariga, undaunted, 'they must all have been in the underground.' (Another member of the same expedition, George Stacpoole, was subsequently quoted in *The Irish Times* saying that native Russians 'thought we were Georgians, exiled to Ireland, and now returning to our native land'.)

In September 1966 a trip to Bordeaux was arranged, this time with both Desmond and Mariga Guinness in attendance. Once more, thanks to their contacts, in addition to viewing a great deal of architecture the group gained admission to some of the greatest wine-producing châteaux in the region such as Château Latour and Château Mouton-Rothschild where Baron Philippe de Rothschild entertained them to dinner. Brian and Consuelo O'Connor remember that Eoin O'Mahony had insisted the Irish 'Wild Geese' of an earlier era should be honoured and had brought from Avondale, County Wicklow (former home of Charles Stewart Parnell), a wreath of oak leaves for this purpose. The wreath was kept fresh in a hotel bath throughout the tour while discussions took place about where it ought to be laid. Only on the last day did the wreath find a home: on the tomb of the Comte de Lynch who had been mayor of Bordeaux in March 1814 when, at the close of the Napoleonic Wars, the city surrendered to the British army under the command of Marshal William Beresford (illegitimate son of the first Marquess of Waterford).

Four years later, Mariga Guinness led a group to Holland; typically its members were advised that, in addition to comfortable shoes and warm clothing, 'As two picnics are intended, a knife, fork and spoon should also be brought.' Professor Kevin B. Nowlan recalls that one of the houses visited on this trip belonged to a member of the princely Metternich family of Austria. Their hostess was extremely aloof towards the party, informing them, 'We rarely have people here.' However, her manner changed once Kevin Nowlan had explained Mariga's pedigree and 'she showed us around every nook and cranny after that'. From Holland Mariga wrote to Ulick O'Connor, 'We have seen some marvellous things, and listened to the difficulties of cleaning inner moats, outer ones being easier.' In late December 1970, she and the Irish Georgian Society ventured even further when a group went to India for three weeks, taking in Delhi, Agra, Calcutta, Chandanagore, Madras and Pondicherry. As usual Mariga had reconnoitred the place in advance and was able to tell a reporter from the *Sunday Independent* that a Major Cornel, 'who lost 97 soldiers "from drink in excess" had left Kinsale for India in 1754'. Notes sent to the tour's participants prior to their departure advised that they pack plenty of handkerchiefs: 'These should always be on hand for mopping one's forehead, or eating hot curries.'

Top: Tour of South Africa led by IGS president Desmond Fitzgerald, Knight of Glin, and board member Rose Mary Craig. Group pictured on the steps of Land-en-Zeezich House, 2001.

Middle: Tour to Paris and its environs led by the Hon. Desmond Guinness, Mick Jagger's château, Lafourchette, 1990.

Bottom: Jerry Hall and the Hon. Desmond Guinness, tour to Paris and its environs, 1990.

GEORGIAN CRICKET

Major Synnott's cricket team at Furness, Naas, Co. Kildare, 16 August 1958. Standing *(left to right):* Cathal Henry, Thomas O'Brien, Lingard Goulding, Justin Aylmer, Angus Macintyre, William Fennell and Michael Pratt. Sitting *(left to right):* David Pratt, John Blake Kelly, Major Pierce Synnott, David Synnott and Dennis Aylmer.

At least for its first decade, one of the highlights of the Irish Georgian Society's summer programme was the annual costumed cricket match, initiated in August 1958. The costume element of this event was always open to loose interpretation; some players and observers turned up clad, in whole or in part, in eighteenth-century clothing, others used the opportunity for fancy dress. The request for 'period costume' was usually respected, even if the period was left open to interpretation. A photograph from one of the earlier matches shows Mariga Guinness looking like a figure from a Tiepolo fresco in an enormous turban topped with ostrich plumes, and another picture shows the late Agnes Bernelle (then married to Desmond Leslie) mysteriously veiled as though she had just emerged from the seraglio.

The standard of play was similarly elastic as a surviving scorebook indicates, with batting averages being on the low side and more than one participant invariably bowled out without managing a single run.

At least in theory, the game was always played according to the first published rules of cricket dating from 1744 but despite copies of these being printed and distributed, there was rarely evidence that they were being strictly followed. It was usually a case of enthusiasm taking precedence over ability, although a few of the regular participants such as Charles Lysaght, David Synnott and John Bryson could often be relied upon to achieve a double-figure score. It was a condition that players could not be members of any cricket club and most of them appeared only too happy to demonstrate their amateur status. Typically, when playing in the grounds of Crom Castle, County Fermanagh, in August 1965, the Irish Georgian Society team was all out for just seventy-seven runs. By this time, the Society's yearly opposition was provided by a team from the Northern Ireland National Trust (which, at the Crom Castle game, was saved from coming up with an equally dismal performance when rain conveniently stopped play).

The cross-border encounters began in September 1960 with a game at Castleward, County Down; the Irish Georgian Society was the victor on that occasion, with no less than five of the National Trust players successively bowled out without scoring a single run. A kindly press report the following day commented that 'this was leisurely cricket befitting the period, with the bowlers bowling under-arm against two small wickets and a single bail'. Thereafter the norm was for each side to take turns in hosting the event and chances of winning were likewise shared between the two. Aside from those already mentioned, houses visited during this period included Malahide Castle, County Dublin; Mount Stewart, County Down; Castle Coole, County Fermanagh; Drenagh, County Derry; and Lough Rynn, County Leitrim. Because of its deliberately eccentric character, the annual match attracted a good deal of press attention and generated positive publicity for both organizations involved. Writing of the 1966 match in an appropriate style in *The Irish Times*, Bruce Arnold observed that certain aspects of the game were 'the subject of dispute, but there was little enough display of Spleen or Choler and on the whole the vicissitudes of the afternoon were borne by the Players with good grace and courage'.

Unfortunately rising levels of sectarian violence in Northern Ireland led to the suspension of the game from 1969 onwards. It was, however, revived in 1983 (once more at Castleward), with a notable match taking place at Castletown in 1986 when novelist J.P. Donleavy took part and afterwards wrote of the experience for the *Sunday Telegraph* magazine, describing how 'all you do is sit, wait and watch and play cricket while sipping a cool wine of Sancerre between the overs. And I wholeheartedly entered into the fun.' The matches continued for a few more years before finally coming to an end after a game at Drenagh in July 1988. 'I think we were all getting a bit long in the tooth,' remarks John Bryson, who had captained the Northern Irish team for the 1960 game and many times thereafter.

Clockwise from top left: First cricket match at Furness, Naas, Co. Kildare, August 1958.

Audrey Emerson at Furness, Naas, Co. Kildare, August 1963.

J.P. Donleavy (batting), cricket match at Castletown, Co. Kildare, 1987.

The Earl of Rosse (batting), cricket match at Birr Castle, Co. Offaly, 1986.

The Society begins active conservation work — saving the Conolly Folly — Dromana Gateway and Fiddown Chapel — the first volunteer workers — Riverstown House — Panels: the Conolly Folly and Riverstown House

CHAPTER

3

Although the Irish Georgian Society had worked to improve public awareness of the country's threatened heritage through its lectures, tours and exhibitions, during the earliest years it tended not to have any active engagement with conservation. True, on a number of occasions representation was made both to national and local authorities about buildings believed to be at risk, and letters on the same subject were regularly written to the press. In addition, small sums were collected and disbursed to aid the preservation of monuments around the country such as the courthouse in Kinsale, County Cork, Wexford's Theatre Royal, and 9 Henrietta Street in Dublin. But the organization's efforts sometimes met with disappointment. In 1964, for example, the Society, which had already offered on several occasions to pay for repairs to the roof of an eighteenth-century courthouse in Mountrath, County Laois, joined forces with Bord Fáilte to appeal against its demolition by the local authority. To no avail because, as had already been noted in the *Bulletin*, 'it appears to be difficult to arouse local interest' in the courthouse's fate, with the *Leinster Express* observing that in the building's place, 'a public toilet was urgently needed, particularly in view of the fact that Mountrath was the halfway bus-stop between Dublin and Limerick'.

The Society did not undertake direct intervention until 1962 when, at the suggestion of architectural historian Dr Mark Girouard, it was decided to restore the eighteenth-century Conolly Folly. Built in 1740 on the instructions of Speaker Conolly's widow, Katherine, to give employment after the previous year's harsh winter, this remarkable obelisk, which stands on high ground at a distance of two and a half miles to the rear of Castletown and soars 140 feet above the surrounding landscape, had from the very start served as the Society's logo; an early engraving of the folly appeared on the cover of the first issues of the *Bulletin* in 1958. Even then it was apparent that the monument was in serious disrepair, much of it smothered in ivy with the decorative sandstone pineapples fallen to the ground and a section of the tapering spire lost barely a yard from the summit. As one local wit commented, 'When the top falls off, it will lose its point!'

Four years after the Society had been established, the folly was in worse disrepair than ever and it was plain that unless something were soon done the entire structure would collapse. 'It would be very sad if this well-known landmark in Co. Kildare, the only one of its kind in the world, was allowed to disintegrate,' commented the summer edition of the *Bulletin*. A pamphlet published by the Society more bluntly warned that the spire 'has become so unsound that it may not survive another winter and the beautifully cut coping stones etc. that have fallen off must be put back as soon as possible'. It would, of course, have been perfectly understandable if the organization had merely badgered the government and the folly's owner, Lord Brocket, into embarking on a programme of essential repairs. That, after all, was what had hitherto been its policy in similar circumstances. But perhaps there was an awareness that this approach would not be successful; after all, six years earlier the state's National Monuments Advisory Council had strongly recommended that the folly be taken into the care of the Commissioners of Public Works but the suggestion was turned down 'due to lack of funds'.

Rather than face a similar scenario and in the interim watch the monument suffer further, the Irish Georgian Society chose to act: it would launch an appeal, raise money and employ workmen to restore the Conolly Folly. A notice to this effect was duly published and the first fund-raising event, a 'Steel Band Party', was held beside the folly on the rainy afternoon of Sunday, 5 August 1962, with tickets priced at ten shillings. Molly Keane's daughter, Sally Phipps, remembers this as the first Society function she attended: 'Mariga gave me a fruit cake to hand around the company and I remember she gave a hat to Garech Browne's beautiful brother who was killed (the Hon. Tara Browne) to make a collection. He returned with it empty saying everyone looked so poor he could not ask them for money.' Fortunately it was discovered that a government Amenity Grants Scheme, which had come into operation in 1960, would provide half the cost for what turned out to be an extremely complicated and, for the time, expensive, restoration. A Belfast firm of steeplejacks, Rainey and Sons, quoted a price of £358 for rebuilding the top fifteen feet of the pinnacle but more than this was going to be needed if the lower sections were also to be repaired. And, of course, the Society had to find 50 per cent of the final sum.

By the end of September 1962, some forty-eight individuals had made donations totalling £220 but this amount was still insufficient and another push had to be made for contributions; an updated list of subscribers printed at the end of 1963 showed plenty of donors giving £1 as well as larger sums from people like Lord Moyne (£150) and Sir Alfred Beit (£100); the smallest amount came from Desmond and

Portrait of Lady Louisa Conolly, wife of Thomas Conolly, by Hugh Douglas Hamilton, *c.* 1770.

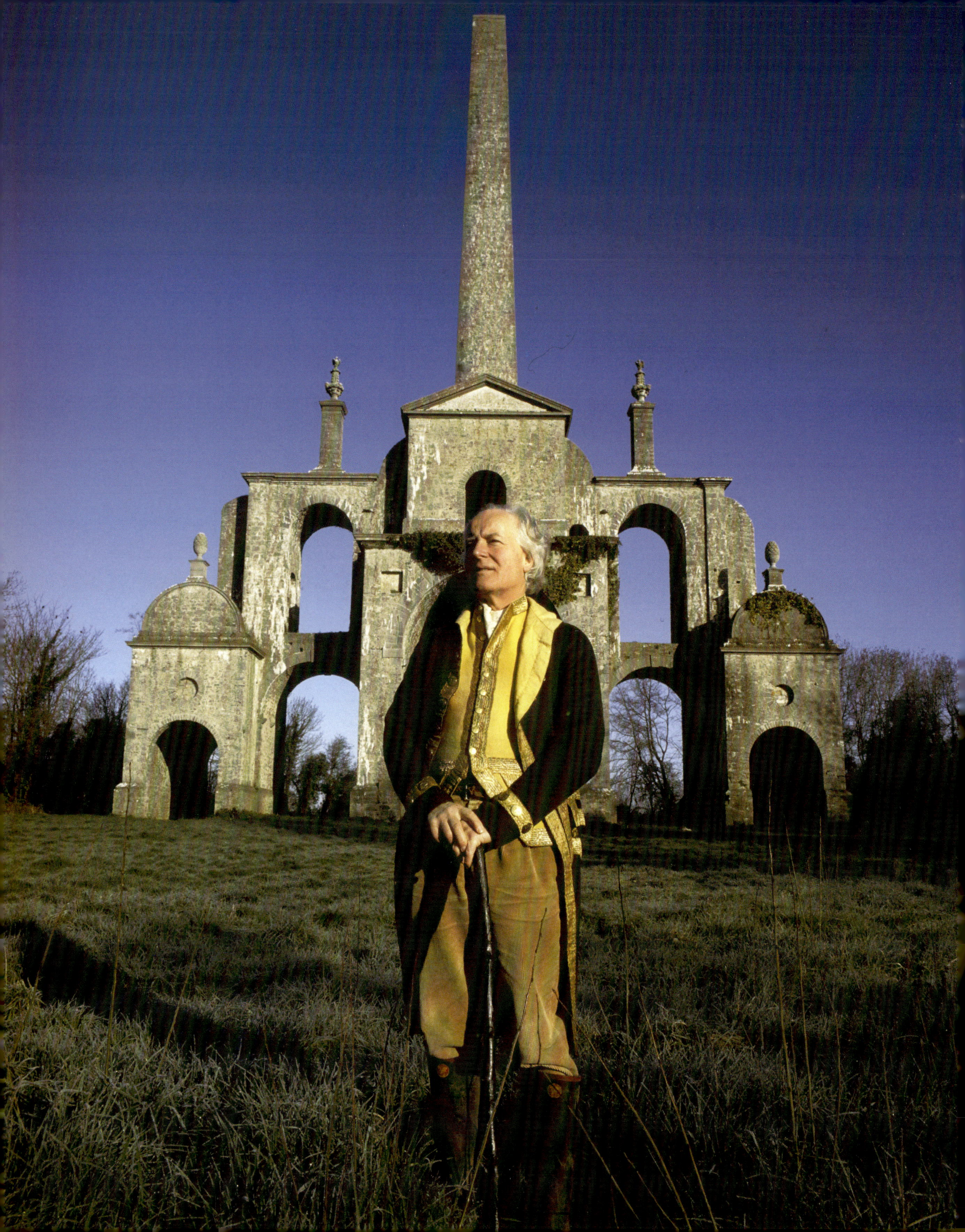

Mariga Guinness's seven-year-old son, Patrick, who offered five shillings. In addition, the state tourism board, Bord Fáilte, also provided £50. By spring 1964 the *Bulletin* was able to report that 'The first stage of the restoration of Conolly's Folly has been completed at a cost of £540; the 70-foot shaft has been repaired and completely repointed, as well as the plinths that carry the carved urns. The restoration fund is still open, and we hope to finish the work in 1964.' In fact the job took a little longer and cost rather more, but at the end of 1965 it was announced that after spending £2500 the Society had completed the work on the Conolly Folly, 'which is now safe for many years to come from the ravages of wind and weather'.

This project was significant not simply because it ensured the future of a major historic monument but in addition because for the first time the Irish Georgian Society had been directly responsible for preserving part of the national heritage, thereby setting a precedent for many similar operations over the coming decades. In fact, the next such undertaking began even before work on the Conolly Folly had finished. The Dromana Gateway in County Waterford dates from 1849 and is the only example of 'Brighton Pavilion' architecture in Ireland. An eccentric mix of Hindu and Gothic styles, the gateway dominates a bridge spanning the River Finisk and features a pale-green onion dome surmounting a pointed arch flanked by slender minarets. It was built by Henry Villiers-Stuart, first and last Lord Stuart de Decies at the entrance to his estate, replacing a similarly styled temporary structure that had been erected when he and his bride had returned from their honeymoon.

A century later the Villiers-Stuart family was no longer affluent; indeed, for financial reasons they were forced to demolish the greater part of Dromana House in 1966. By this time, the gateway stood empty and in a dangerous condition, its ogee Gothic windows required repair, its roof was leaking and ivy had overrun large parts of the exterior. The Irish Georgian Society undertook to save the building and to this end launched an appeal, beginning with that staple of the fund-raising circuit: a fashion show held in Leixlip Castle in May 1964. A Waterford architect, Don O'Neill Flanagan, offered his services for free and by the end of the year John Costin, a builder from nearby Cappoquin, had prepared an estimate of £550 for the job, with about half of that money already collected. The work was completed before the summer of 1966 and the Dromana Gateway still stands.

The next restoration project once more altered the character of the Society since it required active participation from willing members. The apse of what had once been a church, the little chapel at Fiddown, County Kilkenny, had been rebuilt in 1747 by then-vicar of the parish, the Revd Robert Watts, who commemorated his deed with a plaque inside the building. It is only one of the chapel's many eighteenth-century memorials, several of which are dedicated to members of the Ponsonby family whose seat, Bessborough, lies not far away. In the Society's *Bulletin* at the end of 1965, it was noted that some of the chapel's windows were broken and 'at present birds fly in and out'. More worryingly, the ground level outside was about three feet higher than the building's internal floor with the result that the elegant plaster decoration was rotting away. The following spring the Society asked for volunteers to help with the chapel's restoration. 'Please bring picks and spades,' the notice requested, 'as we hope to dig a ditch around it.'

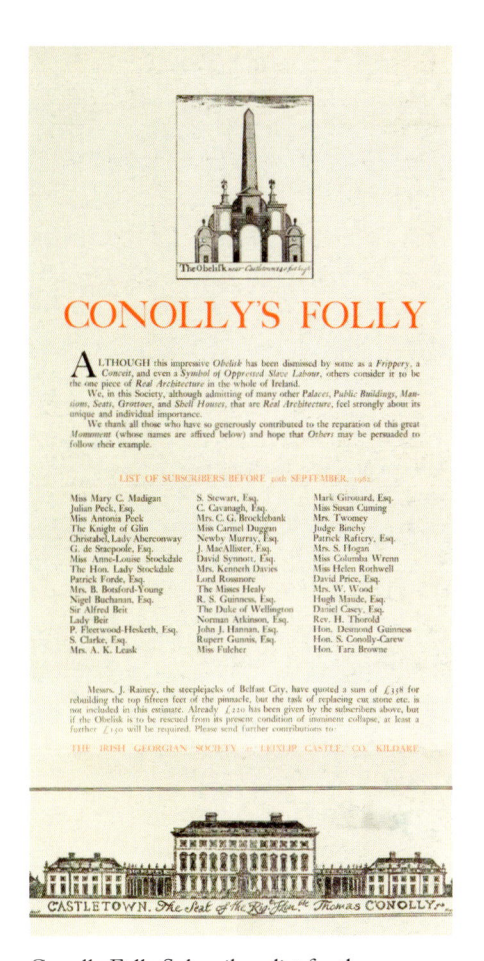

Conolly Folly Subscribers list for the restoration of the folly, 1962. Drawing of Castletown by the Knight of Glin.

Opposite: The Hon. Desmond Guinness in front of the Conolly Folly, Co. Kildare.

Hindu Gothic bridge at Dromana, Cappoquin, Co. Waterford, before restoration, 1964. Built in 1849 by Lord Stuart de Decies to give employment after the Famine.

Led by Desmond and Mariga Guinness, a small and hardy band tackled the task in June 1966, among those involved in the work being Peter Smithwick, Alison Cooke-Hurle – now Countess of Rosse – and Brian Molloy who was to play such a crucial role in the Society over the next twelve years. Exactly a decade later, the Society would restore another important funerary monument: the mid-eighteenth-century mausoleum carved by David Sheehan and commemorating the Earl of Barrymore at Castlelyons, County Cork. And in 1986 the Irish Georgian Society arranged for a group of volunteers to take care of the memorial to Sir Cornelius O'Callaghan in Shanrahan graveyard, County Tipperary, which had suffered badly from vandalism. Meanwhile, twenty years before in 1966, immediately after finishing work at Fiddown another voluntary work party spent four days mending and cleaning the roof and windows at Charleville Forest, County Offaly. Francis Johnston's most important Gothic building in Ireland, the house had stood empty and unoccupied since a sale of contents in 1948 but, readers of the *Bulletin* were assured, 'it only needs to be made watertight to survive until a suitable use can be found for it'.

The Fiddown Chapel and Charleville Forest voluntary ventures set the pattern for many to follow. Given the Society's limited financial resources (by 1966 membership had grown to around 3000 but the annual subscription remained just £1) and an ever-growing demand for its services, inviting volunteers to provide manual labour made sense. Unpaid work, whether clearing away undergrowth or painting woodwork, encouraged a spirit of camaraderie and a feeling of participation in realizing the organization's ambitions that was quite different from making a monetary donation. Especially for younger, more physically active members the causes championed by the Irish Georgian Society didn't have to represent some worthy but abstract ideal; they could become tangible with results the volunteers had personally helped to achieve. This was most easily done when the job being done was either on an uninhabited site

Hindu Gothic bridge at Dromana, Cappoquin, Co. Waterford, after restoration.

or, as would later be the case, on properties that had come into direct ownership of the Irish Georgian Society. It was more difficult where the building in question remained in other hands or the task in question demanded professional skills and training. In those cases, the Society had to revert to seeking donations from its members and other well-wishers.

This was what it did during the first half of the 1960s for two other properties deemed to be at risk without active intervention. Gill Hall in County Down was a three-storey, seven-bay building dating from 1670–80 and therefore one of the country's earliest unfortified domestic structures. Reputedly also the most haunted house in Ireland, Gill Hall had been abandoned by its owners around 1910 and though retaining seventeenth-century panelling and other decoration the house had been permitted to fall into serious decay. Although in Northern Ireland, and therefore outside the Society's unofficial bailiwick, nevertheless the case of Gill Hall was too important not to command attention. As architect Desmond Hodges wrote, 'For years the ceilings and roof timber have been exposed to wind and rain, loose slates have been lifted and the heart of the building was laid open.' In 1966, £600 was provided by the Society for certain essential work: crumbling chimneys were removed within the centre wall; new, sound brickwork inserted to carry the load of sagging trusses reinforced with steel angles; and sections of roof slating replaced. 'The rain can still enter the building through the broken windows,' warned the *Bulletin* at the end of the year, 'and spores of fungus still remain among the timbers, but at least the fabric will stand for a few more years.' Unfortunately, a few more years was all the time remaining for Gill Hall: not long afterwards it was ravaged by fire and subsequently demolished.

A happier outcome awaited another of the buildings benefiting from the Society's attention during this period. Just a few miles outside the city of Cork, Riverstown

CHAPTER 3

Volunteer restoration work at Fiddown, Co. Kilkenny, on the monument to the Earl of Bessborough by William Atkinson, 1758. *Left to right:* Chris Anthony; Kevin Pakenham; Mariga Guinness; Brian Molloy; Alison Cooke-Hurle, later Countess of Rosse; the Hon. Desmond Guinness.

House was built during the 1730s by Dr Jemmett Browne who became Bishop of Cork and Ross in 1745. Its most notable feature has always been the dining room, the walls and ceiling of which are decorated with plasterwork by the Italian Lafranchini brothers, possibly the first commission they executed in this country and ever since much admired. Nevertheless, although Riverstown remained in the possession of the Browne family until the middle of the last century, by the 1950s it stood empty and the threat of irreparable deterioration seemed so likely that moulds of the dining room were made under the direction of Raymond McGrath of the Office of Public Works (thanks to the close friendship of President Sean T. O'Kelly and Dr C.P. Curran, the authority on Irish decorative plasterwork); these were installed in the Irish president's residence, Áras an Uachtaráin, where they can still be seen today.

Not long afterwards Riverstown and its surrounding land were bought by a Cork market gardener, John Dooley, whose interest at the time was agricultural rather than aesthetic. Mr Dooley used the house for storage; a photograph published by the *Cork Examiner* in February 1965 shows boxes of potatoes neatly stacked on either side of the dining-room fireplace. Nevertheless, he was not unaware of Riverstown's importance or unwilling to see the building refurbished. On the contrary, he willingly collaborated with the Irish Georgian Society in this project and within a few years the house had once more become a family home – and has remained so ever since. The Society initially drew its members' attention to Riverstown in late 1964, a *Bulletin* advising that John Dooley had accepted that restoration of the dining room was necessary, 'and has agreed to remove the contents (though needing the space). He will permit the public to use the elegant semicircular entrance hall through which the plaster room is reached, which is most generous of him.'

Within a month of the appeal's issue, no less than 128 contributions had been received. Work began on the site early the following year when the walls were stripped of paint and cleaned, fretwork re-gilded, new windows installed and electric wiring renewed.

40

Though some of these tasks had to be left to professionals, much of it was done by volunteers. Four years later, for a feature in the *Irish Woman's Journal*, John Dooley's wife remembered that Mariga Guinness 'could stand for hours on a ladder carefully cleaning every speck of dust from the gold-leaf decoration'.

By the end of 1965 Riverstown's dining room had been 'restored to its former beauty' and furnished with a number of pieces of furniture provided by the Society, including a fine hunting table that had come from Doneraile Court (itself soon enough to become a cause for concern). The drive up to the house had also been overhauled so that visitors could come to see Riverstown. The initial work cost £717, the sum once more being collected from individual donations and at fund-raising events such as yet another fashion show, this time held at Major Synnott's home, Furness, County Kildare. By spring 1966, the amount had climbed to £1777 but the investment can be considered worthwhile because it had the effect of inspiring the Dooleys both to make Riverstown their home and to continue restoring the building at their own expense. In the Society's January–March 1970 *Bulletin*, it was reported that one of the house's two late-eighteenth-century drawing rooms adjoining the dining room

> has been given a new dado, architraves, chimney-piece, overdoors and overmantel. These have been collected by John Lenehan of Kanturk, who rescued them from houses in Dublin that were being demolished and inserted them at Riverstown. The farm implements have been banished once more to the farm, and in their place is elegant eighteenth century and Regency furniture. Some pictures, busts and an Italian statue have kindly been lent by the Cork Municipal School of Art and others.

Meanwhile, in the surrounding garden, John Dooley had drained a swamp and restored the river to its original course. 'A very fine ice house was discovered when brambles and briars were cleared away; telegraph poles are being moved to less conspicuous positions, and a new driveway is being made to give a more impressive view of the house on arrival.' (The latter work was paid for by Bord Fáilte.)

Ten years after the Society's initial involvement with the house, still more work had been achieved, as a feature in the Cork *Evening Echo* noted, with the drawing-room walls covered in green silk and hung with eighteenth-century pictures. The success of Riverstown suggests the Irish Georgian Society might have undertaken many similar collaborative projects with other owners of historic houses. And perhaps it would have done so, had not so much of the organization's time and effort been taken up over the next few years by another campaign: the fight to save Georgian Dublin.

Riverstown House, Co. Cork, entrance hall.

THE CONOLLY FOLLY

Top: The Conolly Folly, built in 1740. Taken from Noble and Keenan's map of Co. Kildare, 1752, used as a symbol by the IGS.

Bottom: Rose Saul Zalles, goodwill ambassador to Ireland, with Irish ambassador to the USA, William P. Fay, 1969.

'My sister is building an obleix to answer a vistow from the bake of Castletown House,' wrote Mrs Jones to another sibling in March 1740, adding, 'it will cost her three or four hundred pounds at least, but I believe more. I really wonder how she can dow so much, and live as she duse.' The sister referred to in this erratically spelled letter was Katherine Conolly, widow of the late Speaker Conolly who had begun building Castletown prior to his death in 1729. Mrs Conolly, who continued to live in the house, undertook the construction of the folly in early 1740 in order to provide local employment after a particularly harsh winter the previous year. In 1743 she was also responsible for commissioning the Wonderful Barn, which closes the vista from Castletown to the east as the folly does to the north. Standing two and a half miles on a direct axis from the house, the folly rises 140 feet and comprises a 70-foot obelisk supported on a series of arches, the whole decorated with cut-stone pineapples, urns and other ornamentation. Lying on the highest ground in the vicinity, the structure can be seen from twenty miles away. In 1978 its distinctive image featured on an Irish postage stamp.

Though built at the request of Mrs Conolly (who bore the full cost of its erection) and intended to be best seen from the rear of Castletown, the folly actually stood inside the estate of her immediate neighbours, the FitzGeralds, subsequently Dukes of Leinster at Carton; local tradition held this was the reason an avenue was never planted all the way to the structure. It is therefore agreed that the architect responsible was the German-born Richard Castle who at the time was employed on extending and improving Carton and who would later work at Belan, County Kildare, where two obelisks were built in the grounds, one of them not unlike the Conolly Folly, both restored by the Irish Georgian Society.

More than two centuries after its initial construction, the Conolly Folly had badly deteriorated and threatened to collapse until restored by the Irish Georgian Society between 1962 and 1965 at a cost of £2500. In 1968 the Society bought the monument and immediately surrounding land from the owner of Carton, the Hon. David Nall-Cain, for £1000; this money was provided by Rose Saul Zalles, a Washington resident and long-time supporter of the organization. Twenty-five years later the Irish state assumed ownership of the Conolly Folly from the Castletown Foundation and has been responsible for its maintenance ever since. After her death in 1989, Mariga Guinness was buried beneath the Conolly Folly.

Clockwise from top left: The Conolly Folly.

The Conolly Folly before restoration.

The Conolly Folly after restoration.

The new IGS logo, drawn by Michael Craig and designed by Vermillion, in use since 2007.

The Conolly Folly.

RIVERSTOWN HOUSE

Riverstown House, Co. Cork, dining room.

The earliest reference to Riverstown is in Smith's *History of Co. Cork*, published in 1750, where it is described as a 'pleasant seat' and 'a house beautified with several curious pieces of stucco performed by the Francini brothers'. Clearly by this date the house and its interior had been finished on the instructions of Dr Jemmett Browne, appointed to the Bishopric of Cork and Ross five years before. In a feature on Riverstown written by C.P. Curran and published in the Society's *Bulletin*, Volume IX, No. 1, Bishop Browne is summarized as 'an amiable man of no great distinction though he occupied two sees before Cork and two others before his death in 1782'. But he surely merits a little more praise than this, if only for commissioning the dining room at Riverstown. The rather plain exterior of the house gives little indication of the glories lying within and indeed these are largely confined to one room, although the entrance hall with its columns and curved inner wall is also charming.

However, the dining room is unquestionably Riverstown's chief glory thanks to its elaborate plasterwork decoration by the Swiss-Italian Lafranchini brothers, Paul and Philip, who having already worked in England came to Ireland in 1738 at the request of the Earl of Kildare (father of the first Duke of Leinster) for whom they executed the great saloon ceiling at Carton. They also found work at a number of County Cork houses including Kilshannig and Castle Saffron; while the latter was destroyed by fire in the second half of the eighteenth century, the former still happily survives with its magnificent interior decoration intact. At Riverstown the Lafranchinis covered the dining-room walls with a series of panels, eight of which feature classical figures as diverse as Aeneas the founder of Rome, the goddess Ceres and a draped female representing Grammar. Curran's research demonstrated that the source of inspiration for these figures was equally varied. On the ceiling the brothers represented Time rescuing Truth from the assaults of Discord and Envy, a direct translation into plaster of a ceiling painted by Nicholas Poussin for Cardinal Richelieu in 1641 and now in the Louvre. The work at Riverstown is more severe than that undertaken by the Lafranchinis elsewhere in Ireland, perhaps because their patron was a senior member of the established church, perhaps because it was carried out at the start of their time in this country. But whatever the explanation, it does not detract from the splendour of the room.

Riverstown remained in the ownership of the Browne family until the middle of the last century, after which it was left empty until being bought by a Cork farmer, John Dooley. He died in 1987 and today his son and daughter-in-law, Denis and Rita Dooley, live in the house. The third country house in the Republic to open to the public (after Bantry and Westport), Riverstown continues to receive visitors.

Top: Riverstown House, Co. Cork, dining room. Formerly used as storage for potatoes as published in the *Cork Examiner*, February 1965.

Bottom: Riverstown House, Co. Cork, dining room with ceiling and wall panel plasterwork by Philip and Paul Lafranchini, the third house in the Republic, after Bantry and Westport, to be open to the public.

Georgian Dublin at risk ~ public indifference or hostility towards eighteenth-century architecture ~ the fight to save Lower Fitzwilliam Street ~ the Tailors' Hall ~ St Catherine's Church ~ Panels: the Tailors' Hall and the kindness of donors

CHAPTER

4

It is well-known that, as far as the central city is concerned, the days of Dublin's Georgian heritage are numbered and that when these decayed and obsolete monuments of a past age come to be demolished, many of their sites will be redeveloped with buildings much larger in bulk and greater in height than the present ones. This change of character must be faced; it is not, of itself, a good or a bad thing.

These words from the architectural correspondent of *The Irish Times* on 31 December 1959 turned out to be unhappily prophetic of what would happen over the next few years, and of the kind of attitude the Irish Georgian Society persistently encountered in its battle to preserve Dublin's eighteenth-century buildings. There were, it is true, a few citizens aware of their capital's particular charm. An editorial in the *Dublin Historical Record* of March–May 1958 insisted that the neglect of buildings, 'which give Dublin its character and civilisation, must cease lest it deteriorate into a mere middling city of mediocre domestic dwelling houses'.

Until the start of the 1960s the city had preserved the greater part of its Georgian heritage intact although the main reason for this lay not in a widespread enthusiasm for conservation but in poverty; the state, the local authority and the residents generally lacked funds to replace what was already there with anything else. The city's largely unaltered appearance since the mid nineteenth century was much commented on and admired by visitors and also by some natives; in 1963 novelist Sean O'Faolain wrote of how the brickwork of Dublin houses 'has been chromatized and mellowed by centuries of wind and weather into a shifting array that glows now like a ruby port, now like a saffron sherry, now like a primrose muscatel'. In fact a certain amount of official effort had been made to preserve the character of Dublin. During the 1940s and 50s, the corporation reconditioned some of its Georgian properties into flats for rent. However this was primarily because of the difficulty of undertaking new work owing to shortages of skilled labour and material. And while some of the city's own housing stock was refurbished, the great majority of properties in private hands were not. Instead these houses had gradually deteriorated to the point where they were frequently beyond restoration.

Two disasters in June 1963 made the degeneration of Dublin's Georgian heritage abundantly clear. One night at the beginning of the month, No. 20 Bolton Street, a house on the north side of the city, collapsed, killing an octogenarian couple Leo and Mary Maples who were asleep in the building at the time. Ten days later, in the middle of the afternoon and on the other side of the Liffey, two early-nineteenth-century houses on Fenian Street fell down; two little girls walking past on their way to buy sweets were buried in the rubble. The effect of these twin tragedies was to make suspect the security of every old residential building in Dublin, especially after there had been protest marches by women and children through the streets with placards that read, 'Don't Wait for the Houses to Fall'. In a panic, the corporation began evacuating residents from many of its own properties and private landlords did likewise. Nobody thought to point out that the Bolton Street house had been left unprotected after the demolition of its neighbour or that warnings had been given weeks beforehand that the Fenian Street houses were in a vulnerable state. The general consensus was that old buildings were unreliable and unsafe and ought to be condemned to demolition before they killed anyone else.

This viewpoint was articulated by young architect Sam Stephenson, who wrote to *The Irish Times* a few days later, decrying Dublin's Georgian houses and claiming that 'the shoddiness of the construction would horrify the average layman brought up on the pious myth about the robust good sense and the innate good taste of the 18th century'. He also took a swipe at organizations like the Irish Georgian Society, insisting, 'A considerable disservice to the future of Dublin is performed by the antics of the so-called responsible citizens who call for a unilateral preservation of the city.' The point was plain: Dublin's old buildings should be regarded as potential deathtraps. Over the next year, the corporation's Dangerous Buildings Inspectorate, which had been hastily expanded, condemned 900 houses and by 1965 this figure had climbed to 2000, of which more than 1200 were actually demolished. It did not help that the government's Planning Act of 1963 did not include demolition under its definition of 'development', meaning only the tiny number of buildings specifically listed for preservation were safe.

Although undertaken for reasons of public safety, the clearances often suited Dublin Corporation, which had begun quietly making plans to sweep away much of the old city years before. For instance, the scheme to build new civic offices on Wood Quay, the subject of so much controversy in the late 1970s, actually dated back to a decision taken by the authority in January 1956. Similarly, the windswept highway that now lies to the immediate west of St Patrick's Cathedral was originally proposed as part of a road-widening project as long ago as 1954. There was relatively little interest in preserving the older parts of the city when these were perceived as impeding progress and development. So the earliest new buildings constructed at this time were broadly welcomed as heralding a new era of prosperity. Aside from the national bus terminal Busáras built from 1946–53 to the immediate rear of James Gandon's Custom House, among the most notable and intrusive examples of what was then regarded as 'modern' architecture in Dublin were Liberty Hall on Eden Quay and, across the river on Burgh Quay, O'Connell Bridge House, which unnecessarily replaced the early-nineteenth-century Carlisle Building.

The function of these two structures, and countless others like them, provides a further explanation for why older buildings became so vulnerable to demolition during the 1960s: that era's office boom. Central Dublin had increasingly come to seem an unattractive place in which to live and the greater part of the population, as well as new arrivals in the city, preferred to settle in the suburbs. Between 1936 and 1971, the inner-city population halved, falling from 266,511 to 131,501. The heart of Dublin became somewhere to work and accordingly more and more of it was given over to offices. But old houses intended for private residence were awkward to adapt to this purpose; it was easier to knock them down and put up something specifically designed to accommodate workers, whose numbers in Dublin doubled between 1946 and 1972.

More than 300 office blocks were constructed in central Dublin during the twenty-five years after 1960, the majority of them first requiring the demolition of several old houses. And after completion many of the new offices were leased by the government to house its ever-expanding bureaucracy; in the ten years up to 1973, the state's annual outlay on rental of privately owned office space grew from £200,000 to £1.5m. and a decade later had increased to £15m. Thus there was an incentive for property speculators to enter the office market. Their emergence reflected Ireland's increased affluence, particularly during the first half of the 1960s, as well as a growing sense of national self-confidence that followed the publication in 1958 of the first programme devised by T.K. Whitaker, secretary of the Department of Finance, and implemented by the government of Taoiseach Sean Lemass. After a long period of recession, national employment and incomes finally began to rise and with them came the expectation of material betterment. The shabby Dublin of the 1950s might have had its charm for overseas visitors but few residents were sorry to see it go.

One of the principal sources of employment (both then and ever since) was the construction industry, which has always had close links with the Irish political establishment and has, therefore, rarely faced official censure. The promise of jobs on a building site, no matter what the consequences to the national heritage, has consistently been thought too good to overlook. Besides, back in the 1960s a large percentage of the population would have questioned whether Dublin's Georgian buildings – and indeed those throughout the country – should be considered truly Irish. After visiting Dublin in the 1930s, the Italian art historian Mario Praz wrote in his 1941 book, *On Neoclassicism*, 'Vandalism and decay confer, almost, a greater value on such places; one is conscious of a bitter pleasure of admiring what most people do not admire.' Most of the city's population, struggling with the more pressing question of earning a living in a persistently depressed economy, did not admire Dublin's Georgian buildings. The aesthetic merits of these structures was deemed irrelevant. But did it need to be so?

Writing in *The Irish Times* in January 1989, Molly Keane compared the situation in this country to that in Russia, 'which suffered many wrongs at the hands of her aristocracy and land-owning classes before she overthrew a great dynasty'. Nevertheless, the author remarked, the Soviet regime had preserved the old treasures 'as a purposeful attraction to tourists, a strong link with the outside world long before glasnost was a thread of hope in one man's mind'. Somehow a similar awareness never occurred in Ireland where those citizens not indifferent to the fate of the country's old buildings were often vocally hostile towards them. One (unnamed) Irish minister of state was quoted as saying at the time of the Kildare Place debacle, 'I was glad to see them go. They stand for everything I hate,' and in his 1983 book on Dublin's beleaguered legacy of eighteenth-century architecture, *Georgian Dublin: Ireland's Imperilled Architectural Heritage*, Kevin Corrigan Kearns quoted a correspondent to *The Irish Times* who wrote,

13–28 Lower Fitzwilliam Street, Dublin. Owned by the Electricity Supply Board.

Meeting held at the Pillar Room, Rotunda Hospital, Dublin.
Left to right (in front row): Lady Moyne and Catriona; Nell Tormey; Desmond Guinness and Lord Moyne seated on the floor.

'Georgian buildings are an offence to all true-blue Irishmen, they are a hangover from a repressive past ... and they must go.' Likewise in 1977, after the Irish Georgian Society had restored the early-eighteenth-century Damer House in Roscrea, County Tipperary, it could still be described by an elected member of the local council as a 'bastion of British Imperialism'. At worst Dublin's eighteenth-century buildings were reviled, at best the subject of general ignorance despite the publication in 1952 of Maurice Craig's magisterial work, *Dublin 1660–1860*, and the ongoing research of organizations such as the Old Dublin Society, founded in 1934.

These were just some of the difficulties faced by the Irish Georgian Society when it sought to prevent the obliteration of large swathes of Georgian Dublin. A struggle that would last decades began with the fight against a plan to knock down sixteen houses on Lower Fitzwilliam Street, immediately to the south-east of Merrion Square. From 1927 onwards these buildings and their immediate neighbours had been gradually acquired by the national Electricity Supply Board as its duties and staff swelled. In December 1961 the company announced its intention to demolish 13–28 Lower Fitzwilliam

Street and replace the terrace with a purpose-built office block designed by the winner of an architectural competition. Although this would mean the destruction of Europe's longest unbroken line of Georgian houses (running from the northern end of Merrion Square to the top of Fitzwilliam Place) various justifications were given for this gratuitous act of vandalism. These ranged from declaring the buildings 'structurally unsound' to claims that dry rot had been discovered in their roof timbers. But as the Irish Georgian Society's *Bulletin* noted, if structural problems did exist, then 'the ESB, having used these buildings for 20 years cannot entirely disclaim responsibility for this'. More significantly, in 1962 the ESB's chairman in an interview carried by the Society's *Bulletin* admitted his organization had envisaged rebuilding the terrace more than twenty years earlier: 'Rules for an architectural competition to provide a replacement were drawn up in 1938, but the competition was abandoned because of the war.'

Lower Fitzwilliam Street, Dublin. Sixteen Georgian houses being demolished, 1965.

The ESB's plans attracted widespread opposition, both at home and abroad, with *The Guardian*'s correspondent asking, 'Is there a public opinion in Ireland sufficiently concerned to put a stop to this vandalism; and if not, why not?' In an editorial on the subject, *The Irish Times* invited readers to 'stand outside Holles Street hospital and look towards the Dublin Mountains. What would Canaletto have made of the view?' A public meeting called at Dublin's Mansion House attracted some 900 people, with 300 more having to be turned away at the door and therefore being denied the opportunity to hear the ESB denounced by people like actor Micheál Mac Liammóir and artist Sean Keating, then-president of the Royal Hibernian Academy, who warned that if Fitzwilliam Street's destruction went ahead, 'the next move will be to feed the books in the Library of Trinity College to the boilers of the Pigeon House'. (Similarly in a report written by Dublin City Architect Daithí Hanly – one of the Irish Georgian Society's original committee members – the question was posed, 'How important is the Book of Kells? At what price and for what convenience would we divide it and allow 16 pages of it to be destroyed?')

The audience at the Mansion House meeting also heard read the contents of a telegram of objection to the ESB's scheme, sent by the ground landlord of Fitzwilliam Street, the Earl of Pembroke whose forbears were responsible for the original development of the area. In an attempt to preserve the Fitzwilliam Street buildings, he now offered the ESB an alternative site nearby on James's Street East. This proposal was not only declined but a compulsory purchase order was served on the Fitzwilliam Street houses, for which Lord Pembroke was paid a derisory £1000; he immediately donated half the sum to the Irish Georgian Society to help its campaign.

But there were as many voices heard in favour of the terrace's destruction. For example, two groups of architectural students attended the Mansion House meeting to demonstrate their support of the ESB's intentions and in February 1962 the council of the Royal Institute of Architects in Ireland declared itself 'satisfied that a new building need not destroy the beauty of the existing environment', despite the fact that the design of the new building had yet to be seen. It was only in November 1962 that the winner of the ESB's architectural competition was announced: Stephenson Gibney and Associates in which Sam Stephenson – the same man who would write

Lower Fitzwilliam Street, Dublin, before demolition.

to *The Irish Times* the following summer denouncing Georgian buildings' general shoddiness of construction – was a partner. Sir John Summerson, the distinguished English architectural historian, was now hired by the ESB to champion their cause. Having already pronounced that the only reasonable course was 'to build to an entirely new design', in an interview carried by the Irish Georgian Society's spring 1962 *Bulletin* (which was entirely devoted to the subject of Fitzwilliam Street) he went further, calling the existing houses 'a sloppy, uneven series' and declaring, 'It is nearly always wrong to preserve rubbish, and by Georgian standards these houses are rubbish.' Meanwhile the Society had retaliated by inviting an expert of its own, another architectural knight, Sir Albert Richardson. His retort to Summerson's dismissal of Fitzwilliam Street was to argue that 'no eighteenth century houses were substantially built – does that lessen their merit?'

The battle went on for more than two years. At the end of 1962, Desmond Guinness wrote that if the ESB's scheme were to go ahead, 'it will show the complete disregard which there is for our architectural heritage, and the scant attention that has been paid to the outburst of public opinion against demolition'. Both the Irish Georgian and Old Dublin societies organized petitions against the ESB's plans but no matter how much support they mustered or how vocal their objections it made no difference, not least because the government of the day had no objections to the buildings' demolition. In late September 1964 on the day before the new Planning Act – which might have provided salvation for the terrace – came into effect, the Minister for Local Government, Neil Blaney, signed an order granting full planning permission for the new office development on Lower Fitzwilliam Street. The following summer the sixteen houses were knocked down and work began on their replacement, which still continues to break the unity of the area's streetscape. In 1988 the ESB, by way of restitution for the earlier act of vandalism, spent £4m. carefully restoring the remaining properties it owned on Upper Mount and Lower Fitzwilliam streets, opening one of the latter as the Georgian House Museum.

Lower Fitzwilliam Street, Dublin, replacement office development.

Desmond Guinness later described the Fitzwilliam Street debacle as the 'onset of the rot' and it is true that in the following years there was widespread and wanton destruction of historic buildings throughout Dublin. But preservationists like the Irish Georgian Society, though they lost some battles emerged victorious from others. Among the most important successes of the 1960s was the salvation of the Tailors' Hall on Back Lane. Not long after its foundation, the Society had recognized both the significance of this building and its extreme vulnerability, especially since it stood in a part of the city where Dublin Corporation planned to implement sweeping clearances in pursuit of a road-widening policy. Built in 1706 and the capital's last surviving guildhall, the Tailors' Hall was the subject of a well-researched paper written by William Dillon (then a student) and published in the Society's *Bulletin* in spring 1960; this warned that the building would be lost within a decade 'unless it is restored in the immediate future'. The following year the *Bulletin* was pleased to announce that 'a preservation order has been made so that the Tailor's Hall is now out of danger'.

Would that this had actually been the case. By now the hall had passed into the ownership of Dublin Corporation, which displayed no interest in the building other than to instruct the last tenants, the Legion of Mary, to vacate the premises, which were classified as being in a dangerous condition. In 1964 the Society's *Bulletin* reported that despite being officially listed for preservation, the Tailors' Hall was to be demolished. Photographs of the exterior show just how dilapidated it had become, with the walls shored up by timber buttresses, almost every window broken, slates missing from the roof and the door boarded up. Many of the original interior fittings had been stolen; the fine marble chimney piece presented by then-Master of the Guild, Christopher Neary, in 1784 would later turn up in Cork. Since the local authority was not prepared to do anything, it was plain that without third-party intervention the hall would either fall or be pulled down. In its spring 1966 *Bulletin* the Irish Georgian Society advised that the building, which had stood empty for the past six years, was by then shored up 'and will only be saved if enough people show an interest in it and act now'. Members were invited to demonstrate their interest by attending a meeting at Ely House in early June where they were told that Dublin Corporation had agreed to allow the Society, or any other responsible organization, to assume responsibility for the restoration of the Tailors' Hall, estimated to cost in the region of £20,000.

This was a considerably larger sum than the Irish Georgian Society had ever before tried to raise and indeed the whole project was by far the biggest it had yet considered tackling. But the opportunity to save the Tailors' Hall from what was otherwise certain destruction could not be ignored and so it was agreed to call a further meeting in late July when other individuals and groups would be invited to join forces with the Society in a common cause: saving the Tailors' Hall. Held in the Royal Hibernian Hotel, the event attracted extensive press coverage, with all the following day's newspapers reporting the formation of a new association called the Tailors' Hall Fund. Its committee was chaired by Desmond Guinness and featured such familiar names in the cause of conservation as Professor Kevin B. Nowlan, Uinseann Mac Eoin and Daithí Hanly. Disproving any notion that the Irish Georgian Society and its ilk were snobbish or elitist, the fund's honorary treasurer was a long-standing Republican, Máire Comerford, who had just retired from thirty years as a journalist with *The Irish Press*. Born in 1892, she had participated in the Easter 1916 Rising and in the Irish Civil War on the anti-Treaty side, for which she then spent some time in prison. Máire Comerford's involvement in the campaign to save the Tailors' Hall demonstrated that Ireland's burgeoning conservation movement was by no means the preserve of one particular social group or class. And the fund's plan for the building was equally democratic: when restoration was complete, the premises would 'once more be available for meetings and exhibitions for the citizens of Dublin as in the past, and it will stand as a lasting tribute to all those who worked there to secure the rights and liberties of Irishmen'.

Efforts to find the necessary money began almost immediately and no endeavour was deemed too modest. In late October, for example, the Tailors' Hall Fund organized a bring-and-buy sale at the Mansion House; a photograph of Mariga Guinness in a sandwich board publicizing the event was carried by most of the national newspapers, astonished that a princess would engage in such behaviour. More money was raised at the end of the year thanks to a masked ball in the Rotunda Hospital's Pillar Room, with prizes offered for the most original costume, and 1967 saw a spate of functions arranged for the same purpose, such as an 'Afternoon Promenade' around central Dublin ending in wine and cheese 'at Mr Elliott's Poplin Mill, the Coombe' and, on another occasion, home-made tea and ballads at Sandyford House, County Dublin, 'by kind permission of Mrs Patrick David who wishes to know numbers'. By December 1967 more than £5000 had been collected by the Tailors' Hall Fund but, as a notice sent out to supporters advised, 'We are at our wits' end to think of more ways of raising money, so the work can go right through without a break. If you have any bright ideas for fund raising, go ahead.' By November 1971, a raffle in aid of the fund included 'Three free sauna sessions – including massage – at the Lapland Sauna' and a balloon trip over Dublin.

Dublin Corporation had by now agreed to lease the building to the group at a nominal rent for ninety-nine years; a limited liability company was formed for this purpose with

The Tailors' Hall, Back Lane, Dublin.

the relevant documents carefully drawn up by long-standing Irish Georgian Society member and solicitor, Brian O'Connor. 'There's no doubt in my mind,' he says, 'that if it hadn't been identified by Desmond and Mariga as a place to be saved, it wouldn't be still there today.' On 31 May 1968 the keys to the Tailors' Hall were officially handed over to the fund by Dublin's Lord Mayor, Thomas Stafford. Only now could restoration work begin on the building but a two-year delay meant the amount of money required had increased. Roof repairs alone were estimated to cost over £1700 and new windows more than £760. The Merchant Taylors Company of London gave £210 and Bord Fáilte £500, while a fund-raising lecture tour of the United States given by Desmond Guinness in early 1967 delivered another £1000. But it was a slow, gruelling process, particularly during a period when fund-raising campaigns were being waged on behalf of so many other historic Irish buildings at risk.

Once started, the restoration programme seemed to take on its own momentum and by 1971 the Tailors' Hall Fund could declare, 'We've Done It – (almost)' and display pictures of the building looking infinitely better than it had just five years before. By then £15,000 had been raised, much of it from American well-wishers. Nevertheless, thanks to ever-spiralling costs during the period of restoration, an additional £7000 was needed to pay off the fund's deficit (it had climbed still further to £10,000 the

CHAPTER 4

Above: Uinseann Mac Eoin, architect, town planner and conservationist, lecturing on the Tailors' Hall in St Catherine's Church, 1972.

Right: St Catherine's Church, Thomas Street, Dublin. Pool and Cash engraving of the front of St Catherine's Church, 1780.

St. Catherine's Church
Thomas Street, Dublin

FRONT of ST CATHERINE'S CHURCH.

St. Catherine's Church, Thomas Street, was built in 1769 by John Smyth, architect of the Provost's House in Trinity College. A plaque recalls the fact that Robert Emmet was hanged in front of the church in 1803 and the surroundings have changed little since then. Closed in 1965, St. Catherine's is at present being restored as a cultural centre by a voluntary trust.

Sixth of the Series – Autumn 1974
Limited Edition of 750

following year when additional restoration work was forced to come to a standstill). In the end, the total cost of restoring the hall and its surrounding area was about £40,000. Ever loyal to the Irish Georgian Society, architect Austin Dunphy oversaw the job without charging for his services. Though still in need of more work, the building officially reopened on 17 April 1971 and despite a few intervening vicissitudes has remained open ever since. While much of its old neighbourhood has disappeared, the demolition of the Tailors' Hall is now unimaginable.

So too is the loss of St Catherine's Church not far away on Thomas Street, although this was also once threatened with destruction. Designed by John Smyth (architect

Left: St Catherine's Church, Thomas Street, Dublin, exterior view.

Right: St Catherine's Church, Thomas Street, Dublin, interior detail of capital.

of the Provost's House, Trinity College) and completed in 1769, the church has a particularly fine north-facing facade on high ground that then drops down Bridgefoot Street to the Liffey quays. The United Irishman Robert Emmet was executed in front of the building on 20 September 1803. The church remained in active use until September 1966 when it was closed for services. The following year St Catherine's was deconsecrated and fell into rapid decline. By early 1969, it was in such poor shape that the Irish Georgian Society offered to send a work party to sweep weeds, grass and mud off the roof to prevent any further deterioration of the building's fabric. Astonishingly, the Church of Ireland Select Vestry declined this offer, explaining it planned to hand the building over to Dublin Corporation. 'Not exactly an encouraging prospect for those who wish to see it preserved,' remarked the *Bulletin*, 'judging by the care the Corporation has taken of Tailors' Hall in recent years. There is also a dangerous scheme for road-widening which would destroy part of the church tower.' Nevertheless, the local authority did take over the building and soon enough there was the inevitable talk of demolition.

At this point a number of interested groups, including the Irish Georgian Society, intervened. In 1970 two of the Society's members, Hugh and Maureen Charlton, set up St Catherine's Trust to restore and administer the building on a lease from the local authority. Their plan was to turn the church into Dublin's first arts centre, the Society's final *Bulletin* of 1970 explaining that the main part of the building would 'become a theatre for such things as Shakespeare in the round, and the gallery will be used as an art gallery'. The church's organ, which had been sold to an ironmonger in County Kildare for £200, was repurchased by the Irish Georgian Society for the same amount (thanks to Desmond Guinness's father, Lord Moyne) and restored to its rightful place. Groups of volunteers worked on Saturday afternoons to clear and replant the graveyard while essential restoration work on the church went ahead. In 1975, European Architectural Heritage Year, Dublin Corporation committed itself to spending £18,000–£20,000 on the exterior of the building, including the re-erection of railings and the paving of St Catherine's forecourt. However, the former church never enjoyed great success as a cultural venue since the acoustics were poor and the potential constituency was fearful of venturing into this part of the city. In 1982 vandals broke into, and set fire to the vestry, which had the effect of knocking out the electricity supply.

While the old graveyard was converted into a small public park, plans were drawn up for the building to be used as a local community centre but these progressed too slowly and in the meantime St Catherine's suffered further vandalism, the lead stripped from its roof and the organ destroyed. Returned to the care of the corporation, the church's windows were blocked up and its future once more looked precarious. Yet somehow it has survived and today it is once more used for the purpose originally intended. Following a thorough restoration in the late 1990s, St Catherine's is now in the care of the Church of Ireland's City Outreach for Renewal and Evangelism (CORE).

THE KINDNESS OF DONORS

Top: Daniel Terra (IGS benefactor) of Kenilworth, Illinois, USA.

Bottom: Edmund Corrigan, Knocknamana House, Co. Cork. He contributed to the replacement of Castletown urns and the cost of purchasing gilt wood tables for Castletown.

While the Irish Georgian Society has been privileged over the past half-century to have received substantial donations from a number of wealthy individuals and organizations, much of the money raised during its early years came in small sums from private benefactors. The generosity of these supporters deserves to be remembered and celebrated as without them the Society could not have undertaken such projects as the restoration of the Tailors' Hall in Dublin, Castletown House, Roundwood House and the Damer House in Roscrea. At the start the annual members' subscription was only £1 and even today it is not high, meaning the organization has never been able to raise large amounts from this source. Instead, over successive decades the Society has relied on acts of philanthropy from anyone anywhere in the world who has an interest in preserving Ireland's Georgian heritage. Much of this money has come entirely unsolicited or, particularly in the United States during the 1960s and 70s, in the aftermath of an impassioned lecture by Desmond Guinness.

Typical in this respect was a letter received in November 1968 from B. Carter Randall of Baltimore's Equitable Trust Company: his mother-in-law, Mrs R. Denison Frick, wished to make a donation of $1000 to the Society in the form of stock of General Reinsurance Corporation. The stock was subsequently sold and a sum over the original amount realized. Nine years later, Daniel Terra of Kenilworth, Illinois, transferred 600 shares of common stock to the Irish Georgian Society as a gift. Of course not all donations came in the form of stock. More often they arrived as cheques, such as that for $15 sent by Betty Paxton of Ohio in May 1976. And while the United States was always a generous source of funds, money has come from closer to home too. In August 1974 Edmund Corrigan of Knocknamana House, County Cork, offered £100 towards replacing the urns above the parapet of Castletown and the same sum again five months later towards the cost of buying a pair of giltwood tables that had once been in the house. And then there have been those who remembered the Irish Georgian Society in their wills, such as John Benson who, following his death in March 1975, left the organization £100. Since that time, there have been many other bequests, especially from English and American members, and these continue to be of invaluable help. Over the course of fifty years every donation, no matter how small, has made a difference and helped the Society to accomplish its work.

THE TAILORS' HALL

Dublin's tailors received their guild charter from Henry V in 1419 but are believed to have moved into the premises that still bears their name only in the early eighteenth century. Dublin's last surviving guildhall, the building stands on the site of what had previously been a Jesuit chapel and college endowed by the Countess of Kildare in 1629; it is probable that some elements of the earlier structure were incorporated into the hall, which in its present form dates from 1703–7 when it was erected at a cost of £1022 and 8d. Until the closing decades of the last century, the Tailors' Hall was surrounded by other houses on High Street and Back Lane, and as a result its main, south-facing entrance is reached via a stone arch and forecourt. Built of red brick, the hall's fine, rusticated limestone doorsurround was added in 1770. Internally, the principal room is the great hall with an early-eighteenth-century Ionic reredos at the west end and a large, white marble chimney piece dating from 1784; the east wall features a late-Georgian neoclassical wrought-iron balcony. In addition the Tailors' Hall holds a number of other rooms such as the parlour and council chamber and a stone-walled basement that runs under the whole structure; there is also an elegant staircase with barley-sugar balusters. During the building's restoration, the Irish Georgian Society presented it with three early-eighteenth-century Kilkenny marble mantels that had been removed from Bert House, County Kildare. Until the dissolution of the guild in the early 1840s following municipal reform, the main hall held a fine collection of paintings.

While owned and used by the Tailors' Guild for that organization's own purposes, the hall was always available for rent. In one week alone in the eighteenth century it provided accommodation for a fencing master, a dancing school and a Methodist meeting. Other groups known to have used the building during this period included the Amicable Vocalists' Society, the New Jerusalem Society, the Insolvents' Court and the Grand Lodge of Dublin Freemasons. However, it is best remembered for having provided a home for the 'Back Lane Parliament' of 1792, a convention where it was agreed that Catholics should be allowed to vote in parliamentary elections. Wolfe Tone was secretary of the organization's committee and the United Irishmen subsequently also used the Tailors' Hall for its meetings, paying £9 and 2s. in 1793 for a six-month tenancy. During the uprisings of 1798 the building was commandeered as an army barracks.

After being vacated by its guild, the hall became the Tailors' Endowed School for Protestant Boys. In 1873 it narrowly avoided being used as a distiller's warehouse and instead was taken on lease by another body, which arranged events like temperance meetings and Sunday schools. After coming into the ownership of Dublin Corporation, it was let to the Legion of Mary, which remained in the building until 1960. Once restored and reopened by the Tailors' Hall Fund in 1971, the premises continued to serve an eclectic variety of functions, at one stage hosting banquets for parties of tourists. Since 1984 the Tailors' Hall has been leased to An Taisce.

Clockwise from top left: The Tailors' Hall, Back Lane, Dublin, before restoration.

Mariga Guinness campaigning to restore the 260-year-old Tailors' Hall, outside the Mansion House, October 1966.

The Tailors' Hall chimney piece during restoration, 1971.

Architect Austin Dunphy, then with the OPW, took charge of the restoration of the Tailors' Hall, Back Lane, Dublin. His wife Stella established the Tailors' Hall Fundraisers.

The Hon. Desmond Guinness (left) receiving the keys of the Tailors' Hall from Councillor Tom Stafford, Lord Mayor of Dublin.

Opposite: The Tailors' Hall, Back Lane, Dublin, after restoration.

Challenges faced by country house owners ↔ Castletown is sold to speculators ↔ Castletown is bought by Desmond Guinness ↔ the house is restored and opened to the public ↔ the establishment of HITHA ↔ *Festival of Music in Great Irish Houses ↔ Panels: Castletown House and the Castletown Balls*

CHAPTER

5

Tourism has always been an important industry for Ireland and one that could amply benefit from the revenue generated by visitors coming to admire this country's heritage of eighteenth-century buildings. Not long after its foundation, the Irish Georgian Society began to make precisely this point as an argument in favour of the preservation of significant houses both in Dublin and throughout the state. So many historic estates had already been lost, it was essential those still remaining be offered every possible assistance. As Desmond Guinness wrote in the Society's first *Bulletin* of 1960, for some inexplicable reason in Ireland,

> No attempt has yet been made to attract the many civilised culture-seekers who comb Europe from the Châteaux de la Loire to the Uffizi Gallery. One by one, our natural tourist assets, the country houses and Dublin streets built in the eighteenth century are allowed to disappear without so much as a murmur of dismay from the Tourist Board. We have no National Trust capable of preventing this, and the consequence is that in 30 years time, when some enlightened director of the Tourist Board wakes up to the fashionable 18th century and its national importance, it will be too late.

(At the time, only one property in the Republic, Bantry House, County Cork, was open to the public as a stately home; it had first welcomed visitors in 1946.) In fact, the Society was consistently keen to join forces with Bord Fáilte, proposing that the state's tourism agency recognize that Ireland's Georgian heritage could be better

Bantry House, Co. Cork.

exploited in campaigns designed to attract more visitors to Ireland. One of the 1963 *Bulletin*s, for example, reproduced a feature from *Country Life*, 'House Opening and the Tourist Trade in Great Britain', with the observation that the extract 'may interest Bord Fáilte'. Although hampered by the limitations of its budget, the latter organization was interested in this concept – after all, Bord Fáilte provided funding for the Conolly Folly restoration – but the same could not be said for other state agencies or for local and central government.

This dearth of official support was particularly problematic for owners of large country houses requiring costly maintenance; almost without exception the agricultural land that would once have generated an income for these properties had been divided among former tenants by the Land Commission and its predecessors. Some kind of aid had to be forthcoming. To quote from the same issue of the Society's *Bulletin*, 'Any owner of an historic house who is public spirited enough to open it to tourists should be helped with his upkeep expenses by an abatement of rates.' Such help is now taken for granted, but in the early 1960s no financial assistance or encouragement was available to country-house owners. Writing on the same subject the following year, Desmond Guinness observed that were any owner to open his property to the public, 'he would face increased expenditure in the form of maintenance, insurance, staff, cleaning, advertising, etc., without any guarantee that he would be reimbursed by the proceeds from admission fees, or indeed that these would not be regarded as income for taxation purposes'.

These were important points to make because initially the number of visitors to country houses was relatively small when compared to the costs involved in opening

CHAPTER 5

Westport House, Co. Mayo.

to the public. During its first summer season as a tourist attraction, Westport House, for example, received little more than 2500 tourists, while the four principal National Trust properties in Northern Ireland averaged roughly 1000 visitors each in 1960. Admission charges in the region of half-a-crown a head – about the most that could be charged – would 'not go far to assist owners in preserving their houses after paying for guides, advertising, cleaning, etc., and would be a very small recompense for the inconvenience which must be caused by admitting tourists to the house'. An imaginative solution to the problem of managing an historic house was provided by Lord Brocket who in 1959 bought the early-eighteenth-century former Archbishop's Palace in Cashel, County Tipperary, after this had been put on the market by the Church of Ireland authorities (Dean Robert Wyse Jackson had offered the house and twenty acres to Desmond and Mariga Guinness for £3500). Lord Brocket already owned Carton, as well as Brocket Hall in England, and therefore did not need another Irish residence. However, his property portfolio also included two Irish hotels, the Wicklow in Dublin and Benners in Tralee, County Kerry, and he therefore chose to buy the Palace in Cashel. After a thorough restoration, in May 1962 it opened as a luxury hotel, an example much followed in the decades ahead.

By the time the Cashel Palace began receiving guests, the Irish Georgian Society had been approached both by private businesses and by Bord Fáilte about the possibility of certain historic properties still in private hands opening their doors to the general public. On behalf of the organization and its members, Desmond Guinness and Lord Talbot de Malahide (the Society's president and vice-president) sent a circular to owners of some sixty-five such houses around the country, proposing, among other things, that 'if the owners of the beautiful and historic houses in this country open them to tourists, they are entitled to receive assistance from the government to maintain those houses in a good state of preservation' and in addition that some form of tax relief should be provided. The general feedback to this document was favourable and in 1962 a group of Irish house owners elected a committee chaired by the Earl of Rosse to request financial aid from the government for those among them prepared to open up their houses. However, as is often the case when dealing with state bureaucracy, negotiations progressed very slowly and in the meantime a number of owners followed Lord Sligo's example at Westport and opened to the public.

Others, however, abandoned the struggle, the most significant among them being the Conolly-Carews at Castletown, County Kildare. The largest and earliest of Ireland's great Palladian houses, Castletown had been owned by successive generations of the Conolly family since 1722, the last of whom, Major Edward Conolly, lived on the estate from 1900 until his death in 1956. It was then inherited by a great-nephew, the sixth Lord Carew, whose mother had been a Conolly and who moved to Castletown with his wife and children where they remained for the next nine years. Understandably, Castletown had always been of interest to the Irish Georgian Society and its members. The folly built by Katherine Conolly in 1740 was the Society's first restoration project and the house's print room dating from *circa* 1775 featured on the cover of the 1965 *Bulletin*s, one of which carried an essay by Desmond FitzGerald, the Knight of Glin, on Castletown's architecture and construction. Lord Carew had already sold the estate's woodland for felling and once his intention to sell the house and its surrounding 600 acres was announced, fears began to be expressed about what might happen to Castletown, which lies just twelve miles from Dublin beside the town of Celbridge, then already becoming a dormitory suburb. As a result the demesne land was extremely vulnerable to speculative development. There was a very faint hope that the state might intervene, possibly even buy Castletown because of its national significance and because no historic house in the vicinity of the capital was yet open as a tourist attraction. This, however, did not happen. Instead in late-May 1965 the entire estate and all its buildings were sold for £166,000 to Major James Willson and Julian de Lisle. The house's principal contents, accumulated over a period of more than 200 years, were auctioned over three days in March 1966.

What happened next confirmed many people's worst suspicions. Before long the estate's new owners had secured permission from Kildare County Council for an enormous development of new houses on land lying inside Castletown's gates and immediately to one side of its ancient lime avenue. Meanwhile the old house was left untended and without even a caretaker. Vandals were permitted to break into the building and damage the interior before they climbed on to the roof, which was stripped of much of its lead, later sold for scrap in Dublin. Prior to this, two secondary schools had briefly considered acquiring the property, not least because the surrounding flat land could have served as playing fields, but nothing came of these tentative approaches and Castletown continued to deteriorate(the interest of the secondary schools came prior to the auction; one was a German school and the other the Bluecoat school, keen to move out of Dublin). Windows were broken, lights smashed and handles torn from doors; thankfully none of the chimney pieces were stolen.

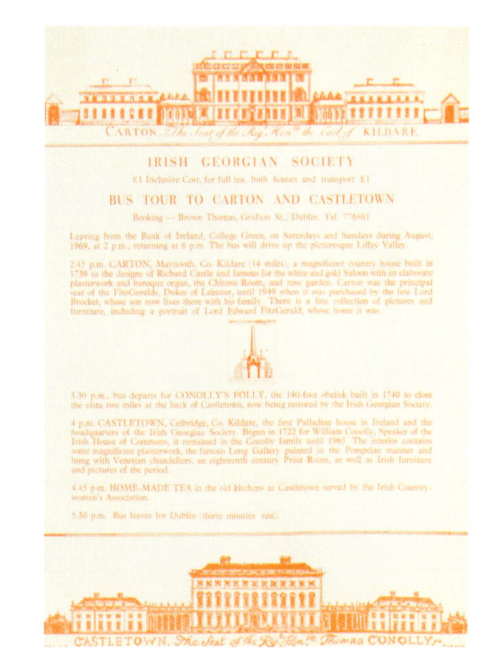

Top: Castletown, Co. Kildare, entrance front.

Bottom: IGS brochure for tour to Carton and Castletown, 1969.

CHAPTER 5

Mariga Guinness and volunteers cleaning Castletown, Co. Kildare, before opening to the public, 1967.

The situation was clearly only going to grow worse and so in April 1967 Desmond Guinness, borrowing against a trust due to come to him a few years later, bought the house and surrounding 120 acres for £92,500. In an interview with *The Irish Press* at the time, he remarked that 'It does not really matter who owns Castletown, so long as it is preserved.' Responsibility for the restoration and management of the house and grounds were invested in a new organization, the Castletown Trust, a company limited by guarantee and enjoying charitable status. Its initial board of directors included not just Desmond and Mariga Guinness but also Celbridge historian Lena Boylan (who published a long history of the Conollys of Castletown in one of the Society's 1968 *Bulletin*s), and a representative of Bord Fáilte. The state tourism board agreed to provide a three-year grant of £3500 to Castletown, specifically for 'upkeep and maintenance, wages, etc'. (The money was well invested because by 1970 over 20,000 people were annually paying to see the restored house, making it one of Ireland's foremost visitor attractions.) It was decided Castletown should now become the headquarters for the Irish Georgian Society, taking over from Leixlip Castle, which, after all, had also been the Guinnesses' family home. Castletown was the first house in the province of Leinster to open its doors to visitors.

Once Castletown had been acquired, a massive programme of restoration and refurbishment began with much of the work undertaken by volunteers. This was, and would remain, the Irish Georgian Society's largest single project and it could not have been accomplished had not so many supporters given their time and labour without the expectation of any monetary reward. The house was due to open to the

Mariga Guinness and volunteers picnic on the steps at Castletown, Co. Kildare, 1967. Marina, her daughter, is on the extreme right.

public at the beginning of July, but, given the poor state of the building after two years' neglect, achieving this ambition required extraordinary effort and dedication. Everyone involved in the programme of work still remembers it with pleasure, despite the long hours and often uncomfortable conditions. Three Trinity College undergraduates – Brian Molloy, William Garner and Andrew Healy – moved in to caretake the house on the very day it was bought, and lived there without light, heat or water for some time. 'When Brian put some daffodils into an old marmalade jar,' Desmond Guinness wrote in 1980, 'he was unconsciously effecting the first "improvement" to the interior.' Not long afterwards, Philippa Bayliss arrived to act as curator of the building; she would be responsible for repainting the Victorian Gothic texts in the old kitchens after the originals had been eaten away by damp and mould. As Jacqueline Kennedy commented when she visited Castletown that summer, 'If you get young people, you can do anything.' A great many of those involved were very young, some still in their teens, and excited by the notion that they were helping to save Ireland's greatest Palladian building.

Carol McGroarty Frazier, who came from the United States as a volunteer during the summers of 1967 and 1968, retains glowing memories of that time: 'Cleaning the brass staircase; polishing and dusting; Sweeney Todd (Desmond Guinness played the minister); the Midsummer's Night Ball; the Chieftains' haunting music rising from the kitchens; Micheál Mac Liammóir's midnight oration; dancing into the morning; catching the early No. 67 bus at the gates into Dublin and Bewleys to warm and wake up.' (She and her husband Captain Samuel Frazier held their wedding reception at

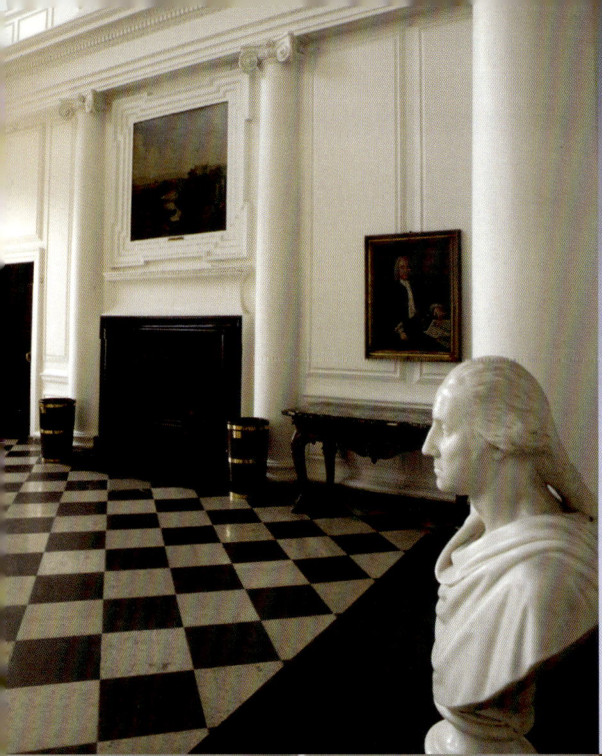
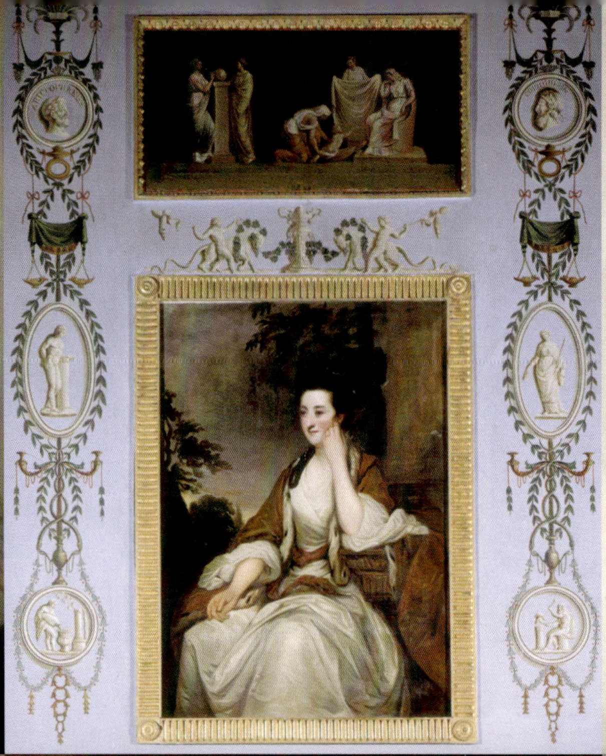
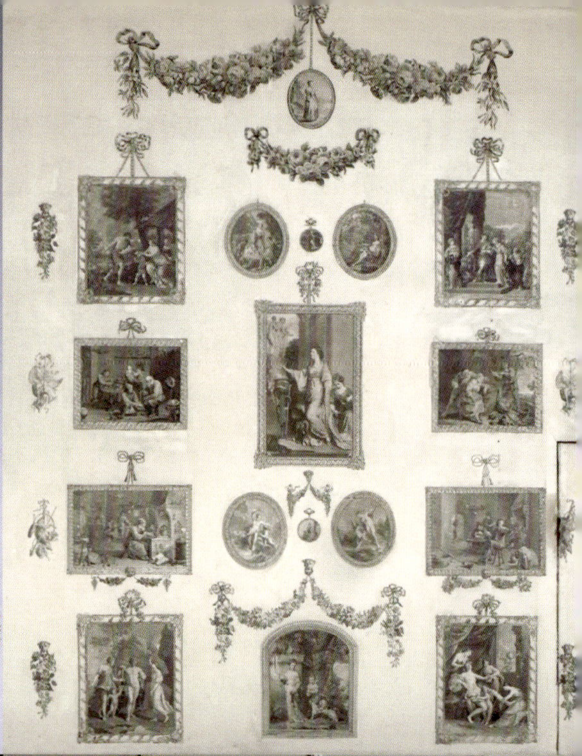
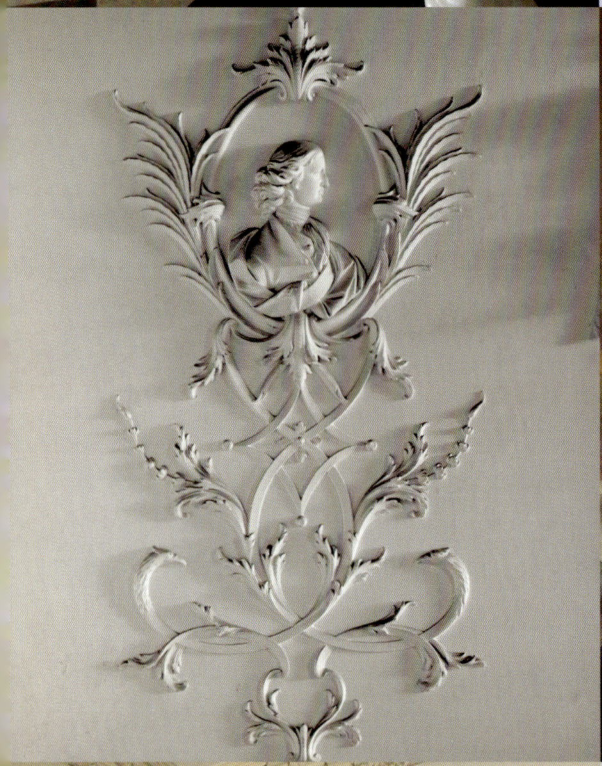
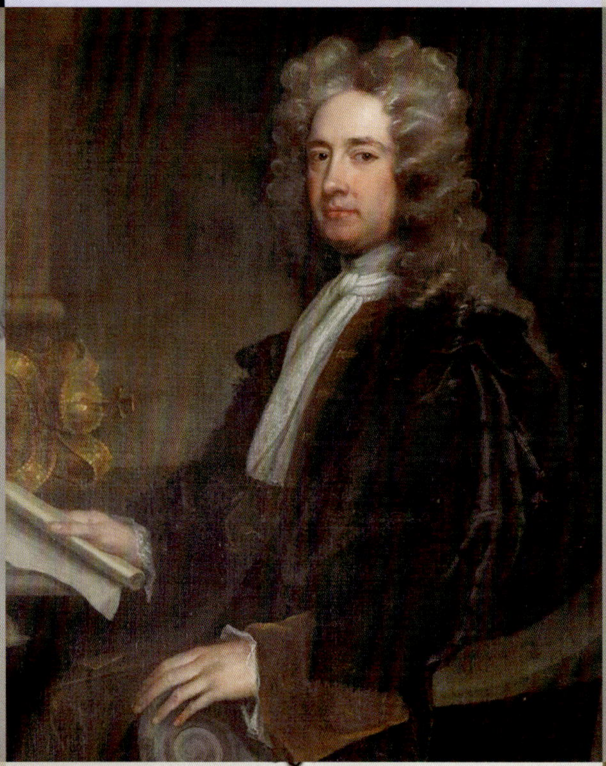
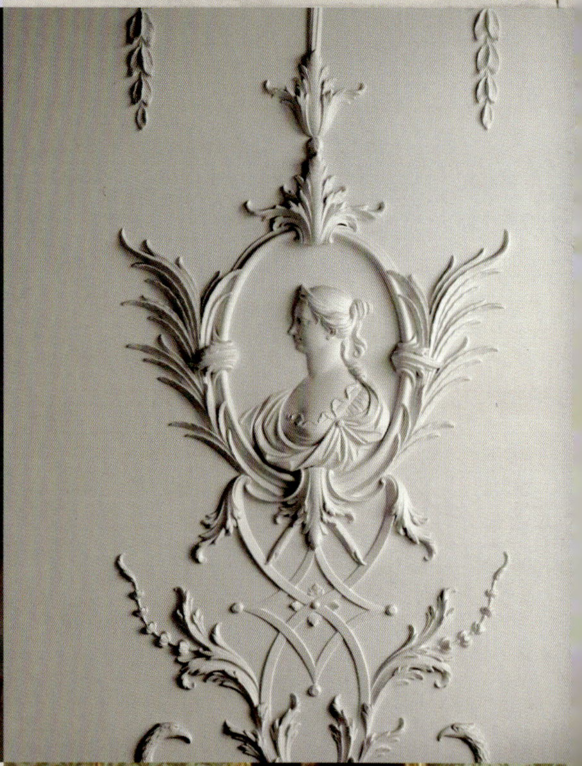
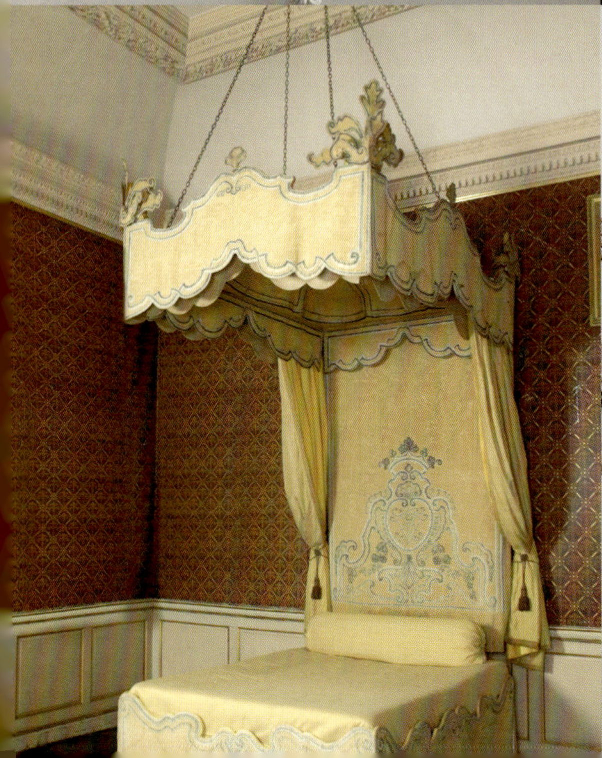
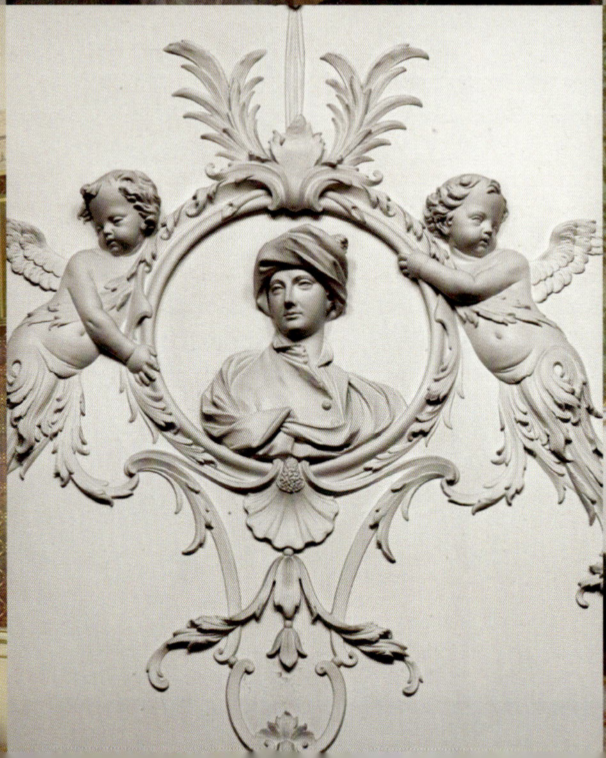
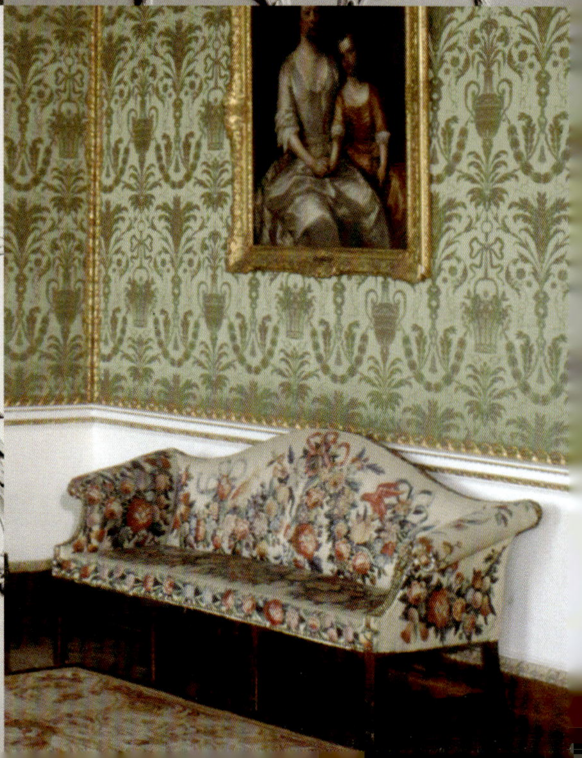

Castletown, Co. Kildare.

OPPOSITE:

Top left: Entrance hall.

Middle left: Detail of the rococo plasterwork by Philip and Paul Lafranchini, showing a bust of Speaker William Conolly.

Bottom left: Canopy bed from Lucca presented to the IGS by the Dallas Chapter.

Top centre: Lady Louisa Conolly by Alan Ramsay after Sir Joshua Reynolds, *c.*1770.

Middle centre: Portrait of Speaker William Conolly by Charles Jervas, *c.*1729.

Bottom centre: Detail of rococo plasterwork by Philip and Paul Lafranchini, showing a bust of Tom Conolly.

Top right: The Print Room.

Middle right: Detail of the rococo plasterwork by Philip and Paul Lafranchini, showing a bust of Emily, Duchess of Leinster.

Bottom right: Part of the tapestry-covered suite of furniture from Headfort, Co. Meath, presented to the IGS by Patrick and Aimée Butler of St Paul, Minnesota, USA.

ABOVE:

Castletown, Co. Kildare, the Long Gallery.

CHAPTER 5

Mariga Guinness painting at Castletown, Co. Kildare, 1967.

Castletown in December 1970.) There was no hierarchy of workers and managers; if a task needed to be done, whoever was at hand did it. A feature on Castletown in the *Irish Independent* noted of Mariga Guinness that when not at Leixlip 'dispensing informal hospitality and discussing such current finds as a document-packed sealskin trunk, or an ancient set of stocks in an ancient Meath courthouse, she's paint-stripping or picture hanging at Castletown'. Likewise Desmond Guinness told a journalist from *The Irish Press* how he and a group of volunteers repainted the house's hall white 'and it was like changing Paddington Station into a Venetian Palace'. Professor Anne Crookshank remembers that one of her assigned tasks was removing modern wallpaper in the dining room:

> I discovered quite a pleasant approach. I went up the ladder, loosened the paper some feet while holding it and then I jumped off the ladder and the whole of the sheet collapsed on top of me. It was much the quickest method I've ever used, but then it's the only wallpaper I have attacked which was attached to rough hessian.

Yet even allowing for the advantage of a free and enthusiastic labour force, money was needed for a large number of essential repairs on the building – as well as to pay for the demolition of an unattractive Edwardian bathroom extension whose upper storey destroyed Castletown's perfect symmetry by jutting out over the east colonnade. Certain practical problems had to be tackled also, not least sorting out the house's unreliable water supply, which, being partly dependent on a well, was prone to drying up entirely during the summer. 'A ram in the Liffey,' Desmond Guinness later recalled, 'deposited a pint of water into the tank beneath the roof once every few minutes, when the pipe was not blocked with mud or fish.' This difficulty was only resolved after a pipe had been laid the length of the avenue, connecting Castletown to the public water supply in Celbridge at the cost of £400. Roof-lead lost to thieves had to be replaced and new frames put into some of the house's 239 windows before all of them could be repainted. Central heating was installed, the plumbing reorganized, public lavatories provided and the gardens tidied, with a flower bed replacing some old lean-to sheds. To meet these and sundry other costs a fresh appeal for funds was launched with the goal of raising £10,000, although that target figure quickly began to climb. In May 1967 Desmond Guinness went to the United States for a fund-raising evening being held by New York auctioneers Parke Bernet and brought back $7000 for Castletown.

American support would be critical in saving Castletown (by the end of the year supporters in the United States had donated a total of $14,000) and in helping to refurnish its otherwise near-empty rooms. After the Parke Bernet event, Mrs George F. Baker arranged to have three marble-topped tables taken out of storage and shipped across the Atlantic without charge to the Society. The following year, Joseph D. Ryle – who set up the Irish Georgian Society Inc. in the United States in May 1968 – arranged for the world premiere screening of *Finian's Rainbow* starring Fred Astaire, Tommy Steele and Petula Clarke, to be held in New York as a fund-raiser for Castletown.

'I hope to be able to stop as many Irish Georgian furnishings as possible from going to America,' Desmond Guinness had told *The Irish Press* in April 1967, 'and maybe

Castletown, Co. Kildare, the Red Room. Furnishings were subsequently rearranged.

I will be able to reverse the traffic and bring them back here to Castletown.' That was precisely what did happen. The Guinnesses themselves had bought a number of items from Castletown's contents privately – notably the chandeliers and statuary in the Long Gallery, and the cabinet, carpet and chairs in the Red Drawing Room – and these were reinstated in the house. But Castletown was so big that even what would otherwise have seemed like a reasonable amount of furniture and pictures was quickly swallowed up without relieving the overall impression of bareness. 'We put all our eggs in one basket,' Desmond Guinness later wrote, describing how the Red Drawing Room was fully furnished, 'leaving the others empty in the hope that people would take pity on the fledgling Castletown Trust and give, or lend, things to furnish the magnificent house.' This they did, Patrick and Aimée Butler of St Paul, Minnesota, for example, agreeing to buy a suite of eighteenth-century tapestry-covered Irish furniture (originally from Headfort, County Meath), which happened to be for sale at the time of their visit to Ireland in August 1968. Over the next few years there were innumerable other gifts from American donors, either of specific items or of money towards the purchase of furniture and pictures. Gradually the main rooms of Castletown resumed something of their former appearance.

During this period, the house's single greatest benefactor was the Samuel H. Kress Foundation of New York but all of the Irish Georgian Society's American chapters were generous contributors towards Castletown's restoration and refurbishment. The Cleveland Chapter paid for the restoration of a chamber organ (originally from Dr

71

CHAPTER 5

Jacqueline Kennedy visiting Castletown, Co. Kildare, with the Hon. Desmond Guinness, 1967.

Steevens' Hospital, Dublin) in Castletown's entrance hall and the Dallas Chapter presented a magnificent canopy bed from Lucca with its original hangings. Gordon St George Mark of the Chicago Chapter lent his collection of family portraits from Tyrone House, County Galway, while Sir J. Paul Getty gave the Society an important collection of eighteenth-century Irish book bindings for display at Castletown. But acts of philanthropy were not confined to the United States. Canadian businessman Galen Weston and his Irish-born wife Hilary, both then resident in Ireland, bought and returned to Castletown an important life-size portrait of its original owner, Speaker Conolly. And one of the most significant financial donations came from a Dublin couple after Castletown's main staircase had been deemed at risk and roped off. A similar cantilevered Portland stone staircase at Slane Castle, County Meath, had collapsed when the building was open to the public and no insurer would provide the necessary cover until that in Castletown had been made secure; Mr and Mrs Lennox Barrow, members of the Old Dublin Society, gave £5000 for this project, which took two years to complete.

Astonishingly, less than three months after its acquisition by Desmond Guinness, Castletown was sufficiently restored to open to the public at the beginning of July 1967, albeit only during the afternoon on Wednesdays, Saturdays and Sundays. Although the house's rescue had been well publicized, the number of visitors paying to see the house was initially not great. Then the project received a welcome boost. That summer the widowed Jacqueline Kennedy and her children had come to spend an extended holiday in Ireland, renting Woodstown, County Waterford, from Major

Opposite: Castletown, Co. Kildare, the entrance hall.

72

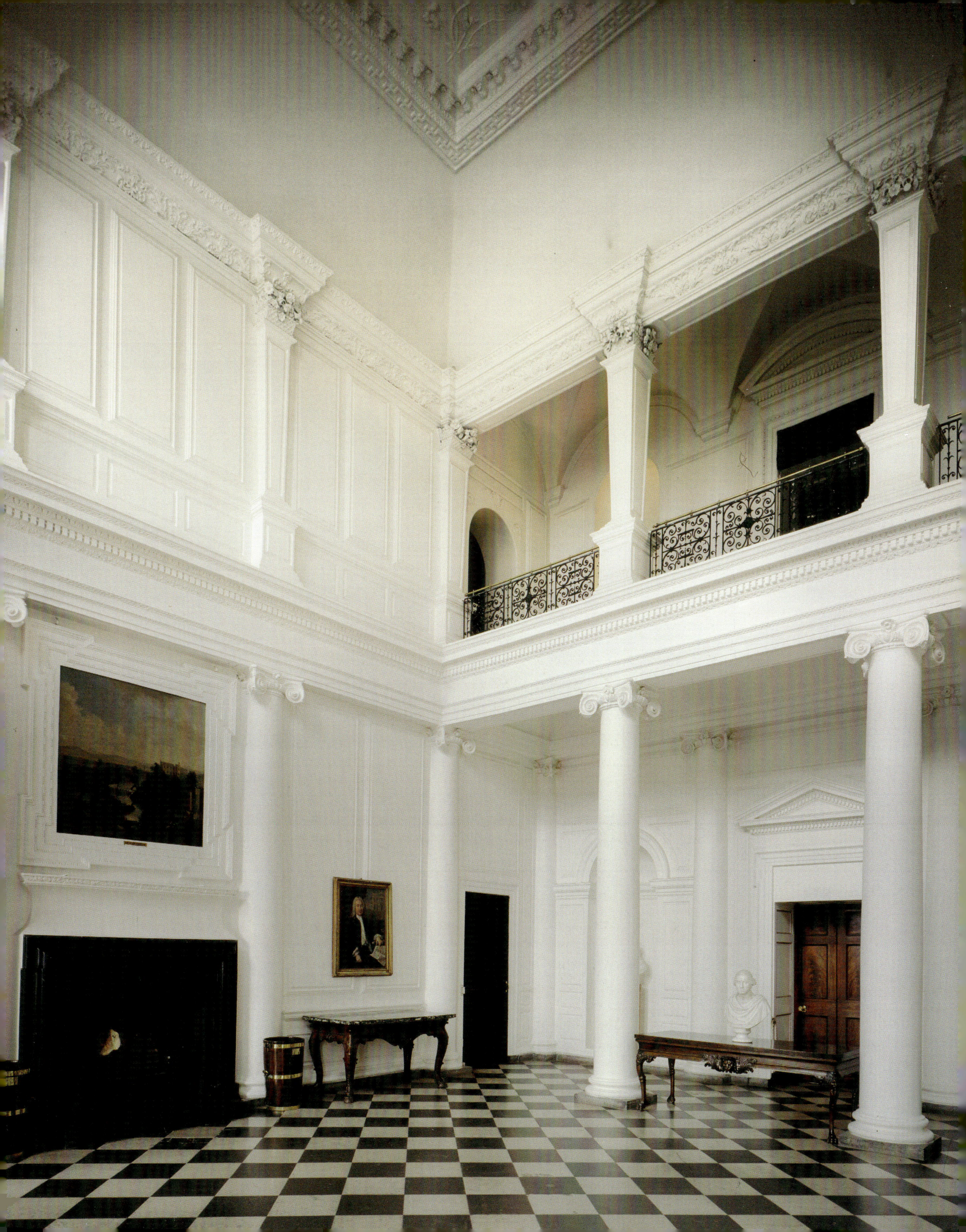

CHAPTER 5

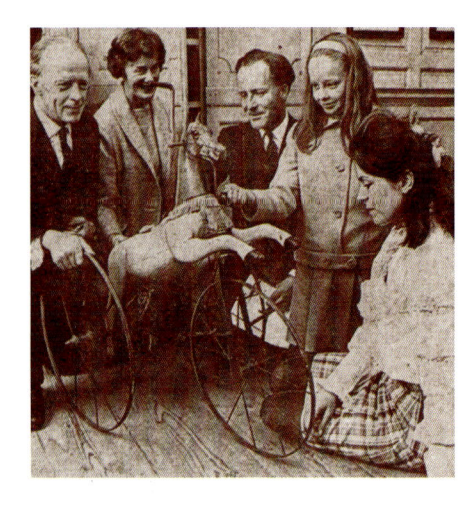

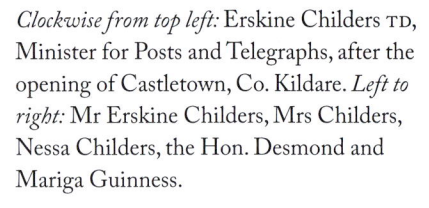

Clockwise from top left: Erskine Childers TD, Minister for Posts and Telegraphs, after the opening of Castletown, Co. Kildare. *Left to right:* Mr Erskine Childers, Mrs Childers, Nessa Childers, the Hon. Desmond and Mariga Guinness.

Jacqueline Kennedy being shown the Long Gallery at Castletown, Co. Kildare, by Mariga Guinness.

Mrs Galen Weston presenting a portrait of Speaker Connolly to the Hon. Desmond Guinness on behalf of the directors of Brown Thomas & Co. Ltd, 1972.

Cholmeley Cholmeley-Harrison (who four years later would buy and restore Emo Court, County Laois). Towards the end of her visit, she drove to Dublin for a lunch in the Merrion Square home of her friend, the Irish couturier Sybil Connolly. Among the other guests on this occasion were Desmond and Mariga Guinness, who subsequently took Mrs Kennedy and her party on a tour of Georgian houses finishing at Castletown where a large crowd had gathered to see the famous visitor. After thoroughly exploring the house, the group moved on to admire the views from the Conolly Folly where, according to a report in *The Irish Times*, 'refreshments were provided' (Desmond Guinness remembers bringing along a bottle of champagne for this purpose).

The following day all Irish newspapers carried accounts of the occasion, the *Irish Independent* quoting Mariga Guinness as saying Jacqueline Kennedy had been 'greatly impressed' by the restoration work at Castletown and that 'she could scarcely believe it had been carried out by voluntary work'. Only many years later did Desmond Guinness admit to biographer Sarah Bradford that he had 'leaked it to the press that she was coming and about seven hundred people came in order to see Mrs Kennedy. We photographed her in every possible room being shown around.' But it was just the kind of publicity that Castletown needed and by the time the house closed for the season at the end of September, visitor numbers had climbed to a very satisfactory 9000.

The following year, on 24 June, Castletown was officially 'opened' by then-Minister for Transport and Power (and future Irish president) Erskine Childers, who, in his speech, described the house as a 'valuable asset to the tourist industry' and observed that 'Great mansions offered tremendous interest to Irish and foreign tourists. There was an instinct to look into the past; to seek an understanding of history.' Once more visitors were welcome on three afternoons each week and during its second season 12,000 people paid to see Castletown during the day, while a further 10,000 passed through its doors to attend plays, concerts and other entertainment supervised by Doreen Moorhead, who had succeeded Philippa Bayliss as curator. At the same time, and for many years to come, restoration work on the building continued, as did the campaign to refurnish its principal rooms. Even after the Irish Georgian Society was no longer officially connected with the house, it continued to support Castletown; in the late 1980s, for example, the organization underwrote the cost of the Green Silk Drawing Room's restoration by paying £22,000 for new fabric to be woven in Lyons by Tissunique Ltd.

More than four decades later the conservation and refurbishment of Castletown goes on and should be considered as a work in progress. At least today the future of both the house and its surrounding parkland is secure. This was by no means the case even after the Irish Georgian Society had assumed responsibility for the property. In the early 1980s, for instance, Castletown Homes, a company owned by brothers Brian and Tony Rhatigan, who, in 1974, had acquired the bulk of the former estate's land, sought permission from the relevant authorities to build more than 2000 houses on their property immediately

Castletown, Co. Kildare. Drawing room with green silk wall covering woven in Lyons in the late 1980s, underwritten by the IGS.

CHAPTER 5

Castletown, Co. Kildare, the Print Room.

to the rere of the house. The scheme was refused and the view from Castletown towards the Conolly Folly remains as unspoilt now as it did 250 years ago.

Since Castletown began welcoming the paying public, many of the country's other historic houses have followed suit. In this way, another of the Irish Georgian Society's ambitions has come to be realized. The first *Bulletin* of 1969 noted that

> the whole question of the opening of country houses in Ireland is in its infancy. The only way to ensure the future of these houses is for the Government to recognise that they are an asset to the nation as tourist attractions. Although opening to the public may bring in a mere pittance in half-crowns taken at the door, both the neighbourhood and the country as a whole stand to benefit out of all proportion.

As already noted, in 1962 a group of Irish house owners had elected a committee to request financial aid from the government for those who were prepared to open their doors to the public. Although the committee urged that nobody 'jump the gun and open' before a satisfactory agreement had been reached with either the Department of

76

Finance or Bord Fáilte, talks progressed so slowly that some owners felt they could no longer wait and began to admit the paying public. Rather than allow matters drift in a haphazard fashion, in November 1968 the Irish Georgian Society took the initiative and hosted a conference for owners and administrators of those historic Irish houses and gardens already open to the public. According to a subsequent report, 'All sorts of mutual problems were discussed, such as insurance, sign-posting, publicity, Bord Fáilte, guides, bus tours, souvenirs and catering.' An association was formed and a subcommittee nominated to work out details such as the new organization's name. Eventually christened HITHA (Historic Irish Tourist Houses Association), it made its debut in July 1969, by which time almost 250,000 people were annually visiting Ireland's stately homes. Brenda Weir was the association's first secretary and Desmond Guinness its chairman, the latter informing *The Irish Times* that HITHA's creation meant 'we can now begin to manage the thing on a professional basis', which would be of benefit to all the group's members. At the beginning there were twenty-five of these in the Republic, HITHA's twenty-sixth member being the Northern Ireland committee of the National Trust, which had responsibility for a further ten properties.

Bord Fáilte was cautious about giving financial assistance to the venture, preferring, as one official remarked, to 'wait a little and see how it jells'. However, following the association's incorporation into a company with trustees in 1971, the state tourism board did provide funds and its director general, Eamonn Ceannt, wrote a fulsome introduction to that year's HITHA guide, commenting that the houses featured should be appreciated not just for their contribution to the tourist industry but equally for their 'value to our own people, young and old alike'. In those early years, Bord Fáilte committed to giving the association a grant of £2 for every £1 it raised, up to a maximum of £3000. HITHA subsequently became Irish Heritage Properties and in 1994 a separate marketing group for Irish gardens was established. Three years later, these two bodies amalgamated and today the organization is known as Houses, Castles and Gardens of Ireland. The most recent available figures show that in 2006 more than 2.1m. people paid to visit one of its properties. An enterprise begun by the Irish Georgian Society continues to thrive.

As does another important feature of Irish cultural life likewise owing its origins to the Society's involvement with Castletown. Particularly in the years immediately following the house's acquisition, an incessant need to find money for the restoration programme encouraged all sorts of fund-raising schemes, not least exhibitions intended to attract additional visitors to the house. Among the most notable of these was one organized in conjunction with the Military History Society of Ireland in June 1969 to mark the bicentenary of the births of both the Duke of Wellington and Napoleon Buonaparte; exhibits included the Marquess of Anglesea's artificial leg made to replace the one he had lost at the Battle of Waterloo. Castletown at this time was also the venue for a film society (spring 1969 screenings included *Brief Encounter* and *All About Eve*) as well as a ceaseless round of lectures and one-off performances of plays written by Ulick O'Connor and Maureen Charlton and others. The Victorian melodrama, *Sweeney Todd, The Demon Barber of Fleet Street*, was regularly seen, not least because it provided an opportunity for extroverts like Desmond Guinness and Marcus Clements to slake their thirst for a stage career. Rose Mary Craig remembers

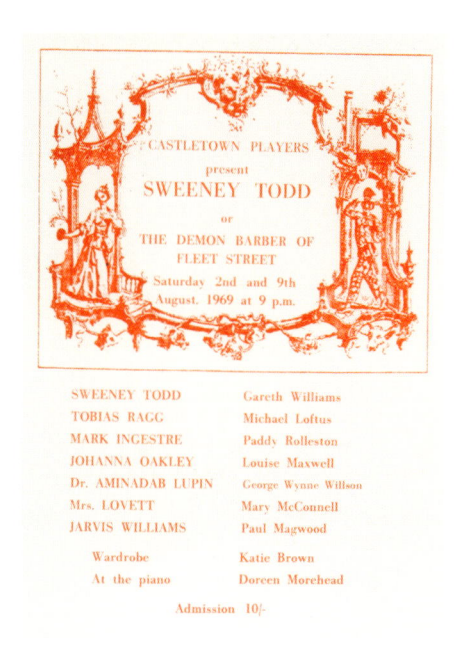

Sweeney Todd notice.

that in those days Trinity College undergraduate Terence Hall, who played a seaman destined for the razor's edge, would infuriate fellow cast member Peter Verity (then a young architectural student-volunteer from England and later a member of the Society's London Chapter) by saying, 'Ah Tobias, what is your name?' To which Peter would have to give the now redundant response, 'Tobias, sir, Tobias,' and hope nobody had noticed the slip-up. According to Rose Mary,

> The truth was that both the cast and the audience had by this time consumed so much wine that anything went and the biggest laugh was when they usually dropped the wooden chair masquerading as the barber's chair and deposited Terence in a heap on the floor – much to his indignation! The audience was supplied with potato and apple peelings to pelt the performers and were encouraged to boo which added to the general sense of anarchy.

Peter Verity confirms that after the initial performance's chaos,

> things could only improve and we thought we went from strength to strength. The secret to this was in keeping the audience waiting as long as possible before a performance in the hope that they would consume more of Philippa Garner's Claret Cup and also through ensuring that the audience was largely made up of friends who made all the right noises. To this was added Brian Molloy shouting out increasingly risqué comments.

These and similar events generated a lot of entertainment and a certain amount of revenue for Castletown. However, in the long term the most successful of all such ventures were the classical music concerts presented from June 1968 onwards. The first two chamber recitals were given in the house's Long Gallery where the acoustics proved to be perfectly balanced and even earned the approbation of *The Irish Times'* notoriously fractious critic, Charles Acton. In a review of the second concert he wrote, 'Incidentally, these two visits have shown me what really valuable work the Georgian Society are doing at Castletown, and how worthy of support; in other countries, the state would gladly cherish it.' Despite the want of state support, the concerts continued and two years later the inaugural Festival of Music in Great Irish Houses was held. This first week-long event established the pattern for those to follow: it offered an opportunity for audiences to hear outstanding performances from some of the world's finest musicians in superlative surroundings.

The event's director was David Laing who would later become curator of Russborough when that house opened to the public; a geology graduate of Trinity College, Dublin, he was working as a London-based concert manager at the time of his first meeting with Desmond Guinness, after a recital by pianist Sviatoslav Richter in November 1968. The two men corresponded about what was originally intended to be a single concert at Castletown but this gradually evolved into a festival with performances divided between that house and nearby Carton. David Laing's programme for June 1970 included concerts by the Amadeus Quartet, the Tortelier Trio, the Camerata String Orchestra and Bernadette Greevy. Although some doubts had been expressed about its viability – the relevant Bord Fáilte representative wrote to Desmond Guinness

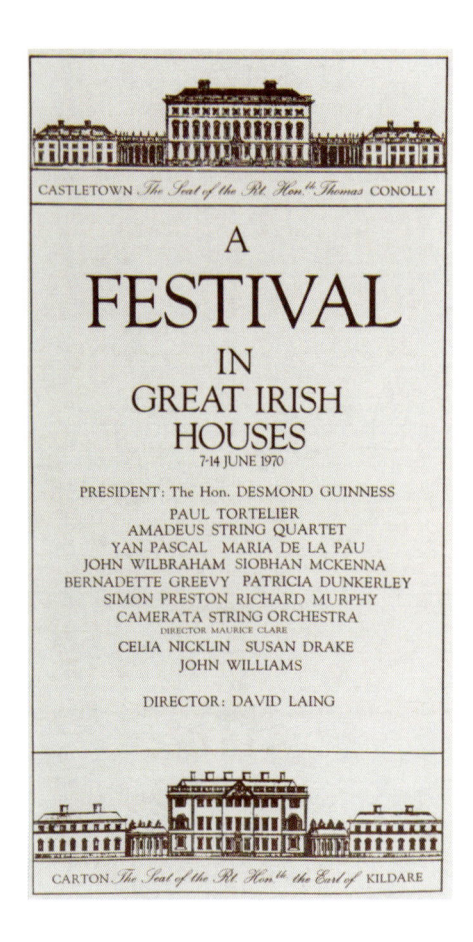

Top: A Festival in Great Irish Houses with the Amadeus String Quartet, 1970.

Bottom: The Second Festival in Great Irish Houses, 1971.

Mariga Guinness at the Festival in Great Irish Houses.

beforehand, 'I feel the prices to be charged are a little high by Irish standards and possibly would not sell' – the festival was an instant success. The *Sunday Independent* reported that hundreds of people had to be turned away from several performances since the greatest number that could be accommodated in Castletown's gallery was 240, and so 'scores sat on the terraces outside listening to the music'.

Opening with a garden party at Castletown and concluding with fireworks at Carton, the festival benefited from exceptionally balmy weather throughout the week. And proselytizing in advance by Desmond Guinness meant a large section of the audience was American; one journalist estimated transatlantic visitors accounted for 40 per cent of the attendance. Thanks to financial assistance from the Arts Council, Bord Fáilte and bankers Guinness & Mahon, the festival was considered sufficiently viable to be repeated the following year, as it has been every summer since. Over almost forty years the venues have changed, with houses around the country passing in and out of vogue, but the essential character of the festival has not altered. It is the pleasure of hearing classical music in intimate and beautiful settings that has ensured the continued existence of an event that began under the auspices of the Irish Georgian Society and arose from that organization's wish to encourage more visitors to this country's great heritage houses. Deservedly, in December 1981 Desmond Guinness was presented with the United Dominions Trust Endeavour Award for the most significant contribution to Irish tourism.

CASTLETOWN HOUSE

Castletown, Co. Kildare, entrance front.

The first and greatest of Ireland's Palladian houses, Castletown was built in the early eighteenth century for William Conolly, the country's richest commoner at the time. The son of a County Donegal publican, Conolly was born in 1662 and quickly rose to prosperity in the aftermath of the Battle of the Boyne (1 July 1690) through the purchase and sale of forfeited estates, resulting in him being called a 'cunning intrigueing spark'. He became chief commissioner of the Irish Revenue in 1709 and, having been a Member of Parliament since 1692, was unanimously elected speaker of the Irish House of Commons in 1717, retaining this post until his death fourteen years later.

Like many self-made men before and since, William Conolly was keen to proclaim his wealth. In 1709 he had bought the lands of Castletown about twelve miles west of Dublin for £15,000, from the attainted Earl of Limerick and his brother John Dongan, but it was only in 1722 that work began on construction of the present house. In July of that year, the philosopher Bishop of Cloyne, George Berkeley, wrote to Sir John Perceval: 'The most remarkable thing now going on is a house of Mr Conolly's at Castletown. It is 142 feet in front, and above 60 in the clear; the height will be about 70. It is to be of fine wrought stone, harder and better coloured than the Portland, with outhouses joining to it by colonnades.' Aside from the house's height and depth being transposed, this is an accurate summary of the finished work. The architect initially responsible was the Florentine Alessandro Galilei who, having spent some time in England, came to Ireland in 1718; however, since he had returned to Italy before construction began, it is believed the young Irish architect Edward Lovett Pearce, who had met Galilei in Florence, designed the house's Ionic colonnades and service wings and also devised the interior layout.

Castletown was still unfinished at the time of William Conolly's death but his widow Katherine remained in residence until she too died in 1752, when the estate was inherited by her late husband's nephew, also named William Conolly. Following the latter's death two years later, Castletown passed to his son Thomas who in 1758 married Lady Louisa Lennox, a daughter of the second Duke of Richmond; her older sister Emily was already living nearby at Carton as wife of the Earl of Kildare (later first Duke of Leinster). The Conollys moved into Castletown in October 1759 and immediately began work on completing the house's internal decoration; the brass balustrade of the cantilevered main staircase is signed 'A. King Dublin, 1760' and during the same period the Lafranchini brothers covered the stair-hall walls with exuberant rococo plasterwork. The Great Dining Room and Red Drawing Room, presumed to be designed by Sir William Chambers, followed shortly afterwards as well as the Print Room, which Lady Louisa herself designed and laid out. Then in the 1770s came work on the first-floor Long Gallery, its Pompeian decoration executed over a number of years by Thomas Riley, a pupil of Sir Joshua Reynolds, Charles Reuben Riley and Thomas Ryder.

Thomas Conolly died in 1803 and Lady Louisa in 1821, after which Castletown passed to another branch of the family and remained in their possession until the middle of the twentieth century when it was inherited by Lord Carew, whose mother had been a Conolly. In 1965 he sold the house and 600-acre estate to speculators and plans commenced to cover the land with suburban housing. However, in 1967 Desmond Guinness bought Castletown and the surrounding 120 acres and established the Castletown Trust to restore and preserve this property. The house was first opened to the public that year and has remained so ever since. In 1979, the year that the Irish Georgian Society turned twenty-one, Desmond Guinness transferred ownership of Castletown and the immediate surrounding land to a new organization, the Castletown Foundation, which took as its model the Alfred Beit Foundation set up at Russborough the previous year. As the Castletown Foundation's second chairman, Professor Kevin B. Nowlan, explains, 'We took on the house without a penny of endowment. We had to live off whatever we could get through fund-raising, charities, etc. We struggled on and got a certain amount of money but never enough to do a proper job on the place.' Fifteen years later the foundation handed over responsibility for the care of Castletown to the state, which subsequently bought from Desmond Guinness the balance of land he still owned. The contents of Castletown continue to be held by the foundation, which adds to the collection as and when possible.

Clockwise from top left: Plasterwork by Philip and Paul Lafranchini in the staircase hall.

The Long Gallery, Pompeian decoration executed by Charles Reuben Riley, a pupil of Sir Joshua Reynolds in the 1770s.

The Red Drawing Room.

Detail of Grisaille drawing, *Lady Louisa Walking in the Castletown Grounds* by Robert Healy, 1768.

THE CASTLETOWN BALLS

Above and opposite: IGS 25th Anniversary Silver Ball ticket. Drawing by Alec Cobbe.

No history of the Irish Georgian Society and Castletown would be complete without reference to the many fund-raising balls held in the house. Attracting up to 500 attendees, the first of these took place the year after the house's purchase by Desmond Guinness when a Midsummer's Night Ball at Castletown was jointly arranged by the Society and the Friends of the National Collections of Ireland. For the price of a three-guinea ticket, guests could dance to the music of either a discotheque run by Kami Fazel, or Dara O'Lochlainn's jazz band, or alternatively listen to the mellifluous voice of actor Micheál Mac Liammóir, who gave an oration at midnight.

Like so much else about those early years, the first balls somehow succeeded despite their lack of meticulous planning and depended in large measure on the support of unpaid labour. 'I don't know how it was put together,' remarks Cormac O'Carroll. 'We'd start a couple of days beforehand and everyone would just row in. There'd be huge cauldrons going and then somehow it all came together. I don't even think anybody was hired to serve; we all helped out.' Rose Mary Craig likewise recalls Philippa Bayliss being in charge of the catering 'with all of us volunteers helping with the organization and dishing out of food and drink – no rules then about only having white cold food and white wine!' while Audrey Emerson remembers Brian Molloy looking after preparations for a ball in 1976 when 'I have never seen such mountains of food, hundreds of cooked chickens waiting to be taken apart before they were served.'

Before long, the annual ball at Castletown, which did much to generate publicity and funds for the house, became a feature of Ireland's summer season and started to attract visitors from overseas. In July 1972 Washington socialite Rose Saul Zalles (who had paid for the Society's purchase of the Conolly Folly four years before) brought a group of almost thirty American friends to a ball at Castletown where, the *Evening*

Press reported the following day, 'the elegance of Castletown was at last matched by its visitors'. Actor Rex Harrison and his wife Marcia attended the 1979 ball, which was co-hosted by indomitable Galway huntswoman Lady Molly Cusack-Smith. In a report on the event carried by *The Irish Times*, Frank McDonald commented that Castletown 'looked positively spectacular last night with practically every window lit up like a fairy-tale palace'. However, a year later the same writer was grumbling because Castletown 'has so many rooms, large and small, and so many nooks and crannies that a crowd of 400 is simply lost in the place'.

By this date the novelty of balls at Castletown had begun to wear off and competition from other social attractions had correspondingly grown. Nevertheless, a Silver Ball was organized by the house's curator, Christopher Moore (now one of the Society's board of directors) and a committee to mark the Irish Georgian Society's twenty-fifth anniversary. This was memorable, not least thanks to the arrival of Mariga Guinness in a cloak and train made of tinfoil. 'Now I know what the knights of old must have felt like when they fell off their horses because they couldn't move in all their armour,' she told the *Irish Independent*'s Justine McCarthy. One further event should be mentioned: the Green Silk Ball held in June 1988 to raise money for new fabric of that ilk in one of Castletown's rooms. This brought another posse of visitors from the United States, including Marylou Vanderbilt Whitney and her daughter Cornelia. According to Suzy in the *New York Post*, 'Marylou wore a white Pat Crowley and emeralds to match Ireland. Doesn't everyone?' Though the house was to host further fund-raising balls, thereafter they steadily became a less important feature of the Society's programme. Anybody who ever attended one of these occasions will cherish the memory of something very special.

Rampant destruction of Georgian Dublin ~ the Hume Street debacle ~ Molesworth Street redeveloped ~ Mountjoy Square ~ the fight to preserve the square ~ opposition to the Society and its work ~ Panels: Henrietta Street and Mountjoy Square

CHAPTER

6

When American academic Kevin Corrigan Kearns published his book, *Georgian Dublin: Ireland's Imperilled Architectural Heritage* in 1983, he calculated that since 1960 nearly 40 per cent of the city's Georgian building stock had been destroyed. Although some sites had been redeveloped – usually as office blocks of at best mediocre design – many others had been left vacant, giving Ireland's capital an appearance not dissimilar to someone missing a lot of teeth. The oldest part of the city, the Liberties, which was granted a charter by Henry II in 1170, contained so many derelict or demolished buildings that it was used to represent bombed Berlin in the 1965 film, *The Spy Who Came in from the Cold*. On 2 February 1966, *The Irish Times* ran an extensive photo essay headlined 'City of Ruins'. The subject was not an Asian or South American metropolis that had suffered bombardment or assault during the course of warfare, but Dublin; during the previous six years the city had undergone an unprecedented attack on its historic centre. Many of the people responsible for this offensive were property speculators who, in the economic boom of the period, eagerly bought up sites and cleared them of any buildings but then put nothing in their place, preferring to wait and see how the market might develop. 'We have enough unavoidable ruins as it is,' commented *The Irish Times*' architectural correspondent. 'We must now stop wantonly creating more merely because the land under them has become more "valuable" than they. We cannot afford, in the name of the city's image, to continue this policy; it is doubtful whether, even in the crudest of money terms, it is worth while.'

Seven months later, the *Irish Independent*'s Des Hickey wrote a long diatribe called 'The Rape of Dublin' in which he proclaimed that 'A disregard for antiquity, good taste and cleanliness has apparently become endemic to our character,' and declared himself 'shamed by what I see in my city, and shamed by what visitors must think of us.' Some of those visitors equally lamented the terrible damage being wrought on Dublin. 'Does anyone care for a noble city?' asked the *Illustrated London News* in an April 1966 double-page spread filled with images of derelict, abandoned and semi-demolished buildings. Similarly, during the same month Ian Nairn in *The Observer* reported that across the city centre, 'houses are being demolished piece-meal; the IRA couldn't have done better in their wildest days'.

In fact, the IRA made its own contribution towards the obliteration of Georgian Dublin on the morning of 8 March 1966 by trying to blow up the 134-foot-high Doric column commemorating Admiral Nelson that had stood midway along O'Connell Street since 1808. The attempt was bungled and the column could have been repaired but with ceremonies to mark the fiftieth anniversary of the Easter 1916 Rising imminent, the government preferred to destroy what remained – curiously enough, this second explosion undertaken by the Irish army was almost as unsuccessful as its predecessor. The lack of public interest in saving Nelson's Pillar – which had been a popular tourist destination – also reflected a general and ongoing lack of concern about the preservation of the capital's architectural heritage. Many of the campaigns in which the Irish Georgian Society participated during this period were not against private speculators but bodies such as Dublin Corporation, which, in the mid-1960s, sought to close the late-eighteenth-century Grand Canal loopline, initially so that sewage pipes could be laid along its bed before the whole thing was covered over and made into a dual carriageway for cars. The public outcry was great enough to stop this plan coming to fruition but despite an equally vigorous crusade, the state's Office of Public Works proved intractable in its determination to build a grotesquely large and visually inappropriate office block within the lower yard of Dublin Castle on a site formerly occupied by stables and a riding school.

Left: Irish Independent 1966 headline: 'The Rape of Dublin'.

Right: Irish Times 1966 headline: 'City of Ruins'.

CHAPTER 6

Illustrated London News 1966 headline: 'Does Anyone Care for a Noble City?'.

With regard to state indifference, the turning point only came in the mid-1970s when Bord na Móna, the national peat development authority, tried to follow the example of the ESB a decade earlier and demolish a row of Georgian houses so that they could be replaced with modern office accommodation. Dating from *circa* 1820, the five buildings on Upper Pembroke Street, just off Fitzwilliam Square, were listed for preservation and known to be in good structural condition but this did not stop their owner from making plans to have the lot pulled down – and from receiving permission to do so from the relevant government minister, James Tully, in March 1975, which happened to have been designated European Architectural Heritage Year. The Irish Georgian Society along with a number of other voluntary groups, and even the Irish Arts Council, all united in opposition to this senseless act of destruction, aided by a band of some seventy architectural students who occupied the Pembroke Street premises even as work began on their demolition. By the time Europa Nostra and the Council of Europe had joined in the outcry, Bord na Móna recognized that it could not hope to win the battle and in April 1976 it sold on the houses to Allied Irish Investment Bank, which pledged to restore them all. (In 1978 Bord na Móna eventually got a spanking-new office building, designed by Sam Stephenson not far away on Baggot Street.)

Dublin Corporation took longer to appreciate the importance of its own heritage. As late as July 1983, for example, the local authority considered building a housing estate on land immediately beside the Marino Casino, the mid-eighteenth-century pleasure house designed by Sir William Chambers for the first Earl of Charlemont. The Irish

CHAPTER 6

The Marino Casino, Dublin, designed by Sir William Chambers for the first Earl of Charlemont.

Georgian Society helped to see off that threat, as it had one some fifteen years before when a religious order, the Sisters of Nazareth, began work on a large-scale housing project for the elderly in the immediate vicinity of the Casino without even troubling to wait for planning permission to be granted. 'One would have expected the fullest public discussion of any plans to build so near the Casino, which is the only non-functional Georgian building maintained by the State,' observed the Society's first *Bulletin* of 1968. The public discussion never took place, but fortunately neither did the nuns' housing scheme.

While the need for new housing might have explained a certain amount of redevelopment in Dublin, speculative office accommodation was behind much of the destruction of the city's historic centre during the 1960s and 70s. As the Society's *Bulletin* commented in 1968, 'Dublin should be lived in again, not killed by office blocks which only add to the traffic chaos as well as defacing our city.' Particularly at risk was the area immediately south of the Liffey as well as St Stephen's Green and all the streets radiating out from it. The Green, Dublin's oldest square, suffered grievous damage in these years, with large sections of the eighteenth-century north and south sides torn down and replaced even before battle was joined between developers and preservationists over the fate of a section of the east side, some of which was under the management of the Office of Public Works and therefore in state care. Early in 1966 Dublin Corporation granted permission for the demolition of a group of houses at the juncture where St Stephen's Green opens to admit Hume Street and creates a vista terminating with Ely House; these buildings were to be

87

Sunday Independent, 18 January 1970: St Stephen's Green/Hume St cartoon.

replaced with a large office development not dissimilar to one already built on the south side of the Green.

This permission was not immediately acted upon, allowing time for opposition from groups such as An Taisce and the Irish Georgian Society to grow and for the establishment of another vigorous conservation body, the Dublin Civic Group, chaired by Kevin B. Nowlan, dynamic Professor of Modern History at University College, Dublin. By the time the developers, the Green Property Company, were ready to realize their plans, a campaign against the destruction of yet more fine eighteenth-century buildings and their replacement by a bland office development was well under way. As Desmond Guinness observed in the Society's *Bulletin*, 'It has been pointed out over and over again that there are vast areas of "waste land" in less fashionable parts of the city where development is needed and good modern buildings would enhance rather than destroy,' before concluding, 'If it is possible for man to reach the moon in 1969, it is surely possible for him to repair a house.'

Throughout 1969, protest over the St Stephen's Green/Hume Street proposal steadily grew, culminating in mid-July in a public meeting adjacent to the site at risk. Here a succession of speakers attacked both the Green Property Company and the government that had given its assent to the demolition of buildings hitherto in state care. Among those who addressed the crowd of more than 1000 were future taoiseach, Garret FitzGerald, Kevin B. Nowlan, Ulick O'Connor and Mariga Guinness, the last of these rhetorically speculating that if Dublin was supposed to be a tourist attraction, 'I can hardly believe that tourists want to come to a third-rate Manchester.' Everyone then marched to Government Buildings to hand in a letter of protest but this made no more difference than had any of the earlier objections. So, at the end of the year with demolition under way on No. 45 St Stephen's Green, a group of architectural students took matters into their own hands and occupied the premises, thereby obliging the workmen to abandon their task. At the Irish Georgian Society's annual general meeting in January 1970, what was described in *The Irish Times* as 'a large sum of money' was subscribed to the cause by the organization's members but it was by no means enough to guarantee the buildings' survival since the developers had by now offered to sell their property to the preservationists for a sum 'in excess of £200,000'.

Given that fund-raising was ongoing for both the Tailors' Hall and Castletown (and for the redemption of Mountjoy Square), finding such a big amount was an impossible challenge. Stalemate followed until June when Minister for Finance George Colley called together the various parties involved and negotiated a compromise settlement: the Green Property Company would be permitted to demolish the eighteenth-century houses but only on condition that the replacement offices were no taller than what had previously stood on the site and were given facades 'in the Georgian idiom'. As the *Irish Independent* noted, the outcome could 'best be seen as a pyrrhic victory for the preservationists and the students', not least because it appeared to suggest that in future knocking down original Georgian buildings would be regarded as acceptable provided pastiche was substituted.

And indeed, this is more or less what happened at the conclusion of another battle between conservationists and speculators that took up much of the early 1970s. A tract of land to the north of St Stephen's Green running to two and a half acres and bordered by Nassau Street, Kildare Street, Molesworth Street and South Frederick Street had been assembled during the previous decade by a consortium called Setanta Investments with the intention that the site be almost entirely cleared for redevelopment. This would mean the loss of some of the earliest extant eighteenth-century houses in Dublin, since Molesworth Street had been laid out in 1727 and South Frederick Street not much later; today, of the former's original twenty-three houses on the north side, only four survive, a pair each flanking the Masonic Hall of 1868. All the rest, which gave Molesworth Street so much character and atmosphere, were swept away, including a building that had been home to the family of the Irish patriot, Robert Emmet. Before this occurred, however, a vigorous war was waged for the house's preservation at the end of which Setanta Investments found itself required to make several concessions on the new office's height and external appearance.

Still, it is a great pity that the Kildare Street house occupied by early-nineteenth-century novelist Sydney Owenson (Lady Morgan), for some twenty-five years, was among the casualties, replaced along with its neighbours by a depressingly bland terrace. Before demolition of the entire area took place, it was arranged that the Irish Georgian Society would be permitted to salvage important architectural features from several of the buildings. It did so with some reluctance since, as the first *Bulletin* of 1971 noted, the ideal scenario would have been to leave the panelling, mantels and doors in situ, 'in the hope that the houses would be spared'. On the other hand, experience had shown that too often 'fittings of this nature, which could so well be used in some restoration project such as the Tailors' Hall, have been smashed by the

Hibernia headline: 'The Midnight Cowboys – The destruction of Dublin'.

Opposite: 50 Mountjoy Square, Dublin, front elevation, 1964.

bulldozer'. Pragmatism prevailed and the fittings were carefully removed and stored for future use.

Towards the end of the 1970s the organization became involved in another battle on Molesworth Street that turned out to be almost as drawn out and unpleasant as that over St Stephen's Green/Hume Street a decade before. Formerly owned by the Church of Ireland, St Ann's Schools and Hall, two mid-nineteenth-century buildings on the south side of Molesworth Street designed by the Victorian era's most famous Irish architects, Deane and Woodward, were acquired by developer Patrick Gallagher with the intention that they be knocked down and replaced by more offices. Once again students occupied the properties in an attempt to prevent their demolition in 1978 but, also once again, their efforts were without success and an office block remarkable only for its want of any character now runs along this length of the street.

More than ten years earlier, Patrick Gallagher's late father Matt had been involved in the most celebrated attempt by the Irish Georgian Society to preserve Dublin's historic centre. Originally from County Sligo, Matt Gallagher was amongst the most shrewd and successful property developers of his generation and like the great majority of them his attention hitherto had primarily been focussed on areas in the city south of the Liffey as this was considerably more fashionable, and hence more profitable. However, over a number of years in the early 1960s and through a company called Leinster Estates, he quietly bought up five houses on the west side of Mountjoy Square, one on its north side and more than half of the south side. A once grand but now rather rundown part of north-central Dublin.

Mountjoy Square had been laid out in 1791 and its houses built over the next thirty years. Long before the 1960s, this part of the city had been given over to tenements, the majority of properties left by landlords were allowed fall into dereliction. The consequence was that they were inexpensive to purchase (sometimes costing as little as £400 each).

Matt Gallagher planned to acquire and clear the square's south side so that he could put up a large office development on the entire site. But he failed to take into account the Irish Georgian Society's long-running interest in the area. As far back as 1958, the last *Bulletin* of the year noted that when Dublin Corporation had announced an intention to pull down two houses in Mountjoy Square, the Society lodged a protest and it was agreed to let the properties remain, 'thus preserving the character of the square'. The following year, a subcommittee of the Society arranged to contact estate agents in Dublin and encourage them 'to bring properties in the square to the notice of good clients for office purposes'.

The corporation would later restore the six houses it owned on the square's north side but over the years the Irish Georgian Society continued to express ever more concern for the area's welfare. There was some reason to hope that Mountjoy Square would yet survive intact. In 1964, for example, the long-established wine and spirit merchants Edward Dillon and Company Ltd moved from premises south of the Liffey to No.

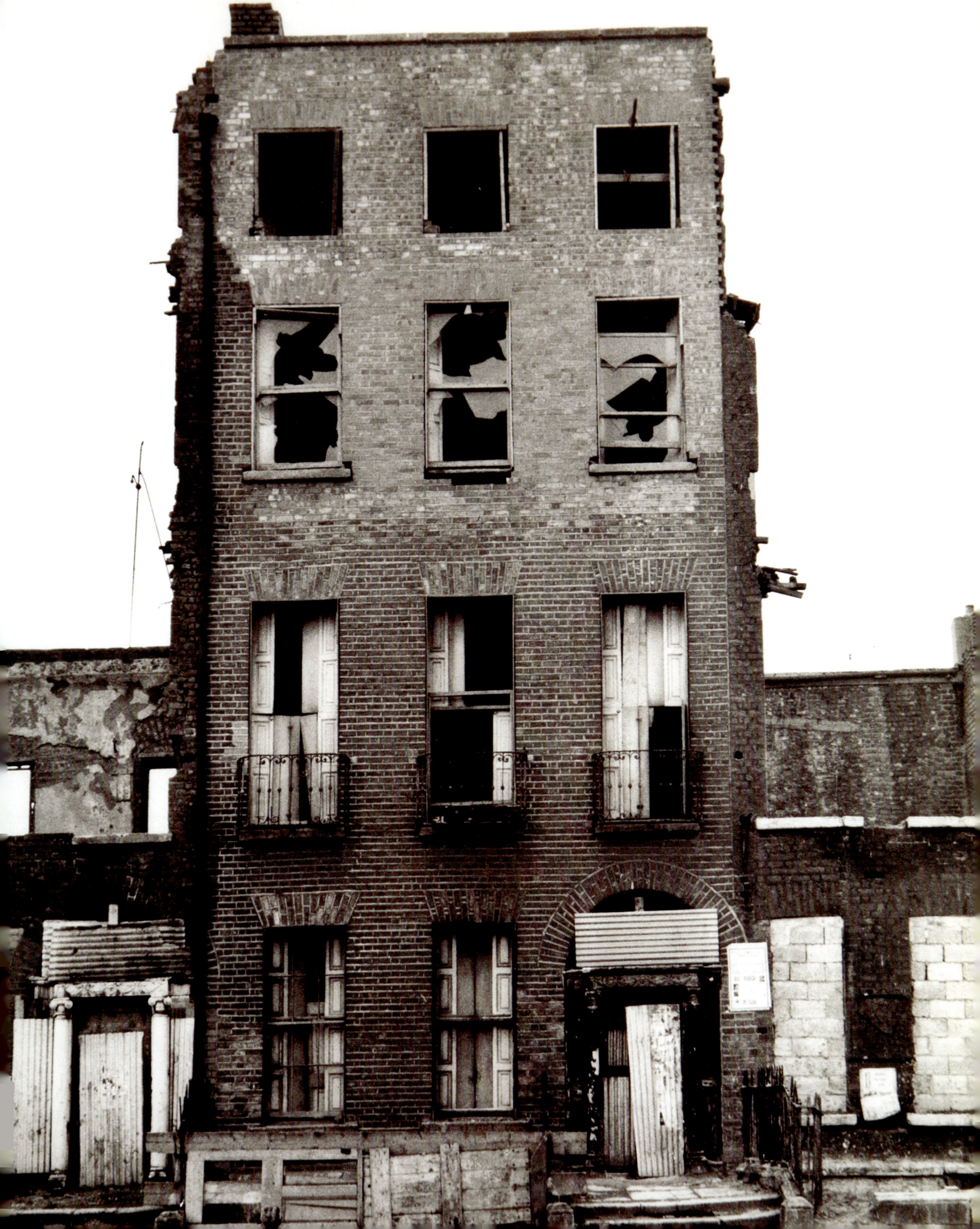

25 Mountjoy Square, a fine house on the east side which, with its neighbours, had been built at the close of the eighteenth century by Frederick Darley senior; soon afterwards a related business moved into the next-door property. These two buildings had for a long time been reasonably well maintained by religious organizations (No. 27 was a Jesuit Club for Teetotalers). However, other sections of the square did not fare so well, especially those falling into the clutches of Matt Gallagher's Leinster Estates. In February 1964, in a pre-emptive strike, Desmond and Mariga Guinness paid £550 to buy a house, at the suggestion of Ivor Underwood (a huge property owner in Dublin), No. 50 Mountjoy Square, right in the middle of that part of the south side owned by Gallagher. He retaliated five months later by demolishing the buildings on either side of No. 50, thereby removing all lateral support from the house and exposing it to risk of collapse.

In February 1966 the Guinnesses went to the High Court seeking an order that Leinster Estates restore necessary support to the outer walls of their property. Giving evidence, Mariga Guinness explained she and her husband had bought No. 50 'simply to save the character of the Square'. Four days into the hearing a settlement was reached whereby Matt Gallagher's company agreed to pay costs and to provide three raking shores on either side of No. 50, so ensuring its survival. Not only did Leinster Estates lose the case – which had been extensively covered in the national press – but it also lost all possibility of proceeding with the wholesale demolition of Mountjoy Square's south side, even though Dublin Corporation granted approval for the company's office scheme in October 1967. As *Build* magazine remarked in June 1966, Leinster Estates' efforts to take over parts of the square had been checkmated, 'and the firm is said to be not anxious to engage in further commitments there'.

For the next few years No. 50 became a kind of urban headquarters for the Irish Georgian Society, very necessary given the number of projects in which it was involved right across central Dublin. At the beginning of January 1968 the Society held a reception to inaugurate the Mountjoy Square house as its office in the capital, author Constantine Fitzgibbon performing the official opening ceremony by candlelight with hundreds of guests crammed into the rooms. Although there were rarely many visitors other than those invited to further parties, the ground and first floors of No. 50 were open to the public, the latter holding an architectural library assembled by Mariga Guinness. David Synnott lived on the second floor: 'In theory, I was the archivist there, but there were in fact very few, if any, archives to be studied.' The top-floor flat was for a while used by Mariga Guinness and later let. But as much as anything else, No. 50's purpose was to act as a symbol, to provide tangible proof that speculators should not assume their ambitions to sweep away old Dublin would necessarily come to fruition. As far back as the last *Bulletin* of 1964, the Society was able to announce that 'Eleven houses have now been bought by the Friends of Mountjoy Square, some on the square and some just off it; our intention is to restore them and do our best to bring the square gradually back to its former beauty.'

In this way, the organization provided inspiration for other would-be conservationists, such as John and Ann Molloy, who, in 1967, bought and moved into No. 47 Mountjoy Square with their young family. The brother and sister-in-law of Brian Molloy, the

John (left) and Brian Molloy, 1968. John and Anne Molloy lived at 47 Mountjoy Square, Dublin, 1967.

couple paid £6500 for the building, which, as Ann Molloy told the *Sunday Express*, was 'what we might have paid for a new suburban detached house'. Initially they were enthusiastic about living in central Dublin and having undertaken a certain amount of restoration they opened their home to the paying public, the first private house in Dublin to do so. Their example attracted other young activists to the area, many of whom ended up living for a while in No. 47. Kevin Byrne, then a student, recalls staying in the house with musically inclined brothers Chris and Richard Davison (the former now better known as singer Chris de Burgh). Kevin Byrne was also associated with nearby No. 43 Mountjoy Square, which had been bought by Carol McGroarty Frazier,

> and I managed it for her. It was a fully tenanted tenement and folk lived in conditions which were alarming. They all wanted to be rehoused and I managed to assist in a number of cases – one ploy was to 'borrow' extra babies before the Housing Officer would visit; a baby in an open drawer was very impressive in the 1960s, but I suspect you would not get away with it now.

Carol McGroarty Frazier herself recalls dinner parties in the Molloy home with its navy-blue walls and white plasterwork ceilings: 'Salmon with homemade mayonnaise; our host's wicked wit; living on the top floor and climbing on to the roof to enjoy Dublin; tossing the key out a window for visitors.' But once the initial zeal had worn off, it became clear that the challenge posed by taking on a big old building in a severely rundown area of the city was enormous. By the time Kevin Corrigan Kearns interviewed John and Ann Molloy for his 1983 book on Georgian Dublin, they had come to feel that 'from a family point of view the sacrifices have been too great'. Inner-city living is now the norm and today many people would relish the chance to rescue an historic property; the Molloys were in the vanguard of what would only much later become a widespread phenomenon.

50 Mountjoy Square, Dublin, rear wall during rebuilding.

One of the problems for the couple was that the fight to save Mountjoy Square was by no means over after Leinster Estates' legal setback in February 1966. As mentioned, eighteen months later Dublin Corporation granted Matt Gallagher's company permission for a smaller office development. This decision was appealed by a number of parties including the Irish Georgian Society, an action that had the effect of deterring any other would-be private buyers from investing in property in the square. At the end of the appeal hearing, Leinster Estates once more attempted to gain the upper hand by making the Society an offer: a chance to buy the seven houses and thirteen sites the company owned at cost price – estimated by Leinster Estates to be precisely £68,000, 17s. and 6d. This was throwing down the gauntlet to the preservationists since the sum demanded was substantial (and probably inflated well above what had originally been paid by Matt Gallagher for the dilapidated buildings).

But the Irish Georgian Society could not afford to ignore the challenge, particularly after Leinster Estates threatened to withdraw its offer when a sufficiently prompt response was not forthcoming. Kevin B. Nowlan remembers that he and Michael Scott accompanied Mariga Guinness on a visit to Matt Gallagher's home in Mulhuddart, County Dublin, where she went on a charm offensive 'and before the day was out he'd agreed to sell to us'. 'Mariga did a good job in vamping him and persuading him to sell the Mountjoy Square houses,' concurs Brian O'Connor. In the summer of 1968 a new company called Mountjoy Square Estates Ltd was set up with Kevin B. Nowlan as its chairman. This entity then exchanged contracts with Leinster Estates, the latter making it a condition of the sale that each house in the square should be fully restored with the Georgian idiom maintained both inside and out.

In theory, everything ought thereafter to have proceeded smoothly. In practice, the venture was simply larger than could be managed by a voluntary organization that, while it had engaged in several restoration projects, was in no position to undertake large-scale urban renewal. Although architectural plans were drawn up, they were not implemented and in June 1972 Mountjoy Square Estates sold on all its properties to a sympathetic farmer and property developer from County Westmeath called Patrick McCrea. He intended to rebuild all the vacant sites on the square's south side and to restore the remaining houses, his architect for this purpose being the ever reliable Austin Dunphy who had already worked for the Irish Georgian Society at No. 50. Work actually began on one section of McCrea's proposed development before his financial backers withdrew and soon afterwards he was killed in a car accident. A period of stasis followed, Mountjoy Square remained semi-derelict and in February 1978, ten years after it had opened as the Society's Dublin office, Desmond Guinness sold No. 50 insisting, as was reported in *The Irish Times*, that the organization had not withdrawn from the fight to save the square 'and that he will maintain a close watch on any future development there'.

Well into the 1980s, Mountjoy Square, which lies on the main route from Dublin Airport to the city centre, continued to present a pathetic spectacle of neglect and dereliction, its southern side largely composed of twenty-year-old empty sites. Only as the decade closed, and in the wake of legislation such as the Urban Renewal Bill of 1986 and the implementation of tax-incentive schemes, did those gaps begin to be filled with buildings, many of them containing apartments and conforming in exterior height and design to what had been demolished. Of course, these recent infills in no way make up for the losses suffered by Mountjoy Square over such a long period. As John Heagney points out in a 2006 essay on the square, 'It is only fair to say that some of the redevelopment schemes are better than others and that both development sponsorship and control benefited from the learning curve.' But whatever the deficiencies of its more recent additions, Mountjoy Square today looks better than it has done for decades.

Analysed in retrospective the Irish Georgian Society's activities in this part of Dublin have to be seen as yielding mixed results. On the one hand, its high-profile intervention ensured that Mountjoy Square's destruction by insensitive developers did not happen, or at least certainly not in the way or on the scale that would otherwise have been the case. On the other hand, the fight to save Mountjoy Square absorbed a great deal of time, energy and funds without ultimately yielding satisfactory results. Furthermore, it made the Society some very powerful enemies who sought every opportunity to belittle and insult it. In February 1966, after *The Irish Times*' architectural correspondent had published the 'City of Ruins' pictorial essay, then-Lord Mayor of

CHAPTER 6

40 Mountjoy Square, Dublin, first-floor drawing-room ceiling centrepiece, 1982.

Dublin Eugene Timmons responded that the capital's ordinary decent citizens 'had little sympathy with the sentimental nonsense of persons who had never experienced bad housing conditions, and who cared little for human misery provided its facade of the Georgian past was preserved for the sentimental present'.

His comments encapsulated a criticism regularly levelled at the Irish Georgian Society during this era: that it was an elitist organization out of touch with the lives of working people and that its aesthetically minded membership had no interest in assisting the residents of old buildings, only in preserving the latter at the former's expense. No matter how often the Society agreed that everyone was entitled to decent housing and that this could be achieved without the destruction of the national heritage, or pointed out that a lot of the buildings being pulled down in the 1960s and 70s were not being replaced with domestic housing but with offices, the stigma of aloof elitism remained. Hence, rather than address important issues of conservation and heritage raised by the Irish Georgian Society, opponents found it easier to accuse the organization of being out of touch and of representing the interests of a vanquished regime.

This allegation was most overtly articulated on 11 March 1970 when the Minister for Local Government, Kevin Boland, attacked the Society's efforts to halt the spoliation of Dublin, and specifically of St Stephen's Green. During the course of an astonishing five-hour Dáil speech, Minister Boland remarked that a 'consortium of belted earls and their ladies, and left-wing intellectuals, who could afford the time to stand and contemplate in ecstasy the unparalleled man-made beauty of the two corners to Hume Street and St Stephen's Green, might very well feel that the unskilled amateurish efforts of Mother Nature in the Wicklow Mountains are unworthy of their attention'. He subsequently made reference to 'the Guinness nobility who pull the strings to which the Georgians dance' and who were keen to preserve 'the reminder of gracious living at the expense of the slavies and lackies subsisting in the less gracious cellars and back lanes'.

Kevin Boland's intemperate outburst provoked a justifiable degree of outrage but his remarks probably represented the greater share of public opinion. Nor did the Society's heavily publicized and hectic annual programme of parties, balls, Georgian cricket matches and the like – although all intended to raise funds for its admirable work – help to dispel a negative image in the public mind. Thus even individuals broadly sympathetic to the Society's aims could show distaste for the organization itself. In his 1985 polemic, *The Destruction of Dublin*, which continues to provide the most thorough and melancholy investigation of this unhappy period in the city's history, Frank McDonald describes the Irish Georgian Society's early members as 'dilettantes'. He is also critical of the failure of this and other organizations such as An Taisce to do more to halt the onslaught of property speculators, asking why they allowed buildings around the capital to be demolished or ugly office developments to go ahead. With regard to the Irish Georgian Society, an explanation is easily provided: this was a small group of well-intentioned, like-minded individuals who had come together just a few years before. The members' initial brief had been to increase public appreciation of Ireland's eighteenth-century architecture, not to take on powerful individuals and institutions. Membership of the Society never rose above 5000 and many supporters lived overseas.

Similarly much of the money that underwrote its activities came from abroad and was earmarked for specific projects such as Castletown and the Tailors' Hall rather than to be used mounting expensive legal challenges or buying parts of central Dublin otherwise destined for destruction. Unlike the property speculators of the period, the Society did not have the backing of banks and other financial bodies and nor was it ever politically well-connected. In fact, the organization never courted political favour, although in retrospect the potential advantages of doing so are self-evident. Other than a wish to preserve Ireland's heritage for the future, it had no vested interest in what was happening to the nation's stock of old buildings; there was never any financial advantage to the Irish Georgian Society whether these stood or fell.

In effect, the Society assumed responsibility for what the government or a state-appointed agency should have done: the protection of an important part of the national heritage. And given the scale of the assault on that heritage in the 1960s and 70s, the Irish Georgian Society often found itself acting like a single fire engine expected to bring under control blazes simultaneously breaking out not just across Dublin but right around the country. Above all, the Society, along with the Dublin Civic Group, which often acted in association with it, had to contend with what Maurice

Above: John and Ann Molloy opened their house in Mountjoy Square to the public in 1967.

Opposite: 9 Henrietta Street, Dublin, stair-hall seen from first-floor landing.

Craig, writing in *The Irish Times* in December 1985, identified as the two most baleful causes of Dublin's defacement: ignorance and greed. 'Even now,' he wrote, 'most Irish people do not look at buildings nor see them in any very conscious way. Nor can they usually imagine the consequences of the loss of a good building and its replacement by an inferior one.' And he went on to note how such ignorance when coupled with inadequate legislative protection made it easy for speculators, both native and foreign, to enjoy 'a quick and lavish financial return' at the expense of everyone else. Under these circumstances, it is astonishing that a tiny organization like the Irish Georgian Society, with no formal management structure and for many years not even a secretary to deal with correspondence, was able to accomplish as much as it did during such a hectic period.

Among the most significant of those accomplishments was drawing attention to the plight of Ireland's Georgian heritage. By the early 1970s, the blanket obliteration of Dublin's historic core was well known and deplored not just at home but also overseas. As the Irish Georgian Society had long predicted, tourists began to complain that the city they visited was lacking precisely what they had come to see: a coherent Georgian centre. Typical in this respect was a letter carried by *The Irish Times* on 21 June 1971 from Mrs Elizabeth H. Salmon of New Jersey, USA, who wrote that 'I cannot leave Dublin without expressing my concern for the survival of the great 18th-century architecture in this delightful country ... It is sad to see evidence of public disinterest in controlling the commercial disfigurement of so many houses and in preventing the decay and destruction of others.' Not long afterwards, internationally renowned urban theorist and historian Lewis Mumford was quoted in the *Sunday Independent* warning after a visit to Ireland that Dublin was in 'very grave danger' of falling into disintegration and ultimately complete destruction if urgent steps were not taken to preserve the city. And comedian Spike Milligan, who was then performing in the capital, told the *Evening Press* that 'the danger to Dublin is so imminent I can't joke about it'. Even if successive governments and developers showed themselves indifferent to censure, the Irish Georgian Society made sure nobody was left in any doubt that the assault on historic Dublin had not gone unopposed.

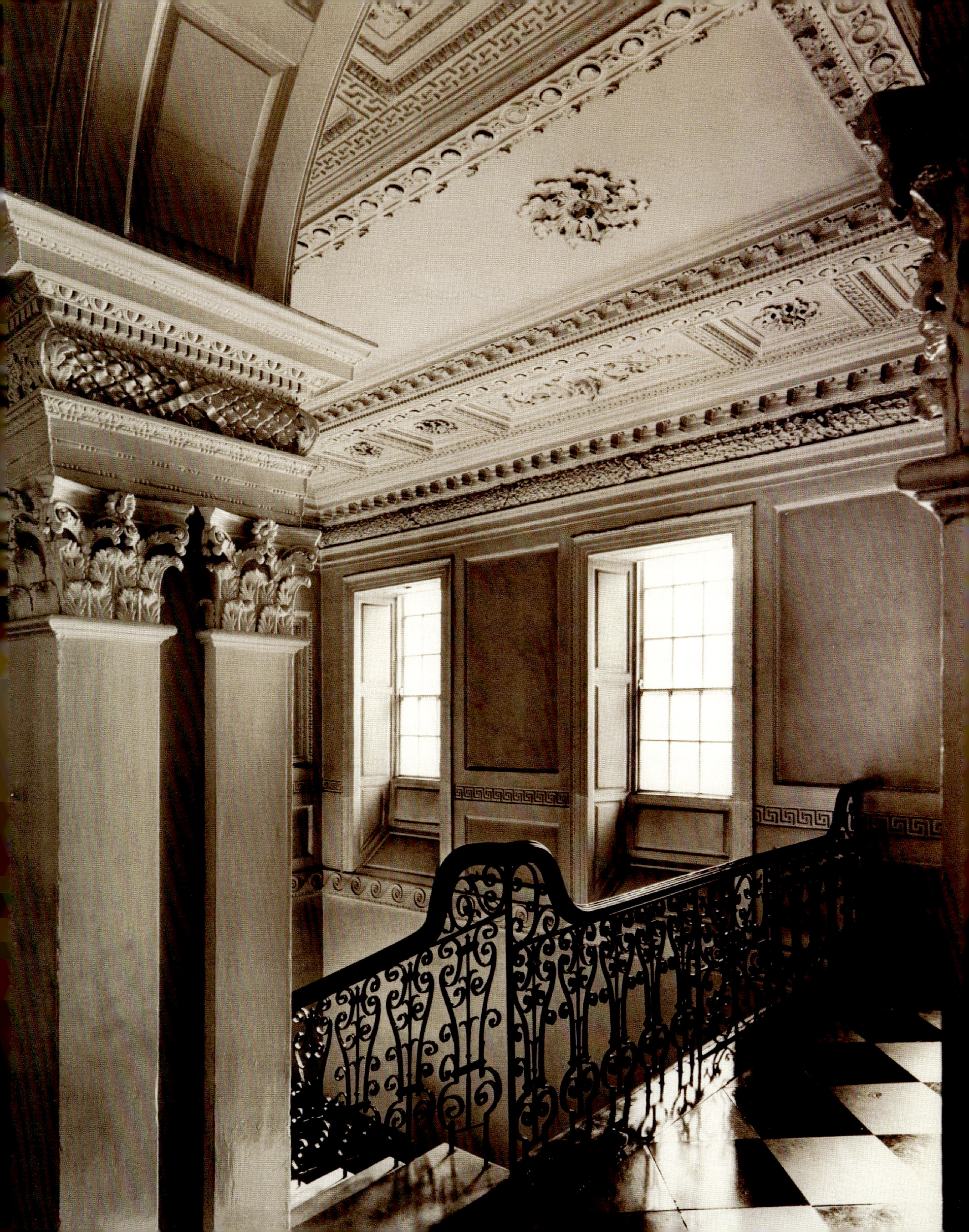

HENRIETTA STREET

Although the Irish Georgian Society's efforts in Mountjoy Square did not bear immediate fruit, the organization enjoyed greater success elsewhere in north-central Dublin. In 1973, it provided an interest-free loan of £13,000 to a young and idealistic student, Michael Casey, enabling him to buy a house on Henrietta Street. Like Mountjoy Square, this part of Dublin had been first developed by the Gardiner family whose own residence at No. 10 still exists on the opposite side of the street. For much of the twentieth century it was an area of run-down tenements; David Synnott remembers visiting the street in the mid-1960s where on one occasion he met an old woman who claimed that one house had accommodated between 200 and 300 tenants, all of them living in squalor. Another day, a pig staggered out of a house, 'so badly kept that it could hardly walk. Every few paces its hind legs gave way and it collapsed into a sitting position.' Writing about the street in *The Irish Times* in March 1982, Frank McDonald reported that until not long before, a horse had lived on the second floor of No. 14 Henrietta Street.

Its neighbour, No. 13, is a palatial four-bay, brick-fronted property believed to date from the 1740s. When Michael Casey and his future wife Aileen took possession of the building, it had long since been divided into eleven tenements and was home to some thirty-six people, all of whom were gradually rehoused elsewhere by Dublin Corporation (which had classified the place as 'unfit for human habitation'). Part of the Society's loan was repaid at the end of 1976 and the balance two years later.

At the time of its purchase, No. 13 was in wretched condition with many of its finest features, including chimney pieces, long since removed. There were holes in the roof, floorboards missing or rotten and sections of wall at risk of collapse. Much of the house's slow and painstaking restoration work was undertaken by Michael and Aileen Casey themselves although where necessary they called on professional help. The original staircase had been pulled out by a slum landlord in the early twentieth century but a replacement was provided by the Irish Georgian Society in 1984; this had come from Lisle House, which was of similar date, when that building was demolished as part of the redevelopment of Molesworth Street in 1974. A donation of $5000 to the Society from the Port Royal Foundation paid for the staircase's installation in No. 13 and for restoration work to be undertaken on the stair-hall's walls and ceiling.

Today the Caseys continue to live in No. 13 where they have raised their family of six children. The house has featured in many films and photographic shoots and is one of Dublin's best-known eighteenth-century buildings. Its restoration programme is ongoing and at the time of writing the owners are about to undertake major work on the facade. The Irish Georgian Society continues to take an interest in the house and regularly brings groups and individuals to see what the Caseys have managed to achieve. Their success in reclaiming a seemingly lost property has been matched elsewhere both in Henrietta Street (where Ian Lumley of An Taisce bought the similarly dilapidated No. 12 in the late 1980s and received a grant for its restoration from the Irish Georgian Society) and in other parts of the city, most notably North Great George's Street, where several loyal members of the Society have made their homes.

Above: 13 Henrietta Street, stair-hall and plasterwork panelling.

Top left: Henrietta Street, Dublin, north side of street, looking east.

Left: 7 Henrietta Street, Dublin, front door, steps and railings.

Opposite: 13 Henrietta Street, Dublin. *From left to right:* James, Aileen, Christina and Michael Casey.

MOUNTJOY SQUARE

40 and 41 Mountjoy Square, Dublin, before restoration.

The only one of Dublin's Georgian squares to justify its title (since each of the four sides measures the same 140 metres in length), Mountjoy Square was laid out in 1791 and built between 1793 and 1818. It was intended to be the centrepiece of the land owned in the capital by the Gardiner family, successive generations of which were responsible for the development of north-central Dublin during the eighteenth century. In 1714 Luke Gardiner had purchased the Moore estate and sixteen years later he started work on the construction of Henrietta Street, which was soon lined with princely residences, including his own at No. 10. Before his death he had also begun work on the northern end of what is now O'Connell Street as well as Cavendish Street, Dorset Street and Rutland (now Parnell) Square. His son and grandson would continue this expansionist policy but by the time the last of the line, Charles Gardiner, Earl of Blessington, died in 1829, the family had little direct involvement in the estate, which subsequently became embroiled in decades of litigation.

In any case, even before the Earl's death the north side of Dublin had already begun its inexorable decline as fashion moved south of the Liffey. On a raised site with views sloping down to the river and the

Above (left to right): Ivor Underwood, Mariga Guinness and Prof. Kevin B. Nowlan at the IGS news conference at 50 Mountjoy Square, Dublin.

Top: Brian Molloy, Castletown, Co. Kildare, and Beth Bryant, New York, preparing for the opening of the IGS office at 50 Mountjoy Square, Dublin.

Left: Side view of 50 Mountjoy Square, Dublin, bought by the Hon. Desmond and Mariga Guinness, 1964.

Custom House, Mountjoy Square, as envisaged by Lord Blessington's father Luke Gardiner II, was to have been grander than anything yet built in the city, a residential development with each side sharing the same integral classical facade centred on a breakfront domed pavilion of cut stone. This ambitious plan was soon abandoned and instead, as had always been the norm in Dublin, individual plots were leased to potential developers who were obliged to comply with certain stipulations regarding their buildings' external appearance. Parapet height; brickwork; position and treatment of windows and doorcases; railings and plinth-wall: all these had to be uniform and ensured that from the start Mountjoy Square exhibited an architectural cohesion

The consistency in external appearance remained unchanged until the middle of the twentieth century, even though behind those uniform doors, many of the square's houses had been altered so that they could be used as offices or, far more frequently, as tenements. Initially the building boom of the 1960s did not affect the north side of Dublin but that situation changed once property developer Matt Gallagher began buying up sites in Mountjoy Square. Thanks to intervention on the part of the Irish Georgian Society, Mr Gallagher's plans for wholesale redevelopment did not go ahead but a great deal of wanton destruction was permitted by the relevant authorities and it was not until almost the end of the 1990s that the outward appearance of architectural cohesion returned. In *The Georgian Squares of Dublin*, published by Dublin City Council in 2006, Mountjoy Square was rightly acclaimed as 'a monument to careful planning and elegant design, and a legacy for future generations to cherish'.

The Society's work around the country ~ Skiddy's Almshouses in Cork ~ Robertstown and its Festa ~ Longfield ~ Roundwood ~ Brian Molloy ~ Damer House ~ Panels: volunteers and Brian Molloy

CHAPTER

7

Although Dublin and Castletown undoubtedly absorbed the greater part of the Society's attention – and funds – during the second half of the 1960s and through the following decade, the rest of the country was by no means ignored. Whenever possible the organization tried to give money to preservation projects and even if these sums were not particularly large, at least they showed the Society was concerned to help as much as possible. Among the many schemes assisted in this way, a few particularly deserve mention here, such as the campaign to restore Wexford's charming Market House and Assembly Rooms dating from 1776. In 1967 the town's corporation intended to rent the building to the county council for use as a Civil Defence Store in which gasmasks, sandbags and the like would be kept. A deputation including Desmond Guinness appeared before the corporation's members to plead that this plan should not go ahead, offering £300 from the Irish Georgian Society if instead the Assembly Rooms were restored and redecorated. Their appeal was successful, the money was provided and since 1974 the building has served as the Wexford Arts Centre.

Around the same time, the Society also contributed £250 towards the restoration of the Georgian Inn, a late-eighteenth-century building in Emo, County Laois, believed to have been designed by James Gandon, the original architect of adjacent Emo Court for the Earl of Portarlington. Now called the Gandon Inn Hotel, the property had been occupied by squatters for some years before being rescued and returned to its intended use. On this occasion, the Society provided financial assistance on condition that all windows should be replaced in the same style (there had been a proposal for squaring them off and inserting metal-framed casements) and that the organization's advice 'should be followed where practicable'. In 1968 the Society, in conjunction with Bord Fáilte, provided help to ensure the preservation of the eighteenth-century Temple at Belan, County Kildare; this, like the long-since vanished house on the estate, had been designed by Richard Castle. It then donated additional money towards the restoration of the nearby Eagle Pillar, which was in danger of imminent collapse.

While the Irish Georgian Society frequently took the initiative to guarantee the survival of a building or monument, there were occasions when it was called upon to provide assistance and support to another group. The fight to save the Skiddy's Almshouses in Cork was one such instance. This extremely important group of arcaded homes had been erected in 1719 and provided sheltered housing until the trustees of the Skiddy's Charity decided to build a new home elsewhere in the city. They sold their existing property for £2000 to a nearby hospital, the North Infirmary, which, in turn, took the decision to demolish the almshouses – until then the oldest inhabited public buildings in Ireland – and replace them with a student nurses' home. A group of local people came together to block this plan and formed the Cork Preservation Society, which was given funding by the Irish Georgian Society for its fight to save the almshouses.

Initially the group's efforts looked doomed to failure; when a case for keeping the building was made to the North Infirmary's committee of management, this body 'questioned its architectural value and tourist potentialities', according to the *Cork Examiner*, 'and explained the technical and other reasons why it would not be possible to preserve the old Almshouses'. The cost of preserving the buildings was estimated to be ten times the price paid for their purchase. Nevertheless, even though contracts for the new nurses' home had been signed, a staying order was secured in August 1967 preventing the imminent demolition of the Almshouses and ultimately, after

The Market House and Assembly Rooms at Wexford date from 1776. Since 1974 the building has served as the Wexford Arts Centre.

Left: Exterior.

Right: Interior.

a struggle lasting another decade, the buildings were saved. Following restoration, Skiddy's Almshouses reopened in 1978 as twelve residential flats.

A similar story can be told about the courthouse in Dunlavin, County Wicklow. Dating from the mid-eighteenth century this Doric structure with its dome of fluted granite was built by the Hon. James Worth-Tynte of nearby Tynte Park; Richard Castle is believed to have been the architect. Although some alterations were carried out in the 1830s and it went through various changes of use, the building remained substantially intact in the centre of Dunlavin until 1966. Then it was badly damaged by fire and subsequently left to moulder for several years. Local pressure forced Wicklow to make a decision on what should happen to the courthouse; not surprisingly, the authority's preferred option was demolition on the grounds that the structure would be costly to renovate and that it was 'a traffic hazard'. Miraculously objectors, including a number of county councillors, succeeded in having this decision reversed and money was procured for restoration to begin. The Irish Georgian Society, which had been involved in the campaign for the courthouse's retention, paid for the exterior to be cleaned. In June 1979 Dunlavin's courthouse reopened as a branch library and market house.

The campaign to preserve a stretch of the Grand Canal was another project with which the Society became associated during the same period, specifically through its association with the annual Festa held at Robertstown, County Kildare. Described in 1966 by writer and broadcaster Stephen Rynne as 'one of the brightest events ever to illuminate the countryside', the Festa had begun in 1964 with the formation of a local branch of Muintir na Tíre (a community self-help movement established in 1937). With a population in the region of just 200, Robertstown was little more than a village but its residents understood that their history – and their future – was intimately associated with the canal, which was then seriously neglected (and in Dublin threatened with being turned into a motorway). The centrepiece of the area, and effectively its raison d'être, was the handsome Canal Hotel dating from 1803 but unused for its intended purpose since the advent of railways led to a sharp decline in canal transport. This building provided a focus for the annual celebration that initially ran for one week in August.

In 1966, when the Irish Georgian Society became involved for the first time, the Festa was extended to a fortnight. To promote its own work, the Society took over a room in the hotel where Brian Molloy managed to sign up some 200 new members. But over the two weeks there were lots of social events, including the annual Georgian cricket match, which, as the *Evening Press* reported, 'was all jolly good fun, even though the wicket was as uncertain as the scoring. Eventually it was agreed that the North had beaten the South by an unspecified number of notches.' There were also eighteenth-century banquets with music and singing in the hotel, which, in addition, hosted exhibitions and a programme of lectures; visits were made to other houses in the area, and a demonstration was given by Desmond Leslie of water-skiing on the canal. What made his activity distinctive was that Mr Leslie was pulled by a horse being ridden at speed along the bank by Desmond Guinness; this alone guaranteed the festival got plenty of publicity in the national press.

Peter Verity also recalls another performance of the perennial *Sweeney Todd*: 'At the insistence of Father Murphy we performed at the Robertstown Festival (the Desmond Leslies much in evidence) but unfortunately without the home base support. To get an audience we had to perform free, the grand piano collapsed and to our great mortification the audience, who had not enjoyed the usual pre-performance claret cup, to a man walked out.'

The Irish Georgian Society retained a presence at the Robertstown Festa for the next decade, a period in which the Kildare town's annual celebrations attracted widespread interest and attendance. A museum containing what was described as 'Canaliana' opened in the old hotel and in 1971 the premises began to offer twice-weekly eighteenth-century-style banquets during the summer season, with diners arriving at the hotel door in a horse-drawn barge. By mid-September of that year, the parish priest Father Patrick Murphy could tell the *Farmer's Journal* that, 'Since May 1 we have had 4000 guests. There has been a lot of building up to do, but I think we're going to make a profit now.' The following year Robertstown was said by the area's tourism chairman to represent the region's major tourism resource.

The Festa also represented what could be achieved when an entire community joined together to save an important part of the national heritage. In this instance the Irish Georgian Society simply offered what support it could to an already dynamic local initiative. But on several other occasions it effectively acted alone to preserve a building of note. In January 1966 a long-standing supporter of the Society, Molly O'Connell Bianconi-Watson, had given a lecture called 'King of the Irish Roads' to the other members about her great-grandfather, whose biography she had written four years before. Born in Italy in 1786, at the age of fifteen Charles Bianconi had come to Ireland and made a living from peddling prints. On his travels around the country he saw the need for better methods of transportation and so began offering a service to passengers. The business prospered and by 1846 annual receipts totalled £40,000 and the Bianconi horse-drawn coaches covered nearly 4000 miles of Irish roads. Bianconi, who became a naturalized Irish citizen in 1831, wisely did not oppose the advent of the railway companies, taking shares in some of them before he sold his own business and retired to a 2000-acre estate he had bought in County Tipperary for £22,000.

This was Longfield, which had subsequently been inherited by Miss O'Connell Bianconi-Watson, her name reflecting that she was also related to the great nineteenth-century Irish politician Daniel O'Connell. At the time of her lecture to the Irish Georgian Society, she was close to seventy years of age and living in somewhat straitened circumstances. The estate itself had shrunk to sixty-two acres while large parts of the house, originally built in the middle of the eighteenth century and by now full of Bianconi and O'Connell memorabilia, were unoccupied. Longfield, which had been run as a hunting and shooting guesthouse in the middle of the century, had poor plumbing and no electricity or telephone line; now occupying just two rooms, Molly O'Connell Bianconi-Watson had written her great-grandfather's biography by the light of an oil lamp. But she was a woman of enormous pluck whose life had been almost as crowded with incident as that of her famous ancestor and her

Brian Lenehan, Minister for Justice, with Miss O'Connell Bianconi who inherited Longfield, Co. Tipperary, and presented it to the IGS in 1968.

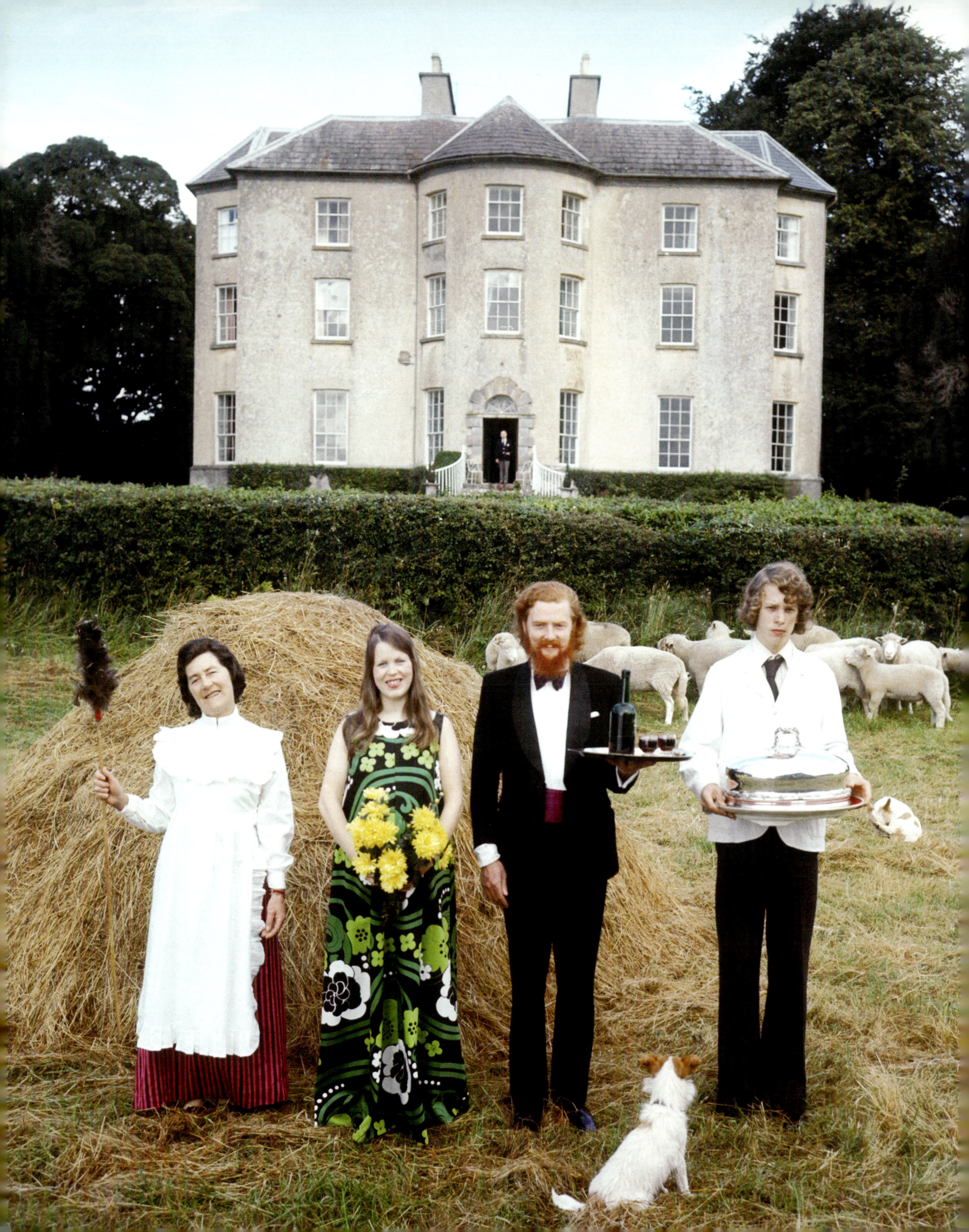

circumstances immediately interested the Society, which provided a grant of £400 for essential repairs to the property's roof. The plan was to turn Longfield, which lies not too far from Cashel, into a tourist attraction once sufficient restoration work had taken place. An early *Bulletin* of 1968 advised that the house

> is at present being restored by the Society with the help of Bord Fáilte, and will be opened to the public officially in 1969 ... Although there is a nucleus of family portraits and mementoes of Charles Bianconi, the transport pioneer, in the house, objects of interest such as would be found in an Irish country house will be most gratefully accepted for display there.

Around the same time, *The Irish Times* announced that Longfield had been presented to the Society by Molly O'Connell Bianconi-Watson. A new company, limited by guarantee, was formed at the time to take possession of Longfield, the Society's first tangible property (both No. 50 Mountjoy Square and Castletown, County Kildare, had been bought by Desmond Guinness). All was progressing well when in late August 1968 Molly O'Connell Bianconi-Watson died, leaving behind a miasma of debts and legal complications. Once these had been adequately, if expensively, resolved, the Society was faced with the responsibility of caring for Longfield, a particularly onerous task since Bord Fáilte, which had provided grant aid worth £4500, now withdrew its support on the grounds that any agreement of support had been made with the house's deceased owner. The first *Bulletin* of 1969, after expressing regret for the death of the organization's generous benefactor, remarked:

> We had hoped that she would continue to live at Longfield and show it to visitors, and with the help of the Irish Tourist Board we were engaged in repairs and reconstruction work to provide her with a self contained flat. We are now faced with having to find someone to live in the house. It has great charm, lovely views, and, although deep in the country, is not far from the historic town of Cashel. Longfield will be open to the public again this summer, and we should like to hear from anyone interested in living there and looking after it.

Electricity, central heating and decent plumbing were installed and a well was sunk. Although restoration work on the house continued, it took a while to find somebody prepared to assume responsibility for its daily management. An update in the following year's *Bulletin* explained:

> Much remains to be done there, but a good deal has been accomplished since the Society took possession of the house in 1968. All the windows in the house are having their proper glazing bars replaced, which should improve the look of it. The roof has been repaired, plumbing, wiring and some decoration completed, and a tenant is being sought for the main part of the house, which now has four bedrooms, two bathrooms and an up-to-date kitchen. The tenant would of course have to be prepared to admit the public, but the rent would therefore be reasonable. There is a light and spacious basement, recently painted white, which the tenant could develop as a tea room for bus tours.

Opposite: Longfield, Co. Tipperary, built in 1770, restored by the IGS and run as a hotel by Kevin and Christa Byrne.

CHAPTER 7

Kevin Byrne in the Drawing Room at Longfield, Co. Tipperary.

Eventually in September 1970 it was arranged that Longfield would be leased to a young couple, Kevin and Christa Byrne, who had been actively involved with the Irish Georgian Society since both were university undergraduates. The Byrnes had already worked on the restoration of houses in Mountjoy Square, at Castletown and, more recently, Roundwood in County Laois, and they were therefore used to tackling projects that demanded single-minded dedication. A long feature in the *Clonmel Nationalist* the following June reveals how much the pair, who were preparing to open Longfield as an eight-bedroom country-house hotel, had already achieved. 'The energy, enthusiasm and courage of this youthful pair is almost beyond belief,' observed the writer. 'You should see the amount of work they have got through in such a small space of time.' Country-house hotels are now commonplace in Ireland but Longfield was among the first of its kind and as such attracted considerable attention and a steady clientele. But there could be surprises for the guests. Kevin Byrne remembers an occasion when Grey Gowrie arrived to stay so late that

> we left a note in the hall, telling him which room (top floor, front, above the front hall), and went to bed. Next morning, serving breakfast, we checked that he had been comfortable. Yes, everything was perfect – but he felt that a neighbouring guest's nocturnal practices had been rather thoughtless and had disturbed his rest. We did not tell him then, nor to this day, that he had been alone on that floor ... Alone, that is to say, but for a former housekeeper who allegedly should have been buried in the Franciscan habit that had been bequeathed to her and which she kept in a trunk under her bed. From time to time, this trunk would be dragged out and opened, preceded and followed by walking up and down the corridor. Lord Gowrie was not the only one to hear her – indeed, Christa and I were completely used to her by then – but he was the only one to actually complain!

The Byrnes remained at Longfield until 1978 when they sold on their lease to another couple and the house continued to operate as a hotel five more years. But in March 1983, the Irish Georgian Society, in conjunction with the house's then-lessees, decided to put Longfield on the market. Insurance costs had climbed horrendously while an economic recession meant a decline in the number of tourists; maintaining the house had become unviable. Longfield was therefore sold to a local stud farmer who already owned the estate's outbuildings; today it is a private home. As mentioned, prior to taking on Longfield, Kevin and Christa Byrne had been involved in the restoration of Roundwood, County Laois. The subject of detailed study by Maurice Craig in his *Classic Irish Houses of the Middle Size*, Roundwood is an exceptionally charming mid-eighteenth-century five-bay house with pedimented breakfront. Its pretty exterior has often been described with reason as being akin to that of a doll's house.

The interior is just as delightful, its most distinctive feature being the double-height hallway containing a staircase and gallery of Chinese-style fretwork; this is lit by a first-floor Venetian window. In 1968 the Land Commission bought the estate from then-owners Chetwode and Elizabeth Hamilton and left the house standing with just fourteen acres. For two years it stood empty and at risk until bought for £6250 by the Irish Georgian Society in the summer of 1970. There was no water supply or electricity but thankfully the building had not been vandalized and its chimney pieces and other features were intact. On 13 July, Brian Molloy moved into the house, along with the Byrnes and Peter Verity. Between them they managed to rescue Roundwood, bringing it back to life at a cost to the Society of approximately £15,000. Peter Verity remembers that on the day this little group arrived at the house, they sat on the front steps and ate a picnic, after which

> Christa Byrne produced coffee much to Brian's amazement as there was no running water. Christa revealed she had made the by-now drunk coffee with the bottled water Brian had thoughtfully brought. Brian's face was the picture of complete and utter horror over what had been done and also for the consequences: we had just drunk the holy water his mother had sent for the purpose of blessing the house (and possibly, for good measure, to exorcise the house of a Protestant squireen).

In 1988 Desmond Guinness described Brian Molloy, who had died ten years before, as 'an amazing leader and organizer' and these qualities were much needed during the period when Roundwood was being restored. A diary kept by Brian Molloy during his first months living in the house indicates just how dilapidated it was and how much had to be done. In an entry for 15 July 1970, he notes that a nineteenth-century extension to the rear of the house 'was consumed with dry rot, wet rot and decay' (it was soon demolished by Kevin Byrne) and three days later, 'Mr Maloney the electrician is coming on Tuesday, thank God. He gave an estimate of £218, very reasonable as it includes 47 thirteen amp sockets.' A constant stream of volunteers came to offer support, some of them by now Society regulars such as David Synnott and Jeremy Williams, others from elsewhere in Europe.

Gradually the house was refurbished and decorated under Brian Molloy's direction. The drawing room's Victorian chimney piece was replaced with a fine eighteenth-century example from Bert House, County Kildare, but otherwise little was added to the building. Similarly the overgrown grounds and stable yard were cleared and tidied. The house was officially opened on 6 June 1971 by Miss Gabrielle Gore-Booth of Lissadell, County Sligo. By the time architect John O'Connell wrote of Roundwood in 1973's final *Bulletin*, Roundwood was being run as a guesthouse. Mr O'Connell was able to report that the building's former dismal condition had been vanquished and that 'with its windows painted brilliant white, the lawns and parkland cleared of overgrowth, an exceptionally interesting example of mid-eighteenth century domestic architecture stands in pristine condition'.

During the summer of 1973 Roundwood had been the focal point for an Irish Georgian Society cultural weekend organized by Brian Molloy; this included an architectural exhibition at Portlaoise and concerts both inside Roundwood and outside where the Chieftains performed. The leader of the Chieftains, Paddy Maloney, had an aunt who kept a grocery shop a mile from Roundwood. That same year Roundwood was bought for £35,000 by a keen American supporter of the Society's work, John L. Tormey of Akron, Ohio. (The profit from this sale was used to provide Michael Casey with an interest-free loan so that he could buy No. 13 Henrietta Street in Dublin.) Some years earlier John Tormey and his wife Nell had taken a flat in Castletown and while there, as Desmond Guinness later recalled, they often entertained visitors by playing Irish songs

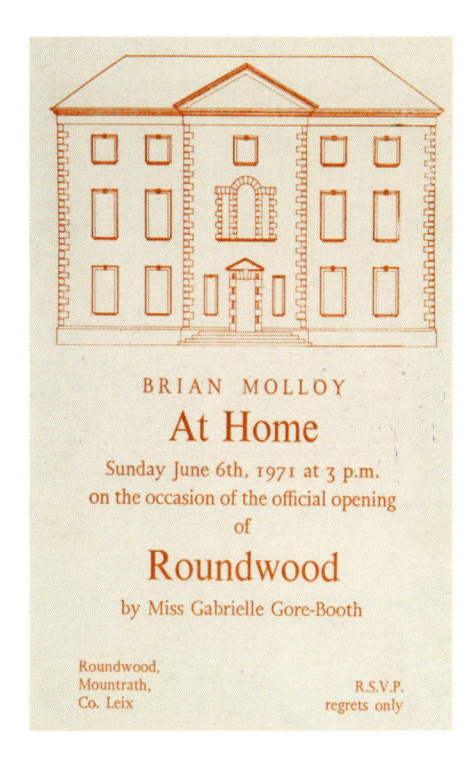

Top: Roundwood, Mountrath, Co. Laois. Invitation to the official opening, 1971, from Brian Molloy.

Bottom: Roundwood, Mountrath, Co. Laois, front doorcase.

CHAPTER 7

Above: Roundwood, Mountrath, Co. Laois, staircase hall.

Right: Roundwood, Mountrath, Co. Laois, entrance front.

and ballads on a piano rented for the duration of their stay from harpsichord-maker Cathal Gannon.

Following their acquisition of Roundwood, they were happy that Brian Molloy should continue to live in the house and soon afterwards it became a centre for volunteers working on the restoration of the Damer House in Roscrea, County Tipperary. Shortly after Brian Molloy died in 1978, Mr Tormey generously donated Roundwood back to the Society and early in the following decade it was leased to two couples who ran the place as a country-house hotel. Eventually in 1988 one of those couples, Frank and Rosemary Kennan, bought Roundwood from the Society for £62,000. The proceeds from this second sale were used to finance restoration work at a number of other historic properties around the country such as Strokestown, County Roscommon; Carrigglas Manor, County Longford; Ledwithstown, County Longford; and Doneraile Court, County Cork. Roundwood continues to be run as a hotel by the Kennans.

Brian Molloy also played a major role in restoring the Damer House. This important building is not only of architectural significance but also highly unusual in that it was built for the Damer family around 1720 inside the walled courtyard of a thirteenth-century Butler castle that stands at the centre of Roscrea town. Of three storeys over basement and with unusually tall narrow windows spread across nine bays, the pre-Palladian house's finest internal feature is a carved pine staircase, in style not dissimilar to that of the slightly later Cashel Palace. The house had a chequered history after the Damers (later Dawson-Damers, Earls of Portarlington) moved to Emo Court; during the nineteenth century, along with the castle, it served as a military barracks before becoming at different times a school, a tuberculosis sanatorium and a library. By 1970 it was empty and unused, and the local authority, Tipperary County Council, announced plans to demolish the house and replace it with an amenity

Above: Doneraile Court, Co. Cork, entrance front.

Left: Damer House, Roscrea, Co. Tipperary, staircase.

centre comprising a swimming pool, car park, playground and civic centre (it had been nurturing this scheme since as far back as 1957). The council's chairman, Tom Shanahan, wanted the demolition to go ahead, arguing that 'as long as it stands it reminds the Irish people of their enslavement to British rule', and dismissing objectors to the scheme as 'a crowd of local cranks'. Most of the so-called 'crowd' were members of the Old Roscrea Society and in December 1970 it was offered help by the Irish Georgian Society in the campaign to save the Damer House.

The following spring the Society arranged for architect Austin Dunphy to survey the eighteenth-century building. His report, published in one of the 1971 *Bulletin*s, concluded that while some restoration work was needed, 'the house is structurally in excellent condition and given normal maintenance, should last for hundreds of years to come. From the architectural point of view, to have such a fine house in the centre of the town is most advantageous, and in my view should form the centre of the social and cultural activities of the town.' A copy of this report was given to the county council, which later that year agreed not to demolish the Damer House.

On the other hand, it did nothing to preserve the building and in November 1973 the authority, on learning that restoration would cost in the region of £40,000, decided to go ahead with demolition after all. So at the start of the following year the Irish Georgian Society once more intervened, this time proposing it take on a lease for the Damer House and assume responsibility for the restoration, now budgeted at £80,000 over five years. In February 1974 the council agreed to this arrangement and the Society took on the house for a period of ninety-nine years at an annual rent of one shilling. The restoration of the Damer House was to be its contribution to European Architectural Heritage Year 1975.

CHAPTER 7

Damer House, Roscrea, Co. Tipperary.
Entrance front, before restoration.

Work on the project began in mid-August 1974 and was once more overseen by Brian Molloy, whose own association with the Society had begun in a similar way eight years before. As with Roundwood, the first task was simply clearing away accumulated rubbish and debris, and removing unsightly additions to the house, such as partition walls. While professionals worked on repairing the roof, the workforce included a dozen architectural students from Dublin and members of the Old Roscrea Society. Volunteers were advised to turn up at the site 'in old clothes, bringing brushes, buckets and handy tools'. Audrey Emerson recalls that the state of the building 'was appalling, with every window broken, the staircase shrouded and boxed in. There was rubbish and debris everywhere and I seem to remember the basement was full of water.' As ever, work proceeded slowly and was dependent on enough funds being raised for this purpose. Some £5400 was spent on repairs in 1974 and at least the same again the next year. In 1976, £8000 was required to repair the staircase, including the replacement of missing balustrades; this work was undertaken some years later by craftsman James Foley of Killaloe, County Clare, who carefully removed sixteen pounds in weight of paint from the staircase's carved frieze.

By June 1977, £22,000 had been spent on the Damer House, which was now deemed ready to admit visitors and host exhibitions, the first of which was opened by then-TD (and future taoiseach) Charles Haughey, who in his speech remarked that state aid was needed for the restoration of buildings of historical or architectural merit. It would be some time before this scenario came about but the support of an influential politician was helpful, if only because Mr Haughey's comments were widely reported and drew national attention to the work done by the Society in Roscrea. Thereafter, while refurbishment continued on both the Damer House and its slightly later

114

Damer House, Roscrea, Co. Tipperary.
Entrance front, after restoration.

annexe, the venue was regularly used for events such as touring exhibitions organized by the Arts Council. In 1980 some of the most influential members of the Old Roscrea Society, notably local teacher George Cunningham, decided to form a new organization, the Roscrea Heritage Society, which later that year organized a large show in the Damer House. Exhibits relevant to the town's history were lent by both the National Museum and the National Gallery.

With aid from a number of public bodies, the house's annexe was next restored for use as a heritage centre; the first of its kind in Ireland, this opened to the public in 1983 and shortly afterwards won a special award from the adjudicators of European Museum of the Year. At the end of 1983, control of the Damer House was handed over to the Roscrea Heritage Society, which subsequently took on the house's 99-year lease (some time later, the Heritage Society leased the premises to the Irish state, which by this means finally assumed responsibility for the building). During the 1990s more work was completed not just on the Damer House but also on Roscrea Castle and its gardens. Today the entire complex has been refurbished and is open to the public. The story of the Damer House's salvation provides another instance of the Irish Georgian Society being ahead of broad public opinion. Once scheduled for demolition, the building is now regarded as a major architectural and tourist asset for the midlands region of Ireland.

CHAPTER 7

Clockwise from top: Ledwithstown, Ballymahon, Co. Longford, after restoration.

IGS group visiting Ledwithstown, Ballymahon, Co. Longford.

The Feeney family in the Drawing Room at Ledwithstown, Ballymahon, Co. Longford.

Ledwithstown, Ballymahon, Co. Longford, before restoration.

VOLUNTEERS

When it came to rescuing old buildings from neglect, much of the work accomplished by the Irish Georgian Society over several decades could not have been realized without support from unpaid volunteers. The first such help was provided in June 1966 for the restoration of the eighteenth-century chapel at Fiddown, County Kilkenny, and soon it became the norm that appeals for volunteers would be issued whenever the Society embarked on a new project such as saving the Tailors' Hall in Dublin or restoring Castletown. The second of these was particularly dependent on voluntary help in the months before it first opened to the public in July 1967. As a rule, participants were young, many of them undergraduates at one of Dublin's universities although a number also came from overseas. Rose Mary Craig, today one of the Society's board of directors, remembers that while still a student at Trinity College, she had met William Garner and through him became involved with work at Castletown:

> The house was being got ready to be opened to the public and I became one of the first voluntary guides going there every Sunday during the summer to guide visitors around. They were exciting heady times and a whole new world, albeit a decaying world, opened up to me … Being at Castletown in the late 1960s and early 1970s was both educational and fun!

Similarly, David Synnott recalls that while professional painters were required for the entrance hall and staircase hall, volunteers such as himself

> did almost, if not absolutely, everything else. Voluntary work continued everyday on the house and its adjacent yards and garden to make it ready for opening to the public. At weekends there were certainly up to 50 volunteers at a time, possibly more, and they were of all ages and backgrounds …

Consequently a fantastic amount of work was done in a few weeks.

Volunteers were primarily responsible for the restoration of both Roundwood House, County Laois and the Damer House in Roscrea, County Tipperary, both these projects being overseen by the late Brian Molloy. Cormac O'Carroll worked at the Damer House where, 'everything was in a dreadful state; we had to pull out sheets of timber boarding that had been tacked over doors and fireplaces – the excitement of finding and exposing the original interiors and the thrill when we got to the wonderful carving on the staircase'. From a slightly later period, Arthur Montgomery remembers that during the 1980s and 1990s there were always regular groups of enthusiastic volunteers to help at Doneraile Court, County Cork. As a rule these helpers were accommodated in the house in groups of four, a large number of them from Italy after a native of that country had one day turned up clutching a page from an Italian newspaper that described the work of the Irish Georgian Society and included a photograph of Doneraile.

Volunteers even came from as far away as Ghana where an organization called the Pan-African Student Congress arranged in August 1988 for a group to come to Ireland, despite being told by Audrey Emerson, then the Society's executive director, that there were no remaining places on any of its work groups. Nevertheless, sixteen visas were issued by the Irish government's honorary consul in Ghana and eight Ghanaians arrived in Dublin. Audrey Emerson managed to find two of them jobs in the gardens of Annes Grove, County Cork, 'where they spent their entire time hiding because they thought there were snakes in the undergrowth'. And while some of the others subsequently returned to their own country, a number of Ghanaians simply 'disappeared'.

Though the organization still occasionally calls on the support of volunteers for tasks such as clearing away undergrowth around historic monuments and houses such as the Fiddown Chapel in County Kilkenny and The Deeps in County Wexford, this source of labour is no longer so central to the Irish Georgian Society's work. Practical matters such as health and safety legislation, and workplace insurance make it more difficult to invite members to provide unpaid help. But the central role played by volunteers in the past should not be forgotten; the Society owes them all an enormous debt of gratitude.

Above: Volunteer group led by Brian Molloy at Damer House, Roscrea, Co. Tipperary.

BRIAN MOLLOY

For the twelve years before his untimely death, Brian Molloy devoted himself to the work of the Irish Georgian Society. As was noted in a memorial notice, during this period he had been the Society's 'practical arm' who tackled 'the various restoration projects undertaken with courage and infectious enthusiasm'. A reminiscence in the *Tipperary Star* observed that 'One could not talk to him without being captivated by his sincerity, charm and utter devotion to the timeless beauty of stone.' Born in Dublin in 1945, Brian Molloy grew up in Roscommon and had begun studying law at Trinity College, Dublin, when he first came into contact with the Society. Desmond Guinness remembers his turning up dressed in a blazer with gold buttons and white trousers to help with restoration work at the Fiddown Chapel in June 1966. Despite this unlikely garb – 'as if about to board a ship' – he was immediately engrossed in the task and later that summer went on to help at both Charleville Forest and the Robertstown Festa.

His legal studies abandoned, the following year he moved into Castletown House as a caretaker as soon as the house had been bought by Desmond Guinness and lived there for the next three years. In July 1970 he moved into the derelict Roundwood, County Laois, which remained his home for the rest of his life. During this period he not only oversaw the restoration of Roundwood but also that of the Damer House in Roscrea and the start of work on Doneraile Court, County Cork. Rose Mary Craig notes that soon after moving to Roundwood, he 'restored the house magnificently. I remember we were all amazed that he was installing bathrooms into the 4 main bedrooms – such foresight!' Among those who helped him on this project was David Synnott, who recollects that

> the grounds there were extremely overgrown, in places totally inaccessible. The trees beside the house were home to a very busy rookery, and Brian remarked that he had not known before then that rooks snored. Nor had I, but on going out of the house late one night one could hear a definite sound of very gentle cawing coming from the rookery.

Once the house had been brought back to life, says Cormac O'Carroll, Brian Molloy 'was an amazingly hospitable person. The first evening I arrived there, the place was candlelit, there were big bouquets of wild flowers and music floating out from somewhere.'

That Brian Molloy was a tireless advocate on behalf of the Society is widely attested by those who knew him. In a tribute after his death, Desmond Guinness recalled that 'starting with a barbeque (in the rain) in Roscommon Castle, his native town, he organized innumerable benefits in aid of Tailors' Hall, Castletown, Doneraile Court and the Damer House. He also arranged the weekend visits to country houses which have become increasingly popular and profitable.' Audrey Emerson remembers that on one of those visits, a bus being supervised by Brian Molloy broke down and rather than leave the passengers grow fretful, he 'went around the bus collecting everyone's commemorative mugs that they had bought in the various gift shops en route, went down the road to a pub not far away, and filled them up with gin and tonic'.

His energy was considerable and so too was the scope of his talents. In addition to fund-raising, tour guiding and supervising restoration work on various properties, he was also an outstanding host and cook; Brian Molloy was responsible for the catering at many Castletown balls as well as dinner before concerts during the early Festivals in Great Irish Houses. That he would have gone on to help with more of the Society's later endeavours cannot be doubted and this made his early death in August 1978 all the more regrettable. A month later he was posthumously awarded a gold medal by the International Castles Institute 'for the splendid restorations he has undertaken on behalf of the Irish Georgian Society'. A fund was established to commemorate Brian Molloy and this money helped to pay for a portrait by Giuseppe Berti of Alessandro Galilei, architect of Castletown, purchased at a sale in New York. The picture now hangs in the hallway of Castletown, a house he greatly loved.

Clockwise from top left: Damer House, Roscrea, Co. Tipperary. At the official opening: Brian Molloy (in charge of restoration), C.J. Haughey TD and the Hon. Desmond Guinness, June 1977.

Brian Molloy photographed at the opening of 50 Mountjoy Square, Dublin.

Memorial plaque to Brian Molloy.

Desmond Guinness starts travelling to the United States ~ Joseph Ryle and the Irish Georgian Society Inc. ~ early American Chapters ~ ongoing American support ~ the Society's indebtedness to the United States ~ Irish regional Chapters ~ the London Chapter ~ its vigorous programme of activity and fund-raising ~ Panels: the Birr, Limerick and Cork Chapters

CHAPTER

8

'No account of the activities of the Society would be complete without acknowledging the help and encouragement of the membership worldwide ...', wrote Desmond Guinness in the Irish Georgian Society's 1988 *Bulletin*. 'In particular the US and Canadian Chapters have been tireless in their fund-raising activities, and the London Chapter events are always fun as well as both enlightening and profitable. These "foreign" efforts are an invaluable addition to the funds raised locally in Ireland.'

The Society's association with the United States dates back to June 1959 when Dr Richard Howland, former president of the National Trust for Historic Preservation, brought sixty-eight members of the Society of Architectural Historians of America to Ireland for a week-long tour. Dr Howland had first come to Dublin in 1958 when he met Desmond and Mariga Guinness through Philip de Burgh O'Brien. He led him up to the roof of the Gresham Hotel and 'showed him the Georgian streets and explained what a threat they were under'. Thanks to this connection, much of the 1959 SAHA trip was arranged and co-ordinated by the fledgling Irish Georgian Society, or more specifically by Desmond and Mariga Guinness.

In addition to visits to all the major historic houses in the greater Dublin area, there were talks given by the likes of Eoin O'Mahony and Percy LeClerc on aspects of Irish art and architecture, receptions in private homes including the Provost's House in Trinity College, and the opening of an exhibition at the Municipal Gallery on

W.B. Yeats; funds for this were inveigled from both the Arts Council and Bord Fáilte. Dr Howland would also remember how his entire party was taken on 'a horse drawn vehicle tour of Georgian Dublin – Desmond and his cohorts found enough cabs, coaches and carriages for all of us to traipse around behind the horses!' The visit was an enormous success and most of the participants willingly joined the Society even before returning home. They also pressed the Guinnesses to come to the United States. 'We should have gone straight there,' Desmond Guinness accepts, 'but we were so busy here. Still, they were the foundation of our American membership.'

It was not until January 1964 that he and Mariga did cross the Atlantic so that Desmond could give a dozen lectures on Irish architecture and plasterwork to various groups around the country; his programme had been organized by Dr Howland who by now had joined the staff of Washington's Smithsonian Institution. Another source of support in this and subsequent years were his uncle and aunt, the Hon. Murtogh and Anne Guinness who lived on East 80th Street in New York. Desmond Guinness insists that as a young man he suffered from terrible shyness when called upon to speak in public; at the Carton tea party of January 1958, for example, he was so embarrassed at the prospect of addressing his guests that Seymour Leslie (from Castle Leslie, County Monaghan) felt obliged to do so. But over the intervening years the shyness dissipated and he soon became renowned as a fluent and entertaining public speaker. Back for a further series of lectures in September 1965, he was already gaining a reputation, as the Nashville *Tennessean* noted:

> In a talk made up of equal parts of historical research on great Irish houses, good-humoured gossip and legendary Irish charm, the Honorable Desmond Guinness spoke last night to an audience that crowded the drawing room at Cheekwood ... Guinness showed slides that made one wonder why tourists ever went anywhere but to Ireland or ever wanted to live in anything less than an 18th-century castle.

Before long, the lecture tours had become an annual, and much publicized, occurrence. 'An old friend of ours, the Honourable Desmond Guinness of Leixlip Castle, County Kildare, Mother Ireland,' ran a piece in the *New Yorker*'s 'Talk of the Town' column in October 1967,

> is making one of his regular semi-royal progresses through the States, putting up in the pleasure domes of wealthy friends and giving illustrated lectures on Irish houses and castles (including his own) for the purpose of drumming up interest in and raising funds for the cause to which he and his pretty wife are devoting their lives – to wit, the Irish Georgian Society.

But entertaining as they might be, there was a strong proselytizing element to Desmond Guinness's talks. Through them, he sought not just to acquire additional members and their financial contributions but also to see whether Irish-American influence might help to prevent the destruction of Ireland's eighteenth-century heritage. Already in 1964, *Washington World* had reported Desmond Guinness saying:

Dublin was in the throes of a modern building boom, but he charged the Irish government and the city 'are doing precious little to save its famous Georgian brick architecture – practically the only architecture we have'. Guinness, like many other critics of the Dublin demolition, feels that American public opinion can be brought to bear to save the buildings ...

Simultaneously, another organization had been established with the same aim in mind. In 1962, Dr Edward Keelan (who had been born and raised in Dublin but was by then living in Westport, Connecticut) set up the Society for the Preservation of Historic Ireland specifically in response to the ESB's plans to demolish Lower Fitzwilliam Street in his native city. Like Desmond Guinness – who he met during the course of the latter's 1964 American visit – his intention was to canvas Irish-Americans for their support in 'preserving the monuments and buildings of historic and cultural Ireland'. And although the battle to save the Fitzwilliam Street houses was lost, the Society for the Preservation of Historic Ireland remained in existence, raising money for other causes and, as a registered charity, gaining tax-exempt status from the United States government. This was particularly helpful to the Irish Georgian Society after Desmond Guinness bought Castletown and large sums of money were required for the house's restoration. Growing numbers of American supporters were prepared to help the cause, but their donations would be liable to tax were they paid directly to the Society. Initially, therefore, all donations were channelled through Dr Keelan's organization; by November 1968 he estimated more than $40,000 had been transmitted to the Society by this means. Even after the Irish Georgian Society set up its own American division and this was designated as tax-exempt, the Society for the Preservation of Historic Ireland continued to provide it with financial support (sending a cheque for $2000 in November 1968), and to help other Irish groups such as the Butler Society.

However, even by the time Castletown was bought it had become evident that if the Irish Georgian Society were truly to benefit from American patronage, then the organization would need to have a permanent presence in the United States. It was at this point that Joseph D. Ryle first became associated with the Society. A well-known public relations executive based in New York, Mr Ryle had been employed by a diverse assortment of clients such as the New York Racing Association, Coca-Cola and the Metropolitan Museum of Art. Moira O'Malley describes him as being 'a fascinating man and a delightful charming spirit ... I can still picture Joe, dapper, delightful, personable.' 'Very chic,' recalls Desmond Guinness, 'rather like an American version of Maurice Chevalier.' In spring 1967 mutual friends had put him in touch with Joe Ryle and by early September of the same year the latter had drawn up a proposal, 'designed to increase the membership and focus attention on the work of the Irish Georgian Society'. Once this was agreed and he began working for the organization from his apartment on East 51st Street, the first and most pressing task to be accomplished was establishing the Society as a legal entity in the United States. To this end the Irish Georgian Society in the United States was incorporated in April 1968 and at the end of the following month it had been awarded the all-important tax-exempt status.

From the beginning the Irish Georgian Society Inc. has had its own board of directors and until his retirement in 1986 Joe Ryle acted as executive director (he would stay on the board for some time and died in July 1997). Even before the incorporation he had started to raise the organization's profile by arranging for it to have a stand at the January 1968 New York Antiques Fair and, once that closed, a display of photographs showing Castletown went on display in Bord Fáilte's Manhattan offices before travelling to Expo in Montreal. But his greatest early triumph was to obtain the world premiere benefit of *Finian's Rainbow* (one of Fred Astaire's last films, and one of Francis Ford Coppola's first). Held at the Warner Bros cinema, the screening was followed by a dinner at the Rockefeller Center's Rainbow Room and the night made over $10,000 for the Society; part of this money was spent on buying Giuseppe Berti's portrait of Alessandro Galilei, which now hangs in Castletown in memory of Brian Molloy. Although in principle this fund-raising night can be perceived as a success, in reality there were a few problems, the most immediate of which was *Finian's Rainbow* – a dreadful piece of whimsical nonsense. Since the film premiere had an interval, many of the guests took advantage of this to slip away and go home. As a result, only about half the number of expected diners turned up at the Rainbow Room and the carefully strategized seating plan had to be frantically rearranged. On the positive side, Desmond Guinness got to dance with Ginger Rogers.

Given his background in public relations, Joe Ryle possessed excellent press connections, meaning the Society was given ample coverage in American newspapers even though its work took place in a small country several thousand miles away. And unlike media attention closer to home, that in the United States was invariably favourable. Typical in this respect is a large feature that appeared in *The New York Times* in May 1970. Headlined 'Battle Waged to Preserve Georgian Dublin', it described how Mariga Guinness swept into 50 Mountjoy Square and informed the reporter that 'developers ripped off my roof and demolished supporting walls to get me out ... But the Georgian Society muddles on firmly, despite this constant opposition.' New York newspapers could be relied upon to cover Irish Georgian Society events, or even just the presence of Desmond Guinness (and later also the Knight of Glin) in the city. One of the Society's most devoted correspondents was the good-looking and witty social columnist Suzy Knickerbocker (real name Aileen Mehle) who, in whatever publication was then running her amusing aperçus, would always devote space to matters Irish. This had begun even before the advent of Joe Ryle; a paragraph she wrote for the now defunct *New York Journal* in March 1966 refers to Anne Guinness,

> who has a terrific nephew, Desmond Guinness, who lives at Leixlip Castle in Ireland and has the most marvellous blue eyes. Desmond is head of the Irish Georgian Society whose aim is to restore the great Palladian houses in Ireland. Anne or 'Go-Guinness' represents the Irish Georgian Society in America and I wouldn't tell you all this if St Patrick's Day weren't just around the corner. Up the Irish! Especially if they look like Desmond Guinness.

Once Desmond FitzGerald took to lecturing in the United States on behalf of the Society, Suzy displayed equal enthusiasm for him, invariably declaring that the

Portrait by Giusseppe Berti of Alessandro Galilei, architect of Castletown, Co. Kildare. Purchased by the IGS with funds provided by Joseph Ryle of IGS USA in memory of Brian Molloy.

CHAPTER 8

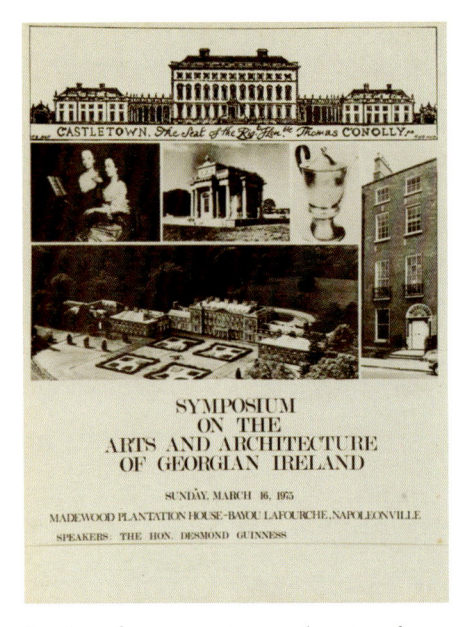

Brochure for a symposium on the arts and architecture of Georgian Ireland, March 1975.

Knight of Glin was 'my favourite title'. Arthur Bassett, who assisted Joe Ryle (and subsequently Arthur Prager) in Irish Georgian Society Inc. work for many years, remembers how, 'every time Desmond Guinness came to town, Joe Ryle would give me copy and I'd take it over to her on East 68th Street'.

Suzy also helped to increase demand for lectures by Desmond Guinness. Initially he relied on friends such as Richard Howland to find venues for these talks because the best-known lecture agency at the time, W. Colston Leigh Inc., already arranged bookings for two Irish speakers, Sir Humphry Wakefield on architecture and Ulick O'Connor on literature, 'and I don't think they were terribly keen about taking on a third Irishman'. But Suzy gave so much advance publicity to a lecture he gave at New York's Metropolitan Museum in January 1967 that when his taxi pulled up outside the building a long queue had formed down the street. By the following September, W. Colston Leigh himself was writing to Desmond Guinness to express the hope 'that you will be interested in making arrangements with us for a tour during the 1968–69 season'. From then on, he made twice-yearly journeys to the United States to deliver talks on different aspects of Irish art and architecture. In March 1975 he was joined on one of these trips for the first time by Desmond FitzGerald, the Knight of Glin, who had recently left his job with the Victoria and Albert Museum and returned to live in Ireland. Speaking to *The Daily Oklahoman*, the Knight warned of the impact that the Irish government's recently imposed wealth tax would have on surviving heritage properties such as his own.

The interest shown in Ireland by groups and societies across the United States was remarkable; during the March 1975 tour, Cleveland arranged an Irish celebration of European Architectural Heritage Year, while New Orleans held a one-day symposium on the arts and architecture of Georgian Ireland. Equally impressive, both then and on later occasions, were the sheer number of cities visited and talks given by both Desmond Guinness and the Knight of Glin. It is a tribute to the two men's stamina and devotion to the Society that over the years they have given so much time to explaining Irish art and architecture to American audiences. Between late-January and mid-March 1967, for example, Desmond Guinness spoke at twenty-five venues in nineteen different cities; he returned to New York two months later for a major fund-raising benefit on behalf of Castletown held at Parke Bernet, and was lecturing in the United States again for much of October.

While the content of these talks was in part amusingly anecdotal and intended to entertain an audience perhaps unfamiliar with Irish history and culture, it was also educational. This was especially evident when either Desmond Guinness or the Knight of Glin, or frequently both, were invited to participate in seminars such as 'The Decorative Arts in Ireland', held over two days at Pennsbury Manor, Pennsylvania, in April 1971. As well as these two speakers on Irish architecture, painting and silver, Suzanne Delahunty from Philadelphia's Institute of Contemporary Art spoke on early Irish art, John Austin talked of Irish delft and Phelps Warren of Irish glass. For the occasion, American museums and private collectors lent items of Irish furniture so that a complete exhibition of the country's decorative arts could be displayed.

Two years later, in April 1973, Boston Public Library was the venue for a day-long symposium on Irish art and architecture organized by the local Chapter; a similar event was held a few days later at the New York Cultural Centre. The Washington Chapter arranged a three-day seminar in early December 1979 to mark the Irish Georgian Society's twenty-first birthday and then in late October 1981, the New York headquarters of Christie's on Park Avenue hosted a seminar for the Society on Irish art and architecture, which had a particularly impressive line-up of lecturers ranging from former Archbishop of Armagh Dr George Simms talking about the Book of Kells, to Professor Anne Crookshank on Irish landscape painting and the Romantic movement. Nicholas Robinson spoke of the Irish Architectural Archive, Desmond Guinness of the Irish origins of the White House, the Knight of Glin on Irish furniture and Professor Kevin B. Nowlan on politics and culture in eighteenth-century Ireland. The thirst for knowledge about Irish culture was seemingly unquenchable.

One advantageous outcome of the yearly lecture trips made first by Desmond Guinness alone and subsequently in the company of the Knight of Glin was that Chapters of the Irish Georgian Society were established right across North America. Massachusetts was the very first and owes its origins to the fervour of hotel executive Michael Neagle and Mary Cunningham, who became the Chapter's chairman and secretary respectively. Mr Neagle paid a visit to Dublin in September 1960, staying at the Gresham Hotel. 'I asked the concierge if there was a walking map of Dublin and was told there was not, but that I could purchase at Hodges Figgis a pamphlet on the subject of Georgian Dublin and containing an appeal to preserve these magnificent buildings. I bought the pamphlet and walked about Dublin. I was hooked forever.' Desmond Guinness recalls that when approached some years later by Michael Neagle and Mary Cunningham with the idea of setting up an American branch of the Society, 'I said to them, look, I haven't got a secretary, I don't even have a typewriter, you can't set up your own Chapter. And they said, it's none of your business; we're going ahead.'

Despite this amicable difference of opinions, the Chapter's inaugural meeting went ahead in September 1965 at the Sheraton Boston Hotel. 'There was a bar and refreshments and Barbara Walker showed slides … A large silver punchbowl was placed at the rear of the room and the princely sum of $380 was donated by the twenty or so guests. The New England Chapter was up and running and has not stopped since.' Membership grew fast, as did a programme of local events, many of which were held to raise money for various restoration projects in Ireland. In October 1971, for example, the Chapter hosted a fashion show at the Women's City Club of Boston featuring five Irish designers (and with Kathleen Watkins as compere) that yielded a profit of $1500 for the Society. Like many other Chapters, it also arranged talks by speakers other than Desmond Guinness and planned tours of Ireland for its members so that they could see the Society's work at first hand and appreciate how their contributions were being spent. The Massachusetts Chapter continues to prosper.

Many American Chapters were set up because there was already a large number of the Society's members in their respective parts of the country. St Louis was typical in this respect. Established not long after Massachusetts, it began when St Louis resident

Prof. Anne Crookshank and Prof. Kevin B. Nowlan, who lectured at a seminar in New York for the IGS on Irish art and architecture in October 1981.

CHAPTER 8

Canopy bed from Lucca, donated by the Dallas Chapter of the IGS, founder Nita Carol Miskovitch.

Kathleen Winter wrote to Leixlip Castle asking for a list of members in the Missouri area: 'According to Mr Guinness's suggestion, we are following the organization of the Massachusetts Chapter as a model for ours here.' That was in mid-April 1967 and by the end of May, Mrs Winter was requesting fifty more membership forms since 'I find the forms with the descriptive literature and coloured pictures most helpful.' Desmond Guinness had already visited St Louis on previous lecture tours and it was a regular stop in the years to come. He was there in April 1973, for example, when the *St Louis Post-Dispatch* wrote that while some fund-raisers deployed overt arm-twisting tactics, Desmond took a more subtle approach, 'by refraining from discussing money. But, he is successful ... Dues for membership are $15 a year, but of course Desmond did not mention this. And that is obviously the best manner to raise money for eighteenth-century houses.'

Women were often the driving forces behind the establishment of a new Chapter. In Cleveland, Ohio, Mrs Robert Hornung (known as Twinks) arranged a party in February 1970 to coincide with one of Desmond Guinness's visits to the city. Her intention was to use this occasion to set up a local Chapter because, as she told a reporter from the *Cleveland Press*, 'we have at least forty national members of the society in Cleveland and it's time we were affiliated'. Mrs Hornung set about her task with gusto and was soon drumming up fresh support for the Society. In November 1970 she and her fellow committee members organized an Irish film festival in the local university and the following April they gave a 'Dessert Tea and Illustrated Lecture' during which Twinks Hornung spoke about the historic houses of Ireland. Thanks to the commitment of long-standing members such as Dottie McNulty, Cleveland continues to thrive. Among the most significant members of this Chapter were John and Nell Tormey of Akron, Ohio. Mr Tormey was the very generous supporter of the Society's work, who in 1973 bought Roundwood House, County Laois, and then five years afterwards donated it back to the Society; he first arranged for Desmond Guinness to lecture in Akron in 1974. Prior to his death in 2006 he also set up a fund that continues to provide revenue for the organization. His son Tom Tormey now sits on the board of the IGS Inc.

Even more Chapters soon followed: in Connecticut; Illinois; Arkansas; Kentucky; California; Baltimore; Oklahoma; Philadelphia; St Paul, Minnesota; and even a Canadian Chapter in Toronto. Moira O'Malley makes an invaluable point about the growing American membership of that period: 'Certainly in the early years, the links are interesting. And it seems to be that Desmond Guinness managed to touch a Who's Who of creativity or money or elegance ... but what's intriguing is that so many were "kindred spirits".' Among those kindred spirits, in Dallas, Texas, the energetic Nita-Carol Cervin (now Miskovitch) did sterling work attracting new members and raising funds; in 1971 the Chapter paid for the purchase of a magnificent canopied bed for Castletown. 'I can hardly believe our luck in finding someone so dynamic to be our woman in Dallas,' wrote Desmond Guinness after she had told him the good news.

Likewise in Miami, Florida, the Society was fortunate in having Constance Pole Bayer as head of the local Chapter, since she was forever discovering new ways to help and retained her enthusiasm for the job in hand. 'Words cannot express the feelings we all have here,' she wrote in April 1971, 'for the work that is being done for this great cause: the work of the Irish Georgian Society.' Also in Florida, the long-standing support of Patrice Cooper and her Society of Ireland (founded in 1970) must be mentioned for all the help, and money it gave the Society over the years.

While Joe Ryle ran an efficient organization in New York, it was thanks to the commitment of these women and many others that the Society developed such a loyal following in the United States. Even by January 1969 from a total membership of 5145, more than 2300 were classified as 'American and Foreign' – and by far the greater part of this number lived in North America. Seven years before, the Society had had only 150 members. (English membership, incidentally, stood at just 437 in January 1969.) Almost without exception, these Chapters arranged for their members to pay regular visits to Ireland. In 1978, for example, a group from the St Louis Chapter spent three weeks in the country, followed almost immediately afterwards by members of the Baltimore Chapter (five days) and then in August the Cleveland Chapter (one week). Astonishingly, despite constant traffic across the Atlantic over many years, it was only in June 2003 that the respective boards of the Irish Georgian Society and the IGS Inc. held a joint meeting; thanks to Sir David Davies, this took place in Abbeyleix, County Laois.

Rose Saul Zalles raised $1000 for the Tailors' Hall, Back Lane, Dublin, and paid for the purchase of the Conolly Folly, Co. Kildare.

Another early Chapter worth mentioning was that based in Washington. Set up in 1968 and run by Susan Kennedy (who, like Richard Howland, worked at the Smithsonian Institution), it benefited from being located in a city that was home to many wealthy potential backers. Their support was sought for the inaugural Ireland of the Welcomes Ball, held at the Mayflower Hotel, Washington, on 7 March 1969. The Irish Georgian Society was one of three beneficiaries from this event, the other two being Edward Keelan's Society for the Preservation of Historic Ireland and the American Irish Foundation. Although organized by these groups and nominally under the patronage of Senator Edward Kennedy and then-Irish ambassador to the United States, William P. Fay, arrangements for the ball quickly came under the sway of Rose Saul Zalles. A wealthy Washington socialite with Irish antecedents (her forbears were Maguires from County Fermanagh), the previous year she had paid for the purchase of the Conolly Folly. Mrs Zalles was a cousin of actor Hurd Hatfield (he played the eponymous hero in the 1945 film, *The Picture of Dorian Gray*) who later bought and restored Ballinterry House, County Cork.

He was just one of 100 guests entertained to dinner by Mrs Zalles at the 1925 F Street Club before they joined some 500 others at the Ireland of the Welcomes Ball where attendees included such Washington social luminaries of the time as Perle Mesta (known as the 'hostess with the mostess' and inspiration for the Irving Berlin musical, *Call Me Madam*) and Gwen Cafritz, along with representatives of other American Chapters, like Kathleen Winter from St Louis. From the profits made by the ball, $1000 was donated to the Tailors' Hall Fund in Dublin. Rose Saul Zalles, who had energy to match her wealth, helped to arrange several other fund-raising balls for the Society over the next few years on both sides of the Atlantic; in July 1972 she persuaded twenty-seven of her Washington friends to come to Ireland for the Castletown Ball, and then flew in legendary dance-band leader Meyer Davis and

CHAPTER 8

his orchestra to play at the event. This was part of a seven-day tour, billed as 'One Fabulous Week in Ireland, with Rose Saul Zalles', which, in addition to its leader's company, included such delights as a visit to the Rock of Cashel, 'Wonder of the World', and a display of horsemanship at the National Stud in Kildare.

But Mrs Zalles was by no means the only member to show exceptional loyalty and generosity towards the Society. In fact, there were a great many others, such as the late Carroll Cavanagh, who was initially given a year's membership of the Irish Georgian Society by his aunt, Mabel Brady Garvan. Not long afterwards he visited Ireland, met Desmond and Mariga Guinness and became involved in the saga of Mountjoy Square. His son, also called Carroll Cavanagh, remembers that the family gradually acquired more and more property in the area, beginning with three houses in Belvedere Place. At the start, the plan had been that he would encourage friends to follow his example and see these buildings as investments that could be restored and then let for mixed residential and office use. Somehow that didn't happen, and as Carroll Cavanagh Jr explains, 'My father went on to own 21 houses on the Square! He was always persuaded that, for instance, "No. 22 is critical lest the whole East side of the Square tumbles like dominos," or there was important plasterwork or something else.' Only gradually did the Cavanaghs dispose of this property portfolio: 'We sold off some into good hands.'

Also meriting mention at this point is the late Sally Sample Aall who, through her Port Royal Foundation, was a munificent benefactor to the Irish Georgian Society. The author of two books on follies and pavilions, she had Irish ancestry and was brought to Ireland by Sybil Connolly. The latter's involvement with the Swiss Cottage in Cahir, County Tipperary, meant that Mrs Aall underwrote the costs of its restoration in the late 1980s. 'She insisted on supplying all the money,' explains Arthur Prager (former executive director of the IGS Inc.), 'because she said that if anyone else donated he or she would want to have some input in the restoration or the furnishings, and she wouldn't want that.' Mrs Aall also contributed funds to a number of the Society's other projects during that period.

Across more than four decades, the Society has been helped by a great many other private and corporate donors, together with charitable bodies such as the Samuel H. Kress Foundation, which provided funds for the restoration of both Castletown and Doneraile, and the Patrick and Aimée Butler Foundation, which provided the Headfort suite of furniture for Castletown, along with much other support. There have also been several substantial bequests such as $100,000 received from the estate of Paul Mellon in 2001; this was granted specifically to help cover the costs of the Society's journal, *Irish Architectural and Decorative Studies*, over the following five years. In 2001 the Society benefited from another major bequest of over $1,000,000, this time from the estate of Andy Warhol's brilliant business manager, Frederick Hughes, who had been a long-standing friend of Desmond Guinness and his second wife, Penelope, as well as a loyal admirer and supporter of the Society's work over many years. For someone who had no direct links with Ireland, this was an extraordinarily generous gift.

Top: Sybil Connolly introduced the IGS to Sally Sample Aall, who underwrote the costs of restoration of the Swiss Cottage, Cahir, Co. Tipperary.

Middle: Gordon St George Mark lent many St George family portraits from Tyrone House, Co. Galway, to Castletown.

Bottom: Fred Hughes, Andy Warhol's business manager, bequeathed over $1,000,000 to the IGS in honour of the Hon. Desmond Guinness and his second wife, Penelope.

Clockwise from top left: Irish table presented to Castletown by Mrs George F. Baker of New York, 1969.

Dr Franklin D. Murphy (left), president of the Samuel H. Kress Foundation, being greeted by Arthur Montgomery, 1982.

Marilyn Perry, executive vice-president of the Samuel H. Kress Foundation, with Arthur Montgomery at Doneraile Court.

Aimée and Patrick Butler of the Patrick and Aimée Butler Foundation, who donated the Headfort suite of furniture to Castletown.

Suite of tapestry-covered furniture from Headfort, presented to Castletown by the Patrick and Aimée Butler Foundation, St Paul, Minnesota, USA.

In February 2000 the American Ireland Fund made the Society one of its 'Named Funds', through which it could receive money. In addition, the AIF announced that it had been offered a major grant for the Society of $250,000 each year for two years. The money was being provided by an anonymous member but it came with the condition that the Society had to match the amount through further fund-raising. 'This challenge grant will propel us forward again,' the Knight of Glin wrote in the Society's next *Newsletter*, 'and the Board is already considering a strategy to achieve the matching funds. We will now be seriously setting our sights on major donors at home and abroad – YOU HAVE BEEN WARNED!' Within a year he was able to report, 'We hope soon to have achieved the goal of $250,000. If you haven't yet responded, please consider doing so – as I have said before, every contribution, however small, helps.'

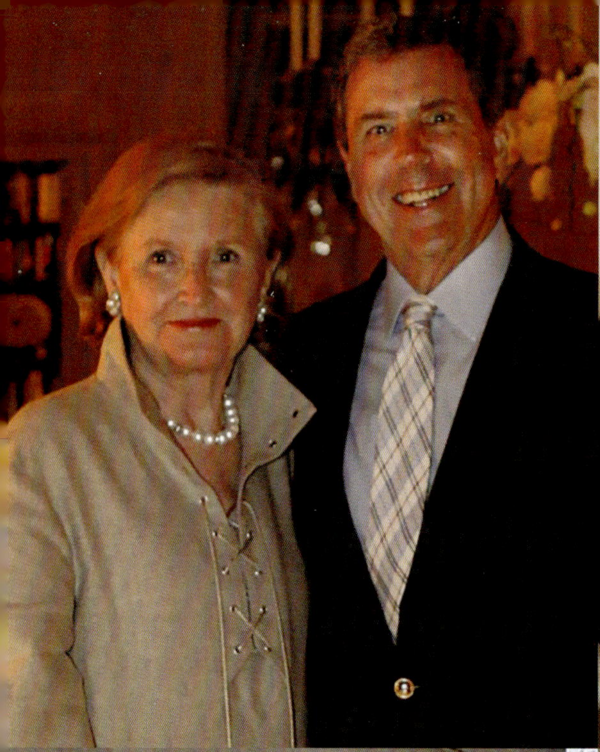
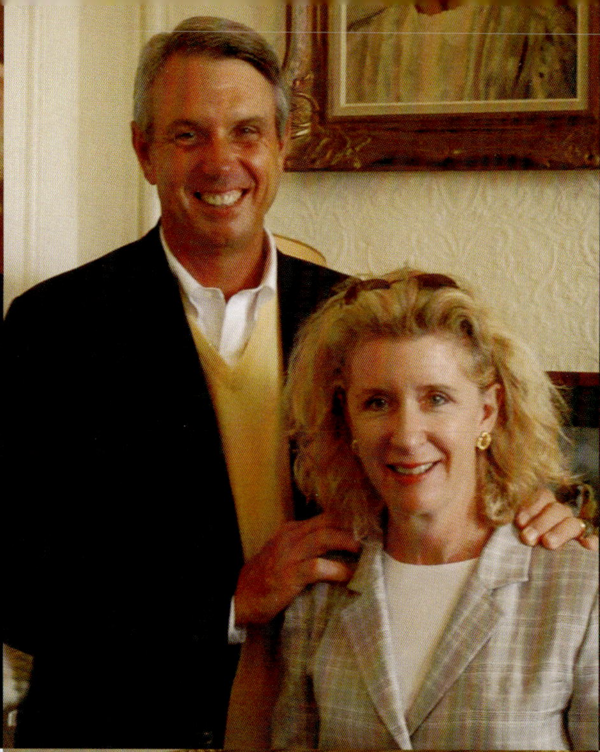
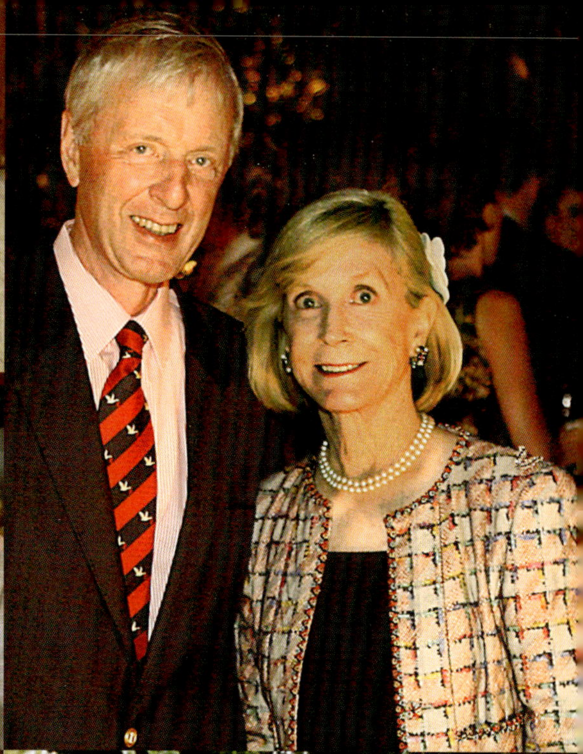
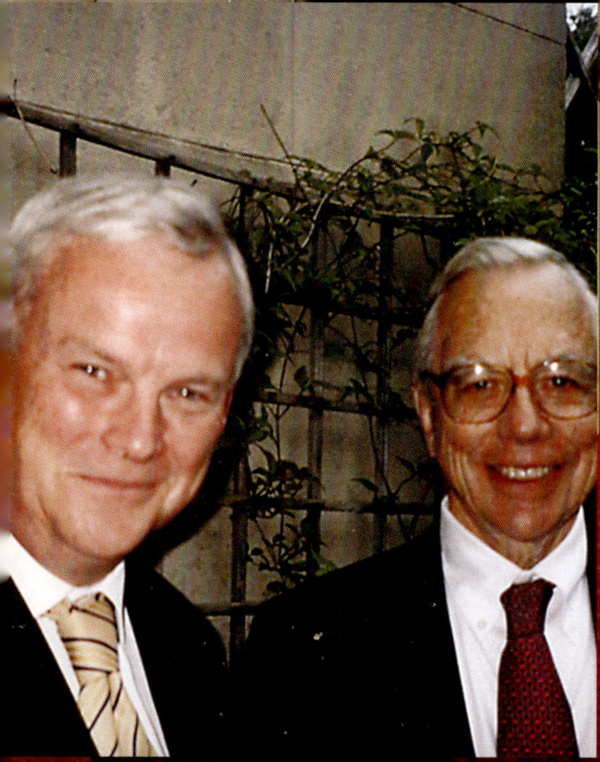
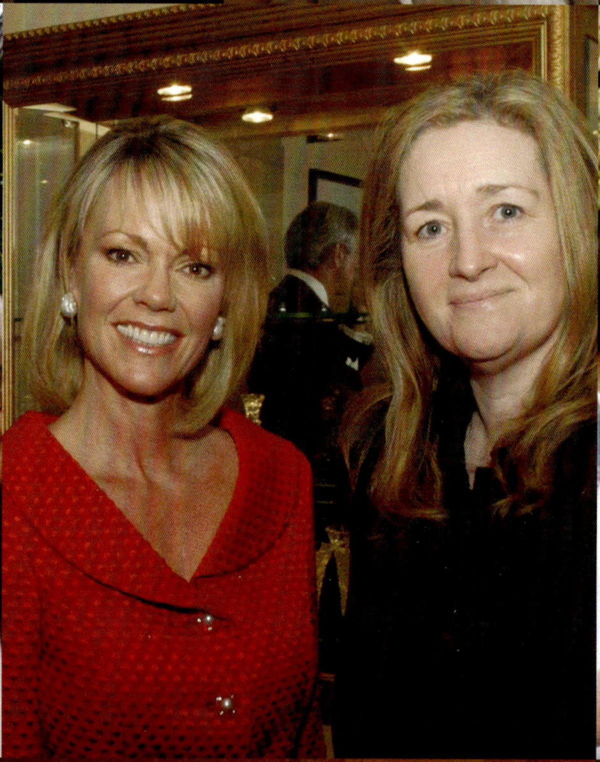
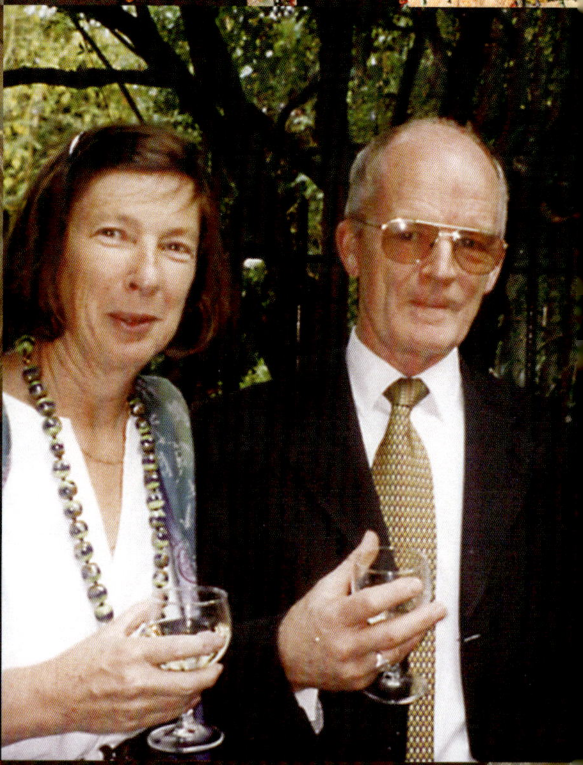
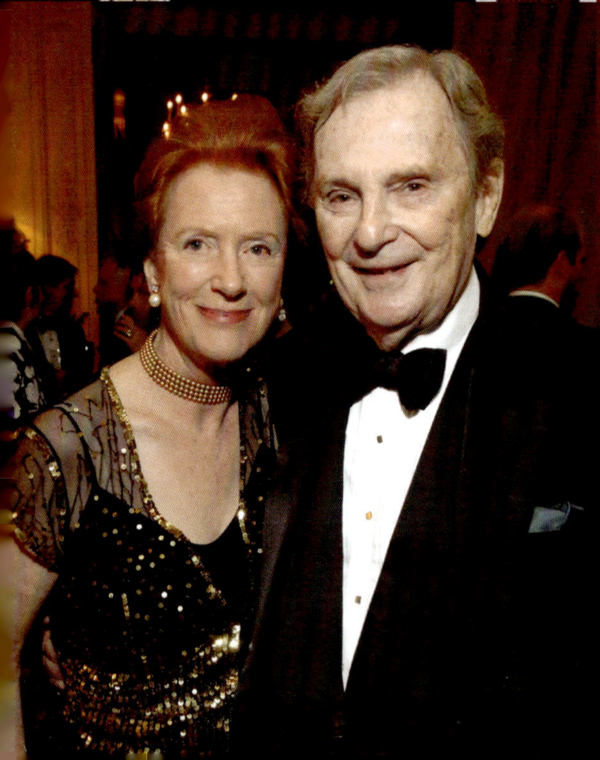
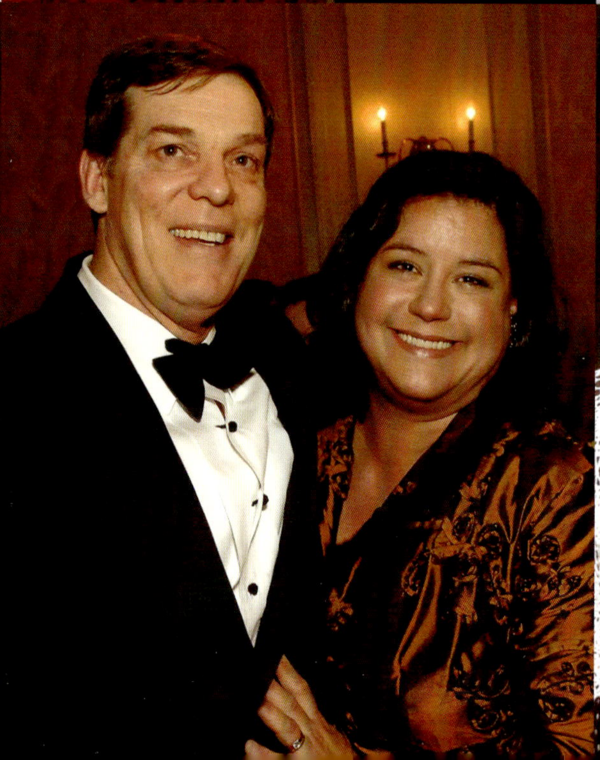
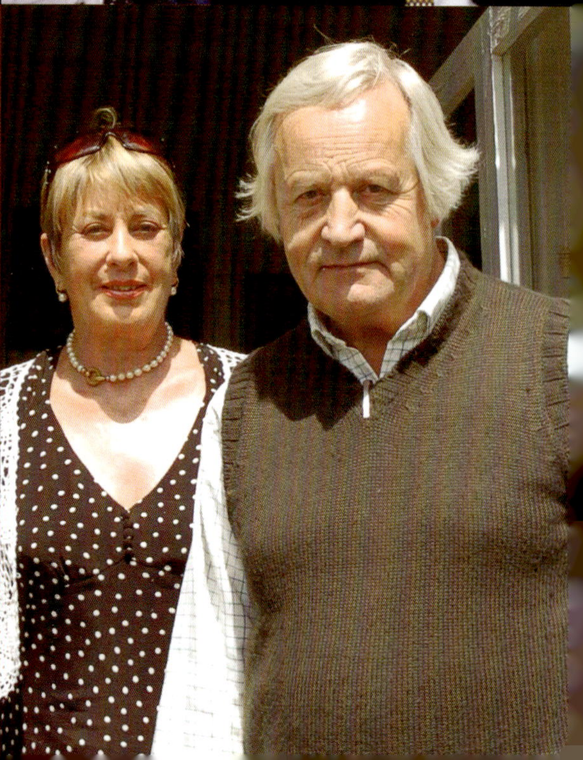

CHAPTER 8

OPPOSITE:

Top left: Kay and Fred Krehbiel.

Middle left: Pyers O'Conor Nash and Gordon St George Mark.

Bottom left: Edwina Sandys and Arthur Prager.

Top centre: Chip and Mary Agnes Quinn.

Middle centre: Paula Fogarty and Chantal O'Sullivan.

Bottom centre: Paul Farrell and Liz King.

Top right: Michael and Pepper Jackson.

Middle right: Rose Mary Craig and Cormac O'Carroll.

Bottom right: Gabriel de Freitas and Stephen Seager.

ABOVE:

Top left: Judy Hadlock, Brian Redmond and John Holohan.

Top right: Mike Neagle, Rosie O'Neill and Desmond FitzGerald, Knight of Glin.

Bottom left: Joe Fuchs, Sheila O'Malley Fuchs and Bill Hart.

Bottom right: Loretta Brennan-Glucksman, Bill Hart and Sheila O'Malley Fuchs.

131

CHAPTER 8

The Malahide Castle dining chair copied by the Kindel Furniture Company, 1983.

Those small contributions have, indeed, mounted up to a significant total. The United States has provided by far the most significant part of the Society's funds. Early records are sketchy but between 1979 and 2007, $4,987,945 has been provided by American supporters. Over this period the amount given has been incremental. In 1979, for example, donations from the United States were worth just $21,000. Ten years later, that figure had climbed to $331,002 (although in 1999 the amount had fallen to $126,900; the second half of the 1990s was not a good fund-raising period for the Society). The Society has of course benefited further since the advent of the American Ireland Fund as a source of assistance, but over a 29-year period the average annual sum provided by the United States has been $171,998.

Nor has this been the only source of transatlantic revenue for the Society. In 1983 Desmond Guinness told members that the Kindel Furniture Company of Grand Rapids, Michigan, had begun making copies of twenty pieces of Irish Georgian furniture – chosen by himself, the Knight of Glin and the president of Kindel, Robert Fogarty – which would be launched on the American market towards the end of the following year in the United States. In fact, there were eventually twenty-three pieces in the initial collection, ranging from dining chairs to a plate bucket, and these made their debut at Altman's in New York in February 1985. Each item was a copy of an existing piece of furniture formerly in an Irish house, such as a sofa from Russborough, for example, or a chair formerly from Malahide Castle. The Irish Georgian Society received a commission from every sale and the amount raised this way proved astonishingly large; within the first two and a half years of operation, $96,000 was made by the Society. In total, the connection with Kindel Furniture profited the Society to the tune of more than $600,000.

During the same period, the organization entered into a similar arrangement with Scalamandré, the well-known fabric and wallpaper company based on Long Island. One of the features of the Irish Georgian range produced was that it included designs by Dublin-born William Kilburn, who, in or around 1784, had produced a mass of innovative work now in an album held by London's Victoria and Albert Museum (in 1981 Ada Leask had written an article on Kilburn for the Society's *Bulletin*). By spring 1986, when Scalamandré's Irish collection had been available for more than a year, the Society had received $16,500 in commission fees. A third source of income generated by sales royalties came from accessories business Chelsea House. Although the Society's association with these companies is now in abeyance, plans are afoot to revive all licensed product programmes with American and other corporations.

But plenty of other clever ways have been found to sustain American members' interest in the Society and its work. In 1986, after nineteen years working with the IGS Inc., Joseph Ryle retired as its executive director. 'We are greatly indebted to him for the keen interest he has shown in our work,' wrote Desmond Guinness at the time, 'and for coming to Ireland each year to see the projects on which the monies raised have been spent.' His successor was Arthur Prager, who had previously worked for the Royal Oak Foundation, the American wing of Britain's National Trust. He was, therefore, a man who could easily understand the nature of the Irish Georgian Society's work and its particular needs. In addition to attracting new members and encouraging them to help the organization as much as possible, Mr Prager came up with a number of fresh fund-raising proposals. The most consistently popular of these has been an annual 'Dinner with the Two Desmonds' (Guinness and FitzGerald) in New York.

The first such occasion was held in October 1997 at Mortimer's Restaurant, whose owner Glenn Bernbaum knew and admired Desmond Guinness. The party proved to be a great social and financial success ($10,000 was raised on the night for the Society). 'All the 120 participants were friends of one or other Desmond,' Arthur Prager afterwards wrote, 'so it was more like an alumni reunion than a fund-raiser.' The venue has since changed but the dinner continues to be held annually each autumn and never fails to draw a capacity crowd, although as Arthur Prager discovered, 'there has always been a problem with seating – everyone wants to sit beside one of the Desmonds. In the end we worked out that the people who gave the largest donations got those seats.' Even after more than a decade, the October Dinner with the Two Desmonds remains a draw.

Another of Mr Prager's innovations was to start tours of American cities for members, again usually in the company of one or both of the Desmonds. Cities explored over a three-day weekend in this way included Savannah, Boston, Chicago and Philadelphia. Although the tours have discontinued, a more recently established annual event in the calendar is the fund-raising dinner, hosted each spring in Palm Beach by long-time Society supporters, Fred and Kay Krehbiel. Since Kay comes from County Kerry, the couple already have strong ties with Ireland but these grew firmer after Fred Krehbiel opened a factory for his family business, Molex Incorporated, at Shannon, County Clare, in 1971. He remembers that the first fund-raising benefit for the Irish Georgian Society that they supported was a dinner in Chicago to mark the organization's twenty-fifth anniversary. Since then they have been exceptionally generous in their support and have hosted many events, both in Palm Beach and in Chicago, where they live for much of the year. They also always welcome seriously interested groups to their astonishing collection of Irish art and the decorative arts at their estate, Churchill, near Tralee in County Kerry.

In many respects, Chicago is today a representative example of an American Chapter. When first established in 1970, its head was the late John Conolly, a Republican State Senator and stockbroker whose family were connected with the Conollys of Castletown (Desmond Guinness presented him with an antique teacup bearing the Conolly crest). Chicago has since been a regular venue for lectures and fund-raising events on behalf of the Society. When John Conolly retired as head of the Chapter in the mid-1980s, his place was taken by another man with strong Irish links, Gordon St George Mark who, through his grandmother, is a descendant of the St Georges of Tyrone House, County Galway; his great-grandfather Christopher St George was one of the founders of the Galway Blazers. (In 1976 Gordon Mark wrote an article on Tyrone House for the Society's *Bulletin*.) He has lent many of his family portraits by Philip Hussey and John Ryan – a primitive Galway painter – to Castletown, where they are now on exhibit.

Gordon Mark remains a stalwart of the Chicago Chapter, as does Rose Marie O'Neill, who has been involved with the Society for so long she no longer remembers

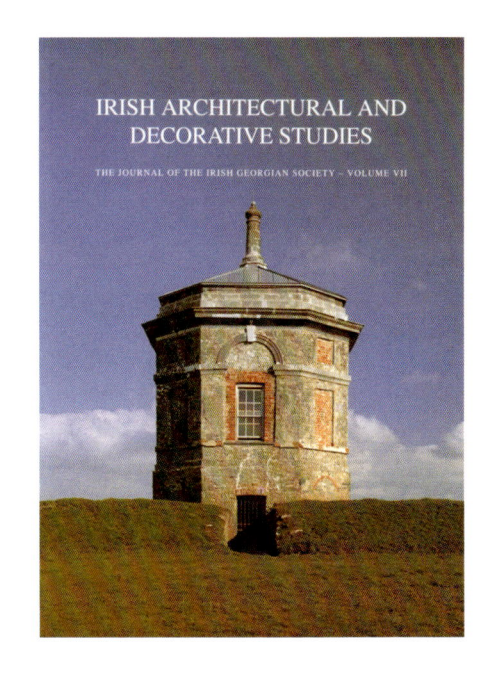

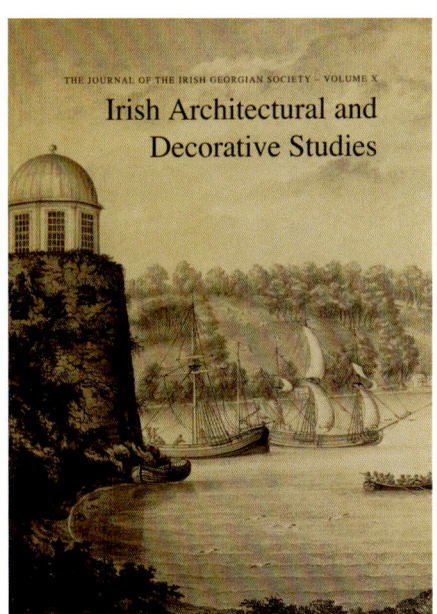

The Society's journal, *Irish Architectural and Decorative Studies*, grant-aided by the estate of Paul Mellon in 2001.

CHAPTER 8

Tyrone House, Co. Galway, family home of Gordon St George Mark, Chicago Chapter. It was burned in 1922. The magnificent shell survives.

how or when this bond began. She deserves credit for finding the funds to preserve the O'Conor library at Clonalis, County Roscommon; this was provided by members of Chicago's O'Connor family. The O'Connor Foundation later gave a $30,000 grant to inventory the Clonalis library. The Chapter has also raised money for a number of other major restoration projects, giving some $100,000 towards the Ledwithstown fund. Other buildings that owe a debt of gratitude to Chicago include No. 20 Lower Dominick Street in Dublin (which was particularly helped by sisters Alice Skilling and Shirley Ryan); Hamwood, County Meath; Killadoon, County Kildare; Birr Castle, County Offaly; and of course Castletown, where the Green Silk Room and the Long Gallery have both been beneficiaries of Chicagoans' liberality. Castletown also contains two Aubusson carpets donated by members of the same Chapter. Chicago even has its own separate junior committee to encourage the participation of younger members; founded by Brian White, this is now chaired by Whitney Templeton.

At the time of writing, in addition to Chicago the Irish Georgian Society has American Chapters in Boston, Massachusetts; Washington, DC; Palm Beach, Florida; and New York City. Astonishingly, the last of these is also the youngest. Although New York has always been the headquarters for IGS Inc., it was only in early 2002 that a separate Chapter was established there under the able chairmanship of Carroll Cavanagh. Following the retirement of Arthur Prager in 2005, the daily management of IGS Inc. has been handled with flair and zest by programme director Maribeth Welsh.

134

Above: Castletown, Co. Kildare, Green Drawing Room, silk wall covering funded by the Chicago Chapter.

Left: Hamwood, Dunboyne, Co. Meath, window glazing funded by the Chicago Chapter.

Desmond Guinness writes:

> It was a lovely day for us when Mike Neagle of Boston picked up an early Irish Georgian Society Bulletin in a Dublin bookshop. When he suggested a Boston Chapter, I tried to reason with him, protesting, 'I have no secretary and have to address the envelopes by hand.' He won the day however, and soon Chapters were formed all over the USA. Next we obtained charitable status in the nick of time with an empty Castletown to furnish. Timing is everything in life. I salute our friends in America for their enthusiasm and for their boundless generosity.

The other important Chapter outside Ireland is based in London. From the start the Society had attracted a certain number of members who were either English or Irish citizens living in England, but for the first twelve years unless visiting Ireland they had little input into the organization's affairs. That situation started to change in April 1971 when Kevin O'Shea, a Waterford-born architect based in London, contacted Desmond Guinness about the possibility of starting a London Chapter. This new group, Kevin O'Shea wrote, 'would serve to keep members of the Society in touch with events in Ireland, who do not normally reside there'. At the time the membership in the greater London area numbered almost 190. All members were notified of a general meeting called for 23 July 1971, at which the proposal of a Chapter could be discussed. It was held at the Irish Club, a rather raffish establishment on Eaton Square that grew steadily shabbier until eventually sold in 2003.

For more than thirty years the Club provided a base for the Society's London Chapter, although John Redmill remembers that 'the rooms had to be cleaned every time before a meeting could start'. Regardless of this handicap, the response to Kevin

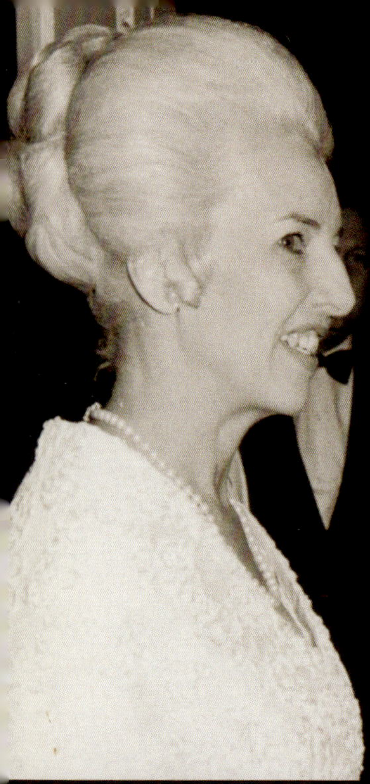
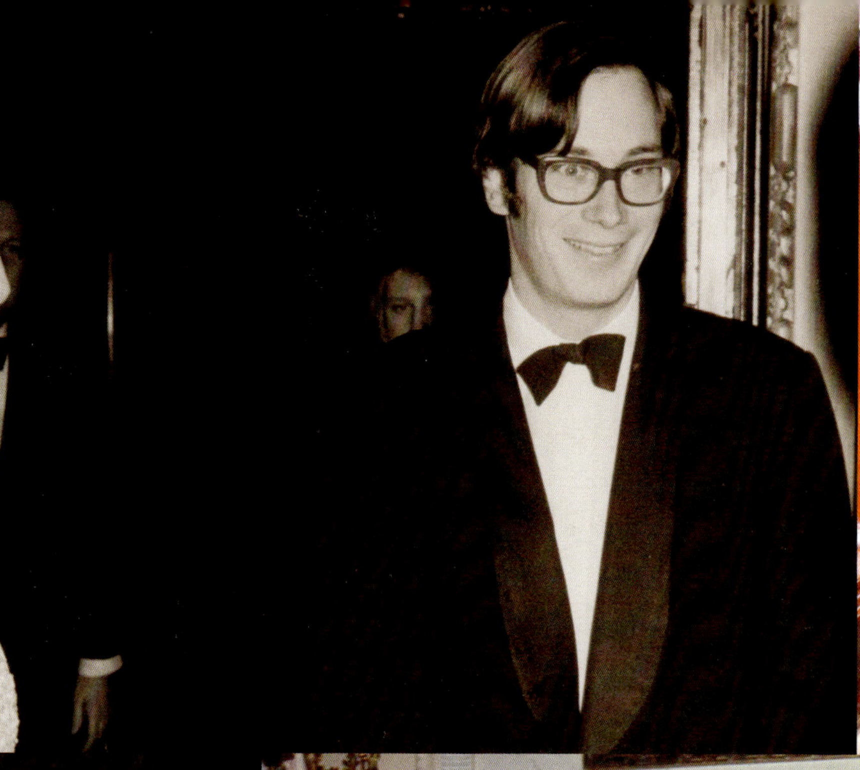
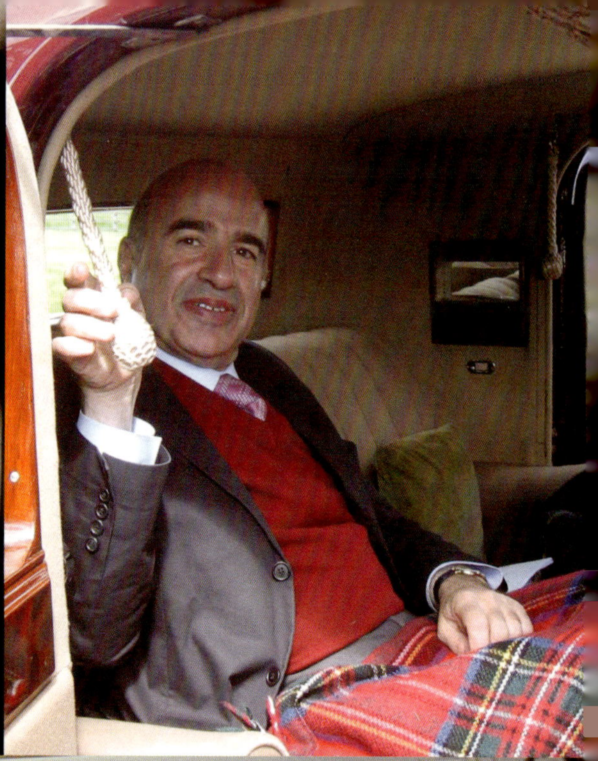
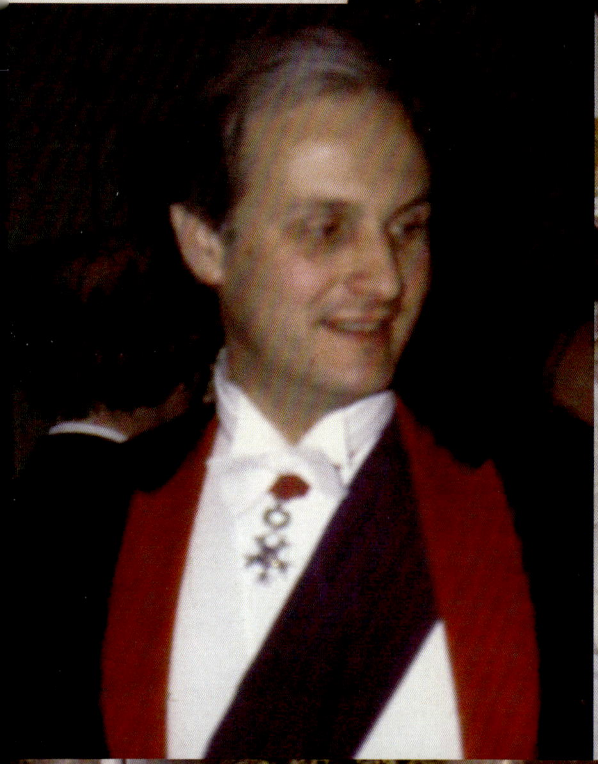
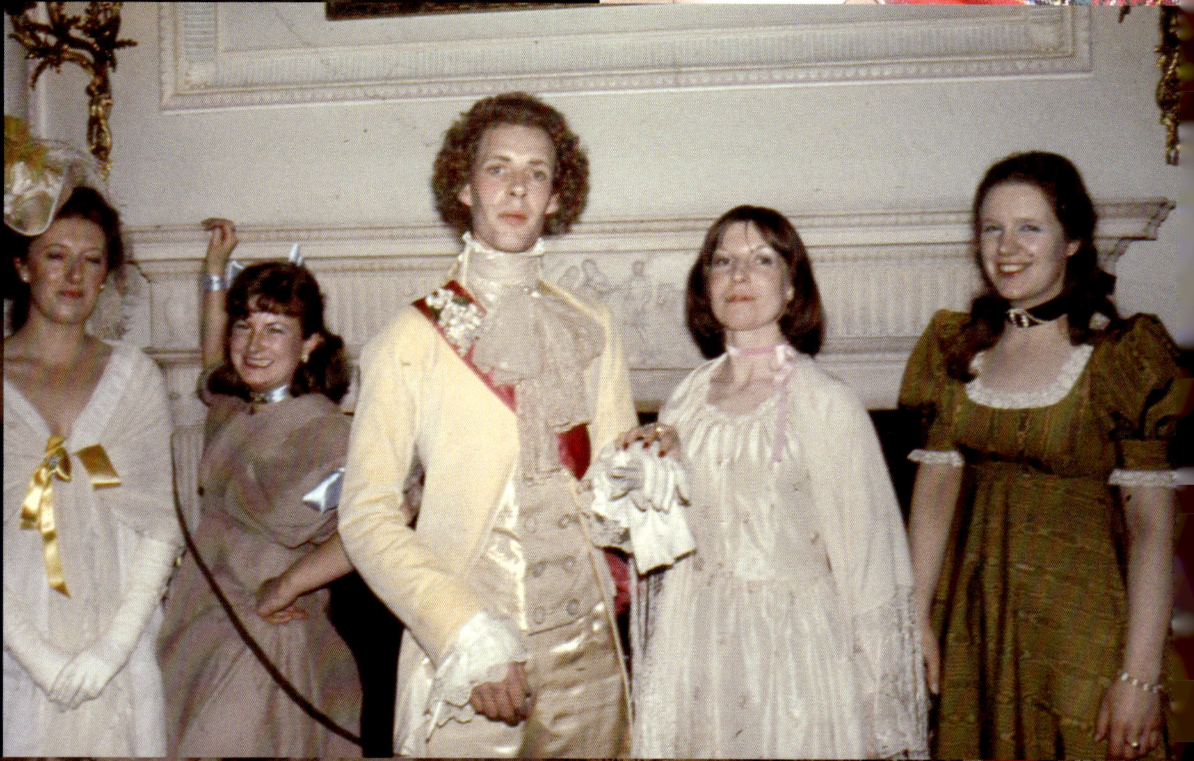
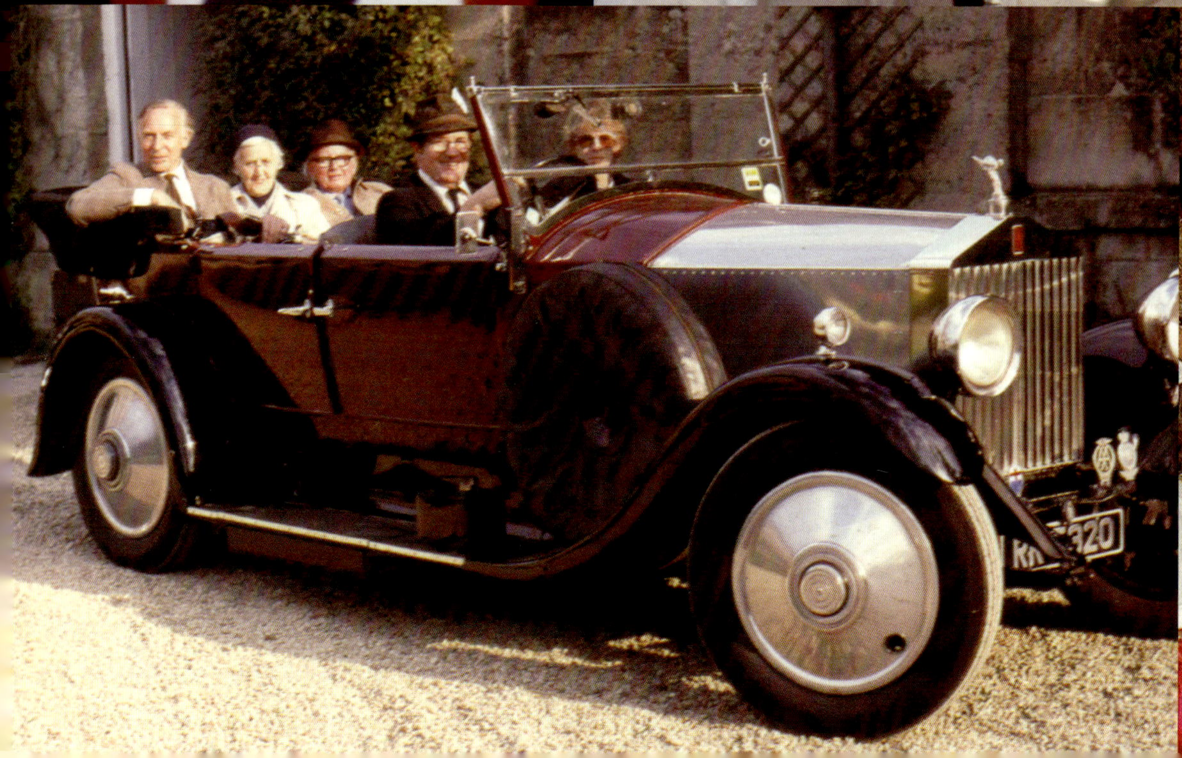
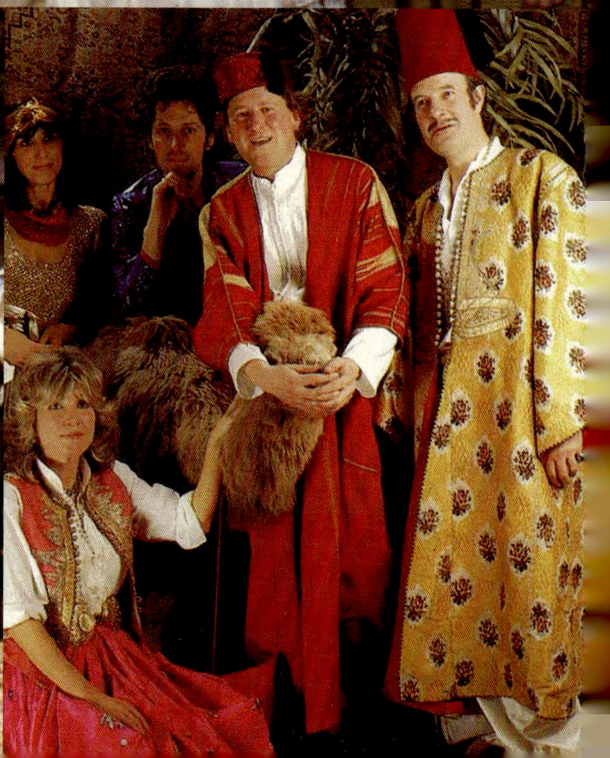

CHAPTER 8

Top row (left to right):

Elizabeth Green, first chairman of the London Chapter, with HRH Prince Richard of Gloucester at the Royal Academy Soirée, 1971.

Nabil Saidi, London Chapter and 20 Ghost Club Tour, 2005.

(Left to right:) John Hardy, Marion Cashman and Adrian Masterson, London Chapter and 20 Ghost Club Tour, 2006.

One of the 20 Ghost Club Rolls-Royces at Barnsley Park, Gloucestershire, 2006.

Middle row (left to right):

Nicholas Thompson, London Chapter chairman (1982–90) at the Ruritanian Christmas Ball in Regent's Park, 1985.

Georgian line-up at Chandos House, including (left to right): Gill Darby, Digby Howard, Phil Rogers, Mary Morgan and Ros Saville, London, 1977.

John Redmill, London Chapter chairman (1990–present) at Wotton House, Buckinghamshire, on the first London Chapter 20 Ghost Club Tour, 1978.

Brian Leask, London Chapter chairman (1975–81) at Chandos House, London, 1977.

Bottom row (left to right):

Brian Leask, London Chapter chairman (1975–81) with Freddie and Norah MacManus in the back of Leo Williams's 1920s Rolls-Royce tourer, 1978.

Desmond FitzGerald, Knight of Glin (second from right) and Madam FitzGerald (seated left) at Christie's, London, for 'The Night at the Kasbah', 1984.

Robert Jennings, London Chapter events secretary since 1982, at Gosford Park, East Lothian, 2004.

Lady Freda Valentine, Michael Barker and Dr Hilary Standish-Barry at Arbury Hall, Warwickshire, 1989.

O'Shea's summons in late June was sufficiently encouraging for a London Chapter to be established. After another meeting on 9 August, a committee was formed with Kevin O'Shea as secretary and treasurer, and the late Elizabeth Green as chairman. The other committee members were Jean Scott, Richard Graham, Felicity Nicholson, Adrian FitzGerald, Brian Leask and Mrs F. Ferguson.

Elizabeth Green was extremely efficient, perhaps a little too much so for some tastes, and she quickly started planning events that would raise the Chapter's profile and bring in some money since the venture had to be self-financing. (The London Chapter was started without any funding and to this day remains entirely dependent on voluntary endeavour, with money for basic costs such as printing and postage derived from the profit on events, most of which is passed to the Society in Ireland.) In late July, Mrs Green told Desmond Guinness, 'I have already put out a "feeler" and find that it would be possible for me to organise a Soirée at a famous Gallery (can't tell you the name in a letter, it's top secret!)' The gallery in question turned out to be the private rooms of the Royal Academy of Arts in Piccadilly where a 'Soirée' duly took place on 26 November, with HRH Prince Richard of Gloucester (now Duke of Gloucester and then an architecture student) as guest of honour. Originally it had been hoped that Princess Grace of Monaco would attend, but she was unable to do so. Nevertheless, Mrs Green managed to attract a number of other high-profile guests, such as the Arts Council's president, Lord Goodman, and Sir Thomas Monnington, president of the Royal Academy. The event received coverage in publications such as the *Evening Standard* and *Tatler*, and managed to make £250 for the Irish Georgian Society; this sum was later sent to Ireland for the purchase of a set of four eighteenth-century chairs for Castletown.

Elizabeth Green's tenure as chairman was brief; after just a year she made way for the Knight of Glin who was then working at the Victoria and Albert Museum. He inaugurated his term by giving a lecture at the Irish Club in November 1972, 'The Irish Interior in the 18th Century'. Nevertheless, Mrs Green's Royal Academy Soirée gave the London Chapter an excellent start and should be considered all the more impressive given the era's problems; this was a time when the Northern Irish Troubles had become especially bad and large sections of the British public were openly hostile to Ireland.

When, for example, Mrs Green invited one Londoner to help the Society, she was brusquely informed by letter, 'I think that the Irish people are constantly helping the IRA who are murdering British soldiers, and whilst I am not accusing you or any member of your society of doing so, I feel more inclined to help the victims of the IRA than to spend money on a purely Irish Society.' Likewise the following year when efforts were made to arrange a weekend visit to Dublin by members of the London Chapter, the response was not encouraging. 'I am not interested because of the way the Irish north and south are behaving,' wrote Lady Dashwood, while H. Stretton of Ottershaw explained, 'We do not want to go to Ireland for a while with the political situation as it is.'

Despite these sentiments and many more like them, the London Chapter persisted in drumming up support for the Irish Georgian Society and by 1977 its own Newsletter was able to report:

Happily the time has come when it is no longer necessary for us to request a discreet London policeman to be posted on the door of an Irish Georgian Society function in case of what is known as a 'backlash', though this may be a matter of regret for the last policeman who went home fortified by much delicious food and a bottle of Irish whiskey which he had somehow by coincidence won with a raffle ticket issued to him by the Hon. Secretary.

Incidentally, at this date the Chapter had nearly 550 members, although only half of them lived in the London postal area – one lived in Venezuela and one was being detained at Her Majesty's Pleasure. The latter member was unlikely to be in a position to attend any of the Chapter's annual series of lectures, such as that given by John Redmill in November 1974, 'Ruined English and Irish Country Houses', or the event held at the start of the same year, 'An Evening with George Moore', held at Lindsay House, 100 Cheyne Walk (formerly the home of Irish art dealer and collector Sir Hugh Lane). Seasons of lectures on aspects of Irish architecture and the decorative arts have since become an element of the Chapter's programme in the early and later parts of each year.

Many of the lecturers have travelled from Ireland to speak to members, notably Desmond Guinness, the Knight of Glin, Professor Anne Crookshank, Homan Potterton, Mark Bence-Jones, Dr Edward MacParland, Thomas Pakenham, Christopher Moore and Patrick Bowe. 'Memorable lectures were held at the Irish Club,' says John Redmill, remembering, 'Anne Crookshank started hers by booming to the startled audience, "I've left ALL my slides on the plane!", and Homan Potterton created havoc by bitterly complaining about the immense height from the floor some pictures of de Valera and Collins had been hung – not the pictures themselves, as misunderstood by the Club Secretary.' More recently, country-house owners such as the Earl of Mount Charles and Sammy Leslie have been invited to speak to the London Chapter about the challenges they face in Ireland.

Nineteen-seventy-four saw the Chapter's first expedition outside London, to view buildings of interest in East Anglia. These tours soon became a fixture of the group and extremely popular. Prior to departure, participants are issued with meticulously prepared notes on all the properties to be seen and the owners to be met. Long-standing member Ronald Porter recalls a visit to Biddesden in Wiltshire:

> We were a bit late but Lord Moyne insisted that the tour of the house and grounds should go ahead as planned. So out we all went, with the elderly Lord Moyne leading us all through the gardens with a lighted miner's helmet on his head and a powerful torch in his hand. When we got indoors we were given 'emergency drinks' of the alcoholic variety, before being taken on a fascinating tour of the interior. I can still remember the superb collection of Stanley Spencers which Lord Moyne collected over many years. After the tour a great party then took place in the hall. We didn't get back to London until eleven at night. I remember having to frantically run off to catch the last train home to Sevenoaks.

Were these seasoned voyagers not already members of the Irish Georgian Society they ought to join the Travellers Club. This is especially true of anybody who has

John Redmill addressing the London Chapter members at The Grange, Hampshire, 1983.

CHAPTER 8

Ledwithstown, Ballymahon, Co. Longford, grant-aided by the London Chapter of the IGS.

taken part in one distinctive element of the London Chapter's trips. Following successful outings by coach to Wiltshire, Kent, Cumbria and the Welsh Borders, the Chapter organized its first joint tour with the 20 Ghost Club in Oxfordshire in September 1978. The Club had been founded shortly after the Second World War to save Silver Ghost and twenty-horsepower Rolls-Royce cars being forced on to the scrap heap through petrol rationing; ownership of such a car was a condition of club membership. The idea of the two groups joining forces came from Lady Freda Valentine, who was a member of both. While the London Chapter would devise an itinerary of interesting country houses, ideally those not usually open to the public, the 20 Ghost Club would provide the means of transport.

The weekends, usually held over the bank holiday in late May, continue to this day. Anything up to a dozen Rolls-Royces have turned out, meaning that around fifty people can take part. By visiting approximately fifteen houses over a three-day period, in the past thirty years more than 360 country houses have been visited – and nearly £100,000 raised for the Society's work in Ireland. Early efforts to bring a group from the London Chapter were frustrated for various reasons: in May 1979 because of a postal strike; and in May 1981 because of political tensions in Northern Ireland. Thanks to John Redmill, the London Chapter eventually came to Ireland with the 20 Ghost Club in May 1998 to celebrate the Society's fortieth anniversary. The two groups returned again in June 2008 for a tour marking the Society's fiftieth year.

At the end of 1975 the Knight of Glin retired as the Chapter's chairman and returned to live in Ireland. His place was taken by Brian Leask, a nephew of Harold Leask who had been involved in the original 1908 Georgian Society. An architect working for the British Home Office, Brian Leask remained as the London Chapter's chairman until 1981 when he too retired and moved to Ireland. His successor was conservation architect Nicholas Thompson of Donald Insall Associates, who held the position for eight years before handing over responsibility to John Redmill; he continues to be the London Chapter's chairman. Already by the mid-1970s many of the group's now-regular features were firmly fixed in the calendar: the annual Christmas Party; the St Patrick's Day Party; and the Summer Party. Until its sale, many of these events took place at the London Club. For a period, John Redmill remembers, Mariga Guinness was part of the committee, and meetings in the Club's bar 'became even more informal and disorganized when she drifted in with her flower basket and grass-hoppered her way around the already vague-enough agenda. Matters were not helped by the delightful and giggly Secretary, Richard Graham, a theatrical agent, who would produce hysterically funny Minutes, more for comic effect than legal accuracy.'

The London Chapter is highly convivial; more than once the suggestion has been made that it should be renamed 'The Gorging Society'. The Chapter had been responsible for organizing a number of memorable parties, some of which involved elaborate costume. These include dinner for 160 in the Waterloo Gallery, Apsley House in 1982 (when the Chapter's honorary secretary, Richard Graham, managed to lock his car on the Marquis of Douro's personal car space – and then lose the key), a Ruritanian Christmas Ball in Regent's Park (1985), a Venetian Carnival Ball at Spencer House (1986) and a Neoclassical Assembly at the Lansdowne Club (1991).

140

Perhaps the most glamorous event of all was the 'Night at the Kasbah' Ball held at the King Street premises of Christie's (transformed for the occasion by David Mlinaric) in January 1984. It raised money for both the Castletown Appeal and for the House of Dun, a project of the National Trust for Scotland. Attracting 400 revellers, dress for the night was 'Arab or Levantine' and as *Tatler* subsequently reported, 'pashas danced with houris, sultanas sat out with hashishim, djinns and viziers and mullahs mingled with King Farouks and Tommy Coopers'.

While these occasions are undoubtedly terrific fun, they do serve a serious purpose, namely to raise money for the Irish Georgian Society. Between 1976 and 1980, for example, the London Chapter helped to provide funds for the restoration of a small Georgian house in Ramelton, north Donegal. It also contributed to the memorial fund set up after the death of Christopher Ewart-Biggs, British ambassador to Ireland who was killed by a landmine in July 1976. For some eight years from 1986 onwards, the Chapter focussed its fund-raising work on helping the restoration of Ledwithstown, County Longford. 'Ledwithstown became something of a London Chapter project,' says Nicholas Thompson, 'and support for it continued until 1994, by which time the exterior had been completely restored, floors and ceilings reinstated, the house rewired, and work started on the finishing and decoration of the principal rooms.' As a consequence of acquiring charitable status (a trust was set up in Britain in 1978), the London Chapter has been able to accept a number of bequests from the estates of Hilary Standish Barry, Rex Britcher and Lord Limerick. The Standish Barry bequest has enabled an annual lecture to be given in his memory. In 2005, Mrs Norah MacManus, whose husband Frederick had died twenty years earlier, bequeathed the Irish Georgian Society a part-share in her estate, which yielded more than £72,000.

Between 1997 and 2005, the London Chapter contributed just over £58,000 to the Society in Ireland; this sum does not include memberships, donations or bequests. Among the Chapter's most steadfast supporters has been Miranda, Countess of Iveagh, who not only welcomed a number of Irish Georgian Society groups to her home, Wilbury in Wiltshire (and then donated all money from these occasions back to the Society) but also is hosting a fund-raising lunch there in 2009 as a belated contribution to the Society's 50th anniversary celebrations. The London Chapter energetically continues to raise money for projects in Ireland at events such as its fiftieth anniversary ball, held at the Merchant Taylors' Hall in the City of London in late June 2008. As an indication of changed times since the Chapter's foundation in 1971, this event's joint patrons were the British ambassador to Ireland and the Irish ambassador to Great Britain.

THE BIRR CHAPTER

Birr Castle, Co. Offaly.

One of Ireland's most attractive and best-preserved heritage towns, Birr in County Offaly, has long enjoyed close ties with the Irish Georgian Society thanks both to the annual Vintage Week Festival (which celebrated its fortieth anniversary in August 2008) and to the participation of the Earl and Countess of Rosse in many of the Society's activities. In 1989 a New York member, Mrs Avery Lichtenstein, sponsored the restoration of a rare Jacobean plaster cornice in the Rosses' family home, Birr Castle. Four years later in January 1993 the town of Birr, which already possessed a vibrant heritage committee, set up what has since become the Society's oldest regional Chapter in Ireland. At the time, chairman John Joyce stated that he hoped the Chapter's primary functions would be to develop an awareness of the area's architectural heritage, encourage conservation and inform local schools through educational programmes. All these ambitions, and more, have been realized in the intervening period.

From the start the Birr Chapter has been diligent in arranging a regular programme of activities for members, not least a summer cricket match that took place every year until 2002 when the game 'had to be cancelled for the first time since its inauguration, due to a waterlogged crease'. An attempt to play croquet during the 2005 Vintage Festival was similarly fraught with problems, this time because it was 'difficult to decide who exactly knew the rules ...'. Social events have included regular Christmas parties and on a number of occasions *a bal masqué*. The Chapter has supported the Oxmantown Hall restoration fund in Birr by staging a number of plays on the premises.

The members of the Birr Chapter are keen travellers and at least once a year organize an expedition to see historic properties elsewhere around the country, such as a day trip to County Laois in June 2000 that took in three houses: Woodbrook, Mount St Anns and Glenmylyre. Sometimes they have ventured further afield, as during the summer of 2003 when a group went to Oxford for the weekend. Amidst all this activity, the Chapter finds time to monitor developments in Birr and the surrounding area and to make sure no untoward damage is done to the local heritage. Again in 2003, for example, the Chapter's main conservation project was the production of a brochure giving guidance on the preservation of wooden-sash windows for householders in the town; Birr, as much as any other part of the country, has recently suffered from the unwelcome intrusion of aluminium and uPVC window frames. It's interesting to note that during the same year the Chapter raised €3000 for the Oxmantown Hall fund while a further €1000 was given towards the cost of producing a copy for the town of the Macregol Gospels, a ninth-century manuscript originally written in Birr and now in the possession of Oxford's Bodleian Library. In May 2005 the Birr Chapter hosted the Society's annual general meeting, attended by many midlands members. The Chapter is now fifteen years old and shows every sign of outgrowing its teenage years.

THE CORK CHAPTER

The baby of the Society's Irish regional Chapters, Cork shows encouraging signs of growing into healthy adulthood. It is somewhat surprising that the state's second city only set up its own Chapter in early 2004 but it has been making up for lost time ever since with an active annual programme of events, many of which seem to involve members travelling to visit houses of significance elsewhere in sprawling County Cork. The city itself has some fine eighteenth-century buildings, such as the former Mansion House designed by Davis Duckart and Skiddy's Almshouses, which had only been saved from demolition in the late 1960s after a vigorous campaign in which the Society had been involved.

Just a year after its establishment, the Chapter was heavily involved in the organization of a traditional building skills weekend, held to coincide with Cork European City of Culture 2005. Presented in the Warehouse, Albert Quay, the event gave Cork citizens the opportunity to see the wealth of local craftspeople available to them in the restoration of old buildings. Over the two days, the Chapter arranged for members Kevin Hurley and Edmund Corrigan, along with Cork City Council's conservation officer, Pat Ruane, to lead walking tours through the historic city centre and highlight examples of good conservation practice on display. As was reported in the Society's subsequent *Newsletter*, 'The weekend really drove home the necessity of good conservation practice. Most significantly, it provided evidence that these conservation skills are available in Ireland today.'

In May 2007 the Cork Chapter hosted the Society's annual general meeting in the Lifetime Lab or the Old Waterworks. Once the formal part of the proceedings had concluded, all present drove in convoy to the gates of Vernon Mount, the 1780s 'cottage-palace' that has been consistently the cause of concern to the Irish Georgian Society for half a century. At the gates, a well-publicized protest was staged against the deplorable neglect into which this important building has been permitted to fall. It must be hoped that further vigilance on the part of the Cork Chapter will help to ensure an eventual happy future for Vernon Mount.

Top: 'Save Vernon Mount' protest outside Vernon Mount, Co. Cork, 2007, with Society members (left to right): Unidentified; Edmund Corrigan; Nick Sheaff; Donough Cahill; John Holohan; Colm Owens; Desmond FitzGerald, Knight of Glin; Peter Murray, director of the Crawford Gallery, Cork; Catherine FitzMaurice; Unidentified; Alicia St Leger; Unidentified; Elizabeth Synge; Doreen McNamara; Kevin Hurley; Geraldine O'Riordan; Rose Mary Craig.

Bottom: Vernon Mount, Co. Cork, front door.

THE LIMERICK CHAPTER

The story of Limerick is a tale of two Chapters, the first of which was established in January 1973 at a time when much of the city seemed doomed to destruction, primarily through neglect and indifference. In particular there was considerable concern over what might happen to the mid-eighteenth-century St John's Square, which had fallen into complete disrepair; happily all the square's houses were restored and the majority of them converted into flats. The Limerick Chapter in its original incarnation did not fare so well and, after an initial burst of enthusiasm, before the end of the decade it had come to an end.

Fortunately in September 1995 the Chapter was revived to coincide with a one-day conference in the city, organized by the Irish Georgian Society on the theme 'Limerick's Architecture: The Way Forward'. Limerick possesses Ireland's largest Georgian architectural urban area outside Dublin, with some 400 houses dating from the late-eighteenth/early-nineteenth century, mainly arranged in terraces and laid out on a grid plan. Patrick Pery, Earl of Limerick, whose ancestors were responsible for building this part of the city – known as Newtown Pery – was present at the Chapter's refounding. At the time, one of the houses in Pery Square was being restored by the Limerick Civic Trust and the local Chapter provided assistance for this project, which concluded when the building was opened in December 1999. The Chapter runs a series of lectures each year and also organizes outings elsewhere around the country. Already by 1998 it had a core of fifty members 'and we hope to attract many more over the coming year'.

Those new members would be needed for one of the Chapter's most important functions: acting as a watchdog against inappropriate redevelopment in the city. As a report in the Society's autumn 1999 *Newsletter* warned, 'The building boom frenzy has taken a firm grip on Limerick, with a number of developers lodging applications with the corporation to demolish perfectly sound Georgian and period houses, replacing them with office blocks, hotels, etc. The Limerick Chapter will be vigorously opposing all such inappropriate applications.' It has done so thanks to a thorough understanding of the city's growth over many centuries. In 1997 one of the Chapter's members, architectural historian Judith Hill, received a grant from the Society to undertake an inventory of Georgian buildings, their exteriors and interiors, in Limerick. Three years later the Chapter published two survey maps of the present-day buildings of Georgian Limerick, based on Judith Hill's survey, carrying information on the houses' condition.

That same year for the first time ever the Irish Georgian Society held its annual general meeting outside Dublin, Limerick's restored No. 2 Pery Square being the venue. By 2002 the local Chapter was involved in campaigning for the city's 'Georgian Preserve' to be extended so that larger sections of eighteenth-century Limerick would be safe from developers. In May 2007, Limerick was once more the venue for a day-long Irish Georgian Society conference, 'Limerick City: Heritage and Regeneration'. Many of the ideas discussed by the seventy-plus delegates at this event already featured in the Society's submission to Limerick City Council's Limerick City Centre Strategy. No doubt one of the local Chapter's roles in the coming years will be to encourage the implementation of these proposals so that Limerick's rich Georgian heritage can be appreciated by future generations.

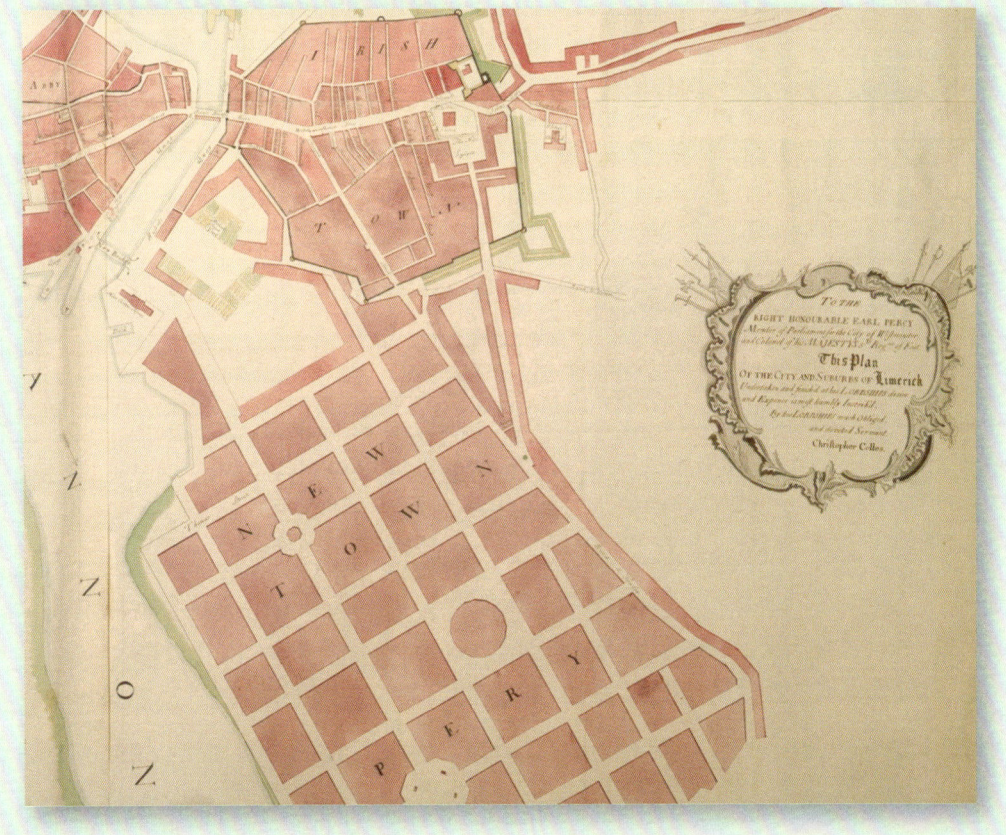

Above: The Tontine Buildings, Pery Square, Limerick, built *c.* 1838.

Left: Plan of the City and Suburbs of Limerick, Christopher Colles, 1789.

Opposite (left to right): Limerick Chapter committee members: David Fleming; Judith Hill, author of the NIAH Limerick County Survey; Liam Irwin, at the launch of the survey, June 2008.

145

Ongoing problems for Irish country houses ~ the threat to their survival ~ houses sold and contents lost ~ Doneraile Court and its restoration ~ Ledwithstown ~ the Swiss Cottage ~ Panels: the St Legers of Doneraile and the Swiss Cottage, Cahir

CHAPTER

9

Despite the best efforts of the Irish Georgian Society and other organizations, country houses in Ireland remained at risk throughout the 1970s and into the following decade. In part this was simply a consequence of ongoing poverty; it remained the case that no state assistance of any kind was provided for owners of historic properties and many of them were forced to sell either their home or its contents and very often both. In fact, an already difficult situation was made worse by the imposition of an annual wealth tax in August 1975 that proved catastrophic for some owners, who were thereby deemed asset-rich even though they had very little money. Eighteen months later the *Sunday Independent* reported that since the new tax's imposition estate agents had observed 'an unprecedented number of auctions of large estates and stud farms as well as major sales of fine art, antiques, furniture and house contents'. The same feature noted how 'the sale of so much fine art and antiques in particular means that countless treasures are lost to the country for good'. In May 1976, Lord Altamont announced that he intended to apply for planning permission to pull down his home, Westport House, 'because of the negative attitude of the Government' towards properties such as his own. He did not, however, act on this threat.

One of the problems was that there continued to be widespread ignorance about Irish houses and their distinctive character. Few of these buildings had yet opened to the public and since the time of the original Georgian Society very little material had been published on the subject of country houses in Ireland. Today many such books are available, but the first to be produced in half a century appeared in 1971. Written by Desmond Guinness and William Ryan, *Irish Houses and Castles* featured thirty-nine of the most important remaining historic homes in the country, at least a dozen of which have since either been destroyed (notably Powerscourt, County Wicklow, by fire) or changed hands and lost their original contents. In this way, the book is now an historic record but at the time of publication, it provided valuable information on a largely unknown subject, not least thanks to the authors' introduction, which discussed not just the architecture of Irish houses, but also the paintings and furniture that had been designed for them and even the gardens, gatehouses and follies that ornamented their surrounding estates. The Irish Georgian Society's January–June 1971 *Bulletin* noted that the organization would benefit financially from the royalty on all sales of *Irish Houses and Castles*, which was published the following autumn. 1800 copies had been ordered in advance but they were not enough to meet demand; the second *Bulletin* of 1972 reported that the full American edition of 2000 copies had sold out within a month.

Desmond Guinness paid tribute to the contribution of William Ryan 'and his wife Mary, who was so helpful in every way, not least in forging his signature two thousand times at the binders in the Hague'. He also remembered one woman approaching him after he had given a lecture in Boston and 'expressing her pride in her Irish background and in the splendid architecture of her native country. "The Yankees think we live in mud huts," she said.' The Society benefited to the tune of £5000 from the American edition alone and the book is now highly prized by collectors; with reprints, it sold 75,000 copies over ten years. 'If ever a book saved a house,' remarks Desmond Guinness, 'ours saved Castletown, where weekly wages somehow had to be paid, and restoration work continue.' In 1993 Jacqueline (Mrs Vincent) O'Brien and Desmond Guinness wrote *Great Irish Houses & Castles* with all the photographs this time taken by Mrs O'Brien. Profits from the works' sales were also given to the Society, it was followed by *Dublin – A Grand Tour*.

Nevertheless, historic properties were still vulnerable especially in the greater Dublin area where demand for suburban housing led to escalating land values. Among the greatest losses during these years were the palatial Kenure Park in Rush (demolished 1978) and Turvey in Donabate (demolished 1987). As far back as 1970, fears had been expressed that the latter house – which included architectural features from many different centuries – was at risk after it had been acquired by speculative builders. Although the Irish Georgian Society was approached by a number of people interested in buying and restoring Turvey and it was marked for preservation by the local authority, in the end the house was allowed to be knocked down. This was a story replicated many times over.

In 1976 An Taisce was responsible for two important initiatives from which many other organizations, including the Irish Georgian Society, would benefit. The first of these was the establishment of an organization to collect and preserve material of every kind relating to the architecture of the entire island of Ireland, and make it available to the public. At the instigation of solicitor Nicholas Robinson and architectural historian Dr Edward McParland, the National Trust Archive, as it was

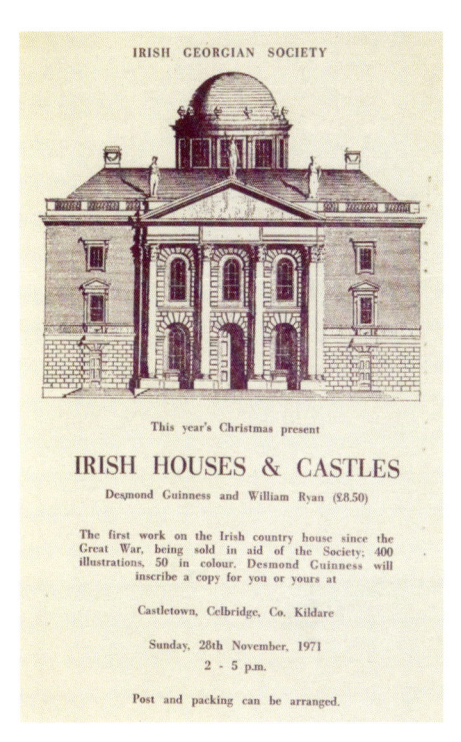

Top: Kenure Park, Co. Dublin, entrance front, 1954.

Bottom: Irish Houses and Castles by Desmond Guinness and William Ryan, order form.

Kenure Park, Rush, Co. Dublin. First-floor interior in ruins.

first called, took premises at No. 63 Merrion Square to provide a central resource for information on Ireland's built heritage, both lost and surviving. It quickly began to acquire material, such as a group of some 6000 items from the architectural firm of Ashlin and Coleman, which, in late-nineteenth/early-twentieth-century Ireland, had designed buildings ranging from churches to Clerys Department Store in Dublin.

Another important early addition was the large collection of photographs of buildings assembled over the previous twenty years by the Irish Georgian Society, including many taken by Lord Rossmore; the archive bought these images from the organization for a nominal sum (the money going towards the restoration of Doneraile Court). The Society has since provided assistance in the acquisition of additional material for what is now known as the Irish Architectural Archive. Based since 2004 in a superbly restored eighteenth-century house, No. 45 Merrion Square, it receives core funding from a number of state bodies. Today the Irish Architectural Archive's holdings include in excess of 250,000 drawings ranging in date from the late seventeenth to the late twentieth centuries, as well as over 400,000 photographs (making this one of the largest collections of photographs in Ireland) and an extensive reference library, with more than 15,000 items of printed matter.

Also in 1976 An Taisce conducted a major survey among owners of 141 heritage properties in Ireland and subsequently published its results. According to the responses from a questionnaire, the annual upkeep costs of these buildings averaged £10,200 and the struggle to find this money meant two-thirds of them were overdue essential repairs, especially to the roof and facade. Lack of sufficient funds also led to many houses and contents being inadequately insured. The full An Taisce report, *Dissolution of the Irish Country House*, was presented to the government and in 1977 a shorter version was published as *Heritage at Risk*. Among the key recommendations was that in the national interest the state should adopt 'a policy of conservation of the national heritage of houses, gardens and collections by making it possible for the bulk of them to remain in private care under conditions favouring appropriate public access'. It would be quite some time before this aspiration began to become a reality but in the interim the government made some concessions to owners of heritage properties. Certain tax concessions were announced in the 1978 Budget and legislation in later Finance Acts permitted the cost of repairs for houses of cultural and historic value to be offset against tax liabilities. Relief from capital tax was also permitted wherever the public was offered a reasonable right of access.

But despite these improvements, houses of significance continued to be lost. As late as 1981, for example, Ballynagall in County Westmeath, a fine early-nineteenth-century building decorated with plasterwork by George Stapleton, was stripped and left a ruin. As Christine Casey and Alistair Rowan commented in their guide, *Buildings of North Leinster* (1993), 'The fate of this elegant house by Francis Johnston – now a gutted shell, roofless, its floors sawn out for their timber and all fittings gone – is one of the most tragic consequences of the laissez-faire attitudes of successive governments towards the architectural inheritance of the State.' The Irish Georgian Society did what it could, but by this time the organization's own resources were severely overstretched. In December 1976, for example, it sent out a notice to

Russborough, Co. Wicklow. Entrance front seen through the colonnade.

members asking for assistance in the restoration of Bellinter, County Meath. This mid-eighteenth-century house designed by Richard Castle was then owned by a religious order, Our Lady of Sion, which had already spent upwards of £80,000 on the building. More still was needed but the Irish Georgian Society was not able to make a significant contribution and therefore suggested, 'Some generous member might take pity on them.' Bellinter has since changed hands and is today a hotel.

Two years before this appeal, 1974 had represented the onset of a particularly bad period for Irish houses and their owners. In late April of that year, members of the Provisional IRA led by a former English debutante, Rose Dugdale, broke into Russborough, County Wicklow. There they tied up the owners Sir Alfred Beit and his wife Clementine before stealing nineteen old-master paintings by Goya, Vermeer, Franz Hals and Gainsborough, the total at the time said to be worth up to £10m. All the pictures were recovered within a week and those responsible eventually caught, tried and imprisoned. (Russborough, which opened to the public in 1978, would be subject to several further raids in the years ahead.) Then in early June another group of dissident republicans broke into Knocklofty House, County Tipperary, and kidnapped its owners, the septuagenarian Earl and Countess of Donoughmore. The couple was released relatively unharmed after four days, but the incident had a traumatic effect on the owners of other historic properties who were left feeling similarly vulnerable (in the early 1980s, for example, Galen and Hilary Weston were the target of an attempted kidnap by members of the IRA and left Ireland soon

CHAPTER 9

Powerscourt, Co. Wicklow. Designed by Richard Castle for the Wingfield family. Destroyed by fire, 1974.

afterwards). Following Lord Donoughmore's death in 1981, his family sold Knocklofty and it is now an hotel.

But in terms of architectural heritage, the greatest loss occurred in early November 1974 when Powerscourt in County Wicklow, which had just undergone a thorough restoration, caught fire and was destroyed along with its original contents. Without question one of Ireland's most splendid houses, Powerscourt had been built in the 1730s to a design by Richard Castle for the Wingfield family, later Viscounts Powerscourt who in 1961 had sold the estate to Mr and Mrs Ralph Slazenger. Quite rightly its destruction was later described in *Vanishing Country Houses of Ireland* (published in 1988 to coincide with an exhibition of the same title) as 'the greatest single loss to Irish country house architecture since the civil war'. As if to emphasize the frailty of these buildings, on 30 December 1974 fire broke out in the upper floor of Castletown's east wing; fortunately it was brought under control before too much damage was done to the building.

Above: Malahide Castle, Co. Dublin, entrance front.

Left: Malahide Castle, Co. Dublin. Drawing room before 1976.

Over the next decade, there were further losses, although none so serious as Powerscourt. More problematic was the invidiously steady sale of family homes and their furnishings. In 1973 Lord Talbot de Malahide, the Irish Georgian Society's original vice-president, died. His family had been associated with Malahide Castle since the reign of Henry II in the twelfth century. In his will, Lord Talbot de Malahide had left the castle and land to the nation but since this will had not been signed, it had no legal validity and as he had no children, the estate passed to his sister the Hon. Rose Talbot. She in turn offered Malahide Castle, its furniture and pictures, and surrounding 265 acres to the Irish state in lieu of death duties. Her extraordinarily generous proposal was turned down and so in April 1976, the castle's eight centuries of accumulated contents were auctioned over a three-day period. As *The Irish Times* reported, 'Dealers from England, Germany, Switzerland, France, Belgium, America and, of course, Ireland, crowded into the marquee to make their bidding.' The total achieved was more than £1m. and some of the castle's most valuable contents left the country forever. The current president of the Irish Georgian Society was in charge of the sale and arranged for thirty-six family portraits to be withdrawn and sold to the National Gallery, which lent them back to Malahide.

But in this instance all was not lost thanks to the foresight of Matt McNulty, manager, at the time, of Dublin Tourism, who persuaded Dublin County Council to purchase the castle and grounds. He then managed to ensure sufficient public money was available to buy back key items of furniture in the sale so that Malahide's interiors would retain something of their original character and atmosphere. Today Malahide Castle is open to the public and an important tourist asset to the greater Dublin region. (In the 1980s, the same local authority – now Fingal County Council – would display equal flair and assume responsibility for the management of two other historic properties lying within its area of responsibility: Newbridge House, which dates from 1736; and Ardgillan Castle, which was begun two years later. Its example was

CHAPTER 9

Fota Island, Carrigtwohill, Co. Cork. Richard Morrison and son, William Vitruvius Morrison, enlarged the house to create Fota Island for John Smith-Barry, whose grandson became Baron Barrymore in 1902.

later followed by Westmeath County Council, which bought and restored Belvedere, designed by Richard Castle around 1740; this is now also open to the public.)

Similarly, in 1975 Dorothy Bell, last member of the Smith-Barry family of Fota, County Cork, died and the estate – which lies less than ten miles from Cork city and had been owned by Mrs Bell's ancestors since the twelfth century – came on the market. It was bought by University College, Cork, which undertook a restoration of the house supervised by architect John O'Connell and, in 1984, Fota, together with its outstanding arboretum, was opened to the public, the house's main rooms benefiting from the presence of Richard Wood's exceptional collection of Irish pictures and furniture. Ensuing problems at the end of the decade, primarily due to government cutbacks, led to the university selling half of the original estate for development as a hotel and a golf course despite the scheme attracting widespread opposition. Another section had been turned into a wildlife park; the demesne's original integrity was thus destroyed. But in this instance, as with Malahide, at least the tale of Fota comes with a happy ending: in December 2007 responsibility for the house and arboretum was passed to the Irish Heritage Trust, which had been established the year before.

The same is not true of Carton, which was offered for sale in January 1976 by the Hon. David Nall-Cain who had inherited the 1000-acre estate – originally home to successive Earls of Kildare and Dukes of Leinster – on the death of his father, Lord Brocket, in 1967. When Carton went on the market an editorial in *The Irish Times* pondered 'the future of such houses as this, the like of which will not be built in this country again', proposing that the government should look at the possibility of acquiring the estate before concluding, 'One thing must be ensured: Carton must not be left to the whim of some wealthy speculator or developer with no responsibility to this country.' However, although given the option of purchasing and preserving Carton intact, once again the Irish state did not intervene to preserve an important part of the national heritage. Instead the estate was left to the whims of the open market and despite valiant efforts by many individuals and groups such as the Irish Georgian Society, it was finally developed as a golf resort and hotel. While the house remains, much of its surrounding parkland has been depleted with two golf courses and housing.

Adare Manor, Co. Limerick, sold in 1982.

One final example of what was happening in Ireland during this period due to government disinterest is provided by Coollattin in County Wicklow. Owned by the Fitzwilliam family for the previous two centuries, in July 1977 the 3000-acre estate was bought by a pair of property speculators who proceeded to break it up. Coollattin's ancient oak forest, one of the oldest surviving in Ireland, would have been cleared away but for a sustained battle mounted by preservationists such as Kathy Gilfillan, the Knight of Glin and Thomas Pakenham, who ensured its eventual purchase by the government. Meanwhile, other important houses were sold and their contents dispersed: Adare Manor, County Limerick, in 1982; Luttrellstown Castle, County Dublin, in 1983; Oldbridge House, County Louth, in 1984; Mount Juliet, County Kilkenny, in 1987. When the last of these came on the market, Kevin Myers of *The Irish Times* remarked,:

> The day is not far ahead when the work of the Republic will be complete, and not a single country house stands in this State. The triumphs of the 18th century will have

been obliterated ... Walls will fall into ruins; ivy will conceal the remnants; grass will break through and vanquish ancient driveways. And then we shall be the glory of all of Europe – a country with no intermediate history between the triumphs of the Gael and the triumphs of the Gaelic revival.

And while none of the properties mentioned above was demolished, the dispersal of their original contents was a serious loss to the national heritage. During the 1970s and 80s many other house owners quietly sold their most valuable items of furniture and pictures, usually through London, in order to pay for essential structural repairs. Since at the time there was no system of export control on works of art, evidence was impossible to gather. Moreover, the faint possibility of a reverse flow was checked by the high rate of VAT charged by the state on works of art and antique furniture being brought into Ireland. A feature on this issue in *The Irish Press* in October 1983 quoted then-director of the National Gallery of Ireland, Homan Potterton: 'There is no effective control over the export of pictures; we never really get a chance; and then we find that we have to buy back our pictures in London paying extra for carriage and the sterling surcharges.'

Lest the history of this period appear too gloomy, it is only right to record some important buildings that were saved for the future thanks to the intervention of the Irish Georgian Society. Principal among them is Doneraile Court, County Cork. As was the case with so many other significant buildings, the Society had long been concerned about Doneraile. One of the earliest non-fortified houses in Ireland, the core of the present building was constructed in the 1720s to the design of Isaac Rothery for Arthur St Leger, first Viscount Doneraile. Doneraile Court has a seven-bay, three-storey facade of cut stone with curved end bows added at a later date in the eighteenth century. Further additions were made in the following century, including a three-bay porch to the front and a vast dining room of 1869 (demolished during restoration work just over a century later). The interior contains an early-eighteenth-century panelled room and an oval late-eighteenth-century staircase hall with Adamesque plasterwork.

The last Lord Doneraile to live in the house was the seventh Viscount who had been born and lived in New Zealand until inheriting the title and estate in 1941. He and his wife had no children and following his death in 1957 she remained alone in Doneraile Court. Then in 1968 a 47-year-old Californian truck driver called Richard St John St Leger arrived in Ireland with his family and claimed to be the Doneraile heir. An application was lodged with the British House of Lords for his claim to be recognized. While this process was under way and despite objections from the estate's trustees, the family moved into the house, initially living with the widowed Lady Doneraile, although she later moved into a cottage on the estate. Around the same time the trustees had reached agreement with the Land Commission for the purchase of Doneraile Court and its lands for £56,800. Richard St Leger meanwhile began refurbishment work on the house with the intention of opening it to the public.

The Irish Georgian Society offered him support in this endeavour and sent a large number of volunteers to help at Doneraile prior to a ceremony planned for late July

Doneraile Court, Co. Cork. Built in the 1720s to the design of Isaac Rothery for Arthur St Leger, first Viscount Doneraile.

1969, when the American ambassador to Ireland would officially open the house. But just a matter of days beforehand, the trustees gained an injunction in the High Court against the public opening of Doneraile Court on the grounds that the house's floors were unsafe. They then proceeded to sell its entire contents to a consortium of antique dealers, even though the Society had made it clear 'that we were interested in purchasing certain objects of St Leger family interest at valuation so as to keep them in the house'. Soon afterwards the Land Commission completed the purchase of the estate. In August 1968 it was announced that Richard St Leger had both retreated from his claim to the Doneraile title and agreed to move out of the house. After some time living in a cottage on the estate, he and his family eventually returned to the United States.

The Doneraile estate now passed into state ownership as part of the Office of Public Works' Department of Forestry and Fisheries. But while care was lavished on the parkland in preparation for being opened to the public, the same could not be said for the house, which rapidly started to show evidence of neglect and deterioration. When Richard Wood visited the place in 1975 (the year the widowed Lady Doneraile died, severing the last St Leger connection with the estate), he reported that 'I saw daylight through at least one hole in a ceiling. Other bedroom ceilings sag with damp and weakness. Ivy has penetrated a few windows.' Elsewhere, panes of glass had been broken by vandals, plasterwork in the hall had come down and the nineteenth-century conservatory had collapsed. In response to press queries about the house's future, the Department of Lands merely pointed out that the building had already been in poor condition when acquired and that 'a very substantial investment would be needed to affect rehabilitation'.

That investment was not going to be forthcoming from the state so, once more, the Irish Georgian Society stepped into the breach. In May 1976 it was announced that Doneraile Court was to be leased to the Society rent-free on condition that the organization undertook to restore the building. Desmond Guinness explained that, while not ideal, this was 'one step forward rather than let the building sit there and get worse and worse'. The Society launched an immediate appeal for financial help, the first job being to make the roof watertight before the end of the year, a job that would cost in the region of £7000–£10,000. Volunteers were also needed and by July 1976 a group of them was already at work on both the garden cottage – where they stayed – and eradicating rotten timbers from the main house's roof. A report in a local paper informed readers:

> Teenage girls from Killarney, Mullingar and Adare wield hammers and crowbars beside Georgian Society members from Dublin, Cork and other centres. Four American girls led by a Mercy nun from Nebraska put in a stint of duty after hearing the Hon. Desmond Guinness speak on Georgian architecture to a campus gathering. And a young French couple camping in the area offered their services for a day after hearing about the work in which some locals are also involved.

At first Brian Molloy oversaw the volunteers but even before his death in August 1978 Eric and June Williams had moved to Doneraile, where Eric replaced all the timber windows on one side of the house. Also involved from the start was Arthur Montgomery, who, as a teenager, would often cycle from his family home to visit the widowed Lady Doneraile. Although he was employed elsewhere until 1986, for twenty years from 1979 (when the Williamses departed) Arthur Montgomery lived at Doneraile Court and was the key figure behind the house's ongoing restoration. For eleven years of that time builders were working on the property; local carpenter Jack Stack had served his apprenticeship for the late Lord Doneraile, the fourth generation of his family employed on the estate.

But a lot of the labour was provided by groups of volunteers who came not just from Ireland and Britain but throughout mainland Europe and the United States. The 1987 *Newsletter* observed that Arthur Montgomery 'must be getting good at Italian, as so many Italians have come to help over the past few years thanks to a listing in the journal of the Touring Club d'Italia. Most write in advance, but sometimes they just walk up the drive.' The arrangement was that voluntary workers stayed in the house for a fortnight; although unpaid and expected to make a financial contribution towards their keep, many of them willingly returned. 'I never asked any of them to do anything I wouldn't,' Arthur Montgomery remembers. 'We did everything from moving rubble to cleaning windows, painting walls and mowing grass.' The builder working on the site during these years was John Doherty and the architect responsible was Frank Murphy, who had also taken care of the restoration of the Skiddy's Almshouses in Cork.

Gradually, Doneraile Court's dereliction was brought under control. By the end of 1978 the Irish Georgian Society had spent £25,000 on structural repairs and that figure would climb steadily; in 1983 alone the Society estimated it had spent some £40,000 on the house. The amount would have been higher but for the fact that much of the work had been unpaid; even Arthur Montgomery only began to take a full wage from 1986 onwards. The Society benefited from a grant of $50,000 from the Samuel H. Kress Foundation. Desmond Guinness remembers that this came about thanks to the intervention of an American supporter, Colonel Jim Gray (who received the Freedom of Venice for helping with the restoration of the ceilings in the Doges' Palace). 'He set me up in a flat in New York with the kind of whiskey Mr Kress's former secretary preferred and a small jug of water on the side. It worked! Her power was absolute.'

CHAPTER 9

In June 1984 the park at Doneraile was opened to the public. On that occasion, Minister of State Paddy Hegarty quite rightly paid tribute to the Irish Georgian Society and acknowledged that without its intervention Doneraile Court 'would by now have become a ruin'. But a lot more still needed to be accomplished before the house could follow the demesne's lead and admit visitors. And so work went on and on with no end in sight. Although it was hoped Doneraile Court would open to the public in 1986, this aspiration could not be realized, not least because shortage of funds meant that at times the professional builders had to be laid off or put on short weeks. By the end of that year, the Society had expended £250,000 on the building's restoration. In October 1987, Professor Kevin B. Nowlan, then the Society's vice-president, met with local residents to see whether they might take over responsibility for the house; the Irish Georgian Society, he said, had done its priming task, 'and it was now up to others to get on with the job'. As Desmond Guinness noted in that year's *Newsletter*, 'There is so much rescue work to be done elsewhere that the Society would like to be free to move on from Doneraile and let its future be handled by people from the locality.' But this did not happen and in the absence of anyone else being prepared to look after Doneraile Court and ensure its survival, the Society stayed on.

In the late 1980s FÁS, a government training scheme, helped by providing a young workforce for the restoration programme. In July 1990 a tea room opened to the public in the house's old kitchen, and finally, on 16 April, Easter Saturday 1992, the ground floor of Doneraile Court opened with a variety of exhibits on show, including photographs of restoration work from the very start. Two years later, with the greater part of the restoration work completed at a cost of £500,000, the Irish Georgian Society was at last able to hand over the house to another body: the Office of Public Works. Since then all should have been well for Doneraile Court but regrettably this has not been the case; after a visit to the once-more shuttered and closed house in 2005, the Knight of Glin wrote that the premises seemed to have reached 'a dead end ... We really need to have some new dialogue with the OPW and if they have no inclination to find a solution themselves for the house, surely a partnership with an organization or private individual could be considered.' At the time of writing, Doneraile Court remains closed and it must be regretted that the Irish Georgian Society's efforts – and expenditure – over an eighteen-year period, should subsequently have been allowed to go to naught. Doneraile Court still stands but lifeless and barren, without even a caretaker.

This is most definitely not the case with another house that has received sustained help from the Irish Georgian Society. A miniature gem, Ledwithstown, County Longford, was built in the first half of the eighteenth century – probably to the designs of Richard Castle – for the Ledwith family who continued to own, although not always occupy, the house until 1911. In that year it was sold to the grandfather of present owner Laurence Feeney, also called Laurence, who had recently returned from Buenos Aires. However, after his premature death just six years later, Ledwithstown was let to a variety of tenants. According to Mary Feeney, none of them took care of the building; a brother and sister who lived there for a while removed all the door and shutter knobs, while another family allowed the chimneys to become blocked and then knocked holes in the walls to let smoke escape. In 1976 Maurice Craig described it as being 'unhappily in an advanced state of dilapidation, perhaps not beyond recovery'. The year before he wrote this, Laurence and Mary Feeney were married and began to consider the possibility of restoring Ledwithstown, which, as Dr Craig noted, is exceptional in that 'there can be few houses of its size in Ireland more thoroughly designed, and with internal decoration so well integrated'. Mary Feeney remembers that the house 'was derelict basically', with part of the roof fallen in, and large sections of the interior decoration lost to damp and rot; 'you could put your hand up and pull out a lump of mould growth from the ceilings'.

The Feeneys, who would have eleven children (five of them born after the family moved into the house), began working on Ledwithstown's restoration in the early 1980s and in 1982 received a visit from Desmond Guinness, after which it was announced that the Irish Georgian Society would give a grant of £1000 towards replacing the roof. The amount was relatively small because there were so many other demands on the organization at this time, not least Doneraile Court. But more aid followed, such as £2700 in 1983 towards the cost of new windows. After the Feeneys moved into Ledwithstown in 1984, Audrey Emerson and William Garner led a number of voluntary work parties to help with the task. 'It was always such great fun when we were there,' Audrey recalls, 'because the Feeneys had such a huge quantity of children. They'd all come along with their buckets and spades to help out.'

By 1987 Ledwithstown had a new roof and parapet and was once more watertight at a cost of £20,000, half of which had been contributed by the Society's London Chapter. Laurence Feeney wrote at the time, 'Mary and I still find it difficult to realise that at last the house is safe from the elements and the trend of decay has been reversed.' Among the schemes devised to help raise funds for Ledwithstown was the sale of a charming box made by Sara Nicholson in the shape of the building. But as Mary Feeney explains, much of the time 'it wasn't just the financial help, but the encouragement we got from the Irish Georgian Society. Everyone was so enthusiastic, it gave us the impetus to go on.'

The Feeneys go on still. Large sections of the ground-floor reception rooms' plaster panelling and other decoration had been lost to damp, but enough remained for it to be copied and replaced. The same is also true of the main stair-hall and sections of the first-floor wood panelling, which has all been replaced; when new floors were installed on this level in 1990, the surviving panelled dressing-room walls had to be suspended in mid-air to facilitate the removal of decayed boards. Mary McGrath subsequently carried out an historical paint analysis and discovered that during a period of 250 years Ledwithstown had only been subject to three complete colour schemes. As recently as 2007, the Irish Georgian Society gave €15,000 towards the conservation and restoration of the house's panelling. Today, a quarter of a century after they embarked on their mission, the Feeneys remain happily living in what is, above all else, a family home. Weather proofing has been completed, as has the interior plasterwork, woodwork and carpentry. Only a certain amount of painting and decoration remains, as well as the possibility of rendering the house's exterior. Described by Mark Bence-Jones in 1978 as 'now derelict', Ledwithstown demonstrates that even the most rundown building can be saved provided the task is approached with enough passion.

THE SWISS COTTAGE, CAHIR

One of the most unusual and charming buildings in Ireland, the Swiss Cottage in Cahir, County Tipperary, was built *circa* 1810–12 for Richard Butler, first Earl of Glengall; the architect responsible is believed to have been John Nash, who designed a similar, but larger, house in Windsor Great Park for the Prince Regent (later George IV) around the same period. A thatched *cottage ornée* with latticed windows and a porch supported by tree trunks, Cahir's Swiss Cottage was intended to be a pleasure pavilion rather than a permanent residence. The principal rooms were decorated with French Dufour wallpapers, 'Monuments de Paris' and 'Rives du Bosphore', brought to Ireland by Lord Glengall's son. An article in *Country Life* in 1966 commented of the building, 'Never has thatch been so enveloping, verandas so rustic, casements so quaint and trellis so variegated.' After passing out of the hands of the Butlers, for much of the last century the building was owned and occupied by a local family who in 1980 sold it to a Canadian, Sheila Hall. Although she planned to restore the cottage, the scale of the undertaking proved beyond her means and so the place was left empty and prey to vandals. Before it became a complete ruin, the local community bought the building in 1985 with the aid of a £10,000 grant from the Irish Georgian Society.

Work then began on salvaging the Swiss Cottage and the greater part of the funds for this project came, via the Irish Georgian Society, from an American benefactor, William Roth. The Port Royal Foundation, and its president Sally Sample Aall (the latter, who served on the Society's American board, also paid for a nearby caretaker's house to be built). The foundation had already donated money towards the cottage's purchase. Restoration work took three years to complete, overseen by architect Austin Dunphy, assisted by John Redmill (today a member of the Society's board of directors). As at Doneraile during the same period, much of the labour was provided under a government youth-training scheme. New tree-trunk posts were put up to support the shingled roof that surrounds the cottage at first-floor level, later internal partitions removed and new wiring and plumbing installed. The building was rethatched (by Hugh O'Neill of Waterford) and the early-nineteenth-century wallpapers restored by David Skinner. Irish couturier Sybil Connolly, a long-term supporter of the Society, was given responsibility for overseeing the interior decoration (she arranged for a set of grotto chairs to be made for the ground-floor rooms) and deserves credit for the superb quality of this work. The restored Swiss Cottage was officially reopened in September 1989 and has since been open to the public under the management of the Office of Public Works.

Above: The Swiss Cottage, Cahir, Co. Tipperary, built *c.*1810–12 for Richard Butler, first Earl of Glengall. The architect is believed to be John Nash.

THE ST LEGERS OF DONERAILE COURT

Originally a Norman family who had accompanied William the Conqueror to England and then settled in Kent, the St Legers first arrived in Ireland in 1537, when Sir Anthony St Leger was sent by Henry VIII to oversee the dissolution of the Irish monasteries. Almost a century later one of his descendants, Sir William St Leger, who was Lord President of Munster, acquired the lands of Doneraile and settled there. Sir William's grandson, Arthur St Leger, was created first Viscount Doneraile in 1703. Seven years afterwards, his daughter Elizabeth became the first woman ever to be made a Freemason. Although the precise details have never been clarified, it is clear that Lodge meetings were held at Doneraile Court and that on one of these occasions it was discovered the seventeen-year-old girl witnessed what had taken place by hiding in a grandfather clock. In order to ensure her secrecy, a decision was taken to induct her into the Freemasons; the room in which this event is traditionally said to have taken place lies on the right-hand side of the house's present entrance hall. The Hon. Elizabeth St Leger, who later married a Mr Richard Aldworth, thereafter was a loyal member of the order and a well-known figure at Masonic ceremonies up to the time of her death in 1755. On the male line failing by the death of her two brothers and nephew, Mrs Aldworth's second son, St Leger Aldworth, inherited the estate, and on assuming his mothers' surname of St Leger was created Lord Doneraile in 1776.

Another notable member of the family was the fourth Viscount Doneraile (of the second creation) whose passion for hunting did not preclude him from keeping a fox as a pet. Unfortunately, on one occasion while out in the carriage, the fox bit both Lord Doneraile and his coachman. The animal was subsequently discovered to have rabies and so Lord Doneraile – and the coachman – travelled to Paris to be treated by Dr Pasteur. A report at the time noted that the Viscount, 'who was bitten through thick dogskin gloves, has not shown any signs of nervousness'. Perhaps it was this that led him to abandon Pasteur's treatment, unlike his coachman who persevered and was cured. Lord Doneraile, on the other hand, duly developed the disease and died a terrible death chained to his bed at Doneraile Court in August 1887; legend has it that the housemaids, to end his misery, smothered him with pillows.

Incidentally, a member of another branch of the same family, Lieutenant Colonel (later Major General) Anthony St Leger, was responsible in 1776 for creating the annual sweepstake race at Doncaster that is still known today as the St Leger. And although the St Legers were not directly involved, Doneraile is associated with the world's first recorded steeplechase, which was run in 1752 for a £100 wager between Cornelius O'Callaghan and Edmund Blake. The race went over natural fences from the steeple of St John's Church, Buttevant, to the steeple of the St Leger Church in Doneraile, a distance of 4.5 miles, and hence the term 'steeplechase' came into being. For several years from 1986 on, the Society's Cleveland Chapter organized a commemorative steeplechase with the opposing team drawn from the English Speaking Union; the Society's team of riders invariably won.

Above: View through the staircase to the ceiling plasterwork.

Top right: View of the staircase and oval landing window.

Bottom right: Appeal notice for the funds and volunteers when the deeds of Doneraile were presented to the IGS in 1976 by the Minister for Lands, Tom Fitzpatrick TD.

Opposite: Doneraile Court, Co. Cork.

Renewal as the Society marks its quarter-century ~ grants to restoration projects throughout the country ~ gains and losses ~ Strokestown ~ Frescati House ~ Drogheda Grammar School ~ Panels: Mariga Guinness and the Thatched Cottage, Freshford

CHAPTER

10

In 1983 the Irish Georgian Society marked the twenty-fifth anniversary of its establishment with a number of events, notably a well-attended and much publicized Silver Ball at Castletown. The previous year the Society organized an important change to its legal status. When founded in 1958, it had drawn up a constitution and regulations, and appointed a committee. Although annual accounts were periodically printed in either the *Bulletin* or *Newsletter*, the Society's activities were generally considered charitable and not liable to tax. In fact, as was noted in a document drawn up for the organization by Maurice Davitt in May 1983, 'Accounts and Returns were not submitted to the Revenue Authorities on the understanding and in the belief that the Society was merely a body of persons who were not trading or carrying out any taxable activity.'

This had certainly been the case until the late 1960s. Although it had raised money and was directly responsible for the initial restoration of Castletown in 1967, the Irish Georgian Society never owned the house; it had been personally bought by Desmond Guinness (and was given by him in 1979 to the newly established Castletown Foundation). But in 1968 the Society acquired Longfield and two years later bought Roundwood, just as in the next few years it would acquire leases on the Damer House and Doneraile Court. Problems were going to arise with a voluntary organization owning property and, under these circumstances, it was thought necessary to look at the Society's rather ill-defined legal status. Maurice Davitt advised that a limited liability company under Irish law be formed and in late-August 1970 the Irish Georgian Society Ltd was incorporated, specifically for holding property on behalf of the Irish Georgian Society.

162

Even so doubts remained over the Society's fiscal position in the eyes of the law, especially if its charitable status was to be made completely secure. So in April 1982, the Irish Georgian Society Ltd became the Irish Georgian Foundation, with Desmond Guinness and Professor Kevin B. Nowlan as the two original directors. Within a few months, a further four directors had been appointed: Desmond FitzGerald, the Knight of Glin; John O'Connell; Nicholas Sheaff; and William Garner. From that time until the present the Irish Georgian Foundation has been the legal entity of the Irish Georgian Society. In October 1983 the Revenue authorities formally recognized the foundation as a charity, thereby ensuring no tax could be charged on its fund-raising activities, and that gifts over a certain sum qualified the donor for tax relief. The Society's autumn 1983 *Newsletter* explained that 'so as to make the most effective use of the charitable status of the foundation, it is planned to channel all contributions and gifts to the IGS through the foundation and the funds so collected will, of course, continue to be applied to the same good causes as in the past'. The Irish Georgian Foundation was permitted to own property and on taking over from the former limited company it assumed responsibility for Doneraile Court and Roundwood. (By this date Longfield had been sold on the open market and the Damer House was in the process of being handed over to the Roscrea Heritage Society.)

While not as overtly exciting as some of the organization's other activities over the years, these changes indicate the Irish Georgian Society's gradual maturation. It had now been in existence for a quarter of a century and had an honourable history of rescuing significant buildings and fighting for the preservation of Ireland's heritage. If this tradition were to be maintained into the future, then the legal and financial standing of the Society had to be clarified and strengthened. This was particularly important in 1983 because during that year Desmond Guinness, in order to meet the terms of his divorce from his wife Mariga, was obliged to offer for sale furniture and pictures from both Leixlip Castle and Castletown. With respect to the latter house, the items in question were owned by Desmond Guinness and he was therefore entitled to dispose of them. Furthermore, he offered the Castletown Foundation – from which he now resigned to avoid any conflict of interest – the opportunity to buy as many of the Castletown pieces as it wished. By the end of 1984 some £250,000 had been raised for this purpose, principally from the Samuel H. Kress Foundation and its chairman, Franklin B. Murphy. The furniture and pictures remain in the house to this day. However, the whole incident attracted widespread publicity and there was considerable confusion about the distinction between the Irish Georgian Society and the Castletown Foundation, between what was owned by a charity and what by a private individual. Desmond Guinness, the Irish Georgian Society and

Left: Celebrating the IGS coming of age in Castletown. *Left to right:* Desmond FitzGerald, Knight of Glin; Mrs Lena Boylan; the Hon. Desmond Guinness; Prof. Kevin B. Nowlan (trustees).

Middle: Geraldine Clarke (left), Co. Sligo; Marion Cashman, Dublin.

Right: Agnes Clarke, California (left); Sally O'Flaherty, Dublin.

CHAPTER 10

Mrs Delany's flower-collage table mats.

Top: Aescalus Hippocastanum (Horse Chestnut).

Middle: Camellia Japonica.

Bottom: Rosa Gallica var. Blush Rose.

Top right: Samuel Dixon, *Foreign and Domestick Birds*, 1755.

Castletown: they had all been intermingled for so many years that in the public mind it was not easy to disentangle one from another. Confusion and factual inaccuracies were commonplace. This is yet another reason why, on the eve of its twenty-fifth anniversary, the Society needed to organize itself into a recognized legal entity.

Changes in name did not mean changes in character and for the rest of the decade the Irish Georgian Society continued to operate in much the same way as had already been the case. It also carried on looking for ways to raise money for the funding of various causes. Among the more imaginative and lucrative of these ways was the production of table mats, the first set of which appeared in 1975, carrying reproductions of Irish sporting artist Robert Healy's 1768 pictures showing the Conolly racehorses and hunters at Castletown. Sold in packs of six (for £12 or $30), the mats sold sufficiently well for others to follow. Two of the most popular sets in the years ahead were those derived from Samuel Dixon's 'Foreign and Domestick Birds' of 1755 and another group based on Mrs Delany's flower collages. Audrey Emerson remembers that when the Dixon mats were first launched in late 1984, 'the demand was phenomenal and they raised thousands for the Georgian Society'. The mats continue to sell today and to benefit the organization, which in the 1980s also raised money by selling reproductions of eighteenth-century maps such as that of Dublin issued by Charles Brooking in 1728, and Noble and Keenan's map of County Kildare from 1752.

Another exceptional project with which the Irish Georgian Society was involved around this time was the publication of a book, *Gold-Tooled Bookbindings Commissioned by Trinity College, Dublin in the Eighteenth Century*. It was described by Maurice Craig in *The Irish Times* in September 1987 as being a 'splendid, solid work of scholarship'.

164

Unfortunately the firm that had originally intended to act as publisher ceased operations. The Society stepped into the breach, with production costs underwritten by a loan from Sir J. Paul Getty; an avid collector of bindings, he had already donated a collection of seven volumes of the eighteenth-century *Irish Statutes* to Castletown and then paid for a cabinet for their storage and display in the house, as well as a collection of book-binding tools.

The ongoing restoration of Doneraile Court absorbed a great deal of whatever funds the Society raised throughout the 1980s and into the following decade. However, thanks to schemes such as those already mentioned, as well as donations from American supporters and money given by members worldwide, it was still possible to provide grants for other projects around Ireland. Among the beneficiaries were quite a number of places of worship owned by the Church of Ireland such as that in Mitchelstown, County Cork, where the Society paid for a new Gothic window to be fitted into the tower in 1983, and St Olaf's in Waterford, once the city's ancient cathedral, which was converted into a community hall. The Irish Georgian Society commissioned surveys of distinguished monuments such as the semi-ruined Temple at Emo, County Laois, in 1985, and also helped to raise awareness of and money for buildings at risk, not least the Governor's House at Nenagh Gaol, County Tipperary (1983); Glencullen House, County Dublin (1985); the James Gandon-designed stables at Carrigglas, County Longford (1986, and again in 1990); and the mid-nineteenth-century conservatory by Richard Turner at Ballyfin, County Laois (1989).

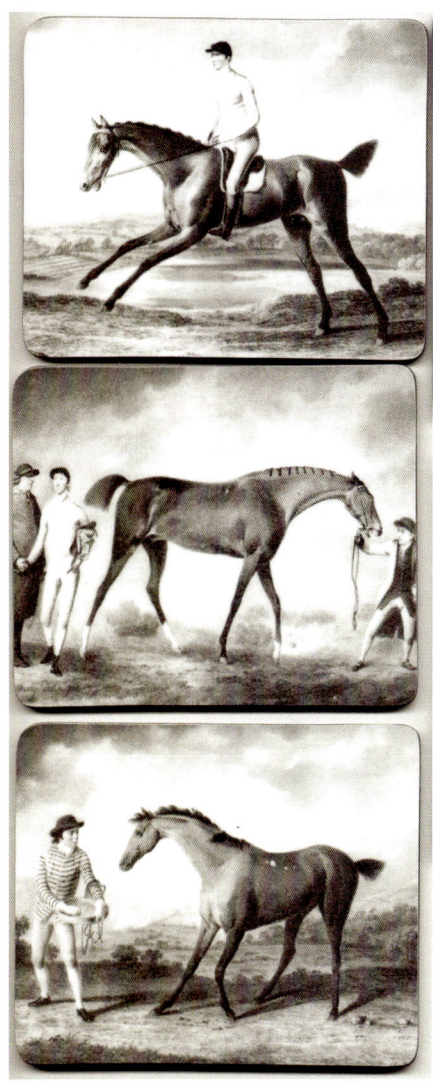

Above: Three IGS table mats carrying reproductions of Irish sporting artist Robert Healy's 1768 pictures showing the Conolly racehorses at Castletown, Co. Kildare.

Top left: Ballyfin, Co. Laois.

Most important of all was the preservation of Strokestown Park, County Roscommon. This house dates back to the seventeenth century, although its wings were designed by Richard Castle in the eighteenth century and further alterations were carried out in the early nineteenth century. The estate had always belonged to the Mahon family until the last member, Olive Hales-Pakenham-Mahon, died in 1979. It might have been expected that Strokestown would then go the same way as so many other similar properties: the land divided up and the house allowed to fall into ruin. That this was not the case is thanks to the imaginative foresight of the estate's new owner, James Callery of Westwood Garages Ltd. Mr Callery's original intention had been to keep the few acres needed to expand his business and then to sell the remainder to recoup his investment. However, he quickly came to appreciate that Strokestown Park was far too important a part of the national heritage to be lost forever. He therefore negotiated with the estate's heirs to ensure that the house's remaining original furnishings should stay in situ, along with the family papers.

In April 1982, the Irish Georgian Society arranged for these documents to be catalogued and not long afterwards restoration work began on the house. Mr Callery was exceptionally fortunate that his nephew Luke Dodd, an art-history graduate of Trinity College, Dublin, who was then working at New York's Whitney Museum, agreed to return to Ireland and oversee the entire project. Strokestown Park opened to the public in June 1987 and during its first four-month season received 8000 visitors. The Irish Georgian Society – which had already provided a grant of £1000 towards the restoration of St John's Church in Strokestown – arranged for a group of volunteers to spend time helping on the estate that first summer. They undertook a huge variety of tasks, everything from manning the reception to painting gates and bringing in the hay. The organization next agreed to underwrite the cost of restoring the plasterwork of Strokestown Park's eighteenth-century still room; although at basement level, the room's fine decoration suggested it had not always been used as a kitchen store and that at some point floor levels within the building had been altered. The cost of the still-room work came to £3746 and a further £1000 was given by the Society towards the general restoration of Strokestown Park, where the splendid and unique galleried kitchen was opened as a tea room.

Over the years that followed more work was done on the estate, with the stable yard developed as a museum exploring the story of the Great Famine during the 1840s and the walled gardens, including Ireland's oldest glasshouse and the longest herbaceous border on these islands, brought back to life. A tribute to the vision of James Callery and Luke Dodd (who would serve on the Society's committee of management for a number of years in the early 1990s), Strokestown Park remains open to the public and is one of the most popular tourist attractions in north-western Ireland.

Would that the tale of Strokestown's redemption had been repeated elsewhere. On the contrary, throughout the 1980s the national heritage continued to be at risk from destruction at the hands of speculators, as illustrated by two noteworthy buildings lost after long struggles. The demise of Frescati House was slow and deeply dispiriting. Located in what is now the south Dublin suburb of Blackrock, Frescati was an eighteenth-century marine villa originally built by a member of the Hely-

Hutchinson family and acquired in the 1750s by Emily, first Duchess of Leinster. It was one of a number of such properties in the area, another being Maretimo, which was built around 1770 for Nicholas Lawless, Lord Cloncurry (and demolished in 1970). Because she and her children spent so much time there, the Duchess greatly enlarged Frescati, with the addition of wings and bay windows. Although its facade was relatively austere, the house's interiors were copiously decorated with marble chimney pieces and plasterwork, a stone staircase ornamented with medallioned walls and, in the Long Parlour, a painted ceiling by Charles Reuben and Thomas Ryder, who were responsible for the decoration of Castletown's Long Gallery.

But aside from its architectural significance, Frescati was also important as the house where Irish patriot Lord Edward FitzGerald, fifth son of the Duke and Duchess of Leinster, had spent much of his childhood and adult life. In 1793, he wrote from Frescati to his mother that he and his young wife Pamela 'are come to settle here. We came last night, got up to a delightful spring day, and we are now enjoying the little book room, with the windows open, hearing the birds sing, and the place looking beautiful.' Crucial meetings of the United Irishmen were held in the house, which was still used by Lord Edward at the time of the failed 1798 Rebellion in which he perished. It is important to appreciate the significance of Frescati House in Irish history when considering its eventual fate. Although its surrounding parkland was gradually covered in housing, the villa and immediate seven acres survived intact into the second half of the twentieth century. In the late 1960s Frescati was bought from its last private owners by a company, Frescati Estates Ltd, which soon passed into the hands of the well-known Irish retail chain, Roches Stores. In 1970 this company applied to the local authority, Dun Laoghaire Corporation, for permission to demolish the house; the plan was to replace it with a department store, office block, hotel and car park.

Astonishingly, approval for the demolition was granted. When news of this proposal became public, an outcry ensued. Mariga Guinness began a letter-writing campaign to the press arguing that even if the developers wished to go ahead with their plans, there was no need to demolish Frescati: 'A practical way in which this charming house could be used with the proposed development would be to make it into a small conference centre with dining facilities, etc.' In early December 1971, Desmond Guinness addressed a packed meeting of more than 400 protestors at Blackrock Town Hall, pledging the full support of the Irish Georgian Society in the campaign to save Frescati. A group was set up specifically to oppose Frescati's demolition and it included representatives from the Society.

By rights, given the strength of public opposition to the Roches Stores' plan, Frescati should have been saved. But the developers threatened to sue Dun Laoghaire Corporation if they were not allowed to proceed with the plan for which permission had been granted and this put the authority on the defensive. In any case, it had not listed the house for preservation but, quite the contrary, both Frescati and its surrounding land had been zoned commercial development. Roches Stores turned down offers from other companies prepared to buy the house – the Irish Georgian Society knew of several interested parties – and instead allowed its condition to deteriorate. In March 1973, *The Irish Times* reported that Frescati 'has suffered further

Frescati House, Blackrock, Co. Dublin, an eighteenth-century marine villa built by a member of the Hely-Hutchinson family and acquired in the 1750s by Emily, first Duchess of Leinster.

CHAPTER 10

Evening Herald, 4 November 1983. Headline on the destruction of Frescati House, Blackrock, Co. Dublin.

damage through vandalism and theft. Ten days ago a large part of the decorative balustrade in front of the house disappeared.' Interior fittings such as chimney pieces were removed, lead was taken from the roof and intruders were allowed free rein to wreak havoc. Some of the damage appeared to have been sanctioned by the owners; at one stage their architect was discovered supervising workmen in the removal of floorboards. No action whatever was taken to secure the house or to repair damage. In 1979, the state planning authority, An Bord Pleanála (which had been established only two years before), granted permission for Frescati Estates Ltd's shopping-centre scheme, without making any reference to retaining the eighteenth-century house, the wings of which were subsequently knocked down.

In 1982 the local authority took a legal action against Roches Stores in the hope of compelling the company to preserve what remained of Frescati House. While the presiding judge said he felt 'the developers have shown a complete disregard for the moral obligations that arose from their course of dealing with the corporation or the planning applications', he pointed out that the original permission granted by Dun Laoghaire Corporation allowed for the house's demolition. In the early hours of 4 November 1983 the shell of Frescati House was razed and, as a report in that day's *Evening Herald* observed, 'one of the most controversial development-preservation rows in the last decade had come to an end'. The site is now a shopping centre and car park. Tucked into a corner lies a boulder bearing a bronze plaque commemorating Lord Edward FitzGerald's association with Frescati House; as a final indignity, the date given for his birth is inaccurate.

A near-identical story can be told about what happened to Drogheda Grammar School. Thanks to its mercantile trade, the County Louth port of Drogheda enjoyed exceptional prosperity during the eighteenth century, when many of the town's finest buildings were erected. Several of these lined St Lawrence Street, including the neighbouring Singleton House and Mr Clarke's Free School. The latter, begun in 1728, is attributed to Michael Wills, who at the time worked as an assistant to Thomas Burgh. The former, possibly designed by Sir Edward Lovett Pearce, was built *circa* 1740 as a residence for Henry Singleton, Lord Chief Justice of Ireland; it contained one of the finest oak-panelled interiors in Ireland, including a magnificent staircase. Both buildings were eventually occupied by Drogheda Grammar School until that institution moved to modern premises in 1975, after which the two houses stood empty for several years. In 1978 a consortium of local businessmen set up a company called DGS Ltd, which acquired the old Grammar School for £70,000 and, as with Frescati House in Blackrock, looked for an opportunity to demolish it even though the buildings had been listed since 1967 as 'worthy of preservation'. Because they stood in the middle of the town's commercial district, the site was clearly worth redeveloping for retail and office use.

The tactics used by DGS Ltd were also identical to those employed by Roches Stores for the destruction of Frescati: calculated neglect to the point that the structure would be deemed irreparably dilapidated. To add insult to injury, in April 1980 DGS Ltd claimed £12,500 from Drogheda Corporation for vandalism to the old Grammar School, a property the company had flagrantly done nothing to protect. However, the developers' plans were stymied by local opposition led by two schoolteachers, Edward O'Doherty and Fergus O'Dowd, who set up the Drogheda Grammar School Preservation Committee, and who received encouragement and financial assistance from the Irish Georgian Society in their fight with DGS Ltd. The Society provided the services of architect John Redmill for more than a decade, through several oral hearings before An Bord Pleanála, as well as a 1986 High Court injunction against the buildings' demolition. On the other hand, as had been the case with Frescati House, the local authority, while insisting it wanted the old Grammar School to survive and discussing the possibility of the buildings' use as a public library, signally failed to utilize its powers compelling DGS Ltd to safeguard listed properties.

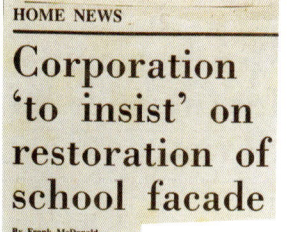

Above: Irish Times 1989 headline on Drogheda Corporation's decision to 'insist' on the restoration of the Drogheda Grammar School facade.

Left: Drogheda Grammar School comprised Mr Clarke's Free School, begun 1728, attributed to Michael Willis, and Singleton House, possibly designed by Sir Edward Lovett Pearce. Built in 1740 as a residence for Henry Singleton, Lord Chief Justice of Ireland.

Because of the Grammar School's architectural significance and because of the ongoing legal battles, the campaign attracted publicity even outside Ireland; *Private Eye* carried a long report on it in November 1981. An Taisce's Stella Dunphy reflected the opinion of all conservationists when she testified at the first Bord Pleanála hearing that same year: 'We feel that to demolish a building of this standard in this day and age would be regarded by the rest of Europe as unbelievably primitive. It is not the behaviour of a developed and civilised country. Countries that are developed don't throw away their heritage like McDonald hamburger wrappings.'

The intransigence of both sides, reported regularly in the Irish Georgian Society's *Newsletter*s by John Redmill, who travelled every few weeks to Drogheda to monitor events, continued even while the two houses' condition further deteriorated. Resolution came early one Sunday morning in July 1989 when a demolition contractor hired by DGS Ltd moved on to the site and began to knock down the old Grammar School. Messrs O'Doherty and O'Dowd immediately went to the High Court in Dublin where the presiding judge, Justice Lardner, issued an order preventing any further demolition or the removal of building materials, requiring the protection of the remains of the building and site, and demanding the careful segregation by hand, salvage and storage of 'the demolished materials on site as can be utilised on the rebuilding and restoration of the Drogheda Grammar School … all this work to be carried out to the satisfaction of Mr John Redmill'. It was the first time such an order had ever been effected, but as John Redmill noted in the Society's 1989 *Newsletter*, 'The point is that the owners blatantly bulldozed through the laws of this country, and allowing them to get away with it would create a precedent for everyone else to ignore what little historic building protection legislation there is in Ireland.'

In February 1992 the Director of Public Prosecutions successfully brought a case against DGS Ltd and their contractor for the unlawful demolition of a listed building in direct contravention of both the 1963 Planning Act and the Drogheda Development Plan. The maximum fine allowable was imposed on the company. Sadly, the damage done during the unauthorized 1989 demolition was so great that not even the original facade could be salvaged. Eventually a replica of the original was built, behind which DGS Ltd developed its intended shops and offices. The battle for Drogheda's Grammar School ended in something of a pyrrhic victory for the local preservationists and their supporters, such as the Irish Georgian Society but, to quote John Redmill once more, 'the legal achievement is a marvellous precedent and an enormous deterrent to potential destroyers of historic buildings'. By the end of the 1980s a change in public attitudes towards the national heritage was palpable and would result in noteworthy legislative changes during the next decade.

THE THATCHED COTTAGE, FRESHFORD, COUNTY KILKENNY

Perhaps the most unusual restoration project ever embarked on by the Irish Georgian Society involved a small thatched cottage in Freshford, County Kilkenny. Although its exterior looked no different from other similar dwellings, the two principal rooms inside contained highly elaborate plasterwork. Both these spaces were quite tiny; one measured six-foot squared and the other was *circa* eight-by-eleven feet. Winged cherubs, clusters of grapes and classical urns holding animal heads were among the stuccowork's more notable characteristics; the smaller room also contained a Gothic-style recess, presumably for holding a religious statue or small altar. Quite who was responsible for giving the cottage its extraordinary ornamentation has never been ascertained. Local residents believed the interiors were created around the beginning of the last century by a local man, Joe Kennedy, who hoped for a career in this field. However, writing in *Ireland of the Welcomes* in September 1979, Desmond Guinness suggested the style of work indicated an earlier date, perhaps *circa* 1840 when the principal rooms of a nearby house, Uppercourt, acquired similar – albeit more sophisticated – plasterwork.

Whatever the origin of its interior, somehow this distinctive little house survived intact until 1974, when the last occupant died and the place was left vacant. Inevitably, the plasterwork began to suffer from damp and neglect since the property's owner, Josie Brown, although originally from the area, lived in London. The Irish Georgian Society contacted Mrs Brown and she announced her intention of returning to Ireland, demolishing the cottage and building a new house in its place. After some negotiation, she agreed instead to sell the building for £8500 to the Society, which at once arranged for a temporary cover to be put over the cottage so as to keep out any further rain. Mrs Brown then announced she had changed her mind and now wanted to restore the cottage herself. All seemed well but unfortunately more time passed and the building was allowed to fall into further decline despite being given a preservation order at the request of the Society. To quote from the spring 1984 *Newsletter*, 'The end of the story is sad. The roof has completely gone, the plaster has been hacked to bits, and a curious little gem of Ireland's dwindling heritage is now no more than a memory …'

Left: The Thatched Cottage at Freshford, Co. Kilkenny.

Right: Ceiling plasterwork from one of the rooms of the cottage.

MARIGA GUINNESS

Mariga Guinness alighting from a carriage.

Opposite:

Top: Portrait of Mariga Guinness by Lydia de Burgh, 1963.

Bottom left: Mariga Guinness in a tricorn hat. Photographed *c.*1962 with Ulick O'Connor (left) and the Hon. Desmond Guinness. Both from an article in *The Irish Times*, 18 November 1997, entitled 'Queen of Georgian Ireland'.

Bottom right: Mariga Guinness photographed by Horst P. Horst for the cover of *Vogue's Book of Houses, Gardens, People*, by Valentine Lawford, 1968.

On 8 May 1989, Mariga Guinness died unexpectedly at the age of just fifty-six. Although latterly she had not been so involved in the daily running of the Irish Georgian Society, many members were shocked to learn of her death, remembering her unstinting devotion to the cause in its early days. Numerous tributes were paid to all that she had done for the Society. In *The Irish Times*, Professor Kevin B. Nowlan noted how, 'In the 1960s and 1970s Mariga Guinness gave a sparkle to the grim struggle to save our heritage of 18th-century architecture.' Indeed, it was Mariga's crusading spirit and her exceptional ability to inspire other people that most deserved to be celebrated. Writing soon after her death, the Knight of Glin commented that 'she had that vital talent of leading every sort of person into the then often unappreciated world of Irish architecture, decoration, furniture and paintings'. During the 1960s the Society's membership ranks had swelled as a direct result of her passionate advocacy of conservationism; she was a force of persuasive charm that could not be resisted. 'Not a painter, not a writer, not a musician,' wrote her great friend Maureen Charlton, 'what she does is to transform life itself into a work of art, to make each passing day a new creation.'

Cormac O'Carroll recalls that 'as a young fellow I was totally infatuated with her; when she spoke to me, I would be tongue-tied. She always had a bevy of young men around her.' Those young men were quickly beguiled by Mariga into working for the Irish Georgian Society, and in a thoroughly practical way too. During the course of an interview given less than two months before her death, she spoke of Castletown's restoration in 1967 when students were at the top of ladders painting cornices, children scrubbed floors, 'and even the oldest of the old were able to polish the beautiful door handles and do something to help'. Although on occasion she could give the impression of being rather vague – she was notorious for introducing even relatively close friends as 'Mr Thingummy' – a strong core of practicality ran through Mariga Guinness's character. This had enabled her to survive a peripatetic and largely parentless childhood and it helped her to overcome sundry other setbacks in later life. But no matter what her circumstances, from the moment Mariga was first introduced to Ireland in the early 1950s she remained committed to the country and to the preservation of its heritage.

This was all the more remarkable given that she had no Irish blood or connections of any kind. As she told *The Irish Times* in March 1989, 'I fell totally in love with Ireland and so I felt it imperative to marry an Irishman.' Having done so, she moved to Ireland and despite periodic departures from its shores, the country continued to be her home up to the time of her death. Likewise she retained her devotion to the Society she had helped to found in 1958, making it her life's work: 'We have no time for anything else at all,' she told an interviewer in the early 1970s, when the organization was involved in a myriad of campaigns. Although memories of Mariga Guinness inevitably include an abundance of amusing anecdotes, she understood the importance of the Irish Georgian Society's mission. As she told *The Irish Times* shortly before her death, 'It was definitely very serious, what we were doing.' She would surely be happy to know that the Society's work is still serious today. Mariga Guinness is buried beneath the Conolly Folly, a monument she helped to save.

'I think the key word that would sum her up is spontaneity — nothing was ever planned and the most marvellous things would just fall into place'

Mariga Guinness in a tricorn hat: 'She certainly brought a lot of colour to people's lives'

Mariga Guinness, photographed *circa* 1962 with Ulick O'Connor (left) and Desmond Guinness

Heritage Council established ~ Knight of Glin becomes Society's president ~ Vanishing Country Houses of Ireland ~ The Irish Country House film ~ seminars on Irish art and architecture ~ Panels: scholars and scholarships and more tours

CHAPTER

11

In June 1988, then-taoiseach Charles J. Haughey set up a committee to advise on the functions and structures of a new body, which would assume responsibility for the national heritage. The committee acted with speed and by early September of the same year the National Heritage Council had been established with a board of fourteen members, chaired by Lord Killanin. Initially the council was accommodated and staffed within the taoiseach's own department but in 1993 responsibility for it was transferred to the new Department of Arts, Culture & the Gaeltacht with Michael D. Higgins as minister. The National Heritage Council's remit was extremely broad and included the formulation of policies and priorities to identify, protect, preserve, enhance and increase awareness of Ireland's heritage in the specific areas of archaeology, architecture, flora, fauna, landscape, heritage gardens and certain inland waterways, as well as to promote an interest in and awareness of the national heritage among the general public. Given the limitations of a small staff and budget – the council received its money via the National Lottery's allocation to heritage and by 1993 the annual allocation stood at £1.55m., of which almost one-third was earmarked for the Archaeological Discovery Programme – nevertheless this initiative on the part of the state could not but be seen as a welcome development in the battle to preserve Ireland's heritage. However, attached as it was to a minister's department, the National Heritage Council did not have independent status nor was its long-term future secure. That position changed in 1995 when the organization was superseded by the Heritage Council, created as a statutory body under the same year's Heritage Act.

Immediately welcomed by the Society as 'a major step forward in the organization of the whole heritage scene', the council has remained in operation ever since with a clear role to propose policies and priorities for the identification, protection, preservation and enhancement of the national heritage. The latter's definition remains extremely broad and includes monuments, archaeological objects, heritage objects such as art and industrial works, documents and genealogical records, architectural heritage, flora, fauna, wildlife habitats, landscapes, seascapes, wrecks, geology, heritage gardens, parks and inland waterways. The council also has a particular responsibility to promote interest, education, knowledge and pride in the national heritage. Based in Kilkenny city, its executive includes an architecture officer and there is also a standing committee on architecture. In this respect, the Heritage Council endeavours to promote an integrated approach to the conservation of historic buildings and to encourage appreciation of the state's architectural heritage by promoting best practice, disseminating information and looking at buildings in a landscape context.

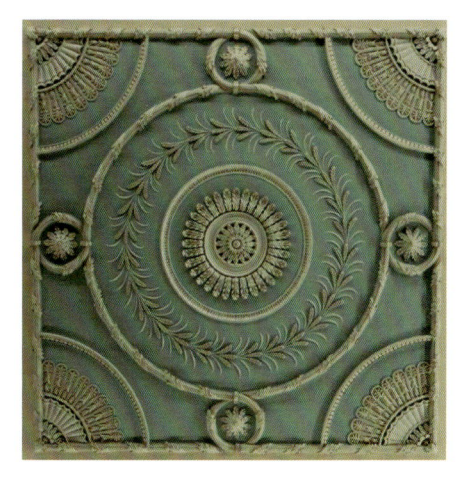

For owners of heritage properties, it can offer practical support in the form of financial aid. The council has an annual budget of around €1.2m. for its Buildings At Risk programme, gives in the region of €1.7m. each year for special conservation grants, runs a small architectural research grant scheme (€40,000) and in 2008 assumed the administration of a new project devoted to the conservation of farm buildings, which will disburse €7m. over seven years. Of late, two of the council's principal beneficiaries have been Westport, County Sligo and Headfort, County Meath, the second of which the Irish Georgian Society has also helped (the Society is marking its half-century by raising the funds needed for the restoration of Headfort's Eating Parlour, designed by Robert Adam in the 1770s). Since 2005 the Heritage Council has given €660,000 to Headfort for a variety of conservation projects and has also bought pieces of furniture that came from the house and that it is holding until circumstances allow their return.

Top: Headfort, Kells, Co. Meath, exterior view.

Bottom: Headfort, Kells, Co. Meath, part of the ceiling design by Robert Adam.

There have been other instances where the Irish Georgian Society and the Heritage Council were called upon to aid the same historic property, an indication that the latter organization's resources are just as finite and just as stretched as those of the former. And the broad sweep of the council's interests means architecture only receives a certain proportion of its attention and annual budget. Despite these limitations, what matters is that the Heritage Council, both in its present and former incarnation, shows the Irish state has finally recognized its responsibility towards caring for the national heritage and no longer leaves the protection of certain historic buildings to voluntary organizations like the Irish Georgian Society. Occurring in the year the Society celebrated its thirtieth anniversary, this was a major breakthrough and indicated a momentous and lasting shift in government policy.

Nineteen-eighty-eight saw another innovation, albeit on a smaller scale than the establishment of the National Heritage Council. That year, a number of owners of historic Irish houses came together to form the Hidden Ireland group. The members of this organization wished to continue living in their family homes but needed to find supplementary sources of income if they were to do so. An obvious means of realizing this ambition was to take in paying guests; after all, most large old houses

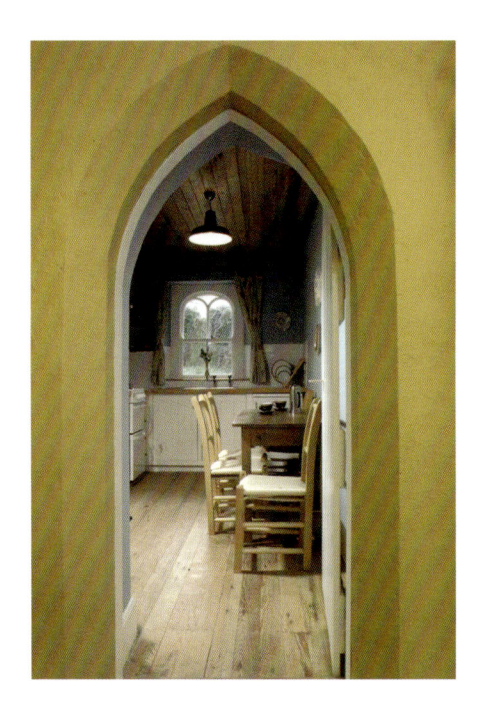

Interior and exterior of Anne's Grove gate lodge, Castletownroche, Co. Cork. Designed by Benjamin Woodward, 1853.

have an abundance of bedrooms and were used to accommodating groups, although until recently these had not expected to pay for the privilege. The buildings and their contents were left fundamentally intact and remained in the hands of the original owners. Although by no means suitable for all circumstances, Hidden Ireland proved itself an imaginative solution to the monetary shortcomings faced by certain houses, especially those where the occupants had a sufficiently sociable disposition. It continues to flourish and offers visitors a special alternative to more conventional tourist accommodation. Among the members who have remained with the group since its debut are Hilton Park, County Monaghan; Enniscoe House, County Mayo; and Temple House, County Sligo. (A similar business venture, called the Irish Country Houses and Restaurants Association but generally known as the Blue Book, had been set up in 1974 and remains in operation today, but its membership is more diverse and includes many venues of no historic significance.)

Also of importance is the establishment in 1992 of the Irish Landmark Trust, a charitable organization that saves heritage buildings either abandoned or at risk of being lost through neglect or inappropriate intervention throughout Ireland, north and south. From inception, and drawing on a wide variety of funds both public and private, the trust has followed a policy of engaging in scrupulous conservation, restoration and maintenance of any property under its care. Once a building has been thoroughly restored, it is made available for short-term holiday lettings, in this way generating an income so that further work of a similar nature can be undertaken elsewhere. The key element in the trust's programme is sustainable development. As the organization itself points out, 'The benefits of our work are enjoyed by more than our visitors. The morale of a village can be lifted by the rehabilitation of its most interesting landmark building. Visitors introduce tourist revenue. Craftsmen and craftswomen are given scope to revive traditional skills. And wasteful decay or demolition gives way to the sensible recycling of Ireland's valuable architectural stock.' At the time of writing, the

Irish Landmark Trust has restored twenty buildings across the island, ranging from a number of gate lodges (including three at Castletown) to several coastal lighthouses, as well as a Merrion Square mews and its own headquarters in an eighteenth-century panelled house on Eustace Street, Dublin.

Meanwhile at the start of a new decade the Irish Georgian Society was undergoing some changes of its own. In June 1990, after thirty-two years at the helm, Desmond Guinness retired as chairman of the Irish Georgian Foundation and the following year as president of the Irish Georgian Society. In these two positions he was succeeded by Desmond FitzGerald, the Knight of Glin, an ideal occupant of both since he had been involved with the organization from its inception and was a member of the Society's original committee (despite being at Harvard at the time). Desmond Guinness by no means severed his associations with the organization he had founded in 1958. Indeed, he continues to sit on its board of directors, returns annually to the United States for his inimitable fund-raising lecture tours and since 1990 he and his second wife, Penelope, have given the Society every assistance they can. Not long afterwards, the organization's executive director Audrey Emerson (who had first come to work for Desmond Guinness in 1973 as successor to his previous secretary, Patricia McSweeney, and stayed for nineteen years, ending as the Society's executive director) left to pursue other interests. Writing in the spring 1993 *Newsletter*, Cormac O'Carroll paid tribute to her indefatigable work over this long period, noting that the many tours around Ireland and overseas 'were largely co-ordinated by Audrey and the success of these and many other events over the years was greatly due to her dedication'.

New personnel now assumed responsibility for the daily running of the Society, including Dr Jane Fenlon, who was initially appointed arts and education consultant but soon became development officer. Her nephew, Declan O'Leary, who also worked

Above: Bianca Jagger and Penelope Guinness, October 1981.

Left: Desmond FitzGerald, Knight of Glin, became chairman and president of the IGS in June 1990.

Prof. Kevin B. Nowlan, vice-president of the IGS.

for Irish Heritage Properties (formerly HITHA), was employed part-time in the capacity of planning officer as the need to monitor the escalating amount of building projects throughout Ireland was identified by the Irish Georgian Society. Taking an interest in planning applications represented an important addition to the Society's already established brief; hitherto it had left such matters to organizations like An Taisce and the Dublin Civic Group. But if the organization was truly concerned with preserving buildings of historic importance, then it needed to be aware as early as possible of any threat to their welfare. Already in the autumn/winter 1994 *Newsletter*, Desmond FitzGerald could write, 'I am particularly pleased that the Society, through our planning officer Declan O'Leary, has made its voice heard on a number of occasions concerning detrimental planning applications.' This would become more and more the case as the decade progressed. Both Jane Fenlon and Declan O'Leary remained with the society until 1995, when she left to pursue academic interests and he took up a position in Cambodia. At that date architect Mary Bryan, who had already been working with the organization for some time, was appointed conservation officer and executive secretary. She subsequently became the Society's chief executive.

Change is an important component of any organization that wishes to have a long-term future and the Irish Georgian Society could not afford to remain static in either its structure or outlook. In particular, it was now realized that the Society had to become more professional in its management. 'Perhaps it was sad for us who had enjoyed those early carefree days,' comments Cormac O'Carroll. 'But you can't run an organization like that, not if it's going to survive.' With the conclusion of Desmond Guinness's time in charge, the Society moved its offices out of Leixlip Castle and into new premises at No. 42 Merrion Square. This was provided for three years at a token annual rent of £1 by the landlord, the Electricity Supply Board, ironically the same body against which the Society had gone into battle over the redevelopment of Lower Fitzwilliam Street some thirty years earlier. Now, however, the ESB was more amenable to the concept of heritage preservation and even agreed to restore the essential eighteenth-century features to the facade of No. 42 Merrion Square, the colour scheme of window frames, entrance door and railings being based on a decorative scheme of 1809 used for the Earl of Meath's house not far away.

At the end of the three-year period, the Society transferred its operations from the east to the south side of the square, settling into the basement of No. 74. In the late 1990s, serious consideration was given to the idea of the Society acquiring its own premises and a subcommittee established to pursue the idea. Alongside its traditional role of fund-raising and saving historic houses, the organization had gained additional prominence through opposing detrimental planning permissions, lobbying for changes in legislation affecting conservation and organizing conferences to highlight practical aspects of conservation. 'With this heightened profile,' announced 1995's *Newsletter*, 'the need for our own headquarters takes on an increased importance.' But in the end the notion came to nothing, not least because of ever escalating property prices in the capital which, as the Knight of Glin remarked in the first *Newsletter* of 2000, led to a concern that, should a building be bought, 'the Society would be overburdened by taking on such a big financial commitment', especially once the costs of refurbishment and upkeep were added. Hence No. 74 Merrion Square continues to be the organization's address. Whether leased or owned, an office in Dublin has been beneficial to the Society by helping to give it a clearly independent identity (Leixlip Castle had, after all, also been Desmond Guinness's private home). As the 1991 *Newsletter* commented, 'The central location makes the Society more available to members and visitors alike and many people drop in to the offices ...'

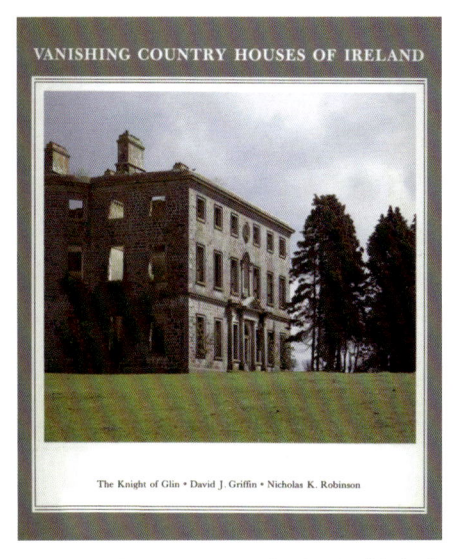

Although henceforth based in the capital and therefore inclined to watch more closely any potential assaults on Dublin's stock of historic buildings, the Society did not ignore what was happening elsewhere around the state. In particular, the plight of the Irish country house continued to be a matter of keen concern. It had already been the subject of a groundbreaking exhibition in December 1988, jointly organized by the Irish Georgian Society and the Irish Architectural Archive and held at the Royal Hibernian Academy. (Coincidentally, at the same time a new edition of Mark Bence-Jones's invaluable compendium of Irish country houses, which had first been published ten years before, now appeared with a supplement featuring 130 additional properties.) Intended to bring to the attention of a wide public the national architectural heritage's precarious condition, *Vanishing Country Houses of Ireland* – which was supported by Christie's of London and the Rohan Group – featured an abundance of photographs depicting ruined houses and interiors from across the state, together with a haunting audio-visual presentation. The show also emphasized that this unhappy scenario would continue to unfold for as long as successive governments failed to establish an historic buildings fund or an adequate system of grant aid for buildings of importance. An accompanying book carried essays by, amongst others, the Knight of Glin and Nicholas Robinson, followed by a catalogue of some 560 country houses already destroyed during the course of the twentieth century.

Vanishing Country Houses of Ireland published by the IGS and the Irish Architectural Archive in 1988.

Both the exhibition and book created a considerable stir (the latter stayed on the Irish best-seller list for several weeks, by which time its entire first edition had sold out; it has remained in print ever since). 'This is a really shocking exhibition,' wrote Frank McDonald in *The Irish Times*, 'and heartbreaking, too ... At the rate things are going, in another generation or so there may not be a country house left in Ireland with its original furnishings and family portraits still intact.' Meanwhile the *Irish Independent*, having commented that the book was 'a faithful, unemotional and unprecedented gazetteer of national neglect, local ignorance and thoughtless destruction', argued that even if the work inspired 'only a tiny number of voices to add their pleas for better terms of preservation nationwide, then it will have served a valuable purpose'.

After closing in Dublin, the Vanishing Country Houses of Ireland exhibition next travelled to London before being seen in New York, Houston, New Orleans, Chicago and Boston; it was also shown at a number of regional Irish venues. Wherever presented, this catalogue of architectural woes was greeted with shock and dismay. In *The Daily Telegraph*, Hugh Montgomery-Massingberd spoke of 'the tragedy and almost unbearable nostalgia' the show evoked while novelist Isabel Colegate in *The Spectator* insisted the accompanying book was 'a well-argued plea for the preservation of what remains and for funding from the Irish Government and/or an independent national property-owning trust'. Must Irish houses vanish? speculated John Cornforth in *Country Life*, noting that 'every year, Ireland slips farther behind general European standards in matters of preservation and planning'.

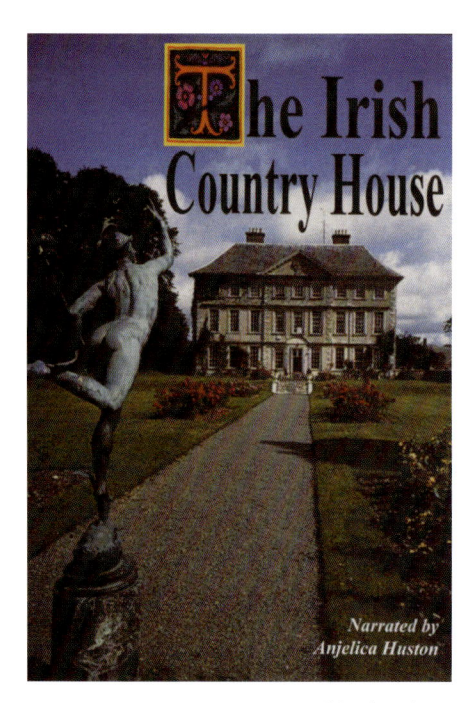

The Irish Country House, narrated by Anjelica Huston, a Wildgoose Films production for the IGS (1993).

It had been a happy accident that the Vanishing Country Houses of Ireland exhibition should have taken place just months after the National Heritage Council was set up, but a lot more campaigning would be needed before the country's remaining stock of historic properties could face a secure future. Early in 1991 the Irish Georgian Society began seeking money from various sources for a fifty-minute film to be made on the subject of the Irish country house. Produced by David Cabot (then environmental advisor to the taoiseach) and Michael Viney, whose weekly environmental column has become an *Irish Times* institution, the film was thought to be 'most useful when approaching Foundations for fund-raising and also for its educational value'. Budgeted at more than £100,000, the project received financial support from a large number of individuals, trusts, foundations and such bodies as Bord Fáilte and the National Heritage Council. Actress Anjelica Huston, who has strong links with Ireland, provided the voice-over and the film contained interviews with Molly Keane, Desmond Guinness, Professor Kevin B. Nowlan, Pyers O'Conor Nash and Luke Dodd.

When finished, *The Irish Country House* was shown on RTÉ television on St Patrick's Day, 1993, and on the same date it was screened for the members of the New York Chapter in the Lincoln Center at what was described by the press as 'the toniest party in town'. Other American screenings had already occurred at Houston and Washington, and would follow at Boston and Chicago, the last of these as part of a fund-raising dinner at the Casino Club organized by the local Chapter. *The Irish Country House* still merits watching; a recent internet reviewer describes the film as a 'loving examination of the long history and surprising variety of these beautiful structures, with gorgeous aerial cinematography captured on lustrous 16mm film ... and tours of the houses themselves featuring illuminating interviews offered by architects, historians, and the people who live in them'.

The Irish Country House's very first public showing took place during a conference jointly organized by the Irish Georgian Society and Irish Heritage Properties in late February 1993. Held at No. 39 Merrion Square, 'The Future of the Country House' was heavily oversubscribed but those who did manage to reserve a place heard from a diverse group of speakers, ranging from Minister of State at the Department of Finance Noel Tracey; Austin Dunphy from the National Heritage Council; MEP Mary Banotti; and Bord Fáilte's director general, Matt McNulty. The last of these, who had already been responsible for saving a number of houses including Malahide Castle, announced his organization's intention of using the next tranche of money for heritage and cultural tourism from the European Regional Development Funds 'on securing and preserving real and genuine heritage'.

Just how necessary this kind of support would be was demonstrated by another speaker, Pyers O'Conor Nash, whose talk on the economics of the historic house in Ireland was subtitled, 'How to Breast-feed a Dinosaur in the Late 20th Century'. Mr O'Conor Nash noted that when Clonalis, County Roscommon (ancestral home of the O'Conors, Kings of Connacht and at various times, High Kings of Ireland), had passed from one generation to the next in 1981, while the house was exempt from Capital Acquisition Tax because open to the public, the estate was not and hence nearly 1100 acres had to be sold, leaving only 600 to provide income for maintenance. He quoted a forbear, Charles O'Conor, who said in 1756 in relation to the Penal Laws, 'I struggle to keep my hold, and if I am left with nothing to inherit but the religion and misfortunes of a family long on the decline, the victim is prepared for the sacrifice resignedly indeed, though not willingly.'

Writing afterwards of the conference, Hugh Montgomery-Massingberd raised a point that had been made by outside observers many times before: 'In a nation where tourism is the second largest industry (after agriculture), the Government should know better than to permit its architectural treasures to disappear.' However, there were signs of a growing awareness within official circles of how threatened this element of the national heritage had become. 'The Future of the Country House' conference was opened by then-taoiseach Albert Reynolds, who, in his speech, assured the audience that architecture of the previous three centuries had as important a position in the state's cultural and heritage policy as did the Neolithic, early Christian or mediaeval. He described as 'misguided' the latent hostility or bureaucratic and commercial indifference towards Georgian buildings that had been a characteristic of previous generations. But while stressing his government's interest in encouraging the preservation of Ireland's heritage properties, he cautioned, 'In all honesty, I have to say that the scope for manoeuvre in the near future is rather limited by current economic and fiscal conditions.' Nevertheless, Mr Reynolds told his listeners, 'I fully accept that the most efficient way of protecting and preserving these houses is to help the owners as far as possible keep and maintain them and that this should be the basic policy objective.'

Even though this aspiration was not immediately realized, its articulation by the head of government was unparalleled and demonstrated that, at last, official attitudes towards the nation's heritage of Georgian architecture had begun to shift. But in the short term, good will and good intentions were not going to be enough to keep more of the country's already shrunken stock of country houses from vanishing. By now the government had made some financial assistance available (notably Section 19 of the 1982 Finance Act, and its subsequent amendments, which provided tax relief from income and corporation taxes to the owners of buildings deemed to be of significant merit in respect of the latter's repair, maintenance or restoration, provided public access was annually afforded for a certain number of days – currently sixty in any one year). But the legislation involved was piecemeal and hard to comprehend, lacked clear guidelines and was often poorly implemented. As the Knight of Glin and Richard Wood stated in a joint introduction to the conference's published proceedings:

> Unless the tangled skeins of tax relief are unknotted and rationalized and the will to help is fostered by government and other concerned bodies, Irish country houses, their gardens, parks and contents will soon be a fading memory ... We must not let the momentum generated by this conference die. It would be appalling if future generations could not celebrate all aspects of their rich, diverse and varied heritage.

For anyone struggling to hold on to and maintain an historic property, the Irish Georgian Society had from its foundation been a source of practical help and advice.

Clonalis, Castlerea, Co. Roscommon.

Frequently the assistance provided took the form of a grant, and these continued to be dispensed whenever possible. The experience of struggling to restore Doneraile Court had shown that assuming direct responsibility for buildings at risk, while admirable, tended to absorb far too much of the Society's limited time and resources. From now on, therefore, the organization adopted a policy of providing financial support to other organizations and individuals engaged in restoration projects. Any money given was always for a very specific purpose and its expenditure monitored. The principle beneficiaries of this procedure have already been mentioned but there were plenty of other recipients of financial help. For example, in 1986 the Society contributed £1000 towards the provision of a new roof on Kilduff, County Offaly, and the following year the organization commissioned and paid for a report on the state of the roof at Borris House, County Carlow. In 1989 the Society provided an interest-free loan of almost £4000 for the restoration of a neoclassical plasterwork ceiling at Ash Hill Towers, County Limerick, and, a year later, Enniscoe House, County Mayo, received a grant of £2000 towards the cost of repairing the late-eighteenth-century plasterwork around the staircase's oval skylight.

But there were other forms of aid available, such as guidance on how best to take care of an old building. Back in September 1969, the Society had organized a week-long seminar on the creation and repair of decorative plasterwork, given by an expert in this field, William Salter from Leeds. The price of enrolling on this seminar was £5 but Mr Salter also gave a free lecture and practical demonstration of his skills to Society members at No. 50 Mountjoy Square. Three years later, he returned to give a second seminar on the same subject, this time without charge for participants since the event's costs were underwritten by a Californian supporter, Alice O'Neill Avery. Some time elapsed before further seminars were arranged by the Society's William Garner, the next being on the valuable topic, 'New Uses for Old Buildings'. Held in early March 1987, its specific focus was on finding an alternative purpose for the former Debtors' Prison of 1794 in central Dublin (for which, incidentally, a new use has still not been found). The following October, Mr Garner organized another, equally practical seminar for the Society, this time on fire precautions for heritage buildings, which offered abundant advice from experts in the field. Likewise in December 1988, a seminar, 'The Building Exterior: New Conservation Techniques', was replete with helpful information for anyone undertaking external restoration on an historic property.

A further means of helping to ensure the survival of historic buildings in Ireland was to increase awareness and appreciation of their distinctive characteristics. From the very start the Irish Georgian Society had arranged an annual programme of lectures for its members. But this was effectively preaching to the converted and so the Society began to host a number of seminars and conferences examining different aspects of the country's art and architecture and brought them to as broad an audience as possible. The first of these events was held at Castletown in late-June 1971, immediately following the second Festival of Music in Great Irish Houses. This six-day occasion featured an astonishing cross section of speakers and subjects, ranging from the late Mrs Leask talking on tombstones to the late John Hunt describing the restoration of Bunratty Castle. There was also a programme of visits to private collections, galleries and museums in the vicinity of Dublin.

Six years later, Castletown was again the venue for a day-long seminar organized by the Society and exploring some aspects of the visual arts in Ireland such as Irish landscape gardening 1660–1845 (speaker, the Knight of Glin) and Thomas Wright's 1746 drawings of Ireland (speaker, Professor Michael McCarthy). By such means as these, the Society sought to broaden its appeal and to reach out to a new membership. Through its first three decades of existence, a handful of individuals, most of them working in a voluntary capacity, had assumed complete responsibility for the Irish Georgian Society's daily management and programme of activities. Now that circumstances had begun to change and a better understanding of the importance of Ireland's heritage prevailed around the country, it was important for the Society to adopt a more inclusive approach.

SCHOLARS AND SCHOLARSHIPS

Nothing better exemplifies the Irish Georgian Society's commitment to increasing knowledge and appreciation of Ireland's heritage than the support it has shown to young scholars. Fifty years ago, the study of Irish art and architecture outside the Celtic period was almost virgin territory, usually classified as a minor branch of British cultural history. Today that is most certainly no longer the case and Irish art history has grown into a thriving field despite the relative paucity of primary source material. The Society has done its share to encourage this development, not least by awarding grants and scholarships to students. For example, during the 1980s the Society sponsored an Irish architect or someone involved in the practicalities of restoration work to attend the annual West Dean Summer School in West Sussex, which specialized in architectural conservation. In 1984 the successful applicant was architect David Sheehan, who had already designed a cabinet to hold the J. Paul Getty gift of Irish bindings at Castletown and has since worked on a number of house restoration projects in which the Society was also involved. The following year the summer school was attended by David Griffin, now director of the Irish Architectural Archive as well as sitting on the Irish Georgian Society's board of directors, while 1989's participant was Dr Paul Caffrey, then curator of Castletown and now a lecturer at Dublin's National College of Art and Design.

In 1996, the Society decided to assist academic study by initiating the annual Desmond Guinness Scholarship, open to anyone resident in Ireland and engaged in research on the visual arts in Ireland, and on the work of Irish architects, artists and craftsmen at home and abroad between 1600 and 1900. Additional smaller prizes have also regularly been given. The first recipient of a Desmond Guinness Scholarship was postgraduate student Nessa Roche, then conducting research on change and development of Dublin windows from 1660 to 1760; she has since published a well-received book, *The Legacy of Light: A History of Irish Windows*. The successful 1997 applicant was Sarah Foster, whose interest lay in exploring the commissioning and purchase of luxury goods in eighteenth-century Dublin; in 1999 the scholarship was awarded to Alison Fitzgerald so that she could continue her work into domestic silver in Dublin during the eighteenth century; and the following year's winner was Aidan O'Boyle, who was examining the history of Aldborough House, the last of Dublin's grand aristocratic freestanding houses to be completed before the 1800 Act of Union.

The most recent recipient, presented with the scholarship in February 2008, was Elmarie Nagle, to assist her research into the life and work of the nineteenth-century Irish sculptor John Edward Carew (the subject of an essay by R.H.C. Finch in one of the Society's 1966 *Bulletin*s). Almost without fail, the results of these scholars' work has been made available to a broad audience through appearing in a volume of the Society's *Irish Architectural and Decorative Studies*. And some of them have followed the example of Nessa Roche by publishing books; for example in 2007 Conor Lucey, who had won the scholarship two years before, published his acclaimed *The Stapleton Collection: Designs for the Irish Neoclassical Interior* (under the imprint of the Churchill Press). Greater research can only lead to enhanced understanding and thus to the better preservation of Ireland's heritage of buildings, their decoration and contents.

Desmond Guinness Annual Scholarship. *Back row (left to right):* Nick Sheaff, director of the IGS; Tony Hand; Hon. Desmond Guinness; Desmond FitzGerald, Knight of Glin; Stuart Kinsella. *Front row (left to right):* Dr Anne Casement, Prof. Anne Crookshank and Livia Hurley.

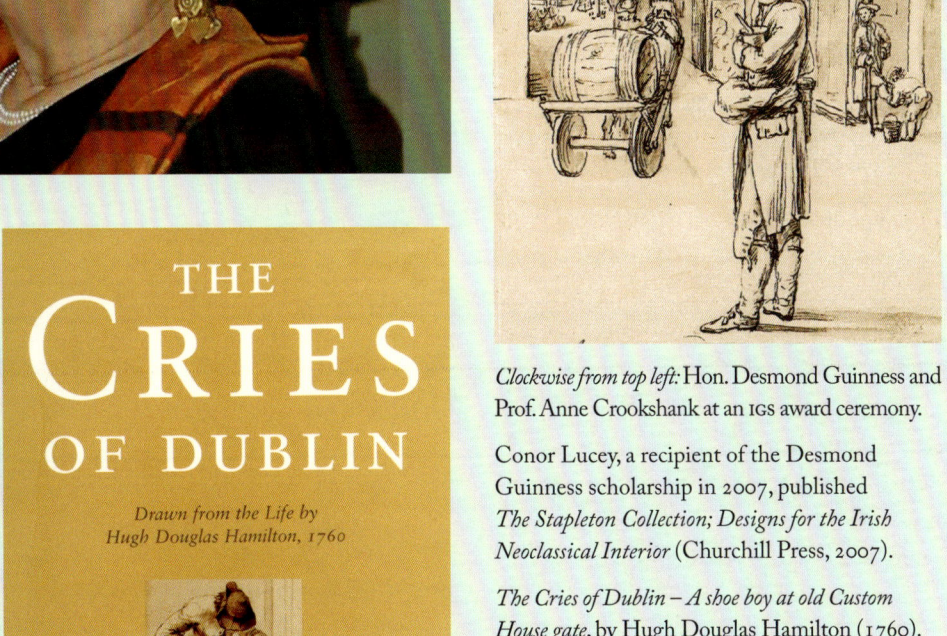

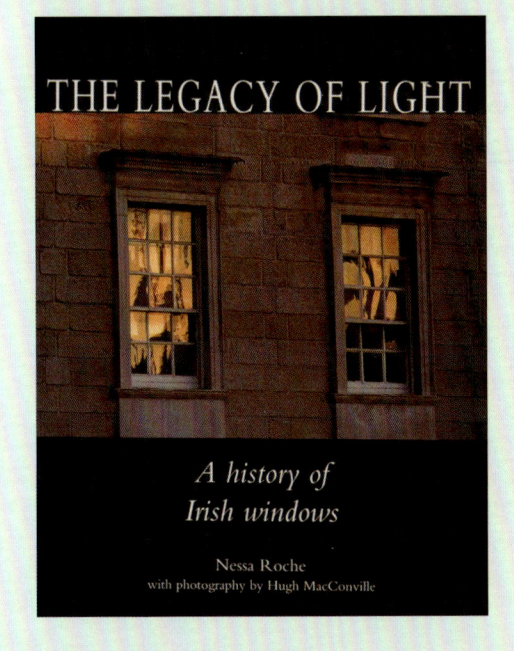

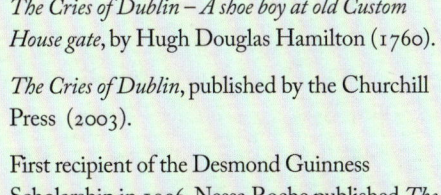

Clockwise from top left: Hon. Desmond Guinness and Prof. Anne Crookshank at an IGS award ceremony.

Conor Lucey, a recipient of the Desmond Guinness scholarship in 2007, published *The Stapleton Collection; Designs for the Irish Neoclassical Interior* (Churchill Press, 2007).

The Cries of Dublin – A shoe boy at old Custom House gate, by Hugh Douglas Hamilton (1760).

The Cries of Dublin, published by the Churchill Press (2003).

First recipient of the Desmond Guinness Scholarship in 1996, Nessa Roche published *The Legacy of Light: A History of Irish Windows* (1999).

MORE TOURS

While certain elements of the Irish Georgian Society's organization and character changed during the early 1990s, one feature remaining consistent was the annual programme of tours. These have also retained their popularity up to the present day and an entire book could be devoted to the subject, not least because of an abiding propensity for mishaps. Audrey Emerson remembers that on one trip around the midlands of Ireland – when participants travelled in a convoy of cars rather than together in a bus – the entire group became lost and was slowly meandering around the small roads when a local man called out, 'Who is it that's died?' Farther afield, Audrey recalls that the April 1978 trip to Iran (then on the very eve of revolution) included an encounter with Margaret Thatcher: 'She thought we were possible votes, as the disappointment in her voice when she asked people where they came from was very apparent on hearing "Co. Kerry", "Dublin", "Co. Cork" even "Qatar" but she eventually struck gold with "Newtownabbey, Co. Antrim"!' This visit had been organized by Peter and Anne Verity, who were then living in the country. 'Little did we realise,' he writes,

> but the Persians rarely receive outside their family and we were prising open doors on private worlds that few outsiders had previously seen. Within months the society that we were privileged to have revealed to us would be no more and no group would ever see again the world and collections that the IGS saw that glorious spring of 1978.

Iran has been one of the more far-flung countries visited by the Society over the years. Others include Mexico, Cuba, South Africa and India, the last of these first explored in 1970 and seen again in spring 2007. But the majority of tours have been to other parts of Europe, with Rose Mary Craig frequently acting as cicerone. 'In 1982 The Export Board sent me off to Amsterdam,' she remembers,

> and one day Audrey phoned me and said, 'Let's do a tour of the houses of Holland,' and that is how my arranging overseas trips for the IGS started. Since that first trip to Holland in 1983 I have organised 21 trips for the Society concentrating on the houses and gardens of Europe and Britain. About 350 properties – at a conservative guess – have been visited and it is rare that the IGS is refused entry. Our credentials are impeccable and the fame of Desmond and Mariga goes far beyond the boundaries of this island and their names, and that of the IGS, certainly help in opening doors – even where the owners did not know either of them or, indeed, the IGS, except by reputation.

According to Rose Mary, members of the Society

> seem to have a propensity for medical dramas and I always say that I am planning to write a guide to the hospitals of Europe as I have, unexpectedly, seen the inside of so many! Over the years I have had to deal with threatened miscarriage, back problems, falls, serious cuts, bone breakages, forgotten/lost life-sustaining pills, threatened comas, allergies, asthmatic attacks – all of which have involved visits to local hospitals.

But despite these hazards, she has memories of many wonderful occasions:

> Some which stand out are the fabulous dinner for over 100 at the Château de Sully where IGS member Dermot Humphries re-enacted the presentation by an ancestor of his, Dr Sigerson, of a jewel-encrusted silver sword to the then Duc de Magenta (the present Duke had the sword in a display case); dinner with the Prince de Ligne in his flower-filled château; a musical evening in the Prince de Chimay's private theatre followed by dinner; a private recital by the Paris-based Irish pianist Miceal O'Rourke in Terry Cross's Bordeaux château; a riotous lunch at the Castello di Trissino where the drinks were so strong (their own brandied cherries and cherry brandy) that people had to be literally helped back to the bus where they slept what was left of the afternoon away; dinner with the Marquis de Breteuil where we sat surrounded by his O'Brien ancestral portraits and he sat surrounded by nine IGS members of the O'Brien clan; the Graf and Grafeine Wolfe Metternich's dinner at Adelebsen where Andy Warhol's Marilyn Monroe portrait and other twentieth-century icons gazed down on us (a change from the usual family line-up); Gilbert and Helen McCabe's atmospheric house in Cornwall where the tree-lined driveway is reputed to have been the inspiration for Daphne du Maurier's Mandalay; drinks and a wonderful buffet supper in Countess Marina Emo's frescoed Villa Emo; Anthony Barton surrounded by adoring ladies at lunch chez lui; drinks by the Mediterranean in Givenchy's Le Clos Fiorentina, formerly owned by Lady Kenmare; the Vatican and the Sistine Chapel at night all to ourselves ... and much more!

Many of the Society's *Bulletin*s and *Newsletter*s contain factual accounts of individual tours, including dutiful lists of museums visited and houses inspected. However, these do not begin to capture the flavour of these occasions in the same way as reminiscences from people like Rose Mary Craig.

For more than a decade the Society's long-standing and indefatigable committee member, John Holohan, has also arranged numerous walking- and day-tours of Irish country houses, towns, cities and suburbs. Recent venues visited under his supervision have ranged from Barmeath Castle, County Louth, and the Dunboyne area of County Meath, to the Artisan Dwelling Company's houses of the Liberties and Alan Hope's modernist house, Meander, in Foxrock village. John has developed a loyal following and the popularity of his tours means they are almost invariably oversubscribed, on occasion leading to requests that they be repeated. Both John Holohan's and Rose Mary Craig's work in this area relies heavily on the excellent organizational skills of the Society's events and membership administrator, Doreen McNamara, who, like accounts administrator Marjorie Malcolm, has worked for the Society for the past twenty years.

Clockwise from top left: IGS tour to Belgium, June 1998: tour leader Rose Mary Craig talking to the Prince de Ligne (right).

IGS tour to Foxrock, Co. Dublin, March 2004. IGS members outside the home of Alan and Mairin Hope, Meander, Foxrock, Co. Dublin. *Left to right:* Dell Lundy, David Boles, Catherine Hardy, Mairin Hope, Hilda Kennedy, Michael Frayne, Dorothy Donnelly, John Holohan, Lochlann Coggin, Charles Duggan, Brian Meyer, Jacqui Donnelly, Avril Larmour, Ursula Lee-McCarthy, Olive Murray, Gabrielle O'Herlihy and Cornelia Legge.

IGS 'Tour to the French Riviera – Art & Gardens', June 2001. Givenchy's Le Clos Fiorentina was formerly owned by Lady Kenmare.

Young IGS tour to Lambay Island, Co. Dublin, 2006 *(left to right)*: Aidan O'Boyle, David Bland, Deirdre Conroy, Enda Sherlock, Victoria Browne, Aoife Kavanagh, Donough Cahill, Tomas O'Connor, Stephen O'Driscoll, Mary Reade and Richard McLoughlin.

IGS tour to Belgium, June 1988. Prince de Chimay (left) and Jeremy Williams.

Urban redevelopment and its drawbacks ~ the Society's conferences on urban conservation ~ Traditional Building Skills exhibitions ~ National Gallery of Ireland and George's Quay: two vulnerable sites ~ the Society marks its fortieth anniversary ~ Panels: Irish Architectural and Decorative Studies *and 20 Lower Dominick Street*

CHAPTER

12

In 1994 the Irish Georgian Society embarked on its first-ever membership survey, asking those people who had sustained the organization for the past thirty-six years how they thought its work could be improved. The response to this opportunity for active participation in determining the Society's future direction was disappointing: of 3322 questionnaires distributed, only 282, or 9.4 per cent of the total, were returned. When equivalent bodies in London such as The Georgian Group and the Society for the Protection of Ancient Buildings (SPAB) had carried out similar surveys, they had achieved far higher rates of reply – 41 and 25 per cent respectively. The Irish Georgian Society's poor figure of return in itself indicates how unaccustomed the membership was to being consulted on matters of policy. While motivated to join the Society by an interest in heritage preservation (as was stated by 77 per cent of respondents), members had thereafter been given little opportunity to express an opinion on how this might best be achieved.

One reason why they were happy to accept this relative passivity was age: even by 1994, 37 per cent of the Society's membership was over sixty-five and another 31 per cent aged between fifty and sixty-five. Their days of manning the metaphorical barricades had ended and, as many of their comments revealed, they were now primarily interested in the more social aspects of the Society such as outings and parties. Tellingly, comparative membership fell by 397 between July 1993 and July 1994; most of this drop was due to a decline in new memberships, suggesting that when old members died they were not being replaced by the next generation.

188

The spring/summer 1993 *Newsletter* had already reported that a critical area for development in the year ahead was increasing membership among the under-35s and this issue of moving the organization's overall age profile downwards was one that would only grow in importance over the coming decade.

Even before the survey's results were collated and analysed, the society had embarked on the preparation of a five-year development plan. A key feature of this was the establishment of an education subcommittee to encourage the creation of a programme aimed at primary and secondary schools and to work with the staff at No. 29 Fitzwilliam Street, a late-eighteenth-century house restored by the ESB and opened as a museum of Georgian domestic life. Improving membership was another element of the proposed development plan, with the establishment of more Irish regional Chapters, now that one in Birr had been set up. Waterford, Kilkenny and Drogheda were mentioned as possibilities but to date these have remained an aspiration. (Thriving Chapters in Limerick and Cork, on the other hand, have since been founded.) The plan also envisaged improving the Irish Georgian Society's public profile (which had rather slipped since the glory days of the 1960s when the organization consistently made headlines) as this in turn would draw attention to its important work.

One aspect of that work was touched on by a member whose response to the 1994 survey included the telling remark, 'I believe very strongly that the Society's efforts today must be directed at eighteenth- and nineteenth-century architecture in Irish towns and cities … If the Irish Georgian Society really wishes to do good work in this direction then it should seriously consider entering into projects for the restoration of houses, or even terraces, in Irish towns.' It is undeniable that following the battle to preserve Mountjoy Square in Dublin, more and more of the Society's attention had been focussed on restoring or assisting in the restoration of a number of country houses. Towns and cities, and especially the capital, had been paid relatively little attention but that was no longer to be the case, not least because from the mid-1990s urban renewal and redevelopment became a widespread phenomenon in Ireland.

The Society made its own interest in the matter plain in late May 1993 when it made an oral presentation to the conservation subcommittee of Dublin Corporation; this was the first time a local government body had requested a deputation from the organization. In the course of its submission, the Society proposed the establishment of a conservation section within the corporation that would advocate preservation rather than demolition, the commissioning of a survey and inventory of important buildings' interior features and the establishment of a civic forum whereby matters of concern to groups such as the Irish Georgian Society could be raised. Above all, the Society was anxious that Dublin's local government should be more actively interested in conservation, especially since the city was undergoing significant commercial redevelopment.

In fact even without prompting, the private sector, hitherto notoriously indifferent to the concept of national heritage and its preservation, had already started taking some inventive steps in this direction, as exemplified by what happened to Powerscourt

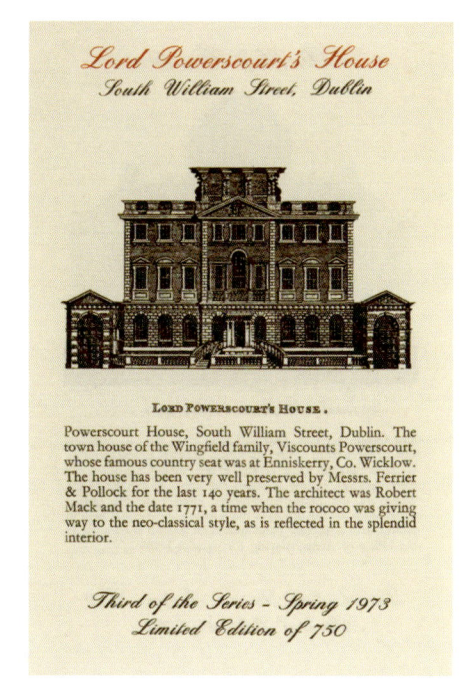

Lord Powerscourt's House, Dublin. Designed by Robert Mack in the 1770s as a Dublin residence of Richard Wingfield, third Viscount Powerscourt. Engraving by Pool and Cash, 1780.

House. This palatial building had been designed by Robert Mack in the early 1770s as a Dublin residence for Richard Wingfield, third Viscount Powerscourt (who, it was said, spent most his life wishing he were instead an earl and whose County Wicklow seat would be tragically gutted by fire in November 1974). Its vast four-storey, nine-bay frontage dominates South William Street, while the principal reception rooms feature superb neoclassical stuccowork by Michael Stapleton; the slightly earlier plasterwork of the hallway and stairs is by James McCullagh, assisted by Michael Reynolds. The Wingfields would occupy the house for less than forty years, selling it to the government in 1807 for £7500 (which was £500 less than it had cost to build). Francis Johnston added a large brick courtyard to the rear so that the property could serve as a stamp office but in 1832 the government sold the entire site, which thereafter was used as a wholesale warehouse until the last quarter of the twentieth century.

Somehow throughout this long period the building survived unaltered and so when it was put up for sale by the drapers Ferrier Pollock & Co. in January 1977, hopes were expressed that Powerscourt House might be bought by the state, perhaps for use as an extension of the National Museum. Alas, in an era of government cutbacks (the museum's own budget that year was severely trimmed) it was not to be and so the building was left to take its chances on the open market. Happily the eventual purchaser proved to be Cork-born dentist-turned-developer Robin Power whose company, Power Securities Ltd, made a point of consulting the Irish Georgian Society and other groups before embarking on a £3m. restoration and conversion of Powerscourt and its courtyard into a smart shopping mall. Even the most hardened opponents of speculative development were stunned at this turn of events; writing for *In Dublin* magazine, Fintan O'Toole wondered whether 'after all, there is such a thing as a property developer with taste'. Obviously the entire property development profession did not follow Mr Power's example (and he was himself guilty of some heinous aesthetic crimes in the years ahead, such as the abysmal St Stephen's Green Shopping Centre) but Powerscourt House's sensitive restoration showed that demolition was not inevitable.

Accordingly, the Irish Georgian Society's five-year development plan of 1994 included a programme of restoration initiatives in urban areas, beginning with work at No. 20 Dominick Street. An astonishing survivor in what had been one of the most neglected parts of Dublin for at least a century, No. 20 is owned by the National Youth Federation, a voluntary body that would not have the funds to restore the house's mid-eighteenth-century rococo interiors by Robert West and others. In 1994, the Irish Georgian Society commenced its association with the building by raising the necessary funds so that historically correct wooden window frames and granite sills could be reinstated in the facade. Similarly, in 1995 the Society gave a grant towards the installation of appropriately designed new windows, copied from a surviving example, for Nos 3 and 4 Fownes Street, two mid-eighteenth-century houses in the Temple Bar district of Dublin, which was then undergoing a resurgence.

The rampant virus of architecturally incorrect modern windows inserted into old buildings was to preoccupy the Society over the years ahead. In 1993 it noted with satisfaction that An Bord Pleanála had ruled a local authority could now demand planning permission be required before sash windows were replaced with aluminium or uPVC frames (until around this date, government grants were available for replacing wooden windows with aluminium or uPVC framed units). Three years later, the *Newsletter* reported that Dublin Corporation had taken the step of contacting owners of listed buildings, and the manufacturers of such windows, and alerting them to what was and was not permissible for historic properties, as well as beginning legal proceedings in a number of cases where An Bord Pleanála's ruling had been flouted. In 1994 the Society undertook a sample survey of the core conservation area in Dublin and 'we were shocked to see the number of aluminium/uPVC windows in listed buildings in these areas ... The Society are [sic] currently developing a conservation policy document which will be used to promote a correct approach in terms of architectural conservation.'

Emphasizing its re-engagement with questions of urban development and preservation, in February 1995 the Society organized a major three-day conference at Dublin Castle on the theme, 'The Town – Conservation in the Urban Area'. As with the conference on the future of the Irish country house two years before, this event was opened by the current taoiseach, John Bruton, who, like his predecessor in office, acknowledged the taxation problems facing owners of historic houses and stressed the benefits of having those owners living in their own property. He confessed, 'It is obvious that past generations since the foundation of the state have not served us particularly well as far as urban planning is concerned. We have lost through dereliction and neglect some very beautiful urban vistas and some very fine buildings.'

The IGS's restoration initiative in 1994 to restore Robert West's plasterwork at 20 Lower Dominick Street, Dublin. Desmond FitzGerald, Knight of Glin, and Mary Bryan, director of the IGS, inspect plasterwork restoration in progress.

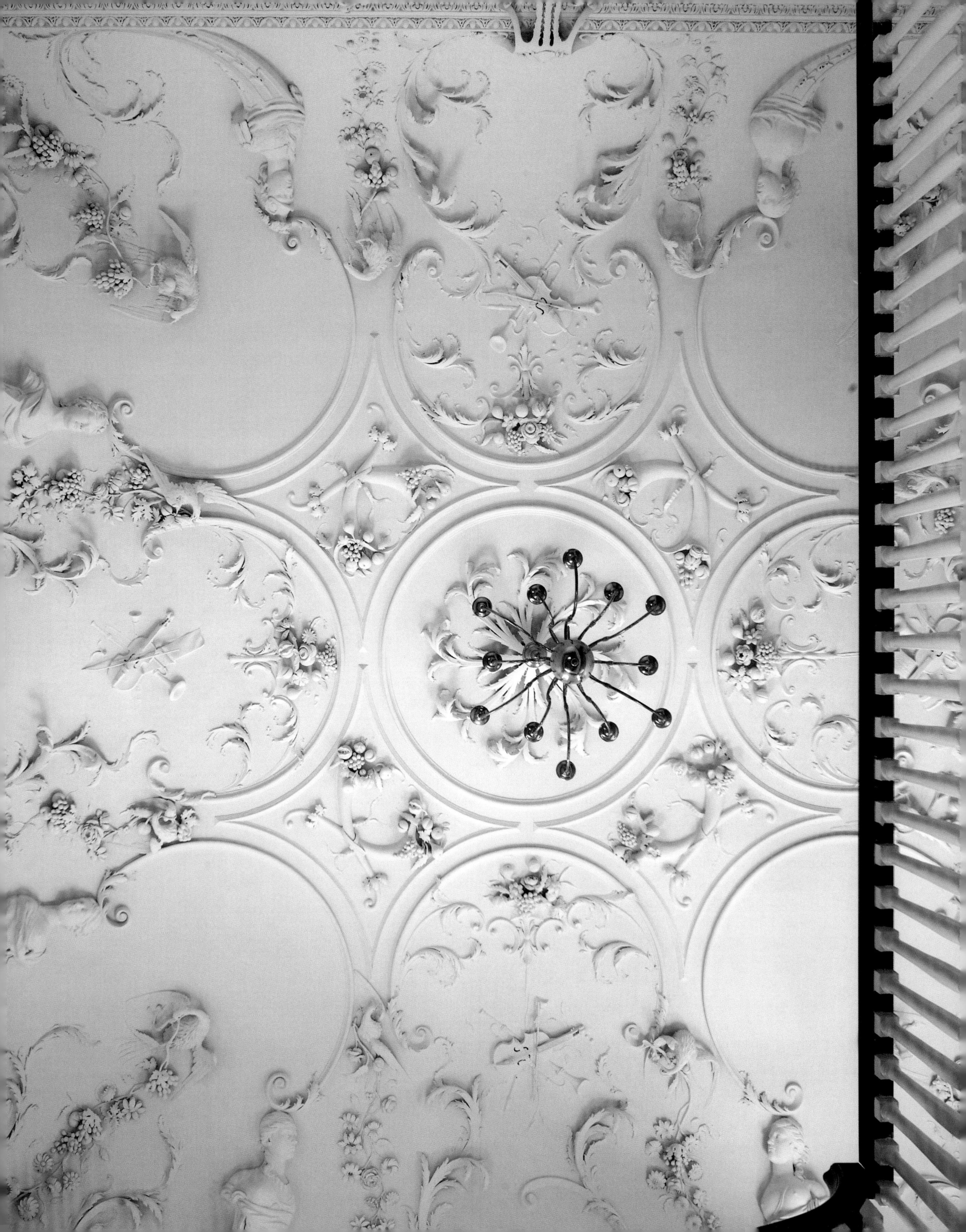

These included, of course, the terrace of houses on Lower Fitzwilliam Street demolished by the ESB in the mid-1960s and, at the conclusion of his speech, the taoiseach received a mediaeval deed and an eighteenth-century map from the Earl of Pembroke; these two items were representative of the extensive archival material relating to the Pembroke/Fitzwilliam estate in Ireland, which the Earl now presented to the National Archives. Mr Bruton was followed by a long list of other speakers including the president of the Royal Institute of the Architects of Ireland, Joan O'Connor, whose conclusions included the argument that 'The planning approach must change – from the pro-development administrative structure which suited the 1960s and 1970s, to an approach which suits the small-scale community-oriented needs of conservation.' She ended by ruefully noting that the government's own recent and much-heralded Arts Plan for 1995–7 had merely made passing reference to architecture, a grave oversight because 'Unless and until architecture and the protection of our architectural heritage are acknowledged as a cornerstone of a developed arts policy, awareness and appreciation of quality in architecture and conservation will not develop, to the detriment of all.'

Among those who also gave papers were Dublin City Architect James Barrett, architectural historian Dr Christine Casey and Dr Edward McParland. The subject of their talks ranged from conservation consultant Nigel Green's discussion on the use of traditional materials for paving, to Cork City Manager Maurice Moloney's report on a policy framework for urban conservation. Dr Jane Fenlon spoke of the Irish Georgian Society's own initiatives in the field of urban restoration. She warned that on occasion the removal of even one building could alter the entire focus of a town and gave a timely warning that, 'Paradoxically, the promise of large sums of money from the European Structural Funds for use on various construction projects in urban areas may in fact hasten the destruction of historic town properties.' Since 1989 these EU funds had part-financed Ireland's National Development Plan (NDP) and their impact on the improvement of state infrastructure over the next twenty years was to be considerable but, as Dr Fenlon had presaged, this would be at a heavy cost to the existing heritage.

Following the February event in Dublin, the Society organized a one-day seminar in Limerick city in September 1995 with the title, 'Limerick's Architecture – The Way Forward'. Limerick is particularly blessed with a large stock of Georgian buildings but these had long been as vulnerable to neglect and demolition as their equivalents in Dublin. The seminar attempted to find new ways to preserve and enhance the city's historic core, with case studies offered from elsewhere. The event coincided with the establishment of a new Limerick Chapter of the Society, which also showed its support for the existing Limerick Civic Trust, which was then restoring No. 2 Pery Square as the Georgian House Project. This received a grant of £7000 from the Society, one of the largest it had given in this period and yet another indication of its growing interest in urban regeneration. (In May 2007, the Society, in association with the city council, held another conference in Limerick on the theme, 'Heritage and Regeneration'.)

The question of urban regeneration had also finally arrived on the Irish political agenda. In February 1996, Fianna Fáil issued a position paper on Georgian Dublin during the

Opposite: 20 Lower Dominick Street, Dublin. The restored Robert West ceiling plasterwork, 1755.

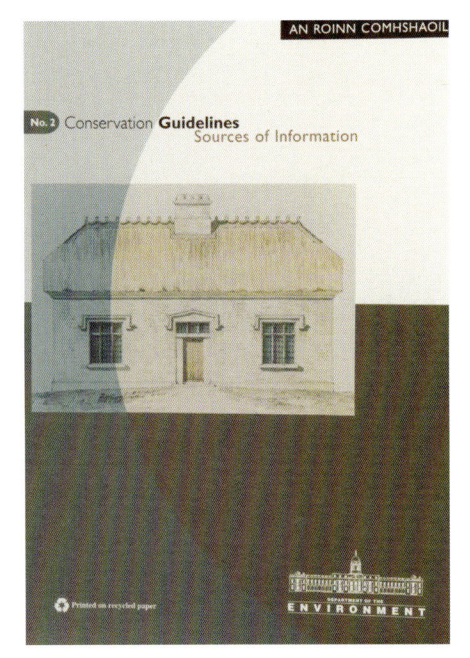

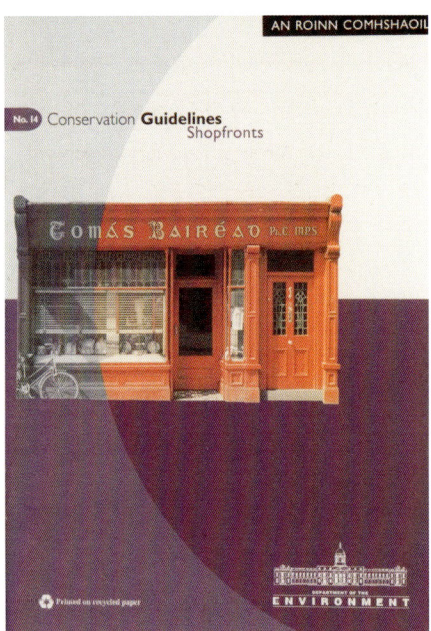

Department of the Environment conservation guideline booklets, which were edited by Mary Bryan, director of the IGS.

formulation of which the Irish Georgian Society had been asked for information and advice. The paper included a number of major commitments should the state's largest party be returned to government (it was not long afterwards, but the promises were not honoured). Of especial interest was a proposal that the capital's core of eighteenth-century building stock should be returned from office use to the originally intended purpose of domestic housing, with Fianna Fáil promising to 'provide a package of tax incentives for refurbishment of Georgian houses for residential purposes', as well as the adaptation of building and fire regulations to take account of the properties' design and character. The party also announced its intention to establish a single office to exercise control, give advice and administer financial aid; the Irish Georgian Society was to be one of the nominating bodies to this office. Naturally the Society welcomed this initiative, commenting at the time that 'too much of the preservation of our stock of Georgian buildings, particularly the squares and streets, is being left to chance and to the goodwill of owners and developers'.

That Fianna Fáil failed to honour its pledges once returned to government is a matter of regret, yet the fact that it had gone to the trouble of producing a paper on Georgian Dublin shows that heritage matters were now of interest to politicians. In fact, the following spring Fianna Fáil's spokesperson for Arts, Culture and Heritage (and subsequently minister for the same), Síle de Valera, produced a wide-ranging paper called 'Caring for our Heritage', in which she stated that her party was 'conscious that there is a need at present for a comprehensive vision of the care and management of heritage for the future'. 'The climate for conservation improves all the time,' remarked the Knight of Glin in the spring 1996 *Newsletter*, citing such instances as the conversion of St Andrew's Church in central Dublin to house offices for Dublin Tourism, the restoration of Limerick's eighteenth-century Custom House for use as the Hunt Museum and, on an even larger scale, the refurbishment of Dublin's Collins Barracks for the National Museum.

In September 1996 the coalition government published a report submitted by the Inter-departmental Working Group on Strengthening the Protection of the Architectural Heritage. The group had been charged with assessing the effectiveness and deficiencies of the existing system to conserve buildings of architectural and heritage interest. Among its sixty-four recommendations were that 'Listing should be a mandatory statutory function of planning authorities'; that 'Buildings should be listed in their entirety, including interior and curtilege'; and that as well as legislation being enacted to oblige owners to maintain listed buildings, 'Permission should be required for any material alteration to a listed building'. There were also further proposals for the improvement of tax relief and for financial incentives. Of course, these were only recommendations and had no legal validity; it would be another three years before a new Planning Act saw at least some of the suggestions become reality. In the meantime, the Department of the Environment issued a series of guideline booklets, the first of their kind developed specifically for Ireland, in the preparation of which the Irish Georgian Society had been closely involved (Mary Bryan edited the work). Each of the sixteen titles had been written by an appropriate expert and though relatively short, contained a great deal of practical advice and information on subjects such as mortars and renders, rising damp and timber decay, and interior joinery.

These publications were soon complemented by the inauguration of the Society's Traditional Building Skills exhibition. Increasingly, the organization had been receiving calls from house owners around the country seeking help in finding specialists for such tasks as the repair of wooden window frames or damaged plaster and brickwork. First held over two days in September 1998 in the eighteenth-century Riding School attached to Collins Barracks, the Traditional Building Skills exhibition featured eighteen areas of expertise ranging from thatching to historic lock repair, as well as restoring old joinery and fanlights, and recreating eighteenth- and nineteenth-century wallpaper. There were also free lectures and a display of items from Peter Pearson's unique collection of architectural salvage. More than 5000 visitors attended the event which, like its successors, received financial assistance from the Heritage Council and the Department of the Environment, as well as a range of other private and public bodies.

Twelve months later, even bigger crowds turned out for a second Traditional Building Skills exhibition staged in Cork with help from the local Civic Trust and Cork Corporation. Highlights this time included traditional signwriting and a forge where the skills of an ironworker were on show. The grounds of Kilkenny Castle was the setting for a third event in September 2000, while the next year the Society arranged to hold its exhibition as part of the main trade fair for the building industry, PlanExpo at the RDS's Simmonscourt Pavilion, the first time a conservation section had featured at the fair. The Society used this occasion to launch its internet service, Traditional Building and Conservation Skills – Register of Practitioners. After the first exhibition, it had put together a listing of those people with the necessary expertise in various restoration techniques and the result, containing some 450 names, was published with help from the Department of the Environment. Its online successor can be found on the Society's website. An invaluable asset to anyone undertaking restoration work on an old property, this regularly updated database contains over 1000 entries from specialists in a wide variety of fields and based throughout the country.

IGS Traditional Building Skills exhibitions.

Left: Eoin O'Donnell, bodger, at Adare 2007.

Middle: David Skinner, historic wallpaper specialist, at Dublin 2006.

Right: Thomas O'Collins, thatcher, at Adare 2007.

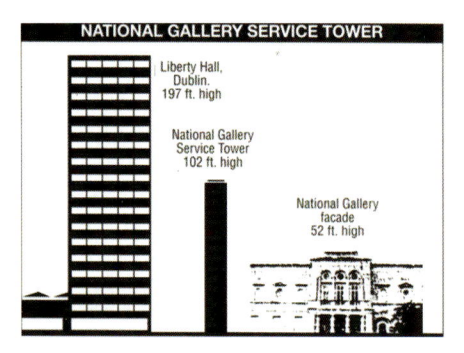

The Society has since organized three further exhibitions (2005, Cork, with Cork City Council; 2006, St Anne's Park, Dublin, with Dublin City Council; 2007, Adare, with Limerick County Council; and 2008, Cuffesgrange, County Kilkenny) allowing interested parties an opportunity to see these skills put into effect at first hand. Equally worthy of mention is the Society's *Catalogue of Irish Theses and Dissertations Pertaining to Architecture and the Allied Arts*, launched in 2005. Devised by the organization's conservation research manager, Emmeline Henderson, and made possible through Heritage Council funding and the cooperation of Ireland's universities both north and south, the catalogue complements the Society's other scholarly initiatives. Acting as an academic research tool, it provides a centralized database of Irish theses and dissertations relating to architecture and the allied arts, which have been submitted as part of an academic qualification awarded on the island of Ireland.

At the same time, the Society has grown steadily more active in monitoring buildings and lands around the state that are at risk from insensitive or inappropriate development. A respondent to the 1994 members' survey had suggested, 'The IGS should make itself more of a watchdog ... and also do slightly more practical work.' From the mid-1990s this increasingly came to be the case, with the Society – through its planning officer – scrutinizing building applications to local authorities whenever the former might impinge in any way on the existing heritage. Sometimes the threat could come from the most unexpected source. The National Gallery of Ireland dates from the 1860s and lies on the west side of Merrion Square where all opportunities for expansion had been exhausted by the late 1960s. Almost thirty years later, the Gallery wished to increase its exhibition space and therefore acquired a site to the immediate north-west with a frontage on Clare Street. In 1996, it held an international competition for the new development, budgeted at £13m., without specifying that the site held an eighteenth-century house with rare Regency ballroom to its rear and that these should be retained.

The commission was duly won by British architects Benson & Forsyth (who had already designed Edinburgh's controversial Museum of Scotland) and their proposal was sanctioned by Dublin Corporation, even though it involved the demolition of the eighteenth-century house and ballroom, and the erection of a 102-foot service tower destined to loom over every other building in the vicinity. The Irish Georgian Society vociferously objected to the project going ahead and in August 1997 demonstrated the reasons for its hostility by flying a commercial balloon over the site at the height of the proposed service tower. Five months later, following an oral hearing, An Bord Pleanála refused planning permission to the scheme on the grounds that the demolition of the old buildings and their replacement with a new structure would materially contravene its policy of protecting the area's architectural and civic design character. The architects were required to come up with a new design that preserved the eighteenth-century house and ballroom (and featured a service tower much reduced in scale) and only then could the National Gallery of Ireland's new Millennium Wing be built.

If one of the country's foremost cultural institutions could attempt to ignore the basic rules of heritage conservation, how much less likely was it that private developers would

Top: IGS Traditional Building Skills exhibition. Andrew Smith, decorative plasterwork restorer, at Cork 2005.

Middle: IGS planning objection balloon, 1997.

Bottom: IGS planning objection drawing, 1997.

show any interest in the subject? Or that they would trouble to think of context when planning a new scheme? This want of consideration for the surrounding environment was epitomized in the 1990s by building company Cosgrave Brothers' attempt to foist a Manhattan-style skyscraper on central Dublin. The two-acre site on George's Quay for which this monster was intended had been assembled twenty years earlier by another business, Irish Life. In 1991 they had been granted a ten-year planning permission by An Bord Pleanála for a group of seven moderately high-rise office blocks.

Six years later, having not acted on the permission, Irish Life sold the land to Cosgrave Brothers, who hired the international architectural practice of Skidmore Owings & Merrill to design another scheme with a central tower rising to almost 100 metres – almost twice the height of Liberty Hall, still the city's tallest building since being built in 1965. It was also more than three times higher than the Custom House, James Gandon's iconic masterpiece, which lay directly opposite on the other side of the Liffey and would be entirely dwarfed were the scheme to have gone ahead. Cosgrave Brothers lodged its planning application with Dublin Corporation in April 1998 and just five months later the authority went against the advice of its own planning officer and granted permission, the only significant proviso being that the central tower be reduced in height from 100 to 80 metres.

Yet another outcry followed this iniquitous decision, with the Irish Georgian Society being one of the principal voices heard raised in disapproval. 'This is probably the most important planning decision made in the history of the State,' commented the autumn 1998 *Newsletter*, 'as, if built, the building will alter forever the historic skyline of Dublin, and change the attractive low-rise ambience of the city completely.' Dublin Corporation's decision to grant permission was appealed by a large number of individuals and organizations, including the Society; there was also strong opposition from local residents. In the United States, the board members of IGS Inc. started a Save Dublin's Skyline fund and this proved of immense value in enabling the Society to put together a detailed and comprehensive appeal for An Bord Pleanála.

That body first requested an Environmental Impact Statement from Cosgrave Brothers and in September 1999, after a four-day oral hearing, turned down the scheme on a number of grounds, not least that it would 'detrimentally affect the historic precincts of the Custom House, Trinity College and the Liffey Quays'. The autumn 1999 *Newsletter* told its readers that 'The Society is naturally delighted, as it had worked hard in opposing the scheme, but the overriding feeling is one of relief – that the future of historic Dublin has been saved – at least from this particularly dangerous threat.' Cosgrave Brothers was forced to revert to the 1991 planning permission and developed the site accordingly with the highest tower rising eleven storeys.

The history of attempts by both the National Gallery of Ireland and the George's Quay developers to ignore issues of heritage and conservation are just two of many from this period. The Society was involved in fights to stop many other insensitive building projects, not least the long struggle to prevent overdevelopment on the north side of the river in an area known as Spencer Dock where, once more, plans were drawn up for buildings totally out of scale with the rest of Dublin. Happily for the

CHAPTER 12

Cleveland Chapter event, 2006.
Left to right: Skip Watts, Eileen Mullally, Dottie McNulty and Nick Sheaff.

capital, in 2000 this proposal was comprehensively turned down by An Bord Pleanála. It is important to emphasize that the Society never opposed high-rise development as a concept, but consistently argued that context needed to be taken into account, pointing out that while Rome and Paris had tall buildings, these were always located well away from the historic city centres.

The organization also objected to many other, albeit smaller speculative building schemes not just in the capital but in other towns and cities, making submissions to the relevant local authorities and where necessary to An Bord Pleanála, being vocal at public oral hearings and, as a result, frequently achieving success. As Mary Bryan notes, although this kind of work was not as overtly exciting as the rescue of individual buildings, it 'showed the Society in a different light from previously. As time went on IGS came to be recognized as a serious player in the game and a new dimension was added to the work of the Society.'

Underlining this nuanced shift in the direction of its work, in 1997 the organization took the decision to make an addition to its title. Ever since, it has been called the Irish Georgian Society, Ireland's Architectural Heritage Society. The Society had for some time shown interest in helping to preserve more than just the architecture of the Georgian period, looking back to the seventeenth century and forward to the nineteenth. Professor Kevin B. Nowlan, then vice-president of the organization, wrote that he felt 'we have to go further and see it as our task to defend examples of good architecture from all periods right down to the present century' and at one point he even suggested the Society's name should be changed completely so that it might become the Irish Architectural Heritage Society. But the Irish Georgian Society was, by now, an established brand with a clear identity and international recognition. Changing its name would have involved a great deal of explanation, especially among supporters outside Ireland for whom the Society had become synonymous with the appreciation of eighteenth-century architecture. Eventually it was deemed best to retain the existing appellation and simply to add a secondary title to explain better the Society's purpose.

Besides, in 1998 the Irish Georgian Society was able to mark forty years of achievement. Anniversary celebrations began in mid-January with a lecture in the Tailors' Hall by Desmond Guinness, who provided a customarily amusing account of activities over the previous four decades. The following month, 170 guests – many of whom had travelled from overseas for the occasion – attended a gala dinner in the King's Inns, which, while highly entertaining, served to raise funds so that the Society's work could go on. Desmond and Penelope Guinness hosted a summer party in the gardens of Leixlip Castle and the Christmas party took place at Dublin Castle. The various Chapters organized their own events, not least London, which in December 1998 held a Ruby Anniversary Ball at 15 Kensington Palace Gardens, formerly the home of Sir Alfred and Lady Beit before they had bought Russborough. But the anniversary programme also contained more serious events, such as the series of lectures on eighteenth-century interiors organized by Dr Edward McParland. While the Society could deservedly congratulate itself on having achieved a great deal since being established in 1958, a great deal more work was needed to protect Ireland's architectural heritage, as the years ahead would show.

CHAPTER 12

Top left (left to right): Deirdre Conroy, Paula Fogarty, Ellen Welsh, Judy Hadlock, Maribeth Welsh.

Middle left (left to right): Ashling Dunne, Doreen McNamara and Aoife Kavanagh.

Bottom left: Victoria Browne.

Bottom centre: Jean Kennedy Smith, US Ambassador to Ireland and Cormac O'Malley.

Top right: Marjorie Malcolm with John O'Brien.

Middle right: Paula Fogarty (left) and Madam Olda FitzGerald.

Bottom right: Emmeline Henderson (left) and Silvie Cahill.

199

IRISH ARCHITECTURAL AND DECORATIVE STUDIES

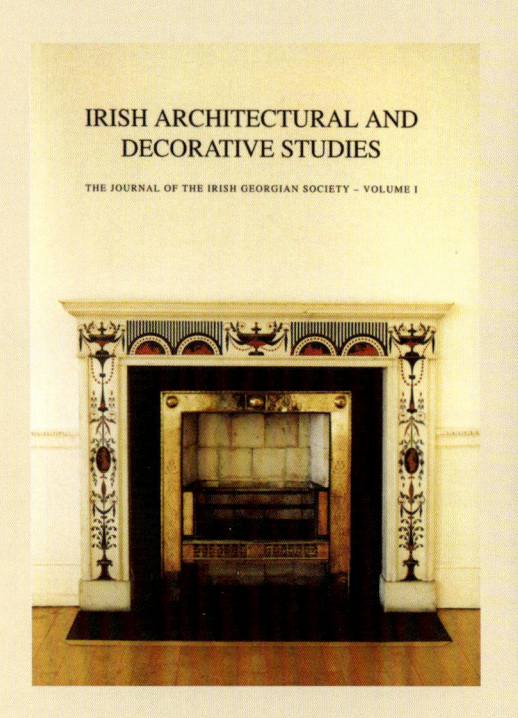

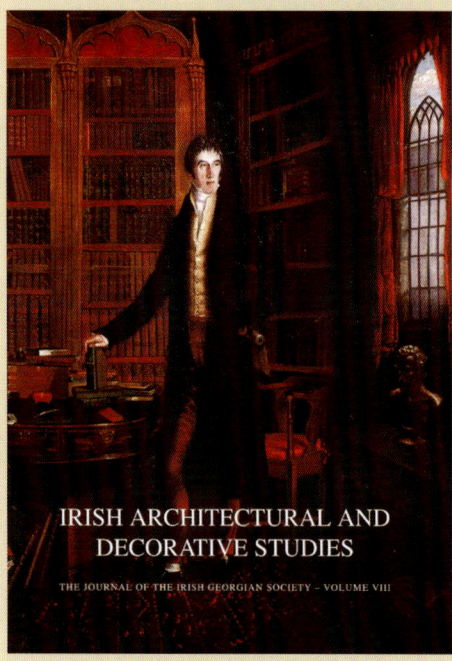

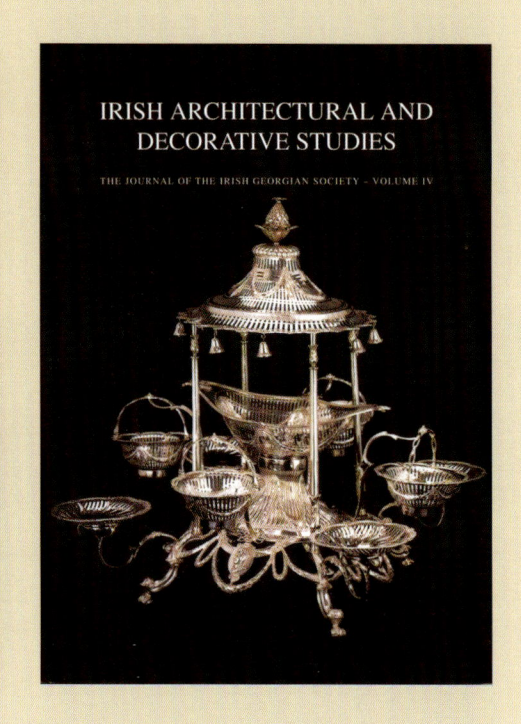

Marking both the Irish Georgian Society's fortieth anniversary, and its widening remit and responsibilities, in 1998 the organization decided to discontinue the *Bulletin*, which had been appearing since 1958. A contents listing of all 113 issues has since been made available on the Society's website (www.IGS.ie) and the full contents can now be found on searchable CD; the latter is invaluable since many of the earliest *Bulletin*s are now extremely rare.

The *Bulletin* was superseded in 1998 by a new annual publication, *Irish Architectural and Decorative Studies*, initially edited by Dr Seán O'Reilly. He was succeeded as editor by Dr Nicola Figgis and since 2005 this role has been filled by William Laffan. The only periodical dedicated to publishing new research on Ireland's architects, craftsmen, artists, garden designers and patrons, *IADS* has never restricted its scope to the Georgian era. The first issue, for example, carried an account by Brendan Rooney of the 1888 Irish Exhibition in London as well as the editor's analysis of George Edmund Street's restoration work on Christ Church, Dublin. An index of the first ten volumes issued in spring 2008 indicated just how diverse the range of subjects has been, from Patricia McCabe's investigation of the accoutrements of the Lords Chancellor of Ireland to Patrick Bowe's study of Irish sporting lodges. Fireworks in Dublin, the arts and crafts movement in Kilkenny, and window tax throughout Ireland: they have all been the subject of essays for *IADS*.

One feature that has remained consistent during the first decade is the very high standard of scholarship provided by all contributors who, through their research, have greatly added to public knowledge of post-mediaeval Irish culture. As William Laffan noted in his introduction to the index, there has always been 'a deliberate policy of encouraging young researchers making their first appearance in print'. Many recipients of the Desmond Guinness Scholarship and prizes have been among the authors to see their work published in *IADS*.

Each submission for inclusion is scrutinized not just by the editor but by a distinguished editorial board and independent experts in the relevant field. Quite rightly, the Knight of Glin could write in his foreword to Volume VIII that, 'The scrupulous scholarship this journal promotes, permeates and informs all aspects of our activities. It is a publication of which the society should be immensely proud.' Volume X was dedicated to the Knight for his seventieth birthday.

From the beginning, the journal's high production standards have required that it be in receipt of sponsorship. This has come from a number of different sources, more recently from the J. Paul Getty Jr Charitable Trust and the estate of the late Paul Mellon. Assistance was also provided by The Ireland Funds, Mark Fitch Fund, Esmé Mitchell Trust and the Schools of Irish Studies Foundation. An anonymous Irish benefactor has already agreed to sponsor the 2008 and 2009 volumes. Although as yet only a quarter of the *Bulletin*'s age, *Irish Architectural and Decorative Studies* has already proven itself a worthy successor, however, funding is needed to continue the journal's publication.

Irish Architectural and Decorative Studies' tenth-anniversary launch at Mahaffy House, 38 North Great George's Street, Dublin, restored by Desiree Shortt.

Top left: Robert O'Byrne (left); Madam Olda FitzGerald; William Laffan, editor of *IADS*.

Top right: Paul Getty, one of the sponsors of *IADS*.

Middle left: Donough Cahill (left), director of the IGS; Desiree Shortt; Dr Edward McParland.

Bottom left: Irish Architectural and Decorative Studies, Vol. II cover.

Bottom right: Irish Architectural and Decorative Studies, Vol. V cover.

Opposite: Irish Architectural and Decorative Studies replaced the IGS *Bulletin* in 1998. It is dedicated to publishing new research.

Opposite left: Vol. I cover.
Opposite middle: Vol. VIII cover.
Opposite right: Vol. IV cover.

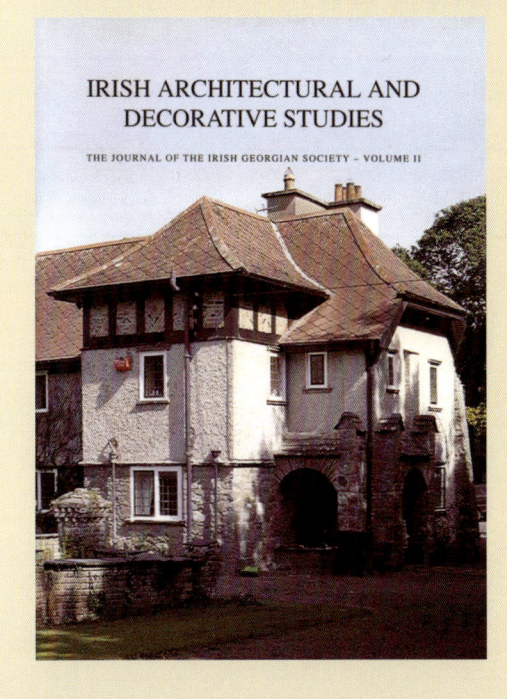

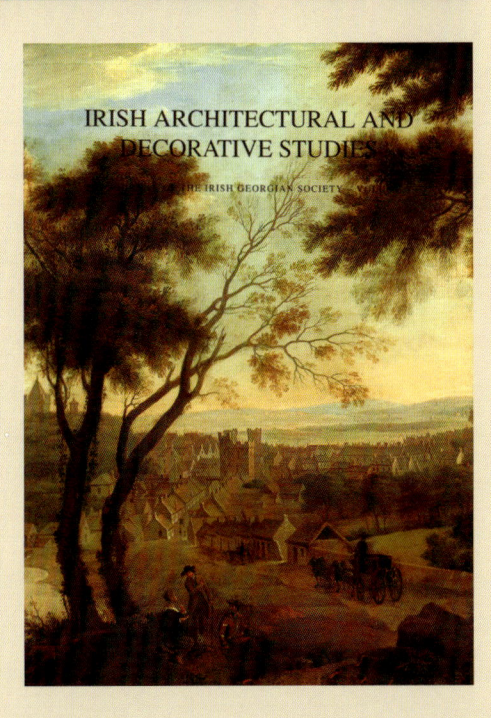

20 LOWER DOMINICK STREET

20 Lower Dominick Street Dublin, decorative plasterwork by Robert West.

Dominick Street derives its name from Sir Christopher Dominick, a physician who in 1709 bought the land on which it stands, built himself a large house there and then leased an adjoining plot to Lady Alice Hine. The rest of the street's houses were only gradually built but by 1785 its residents included two peers and six members of parliament. As Christine Casey has noted, until 1957, this was the grandest surviving Georgian street north of the Liffey, but many of the properties had become fetid tenements and were demolished by Dublin Corporation; of the sixty-six houses recorded in 1938 only ten now remain. The most splendid of these is No. 20 Lower Dominick Street, double the size of its neighbours and one of a number built by the eighteenth-century Irish stuccodore Robert West who sold it to the Hon. Robert Marshall in 1760. In the middle of the nineteenth century the house became a school for the Parish of St Mary and from 1927 onwards it was an orphanage for boys. More recently it has been occupied by the National Youth Federation.

Somehow, through the various changes of ownership and use, No. 20 managed to retain its flamboyant interiors concealed behind a typically plain brick facade of five bays relieved only by a cut-stone Doric doorcase. It remains unclear whether Robert West or someone in his employ was responsible for the decoration of the house's stair-hall, a rococo riot of three-dimensional birds, fruit and flowers, busts and musical instruments, which cover the walls and ceiling in an unparalleled display of the stuccoworker's art. More virtuosity can be found inside the first-floor reception rooms, which, while less overtly exuberant, are more accomplished and lighter in their design and execution. Once again there are birds, fruit and foliage on display as well as an abundance of playful putti.

Although still reasonably intact, by the close of the last century these theatrical spaces were in need of substantial restoration if they were to survive another 200 years. Successive coats of paint had dulled the plasterwork's finer details and it was necessary to strip off the accretions before the whole scheme could be returned to its former splendour. In 1994 the Irish Georgian Society began its association with No. 20 Lower Dominick Street by providing funds so that inappropriate aluminium window frames could be replaced by timber windows with the correct proportions. Beginning in 1997 and together with the Department of the Environment and the Heritage Council, the Society continued to raise money for a meticulous restoration of the reception rooms, starting with the front saloon, and the stair-hall. Repair and restoration of the brick facade and limestone doorcase took place in 1998. By 2002 work had commenced on the plasterwork of the ground-floor rooms. Between 1995 and 2002, the Society contributed over €140,000 towards the restoration of No. 20 Lower Dominick Street. The house continues to be maintained by the National Youth Federation. It is hoped that the rococo carved overdoors, which the Society owns, will be restored to the first-floor drawing room.

Top left: Decorative plasterwork during restoration.

Top: Decorative plasterwork detail.

Middle: 18th-century houses on east side of Dominick Street, Dublin. Demolition in progress, *circa* 1958.

Bottom: East side of Dominick Street, Dublin. After demolition *circa* 1958.

The 2000 Planning and Development Act ~ Ireland's economic boom: the advantages and disadvantages to architectural heritage ~ the Society begins monitoring planning applications ~ further grants and support ~ the Irish Heritage Trust ~ Panels: Headfort and the YIGs

CHAPTER

13

In late 1999, the Irish government enacted a Planning and Development Act that addressed many of the concerns raised by the Society over previous decades. It was, without doubt, a major step forward in the protection of the national built heritage, with money allocated to all local authorities for the distribution of conservation grants within their areas and, even more importantly, for the provision of conservation officers within each authority. A number of such officers had, in fact, already been appointed and were of enormous value since few, if any, authorities had much expertise in conservation. Inevitably, these new powers would lead to a corresponding increase in the workload of local government, especially in the areas of listing and enforcement.

In many respects, the Planning and Development Act, which came into effect on 1 January 2000, deserved a warm welcome from anyone interested in the preservation of Ireland's architectural heritage; owners of buildings listed for protection, for example, could no longer simply allow them to fall into ruin. There were, however, some elements of the legislation that caused justifiable anxiety. In what was presumably an effort to speed up an already cumbersome planning process, the new legislation deprived a third party of the right of appeal to An Bord Pleanála, unless that party had already made a submission when the initial application was being dealt with at local authority level. This meant that if an individual or organization only became aware of a planning issue at appeal stage, it would be too late to do anything. In addition, whereas hitherto all third-party submissions to a local authority had been free, from now on they carried a charge of £20 each (now €20). Meanwhile, an appeal to An Bord Pleanála also comes with a fee, currently standing at €220, although for a fee of €50 it is possible to send a submission in support of an existing appeal.

These elements of the new Act, especially the imposition of fees, undoubtedly served as a deterrent against private individuals and voluntary organizations participating in the active protection of the national heritage, not least because their financial resources would be considerably smaller than those of a property developer. Regular submissions to local authorities and An Bord Pleanála became a costly affair and a drain on the funds of the Irish Georgian Society. In an effort to reduce such costs by directing appeals to the local authority, the spring 2002 *Newsletter* advised members that 'extra vigilance is needed by all – please read planning notices posted in your area, and act immediately on conservation planning issues that may arise'.

In October 2002 the Society, in association with the Royal Institute of the Architects of Ireland, held a one-day conference at the Royal Hospital, Kilmainham, to discuss the consequences of the Planning Act and in particular that part of it that dealt with the protection of the built heritage. The 160 attendees were told that a problem had already arisen with the implementation of the Act owing to a reduction of 45 per cent since 2000 in the level of government funding for conservation grants to local authorities. Even the money originally allocated for this purpose – £4m. – was inadequate, so a cut of this magnitude had catastrophic consequences and made a nonsense of the Act's intentions. By 2004, it had only crept up to €3.9m. and, observed that summer's *Newsletter*, 'When one considers the number of local authorities in the country amongst which this sum is to be divided and then assesses the cost of undertaking repairs to a solitary leaky roof, it is clear that these funds cannot have any great impact on the actual requirements.'

Furthermore by this date many local authorities still had to acquire the necessary staff and skills to ensure the preservation of the built heritage under their control. As County Longford's senior planner, Domnall Mac An Bheatha, explained at the October 2002 conference, the compiling of a record of protected structures, the issuing of relevant declarations to this effect and then enforcing the legislation placed an enormous burden on local authorities, which were already struggling to manage with inadequate funding from central government. In 2004 the Society's planning officer (and now executive director), Donough Cahill, discovered that several local authorities had lost, and not replaced, their conservation officers and that the position of heritage officers was also at risk in a number of instances; government restrictions on employment in the public services meant that when someone left a post, it often had to remain vacant.

These problems were exacerbated by an economic boom – the so-called Celtic Tiger – that Ireland experienced from the mid-1990s onwards. Over a ten-year period, the country was transformed from one of the poorest in Western Europe into one of the richest; from 1994 to 2000, the GNP growth rate averaged 7 per cent and after a dip at the start of the new millennium returned to an average of 5 per cent. Unemployment fell from 18 per cent in the late 1980s to 3.5 per cent, the average industrial salary grew

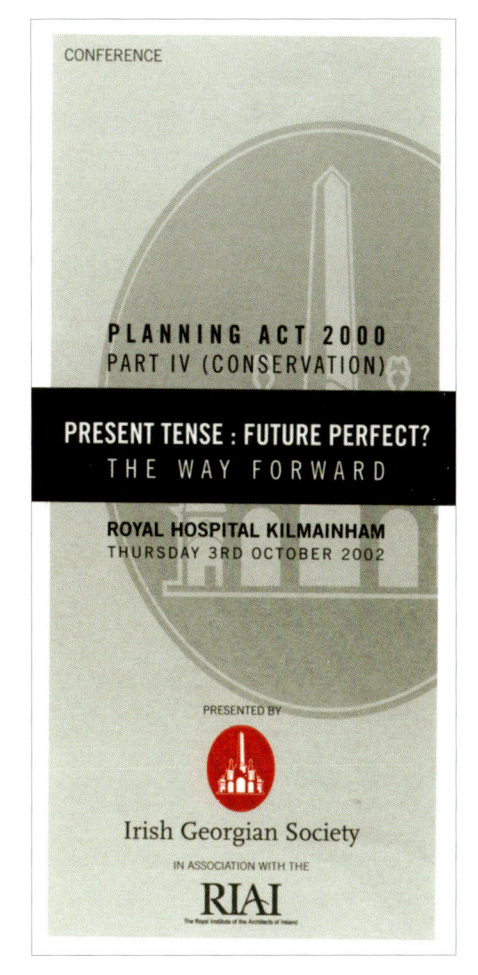

IGS conference in association with the Royal Institute of Architects of Ireland on the 2000 Planning Act at the Royal Hospital Kilmainham, Dublin.

to being one of the highest in Europe, income tax was lowered and disposable income correspondingly increased. One of the main beneficiaries of the boom was Ireland's construction industry and while it delivered many jobs and prosperity for a portion of the citizenry, as ever this came at a price. 'Develop, develop, develop – this seems to be the order of the day everywhere,' observed the Society's spring 1999 *Newsletter*, before enquiring, 'But at what cost? In towns and cities, back gardens are being covered with city dwellings, every spare piece of land being built on; the open spaces, small and large, vital to the wellbeing of the urban environment are being closed off one by one.'

The example of Kilkenny city was cited. Trumpeted as Ireland's 'finest mediaeval city' and home to the Heritage Council, nevertheless Kilkenny suffered from insensitive development that threatened to destroy its traditional character. 'It is a very short-sighted policy,' remarked the *Newsletter*, 'and Kilkenny is certainly not the only place where this is happening in these days of economic boom, but the greater the treasure, the greater the loss.' The following *Newsletter* aptly quoted Maynooth historian John Bradley's response to those developers and speculators inclined to refer to an individual's property rights enshrined in the Irish Constitution. 'I cannot believe,' said Mr Bradley, 'that our Constitution was passed in order that a few people could make a lot of money out of impoverishing the lives of so many.'

Throughout this period the preservation of Ireland's architectural heritage was exposed to several serious threats, the first being that all over the country developers were buying perfectly sound Georgian, Victorian and Edwardian properties and seeking to demolish them so as to cover the site with as many smaller houses and apartments as it could hold. The fact that many of these buildings were not yet listed as a protected structure by the relevant local authority made fighting to save them that much more difficult. But particularly in urban areas, even when the original building was allowed, or legally required, to remain, its surrounding grounds were vulnerable to rampant overdevelopment. Inappropriate development within the curtilege of protected structures – although supposedly covered under the terms of the Planning and Development Act – was especially problematic in cities such as Dublin, Cork, Limerick and Galway. Speculative builders, should their initial proposal be turned down, were prepared to submit another while leaving the original house to fall into disrepair. Shortage of money meant the local authority might not have sufficient staff to enforce the legislation.

Another persistent problem has been the construction of large-scale housing developments on the outskirts of established towns and villages, the former taking no account of the latter's character or history. Particularly in coastal areas, such developments were encouraged by favourable tax-incentive schemes for buyers and as a result large parts of certain counties such as Donegal, Wexford and Kerry that had previously been renowned for their natural scenic beauty were despoiled and many of their smaller towns ruined. Two other issues that were not addressed by government at either national or local level were ribbon development on the outskirts of existing urban settlements and the excessive number of permissions granted for one-off housing in what was supposed to be undeveloped countryside. 'New housing may be needed,' commented the spring 2001 *Newsletter*, 'but the siting and density should take into account the historic landscapes, seascapes and streetscapes involved and be part of a strategic overall plan to provide housing for locals and not just for the profit-making development of holiday homes.'

Counties surrounding Dublin such as Louth, Wicklow, Carlow, Meath and Westmeath have also been adversely affected by poorly conceived and executed housing developments to cater for commuters eager to own their own homes but unable to afford the capital's prices. Towns 80 km or more away from central Dublin now have large dormitory suburbs populated by workers who throng the roads every morning and evening, not least because Ireland's public transport system has been consistently under-resourced and unable to keep pace with housing development. On the other hand, the same has not been true of the national road network, which has benefited from substantial government funding and the vigorous policies of the National Roads Authority.

In this body's rush to improve the state of Irish roads and build more motorways, scant attention was paid to the built heritage. 'As a result of what appears to be a rather piecemeal and incomplete approach by the NRA' to this matter, the Society declared itself in the autumn 2001 *Newsletter* to have 'the pessimistic view that a lot of damage and destruction will have been needlessly inflicted on our landscape and heritage if an overall strategic policy is not put in place at once.' Local authorities were frequently guilty of the same offence.

In 2001, for example, Galway County Council considered running two roads through the grounds of Tulira Castle, a protected structure and once family home of Edward Martyn, one of the founders of Ireland's National Theatre. This proposal did not go ahead (mainly owing to concerns over a turlough at Cook Park and the presence of a bat colony, rather than over Tulira's tower house and Victorian mansion), but more recently Kerry County Council adopted a proposal to run a new ring road through the historic demesne of Kilcoleman – described by historian Roy Foster as 'a Claudean landscape of extraordinary beauty' – thereby separating the town of Milltown from the adjacent remains of a fourteenth-century Augustinian priory and allowing for the construction of new housing units on the priory side of the ring road.

The planning process in County Kerry was the subject of an editorial in *The Irish Times* at the beginning of February 2007: 'Our traditional landscape is being transformed by unsuitable developments and by one-off housing ... A halt must be called. We are no longer an impoverished society. The time when development, any development, was a welcome occurrence in rural Ireland has long gone. We must take steps to protect areas of particular beauty and, through them, the tourism industry.' And yet perversely, it was on behalf, and with the encouragement of the tourism industry that certain areas of particular beauty around Ireland were forever destroyed.

Theoretically, the expansion of the golf industry with its attendant increase in the number of courses (their number effectively doubled to 470 in the twenty years up to 2007) should have been welcomed. However, several of these courses were developed on the site of parklands that had been laid out in the eighteenth and nineteenth

Kilcoleman, Co. Kerry.

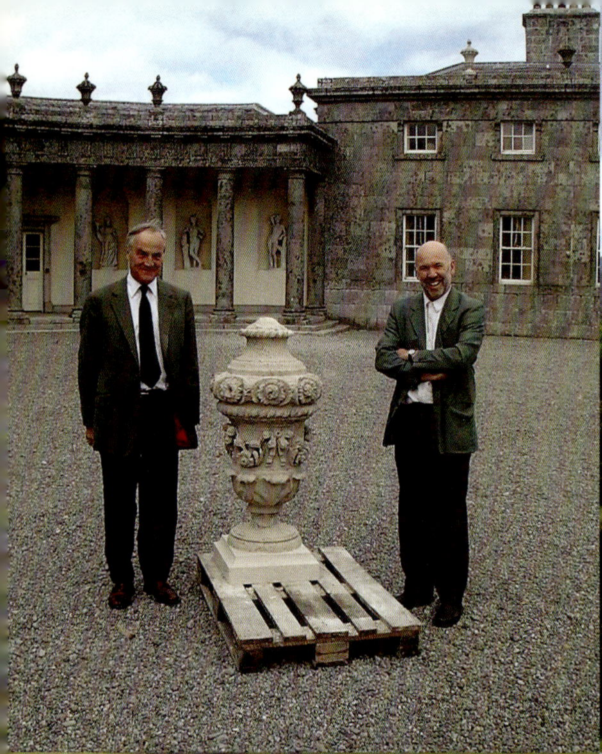
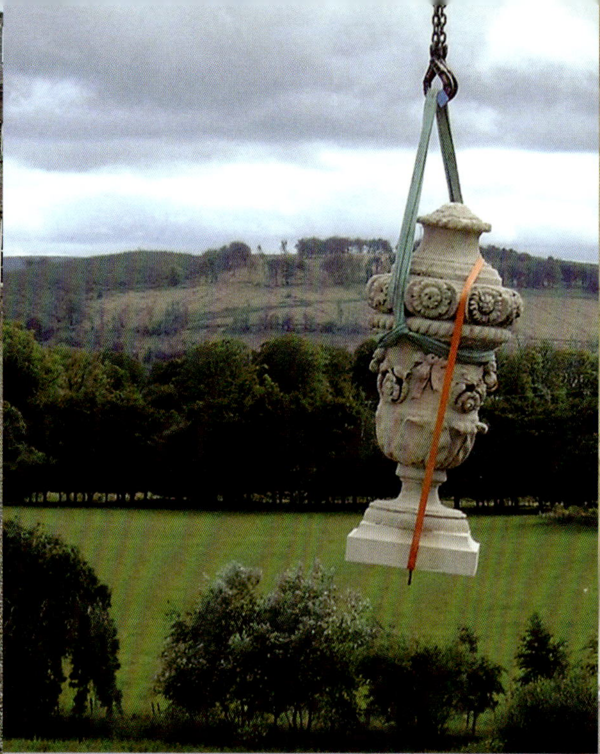
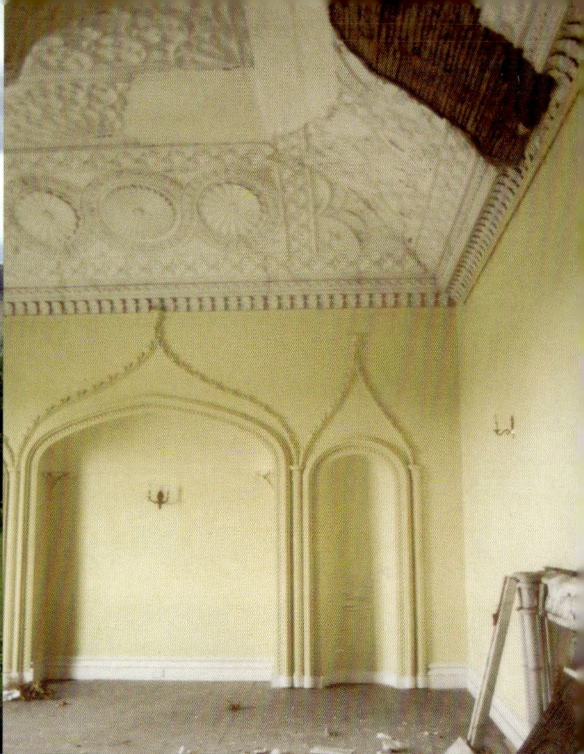
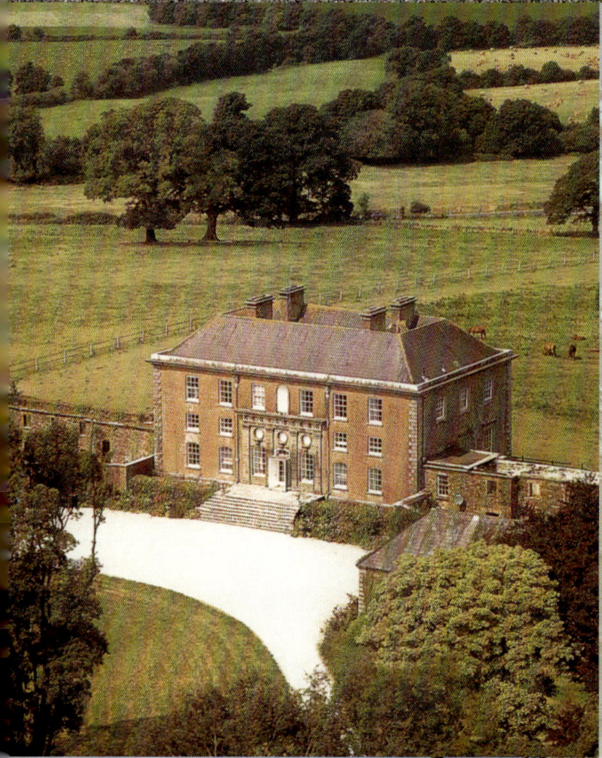
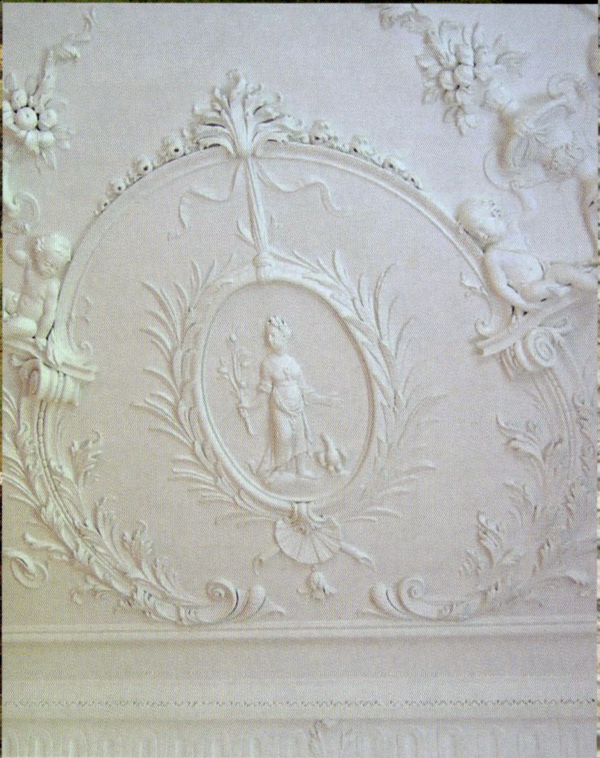
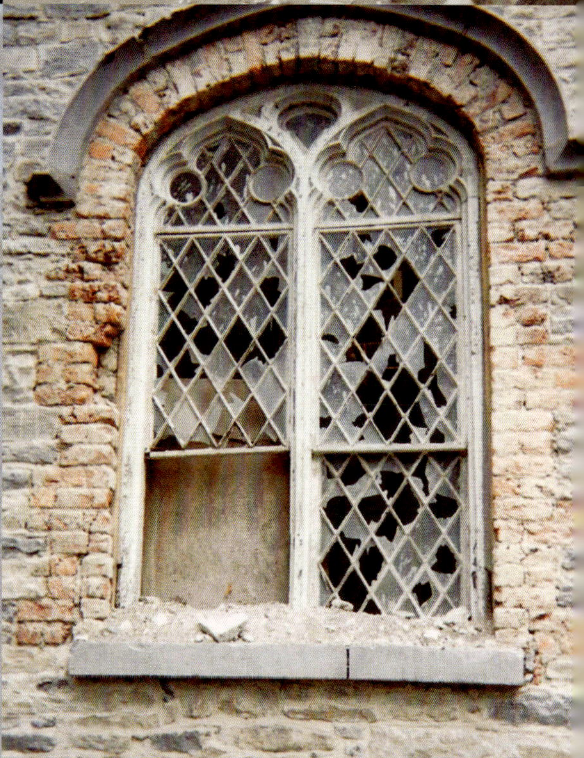
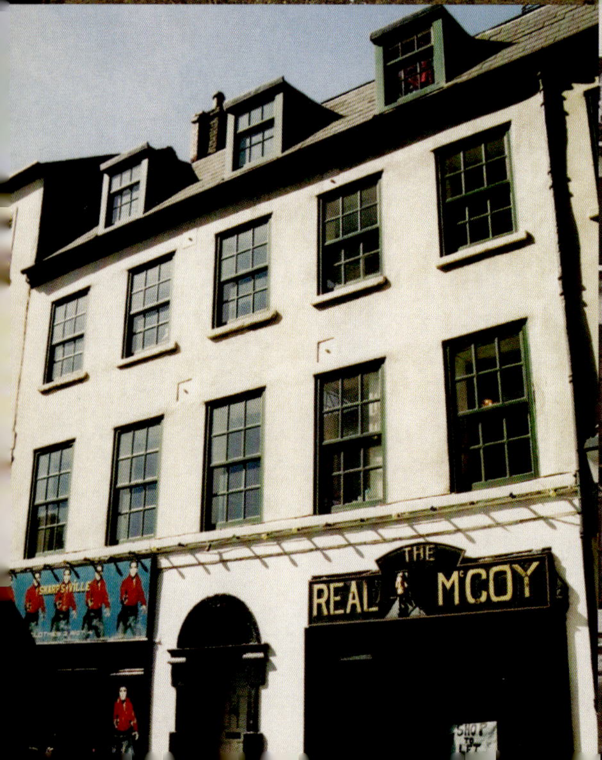
THE
REAL McCOY
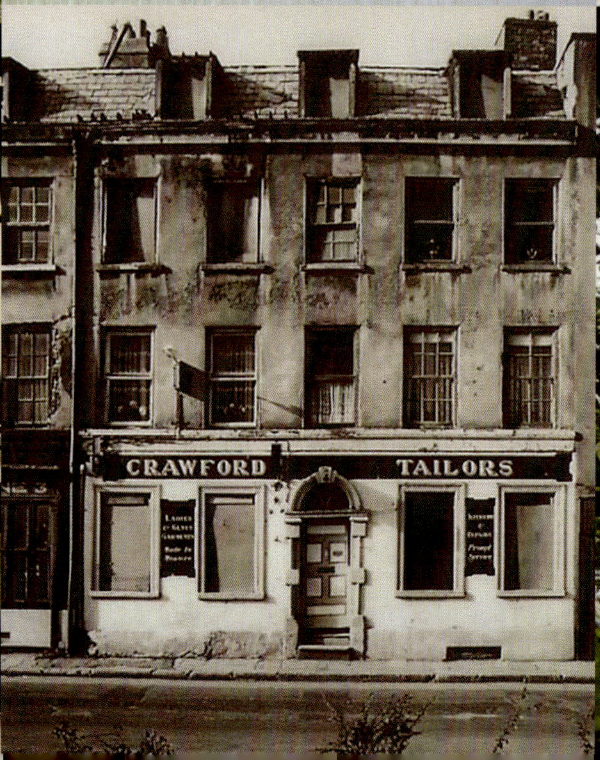
CRAWFORD
TAILORS
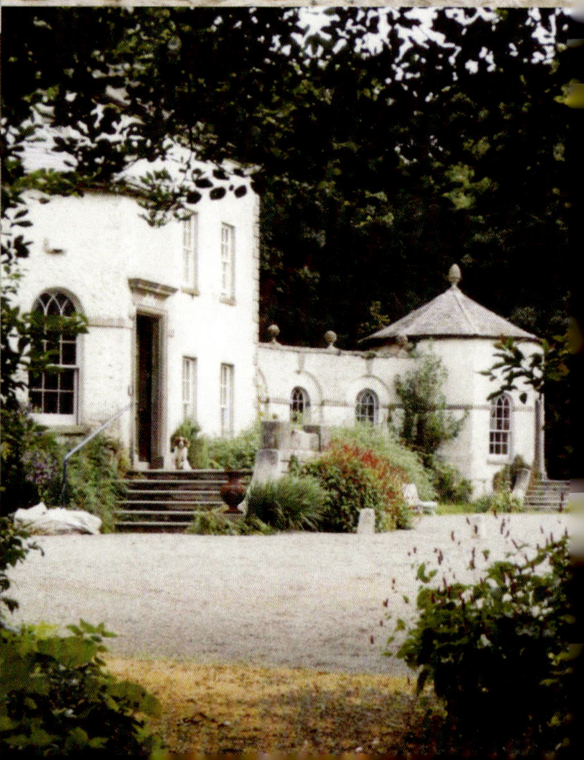

CHAPTER 13

OPPOSITE:

Top left: Russborough, Co. Wicklow. Adrian Masterson (left), IGS benefactor, and architect James Howley.

Middle left: Kilshannig, Co. Cork, pavilion restoration.

Bottom left: Fownes Street, Dublin, after restoration.

Top centre: Russborough, Co. Wicklow, restored urn being hoisted into position.

Middle centre: Kilshannig, Co. Cork, decorative plasterwork after restoration.

Bottom centre: Fownes Street, Dublin, before restoration.

Top right: Annesbrook, Co. Meath. Ballroom plasterwork before restoration.

Middle right: Window of St Mary's Church, Thomastown, Co. Kilkenny, before restoration. Built in 1809, it lay dormant until purchased in 2003.

Bottom right: Hamwood, Co. Meath, sash windows restored with Irish Georrgian Society funding.

ABOVE:

Annesbrook, Co. Meath. Ballroom chimney piece damaged by falling plaster and later restored by IGS. Sasha (left) and Louis McElveen.

209

centuries and preserved ever since; in this respect the greatest loss was the demesne at Carton, County Kildare, which had been planned by the first Duke and Duchess of Leinster but now contains not one but two golf courses. At least the Leinsters' former home at Carton has been sensitively restored but the same cannot be said of many other historic houses, which, as part of Ireland's economic boom, were converted into hotels, most frequently with the addition of large bedroom extensions to the main building as well as holiday homes in the surrounding estate.

Among the worst offenders in this respect are Mount Juliet in County Kilkenny, Farnham in County Cavan and Lough Rynn in County Leitrim. Others are already planned on such historic demesnes as Killeen, County Meath and Humewood, County Wicklow. In November 2005 An Taisce's heritage officer Ian Lumley had produced *Updated Report on Developments Affecting Historic Houses, Gardens and Demesnes* in which he cited the adverse effect of hotel and golf-course development on sixty-five properties around the country. While it might be thought advantageous that this change of use has saved a building of architectural significance, in practice few of these conversions have been executed with any attempt to preserve the house in its correct context or even to engage in a proper process of restoration. Though they remain standing, they have, in effect, been lost.

Since the mid-1990s the Irish Georgian Society has done its best to watch planning applications carefully and to lodge an objection whenever necessary. But the sheer scale of the economic and building boom made it difficult for any organization, let alone a small voluntary body funded by members' donations, to keep an eye on everything that was happening right around the country. Furthermore it has to be noted that successive Irish governments from the early 1960s onwards have looked favourably on the construction industry because of its ability to provide employment and have therefore done little to curb this industry's excesses. As has already been observed, the government has been far less reliable in its support for conservation. Given the continuing inadequacy of conservation grants available from local authorities, the Irish Georgian Society did its best to provide financial assistance to owners of historic buildings who wished to embark on their properties' restoration. Thanks to the generosity of American supporters and donors, to a number of bequests and to money provided by the American Ireland Fund, since 2000 the Society has been able to award larger grants than had ever been the case before. The recipients of this aid were spread throughout the country and were extremely varied in character, as the few now mentioned will indicate.

In 2001, for example, the Society gave £25,000 to St Peter's Church, Drogheda, County Louth, a handsome Georgian building of national importance that had been badly damaged by an arson attack on its interior. That same year, £10,000 was given to Annamore, County Kerry, a rare two-storey seventeenth-century vernacular farm dwelling. As a reflection of the increasing diversity of the Society's grant-giving, the National School in Farnham, County Cavan (designed in the 1820s by Francis Johnston), should be mentioned. It received funds in 2006 for the restoration of the building's windows as did Sligo's Methodist Church and another late-seventeenth-century farmhouse, Coolross, in Roscrea, County Tipperary. Money was raised among the transatlantic membership to pay for the restoration of the only extant Georgian garden in Merrion Square, at No. 63, which is home to the Royal Society of Antiquaries of Ireland.

The previous year funds were provided to help with the restoration of the Obelisk at Killua, County Westmeath (erected in 1810 and believed to commemorate the planting of the first potato in Ireland by Sir Walter Raleigh), as well as for a conservation report on the Lurganboy Mill in County Cavan. So that the Society could expand its work in the area of conservation, in October 2003 Emmeline Henderson (who had previously worked with the Dublin Civic Trust) was appointed as conservation research manager. Since then she has played a central role in providing conservation advice to the public and Society members alike, primarily through the organization of the recent Traditional Building Skills exhibitions and seminars, the maintenance of the Traditional Building Skills and Conservation Register of Practitioners, and the publication of conservation advice articles that respond to members' frequently asked conservation queries.

The Society's diligence in fighting to preserve Ireland's built heritage over almost five decades was recognized by a number of awards it received during this time. In March 2000 the philanthropic Alfred Toepfer Foundation of Hamburg awarded its annual European Prize for the Preservation of Historic Monuments to the Irish Georgian Society. In its citation, the foundation acknowledged that the Society had 'managed to salvage many buildings and ensembles, and also influenced in an exemplary manner the development of both urban and rural architecture'. The following year Desmond Guinness was presented with the Eire Society of Boston's Gold Medal; previous recipients of this honour include poet and Nobel Laureate Seamus Heaney, Senator George Mitchell, film director John Huston and Northern Ireland politician John Hume. Even more significantly, in 2006 Desmond Guinness was presented with the European Union Prize for Cultural Heritage/the Europa Nostra Award for Dedicated Service to Heritage Conservation.

Above: Minister for Foreign Affairs Dermot Ahern TD and the Department of Foreign Affairs hosted a reception to celebrate the Hon. Desmond Guinness receiving the European Union Prize for Cultural Heritage/Europa Nostra Award for dedicated service to Heritage Conservation. *Left to right:* The Earl of Rosse, Consuelo O'Connor and the Hon. Desmond Guinness.

Left: The Hon. Desmond Guinness receiving the European Prize for Cultural Heritage/ Europa Nostra Award from Queen Sofia of Spain in Madrid, 27 June 2006.

CHAPTER 13

Nominated by long-standing Society member Consuelo O'Connor (an elected council member of Europa Nostra since 1993), Desmond Guinness's nomination was supported by three letters of recommendation from the Earl of Rosse, Bonnie Burnham (president of the World Monuments Fund) and the taoiseach, Bertie Ahern. The last of these wrote, 'For over two centuries the Guinness family has made a most important contribution to the quality of life of Irish citizens in the industrial, philanthropic and cultural spheres, none more so than Desmond who is a worthy successor in this tradition. I very much hope that his candidature for this prestigious prize will be successful.' It was successful and, on 27 June 2006, Desmond Guinness received his medal in Madrid from Queen Sofia of Spain. The following October the government hosted a reception for him at Iveagh House (once home to his great-grandfather, the first Earl of Iveagh). In the house's ballroom, Minister of State Noel Treacy enumerated the many achievements of the Society's founder, concluding that 'Desmond Guinness has shown Ireland that our architectural heritage is of international importance ... the presence here of so many friends of his and the Irish Georgian Society is a testament of that achievement.'

But there was a limit to what both Desmond Guinness and the Irish Georgian Society could achieve without state support. This was especially the case with regard to Ireland's greatest country houses, of which fewer and fewer survived with their contents intact because of escalating maintenance costs and inadequate financial help from the government. The Society did what it could, and indeed does so still. Most recently, for instance, it has provided funding to two very important houses, Barmeath, County Louth and Kilshannig, County Cork. Barmeath is a mediaeval castle greatly remodelled and enlarged over hundreds of years but always occupied by the Bellew family, who came to Ireland with Henry II in the twelfth century.

Of late the Society has grant-aided essential works to repair the conical roof of the house's south tower; this will ensure the protection of a Gothic vaulted ceiling beneath a garden room on the ground floor. Kilshannig has been known to Desmond Guinness since the mid-1950s when he and his first wife Mariga considered buying the Davis Duckart-designed Palladian house. Kilshannig's wings and domed pavilions were unroofed at the beginning of the twentieth century, but the present owners Hugo and Elaine Merry have embarked on an ambitious programme to restore these sections of their home. Spring 2008 saw the reinstatement of the copper-clad domes and cupolas. The Society had previously assisted work at Kilshannig with a grant towards conservation work in the main house where the Lafranchini ceilings were at risk of collapse.

The Society is committed to continuing such assistance as its funds allow. However, it has consistently argued that the Irish Republic needs an organization similar in character and purpose to Britain's National Trust, a body capable of taking on and managing historic properties with their contents and demesnes kept intact in perpetuity. The new millennium finally saw just such a trust established, its origins lying in approaches made directly by the taoiseach, Mr Ahern, to one of the Society's members (and now a member of its committee of management), Sir David Davies. A memorandum on the subject was then prepared for civil servants

Belfast Building Preservation Trust Award to Desmond FitzGerald, Knight of Glin. *Left to right:* Desmond FitzGerald, Knight of Glin; Madam Olda FitzGerald; Dick Roche, Minister of the Department of Heritage Local Government; Fionnala Jay O'Boyle; Nick Sheaff, October 2006.

in the relevant departments but, inevitably, progress was slow. In 2002 Sir David agreed to commission a report on the built heritage of Ireland, on the understanding this would be a 50/50 partnership between government and the private sector. The taoiseach accepted this and nominated Dúchas (now merged with the Department of Environment, Heritage and Local Government) as the government sponsor. In turn Sir David nominated the Irish Georgian Society for the private sector and underwrote the latter's costs.

In consultation with the Knight of Glin, it was decided to invite Dr Terence Dooley, an historian based at NUI Maynooth, to author this report following the successful publication in 2001 of his book, *The Decline of the Big House in Ireland*. This task was approved with enthusiasm by Professor Vincent Comerford, Professor of History at Maynooth. In 2003 Dr Dooley organized a one-day conference at Maynooth, 'The Irish Country House: Its Past, Present and Future'. The success of that event led to it being established on an annual basis and spread over two days, with authorities from both home and abroad discussing how best to preserve this critical element of Ireland's architectural heritage.

The latest 'Historic Houses of Ireland' conference took place in mid-June 2008, with Dr Toby Barnard as its keynote speaker. A further development took place in September 2004 with the establishment of the Centre for the Study of Historic Irish Houses and Estates, attached to the Department of Modern History at Maynooth University. A public–private venture sponsored by the Office of Public Works and a number of private benefactors, including the Irish Georgian Society, the centre is co-ordinated by Dr Dooley. One of its main aims is to enhance public awareness of the heritage importance of historic houses through education at tertiary and secondary level. In co-operation with the Department of Computer Science, the centre has created an expanding database of available information on Irish houses and estates, including texts and illustrations of all kinds, as well as comprehensive

CHAPTER 13

Top left (left to right): Dr Terence Dooley, An Taoiseach Bertie Ahern TD and Desmond FitzGerald, Knight of Glin, at the 3rd annual 'Historic Houses and Estates of Ireland' conference where the taoiseach announced the establishment of the new Heritage Trust, September 2005.

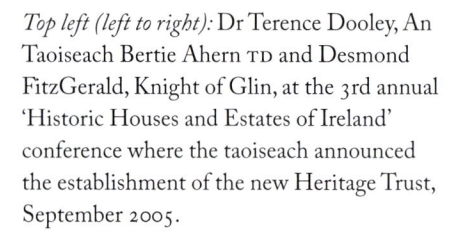

Bottom left (left to right): Dr Terence Dooley; An Taoiseach Bertie Ahern TD; Niall Cullen, Secretary of the General Department of the Environment Heritage and Local Government; Sir David Davies, at 20 Lower Dominick Street, Dublin, September 2003, the launch of *A Future for Historic Houses? A study of 50 Irish Houses*, by Dr Terence Dooley.

Right (left to right): Minister Martin Cullen TD; Mary Bryan, chief executive of the IGS; Desmond FitzGerald, Knight of Glin.

bibliographies of primary and secondary sources available for each property. This will be an invaluable reference resource for those interested in any aspect of historic-house or landed-estate life.

Meanwhile, September 2003 saw the launch of Dr Dooley's report entitled *A Future for Irish Historic Houses?* Fifty historic houses were chosen as a sample group. Twenty-five of these remained in the ownership of the original families who built them; twelve were houses owned by the state (including local government authorities); seven houses owned by organizations and institutions, while six were in new private ownership. The report contained worrying details of the ongoing struggle faced by anyone responsible for the care of an historic property. It also emphasized the national cultural importance of these properties and how their preservation could deliver considerable economic benefits through employment and tourism. The study concluded with sixteen recommendations, the most important of which was that the government should introduce National Trust-type legislation specifically to care for properties of historic and architectural significance, not least because at this time Ireland was one of only four European countries without a National Trust-type body.

The taoiseach, who wrote a foreword to the document, spoke at a reception held in 20 Lower Dominick Street to mark its publication and used the occasion to state that he had requested the relevant minister, Martin Cullen, to undertake a full assessment of what was necessary and what the best approach might be. 'I believe that we must have an open and innovative approach,' said Mr Ahern, 'and that we must explore all the options.' Mr Cullen soon afterwards issued a statement in which he observed, 'The need for a trust to support and maintain major heritage properties is widely acknowledged. The process I am setting in train today will inform me of how we can best establish a trust and what role it should have.'

In 2004 his department commissioned a report from Indecon Consultants: *Examination of the Issue of Trust-type Organizations to manage Heritage Properties in Ireland*. This identified the substantial costs involved in operating an historic property, examined potential tax incentives and how endowment funds could help to sustain the long-term care of these properties. In March 2005 Dick Roche, by that date the Minister responsible for the Department of the Environment, submitted a memorandum to the Oireachtas on the subject of an Irish National Trust but there it seemed to languish. 'I need to express my grave concern,' wrote the Knight of Glin in the Society's summer *Newsletter*, 'over the apparent lack of momentum at government level, in progressing the establishment of a National Trust for Ireland.' However, working behind the scenes it had been agreed that the taoiseach, when speaking at the third Historic Houses of Ireland Conference at NUI Maynooth in September, would announce government approval for the establishment of an independent organization to be known as the Irish Heritage Trust.

This new body would have a mandate to acquire for public access significant heritage properties that the state did not want to acquire directly and where there was imminent risk to their heritage value through neglect, or where an appropriate use could not be secured through a new private owner. Following this announcement, a steering group was established under the chairmanship of Sir David Davies, to advise on the governance and successful launch of the new body. That group produced its report in February 2006, emphasizing that a viable trust could only survive in its first years provided there was adequate financial support from government. This was quantified as an annual contribution of €5m. by way of endowment, €6m. of tax credit and €0.5m. of operating expenses from the Department of Environment, Heritage and Local Government.

The Irish Heritage Trust, a limited company with charitable status and governed by an independent board, was officially established at Russborough on 3 July 2006 and opened its office in Dublin two months later. The board was composed primarily of a mix of men and women with strong business backgrounds to ensure the properties the trust was empowered to protect would be able to draw on committed financial experience. In September 2006 Kevin Baird, formerly Heritage Lottery Fund's manager in Northern Ireland, was appointed as the new organization's chief executive officer and it was thanks to his unstinting perseverance that in December 2007 the trust was able to announce Fota House, Arboretum and Gardens had been acquired. One of the Irish Georgian Society's most cherished dreams had at last been realized. However, the Celtic Tiger is retreating into the kennel and at the time of publishing this book state finances are in deep decline, thus threatening all the advances of the last few years.

HEADFORT

Headfort, Kells, Co. Meath. View of the Eating Parlour designed by Robert Adam, 1771–5.

Situated in a landscaped park on the edge of Kells, County Meath, Headfort exhibits a severely plain stone exterior unrelieved by ornament. The house was built during the 1760s for Sir Thomas Taylour (who became the first Earl of Bective in 1766) to the designs of Dublin engineer and architect George Semple; earlier proposals for the site by Richard Castle and Sir William Chambers had been rejected. Soon after the building's completion, the Scottish architect Robert Adam was invited to devise a neo-classical decorative scheme for Headfort's interior. Dating from 1771–5, these are now among the only surviving examples of his work in Ireland in the classical idiom. The grandest of the Adam rooms is the Eating Parlour, a magnificent double-height space with coved ceilings and highly decorative plasterwork (believed to be by James McCullagh) that looks on to Headfort's gardens. Robert Adam's original drawings for this and the house's other rooms are now part of the Paul Mellon Collection at the Yale Center for British Art.

Until the mid-twentieth century Headfort remained home to the Taylours, who were created Marquesses of Headfort in 1800. The house became a school in the 1940s and is now owned by the Headfort Trust, a registered charity. In 2004 Headfort was selected by the World Monuments Fund for inclusion in its 'List of 100 Most Endangered Sites' due to the significance of the Adam interiors and the urgent need for these to undergo a programme of conservation work. Since then the Headfort Trust has been working with the WMF and Ireland's Heritage Council on essential structural repairs to the building, as well as on a more thorough analysis of the Adam rooms than has ever before been undertaken on this architect's work. As a result, the original eighteenth-century decorative scheme was discovered beneath layers of over-painting; as devised by Adam, shades of verdigris were set against a white colouring to create a truly dramatic interior. Eileen Harris, author of *The Genius of Robert Adam*, described the discovery as 'unique, extremely interesting and very exciting'.

To mark its fiftieth anniversary in 2008, the Irish Georgian Society – which had already provided assistance to Headfort – committed itself to restoring the extraordinary decorative scheme of Headfort's Eating Parlour. Thanks to the generosity of its American membership, already by the early months of 2008 the Society had raised €100,000 for this cause, but at the time of writing a further €250,000 is needed if the Society's goal is to be realized. The London Chapter's Gala Ball in June 2008 was in aid of the Headfort Fund whilst the Two Desmonds Dinner in New York in October is to be for the same cause.

Robert Adam's original drawings, now part of the Paul Mellon Collection at the Yale Center for British Art.

Top left: Ceiling plan.

Bottom left: Section showing elevation of chimney wall.

Top right: Section showing elevation of one end.

Bottom right: Section of the elevation with door end.

THE YIGS

The Hon. Desmond Guinness leading a tour of Young Irish Georgians at Castletown, Co. Kildare, 2005.

As far back as 1993, by which date more than 65 per cent of its membership was aged fifty or over, the Irish Georgian Society was aware of a pressing need to attract a significantly younger demographic. While aspirations to this effect were regularly expressed, not much was done to realize them for another decade and it was only in 2003 that almost simultaneously, and spontaneously, three groups of Young Irish Georgians – hereafter known as YIGs – emerged in London, Dublin and even in Chicago. As Image magazine reported at the time, 'The only official obligation, so far, is that members have to be under the age of 40. Unofficially, you also need to possess an interest in heritage matters and a sense of humour; a pair of wellies wouldn't be bad either as YIGS events do seem to involve a fair amount of tramping across muddy terrain.' In fact, the inaugural outing of the Dublin YIGs required participants to don wet gear in order to descend into a cave at Oweynagat, County Roscommon.

Since then, the YIGs have organized their own annual programme of events with excursions to such varied sites of interest as the Browne-Clayton Monument in County Wexford and Lambay Island off the coast of County Dublin. In August 2006, *The Dubliner* magazine declared YIGs the capital's 'Best Culture Club', with some of its membership 'the posh-elegant sort, others the brainy-academic type, but there are also lots of people like you and me'. As if in memory of the early Irish Georgians' fondness for vin rosé, the YIGs are not immune to taking a drink or two; one especially well-attended evening involved a tour of Dublin's historic pubs (admittedly this was combined with an architectural quiz). And as befits both their age and the Irish Georgian Society's expanded brief to fight for the preservation of Ireland's entire architectural heritage, the YIGs have a healthy interest in contemporary culture, as was shown in November 2006 by their visit to the Donnelly Gallery in Dalkey, County Dublin (although somehow even here the occasion ended with the consumption of Bloody Marys). Likewise a visit to Abbeyleix, County Laois, in September 2007 concluded with time spent in the town's most famous bar, Morrisey's, 'which was of course purely to study the authentic Victorian interior'. Provided their enthusiasm (and livers) hold out, the YIGs ought to continue for many years to come and help to attract more young members to the Irish Georgian Society.

Above: Young Irish Georgian tour of North Great George's Street, led by Conor Lucey, talking to Senator David Norris (front left), 2007.

Left: London Chapter, Young IGS, at Milton Park, Northamptonshire, led by Michael Parsons, 2007.

Changes in Ireland over the past fifty years ~ what has been achieved, saved and learnt ~ what remains to be done ~ the Society in the next fifty years ~ work still to be done

CHAPTER

14

'The past is a foreign country,' wrote L.P. Hartley at the start of his 1953 novel, *The Go-Between*, before adding, 'they do things differently there.' This observation could scarcely be more apposite than when comparing the Ireland of half a century ago with the same country today. It is still Ireland and yet, to quote W.B. Yeats, 'All changed, changed utterly.' Whether a terrible beauty has been born can be the subject of debate on another occasion. Much of the country's eighteenth-century heritage still standing in 1958 has since disappeared, its very existence entirely unknown to younger generations. Buildings of architectural or historic significance like Santry Court and Frescati are gone without trace, only recalled in the names of housing estates or shopping centres. Were the Vanishing Country Houses of Ireland exhibition of 1988 to be repeated today, consternation would surely result and the question be asked: why was this allowed to happen? Equally, were a show mounted of how the towns and villages of Ireland looked fifty years ago, there would be consternation at how much had been lost. *Autre temps, autre moeurs*. What has gone has gone and cannot be brought back.

And after all, a great deal still remains. More, in fact, than might have been expected to survive when, for example, the battle over Mountjoy Square was at its height in the mid-1960s. Had certain planners been allowed to have their way, Dublin's Grand Canal would now carry juggernauts rather than boats. Similarly cars would be parked where Roscrea's Damer House stands, Castletown would be gone and its land covered in suburban homes, the Tailors' Hall obliterated and architectural gems like the Fiddown Chapel or

220

the Dromana Gateway fallen into complete ruin. The survival of these buildings, and very many others besides, can be directly attributed to the Irish Georgian Society. For fifty years it actively participated in the preservation of Ireland's built heritage, often in the face of overt hostility from law-makers (and a few law-breakers). When politicians and civil servants, who were in a position to save the nation's unique collection of historic buildings, failed to do their job, the Society stepped into the breach. When those in power would not, it assumed responsibility for the national heritage.

But there has been another, and just as important strand to the Irish Georgian Society's fifty-year mission. The history of the conservation movement in Ireland is also the history of the Society. For half a century it has worked to change attitudes and legislation so that the mistakes of the past will not be repeated in the future. Persistence has brought rewards and today there is far less likelihood that the demolition of an important house like Bowen's Court would be permitted to go ahead. The Planning and Development Act 2000 was enormously significant in enshrining fundamental principles of good conservation practice and heritage preservation into law. But while the Act deserved the welcome it received, this is not the end of the matter. Legislation is only as good as its implementation and the Planning and Development Act too frequently represents an aspiration rather than a realization of good conservation practice. In part this is because the Irish government has yet to provide adequate funding to guarantee that the country's built heritage is secure from neglect, both premeditated and unintentional.

In late March 2008, Minister for the Environment, Heritage and Local Government John Gormley announced that his department would be giving €6.915m. to the country's local authorities for their programme of architectural protection grants. While this represented a 17-per-cent increase on what had been provided in 2007, it was still only €1.2m. more than had been made available under this scheme in 2001. Allowing for inflation and the rising cost of restoration work, the improvement is negligible. (And, of course, there is no certainty from one year to the next that the money will be forthcoming.) Demand for the grants is enormous and the money provided from central government must be increased substantially if it is to make a real difference at local level. In addition, authorities – which in 2004 were issued by the Department with very thorough guidelines on architectural heritage protection – need to be pressed to apply the Planning and Development Act in full. That means not only appointing heritage and conservation officers but also checking to see that all protected structures in the part of the country under their administration are properly cared for and not subject to any unauthorized alterations. At the moment this does not happen and owners of historic buildings can often break the law with impunity, secure in the knowledge that they will not face prosecution.

Without doubt, much more is known of Ireland's architectural and decorative arts than was the case fifty years ago. In the intervening period, many books and articles have been written on various aspects of the country's heritage (quite a number of them by the Society's president, the Knight of Glin). Since the Society began publishing its *Bulletin* in 1958, there have been other journals exploring Ireland's cultural history in the centuries after the Celtic period; the Society's own publication, *Irish Architectural*

CHAPTER 14

and Decorative Studies, has recently celebrated its tenth anniversary. A number of universities have History of Art departments and Maynooth University is home to the Centre for the Study of Historic Irish Houses and Estates. Meanwhile, Professor Alistair Rowan is overseeing the research and publication of *Pevsner Architectural Guides, The Buildings of Ireland* series. In recent years, the Churchill House Press has published a number of fine works including a volume dedicated to Hugh Douglas Hamilton's *Cries of Dublin* (2003) and *Painting Ireland: Topographical Views from Glin Castle* (2006). Both were edited by William Laffan and proceeds from their sales went towards helping the Irish Georgian Society. Other volumes are in train.

These and other academic initiatives have been undertaken independently of the state, which has been far slower to develop a thorough database of information on Ireland's built heritage, thereby adding to the difficulties faced by local authorities in identifying which structures merit protection. For this information, they rely primarily on the National Inventory of Architectural Heritage (NIAH), a state initiative under the administration of the Department of the Environment, Heritage and Local Government established in 1990 to provide a central record, documenting and evaluating the post-1700 architectural heritage of Ireland. The Planning and Development Act 2000 requires each authority to compile and maintain a record of protected structures in its area; that record is a mechanism for the statutory protection of architectural heritage and forms part of each authority's development plan.

Given the limitations of money and expertise within each local authority, these bodies depend on the NIAH's survey of their respective counties in order to judge which structures under their care should be deemed worthy of protection. But the NIAH's work is still far from complete – information on a great swathe of the country from Mayo to Cork remains unavailable and surveys of only fourteen local authority areas have been published. Without this basic information, planning for preservation is problematic (in its defence, the NIAH has produced a comprehensive survey of historic gardens and designed landscapes based on the first-edition Ordnance Survey Maps of 1833–46 and comparing them with current aerial photographs. This information is available on the NIAH website, www.buildingsofireland.ie).

The argument in favour of preserving Ireland's 'Big Houses' – or at least those that remain – has been won. Hostility towards these buildings on the grounds that they were monuments to a foreign power has gone. If only because they are income-generating tourist attractions, Ireland's great country houses face a secure future. Since the mid-1990s, some of the finest among them have been superlatively restored, often as private homes, the purpose for which they were originally designed. Among the outstanding examples are Castletown Cox in County Kilkenny, Abbeyleix in County Laois, Lyons in County Kildare and Stackallan in County Meath. At the time of writing Ballyfin, County Laois, is being restored by one of the Society's principal benefactors, Fred Krehbiel, and in a fashion that represents the organization's highest ideals. In fact the whole project might be seen as a happy alternative to the kind of rescue operation once regularly undertaken by the Society and, as if to emphasize this parallel, the Ballyfin estate lies almost adjacent to Roundwood. Even were they to change hands and pass into new ownership, it is unlikely anything untoward would happen to houses such as those just mentioned. Their value is now universally appreciated.

Top: Anne Brady, Vermillion Design, with Prof. Roy Foster at the launch of *Painting Ireland: Topographical Views from Glin Castle*, Churchill Press, editor William Laffan (2006).

Middle (left to right): Rose Mary Craig, IGS board; Dr Edward McParland; Camilla McAleese, at the annual 'Historic Houses and Castles' conference, NUI Maynooth.

Bottom (left to right): Mary Bryan, Marion Cashman and Adrian Masterson at Lucan House, Co. Dublin.

But there are lots of other dwellings throughout Ireland, ranging from farmhouses to the homes of that now-vanished social class, the gentry, which, while not showcases of craftsmanship nor big enough to serve as tourist destinations, are still historically important and represent a part of the national heritage that must be preserved. Because they are not open to the public – and never likely to be so – the tax incentives available to owners in this area are not applicable and to pay for structural maintenance they must rely on whatever grants can be provided by their local authorities. To date very little has been done to ensure the preservation of this stratum of the national heritage.

It is, therefore, not surprising that in September 2007 a new organization, the Irish Historic Houses Association, held its first meeting at Castletown, attended by some sixty owners of private houses. Given the Irish state's pitiful history until recently in the field of architectural heritage preservation, quite rightly the members of IHHA remain anxious about their circumstances, and over how little has been and is being done to provide them with support. Like so many others, they are concerned over the ongoing lack of accurate statistics on heritage houses such as those in their ownership. While liaising with bodies like the Irish Heritage Trust and the relevant government departments, they also intend to set up a database of all heritage properties and collections currently remaining in private hands, providing significant information about this important resource for the benefit of the Irish nation.

Ballyfin, Co. Laois.

Owners of historic properties, whether large or small, rural or urban, must often face another difficulty. As Colm Murray, architecture officer with the Heritage Council, explains, although there are now statutory mechanisms in place (however ineffectually implemented on occasion) and grant schemes to help with the cost of a building's repair and conservation,

> Nevertheless, some owners find it onerous to fulfil their obligations under the new legislation to maintain the character of their buildings, especially if they currently have no economic use for them. The new ethos recognizes that heritage buildings are best preserved when their useful purpose is prolonged. The owners may be able to imagine the building paying its own way if they were able to develop it, accepting the constraints imposed by statutory protection. But they may be caught in the trap of not having the capital to make the development happen. Grants tend to be pitched at a level where objectives to conserve the fabric of the building are achieved, but these are not designed to encourage long-term conservation by securing new and appropriate uses, as this is seen as 'development', from which the owner might profit.

In other words, the state's policy of aid in this area is understandably governed by the principle of public benefit and it tends to hold back from facilitating or nurturing the value of any property that will remain in private ownership. 'Thus,' Colm Murray concludes, 'we continue to be faced with what might be called a tragedy of private property owners not being able to serve newly generated public interest in architecture, townscape or landscape.'

And what of the Irish Georgian Society in all this? Over the past few years, the organization has undergone further changes, many of them overseen by Desmond

CHAPTER 14

Mary Bryan, chief executive of the IGS, receiving a farewell gift from IGS president Desmond FitzGerald, Knight of Glin, 2005.

FitzGerald, the Knight of Glin, who has served as president since 1990. He deserves credit and thanks for so deftly handling the transformation of the Society from an organization known primarily as the saviour of individual buildings to one which today has a much wider brief covering all aspects of architectural heritage conservation. In the midst of attempting to secure the future of his own home, Glin Castle, and of writing extensively on all aspects of Irish architecture and fine art, the Knight has found time to be a diligent leader of the Society during the challenging years of Ireland's economic boom. Over the same period and through the same changes, the organization has been equally well served by its staff. In April 2005 Mary Bryan resigned as Executive Director, having been appointed to the board of An Bord Pleanála. As the Knight commented at the time, though the Society would sorely miss her, 'It is, I think, a tremendous compliment to her work at the IGS that this honour has come her way.'

She was succeeded by Nick Sheaff, a Cambridge graduate who, many years before, had been founding director of the Irish Architectural Archive. Following his departure at the end of 2007, the deputy director Donough Cahill became executive director. These changes were paralleled by the Society's own assessment of its future as 2008 and the fiftieth anniversary approached. Prior to her departure, Mary Bryan, with the backing of her board, commissioned consultancy firm Prospectus to conduct a strategic review of the Society and its work, and after extensive in-house work with committees and Chapters, to draft a document outlining what should be done over the years ahead. That strategy was agreed but only in part put into practice. It remains a valuable document when considering the Society's future and its role in Ireland over the next fifty years.

Certain elements of that future are clearer than others. For example, it is evident that the Irish Georgian Society will never again have to take on personal responsibility for the preservation of a house like Castletown, or buy buildings in places such as Mountjoy Square so as to halt their demolition by opportunistic property speculators. Thankfully those kind of high-profile battles are over. But as has been made apparent, this does not mean that Ireland's architectural heritage is safe from any further risk, or that help is not needed in its conservation. Perversely, one positive outcome from the struggles of the early years was that they gave the Society a high public profile; its purpose and modus operandi were universally understood, if not so unanimously admired. The decision in 1993 by the Irish Georgian Society to divest itself of the last such property, Doneraile Court, allowed the organization to concentrate its energy and funds on a wider range of activities. But in recent years, a case has been made for the Society once again to adopt a flagship project that would provide a focus and a showcase for its work. A number of buildings have been considered in Dublin: Henrietta Street; parts of the Liberties; and more recently South William Street. Today's high property values mean the purchase of a building is out of the question. However, there are many properties across Ireland owned by individuals, corporations, local authorities and the state in its various guises, which desperately need restoration.

Kilmacurragh, Co. Wicklow, dating from 1697, managed by the National Botanic Gardens since 1996.

Kilmacurragh, County Wicklow, for example, has a famous garden and arboretum open to the public and managed by the National Botanic Gardens since 1996. However, the house at the centre of the estate, which dates from 1697, has been allowed to fall into ruin. Here is an instance of an important historic building in desperate need of attention. The Irish Georgian Society, which already has an excellent track record in both fund-raising for Ireland's heritage and in active restoration, could oversee the work on Kilmacurragh and then return the building to the state, perhaps to provide a horticultural library and other facilities for visitors to the estate. Such a project would allow the Society once more to practise what for decades it has preached, would offer tangible evidence of the advantages of good conservation and would attract favourable publicity. The example of the Swiss Cottage's restoration during the 1980s offers a model for this kind of exercise.

There are many other Kilmacurraghs waiting for attention from some body like the Irish Georgian Society. In the meantime, since the 1990s the Society has provided advice for individual owners wishing to restore their properties. It has also organized the Traditional Building Skills exhibition, as well as compiling and updating the online Register of Practitioners. More could still be done in this area to make sure correct procedure and best practice are followed whenever an historic building is restored. Too many properties suffer needlessly (and sometimes irreparably) during supposed restoration because the right advice has not been sought. As one of the Society's current board members points out, 'Doing conservation work correctly does not necessarily cost more than doing it badly. For example, at present there is a fashion for repointing brick buildings, many of them actually defacing the bricks and storing up problems for the future.' In a number of recent instances, the Society has paid for a Conservation Assessment Report to be compiled on behalf of the owner of an historic property. The Society continues to disburse grants to projects throughout the country, as and when its own resources make this possible. Until recently, even a relatively small amount of money could make an enormous difference and provide significant moral support to someone embarking on conservation work, not least because there was no such help available from any other organization.

But circumstances have changed of late and while grants from the likes of local authorities and the Heritage Council could, and should be bigger, they have meant that help of this sort from the Irish Georgian Society is no longer so necessary. Furthermore, as the price of proper repair work has climbed, money given by the Society for this purpose has proportionately shrunk as a percentage of the total cost. Perhaps by focussing on specific areas such as Conservation Assessment Reports, the organization would make best use of its own funds and develop a reputation as the preferred source for guidance prior to any restoration being undertaken. In any case, education remains critically important if the cause of conservation is to be better understood and appreciated in Ireland. Hostility towards Georgian architecture may have gone, but in many cases it has been replaced by indifference, which can be equally dangerous. The Irish Georgian Society has long championed the merits of education but due to a scarcity of resources and more pressing demands on whatever time and money it has had, so far the organization cannot claim much success in this matter. The new chief executive is especially keen on establishing a proactive education campaign that would have a number of strands.

One of these would be aimed at primary-school children and intended to engage their attention by focussing on local architecture, in other words on historic buildings already familiar to them through which larger concepts of history, heritage and conservation could be explained. At secondary level, Ireland's long-established and wildly successful Young Scientists competition provides an example of how to engage teenagers in a subject that might otherwise not interest them. For the public at large, Donough Cahill would like to set up high-profile publicity campaigns designed to draw attention to Ireland's best buildings, again with the purpose of placing them into context. To this proposal might be added an annual award scheme intended to encourage and applaud all those involved in conservation and restoration projects, once again whether individuals, companies, local authorities or the state.

Basic education in appreciating the merits of the country's architectural heritage is not required for existing members of the Society (although as the ever-popular annual lecture series indicates, they are always interested in learning more, so perhaps this aspect could be expanded to form a cohesive architecture and decorative arts course associated with some third-level institution). However, members could be persuaded to become more actively involved in the organization's operations. The membership survey of 1994 asked respondents for their opinions, but these have rarely been canvassed since. The funds provided by members and supporters allow the Society to carry out its work, but some of this could be done by them also. Recent calls for volunteers to join work parties in the grounds of historic properties have met with an excellent response and indicate that there is still an interest in physical engagement with restoration work.

This passion for participation, once so central to the Society's work, should be reharnessed and focussed on properties that could benefit from such assistance.

IGS conservation volunteers at the Bath House, Lucan, Co. Dublin. *Left to right:* Christopher Moore, IGS board; Helen O'Neill; Doreen McNamara, IGS staff; Catherine O'Connor; Amy Reilly; Caoillfhionn Murphy; Louise Reilly; Serena Bennett; Nick Sheaff; John O'Connor.

Anyone who was involved in saving Castletown, Roundwood or the Damer House remembers that period with extraordinary clarity and fondness; for many of them, this was a life-defining experience. In the right circumstances, there is no reason why something similar should not happen again, especially if membership of the Society's younger wing, the YIGS, continues to grow. In fact, just as many members were first attracted to the Irish Georgian Society precisely because of a campaign like that to rescue Castletown, so something equivalent now could actually lead to many new young members joining the organization.

Members of the Irish Georgian Society are, of course, already convinced of the need for the national built heritage to be protected and preserved. The same is not necessarily true of a broader constituency in Ireland, which has yet to be persuaded that spending large sums of money on old buildings is worthwhile. Whatever approach is adopted to win consensus on this subject, the Society has to avoid the risk of speaking *de haut en bas*, an offence of which it has been accused, and with reason, in the past. The public must be engaged in dialogue and convinced of the benefits a sound conservation policy can bring to everyone. A stronger case can be made on the grounds of economics rather than aesthetics, which is why the advantages to tourism and employment should be stressed; after all, property developers and builders have been able to destroy parts of the national heritage by advancing precisely these arguments. Broadening the range of properties helped by the Society in whatever way, will help the education process.

If the average citizen associates conservation with preserving a handful of large old houses this will not help the cause; it needs to be understood that the nation's built heritage covers architecture of all periods, sizes and styles and belongs to everyone, not just the privileged few. Even the smallest villages are part of Ireland's heritage, and education would help to preserve them from the kind of rampant and inappropriate

CHAPTER 14

Back row (left to right): Brian Redmond, Christopher Moore, Cormac O'Carroll, Donough Cahill, David Griffin, John O'Brien, John Redmill, Aoife Kavanagh, John Holohan.

Front row (left to right): Rose Mary Craig; the Hon. Desmond Guinness; Mary Bryan; Desmond FitzGerald, Knight of Glin; Prof. Kevin B. Nowlan.

development that has blighted much of the country in recent years. The nuances of conservation must be better explained otherwise, for example, the belief that the development of a golf course has 'preserved' an old demesne will continue to prevail. *Irish Architectural and Decorative Studies*, while without doubt a journal of exceptional quality, is not intended for the general reader; a publication with broader appeal would help the Society's proselytizing role.

The Irish Georgian Society's role as a lobbying body has steadily grown since the early 1990s and it is now regularly consulted by the government on matters of conservation. Yet here once again more could be done, especially in the monitoring of activity at local authority level, making sure urban and county councils are doing the job legally required of them. Much of this work – in lobbying, in education, in monitoring planning applications and lodging objections when architectural heritage comes under threat – is vitally necessary but not very glamorous in character. Finding the funds for it can therefore be difficult. Fred Krehbiel, a long-standing member of the Society's Chicago Chapter and a member of the IGS Inc. board, says he believes the organization's American supporters – by far the greatest donors of money since the late 1960s – will not stop providing funds now just because Ireland is more prosperous than used to be the case. (Although he does concur that more of the Irish new-rich should subscribe to the Society and assist its work.) But, he emphasizes, 'We in the US aren't as interested in programmes to fight your planning issues – we think you should take care of those yourself. It's the restoration and salvaging of some of those wonderful buildings. In terms of financing, you in Ireland should provide the core and we become the add-on.'

As the evidence already presented demonstrates, while circumstances are undoubtedly much better, the future of Ireland's architectural heritage remains insecure. Hence the continuing need for the Irish Georgian Society and its work. Without question, Ireland today ought to be able to pay for the maintenance and restoration of its own architectural heritage, and for the cost of an organization that does so much to help in this task. The country is much richer than ever before and now has enough wealthy citizens in a position to assume the role previously filled by the Society's American supporters: that of providing necessary financial aid. It should no longer be necessary for a tiny voluntary organization to send members of its board across the Atlantic several times a year for this purpose. Likewise today, in place of disinterest and disregard, the Irish government consults the Irish Georgian Society and seeks its opinion on matters of architectural heritage.

However, it is fair to ask whether the state might not consider doing more. After half a century of campaigning and advocacy it seems reasonable to seek some legitimization of the Society's role. One way to provide this is for the organization to be given statutory body status with specific responsibility for the built heritage (thus complementing the role already enjoyed by An Taisce). In addition, should the government perhaps now offer to fund a body which has devoted itself for fifty years to preserving the country's architectural heritage? The Irish Georgian Society has never been officially thanked for all the work it has accomplished on behalf of the nation since 1958. The role it played in saving many important properties from destruction and for restoring significant parts of Ireland's architectural heritage has never been acknowledged. Nor has any formal appreciation been shown for the Society's encouragement of tourism over five decades and for its efforts to better the country's image overseas. One way to make up for this omission would be to provide the funds required to meet the organization's running costs.

In its fiftieth year, the Irish Georgian Society has had the opportunity to explore its past and to examine its possible future. The first is fixed, the second fluid. Over the course of five decades, the Society has evolved in response to an ever-changing Ireland. But in one thing it has remained consistent: the Irish Georgian Society has always fought for the preservation of Ireland's architectural heritage. As the organization's president, the Knight of Glin, writes:

> In 1958 the Irish Georgian Society expressed grave concern about the fate of Vernon Mount in Cork. In 2008 the Society once again found itself campaigning in defence of this exquisite 18th century villa. For as long as buildings of the calibre of Vernon Mount are at risk, the Irish Georgian Society will fight for their survival, and the sight of the banner bearing the words Save Vernon Mount outside the house's gates on the road to Cork airport keeps the fighting symbol of the Society alive. After fifty years of active engagement in the conservation of Ireland's rich architectural heritage for everyone, this fine organization deserves support from the Government and wealthy citizens alike so that its invaluable work can continue for another half-century.

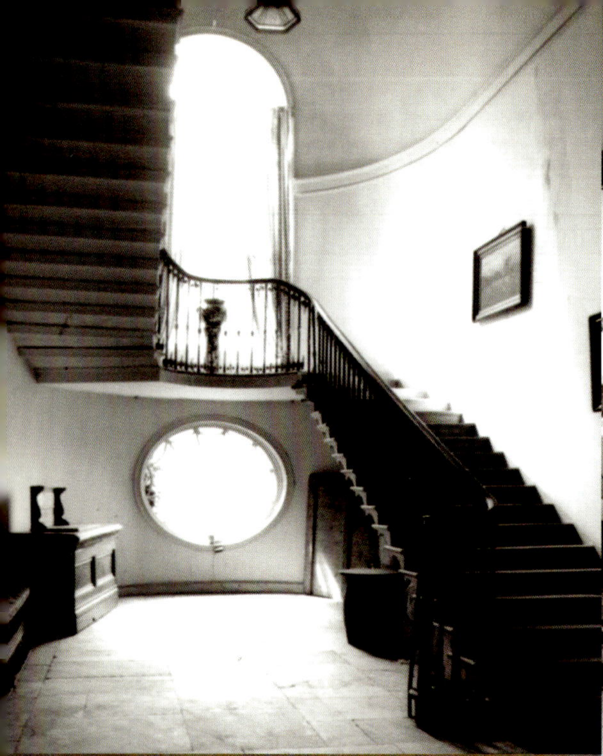
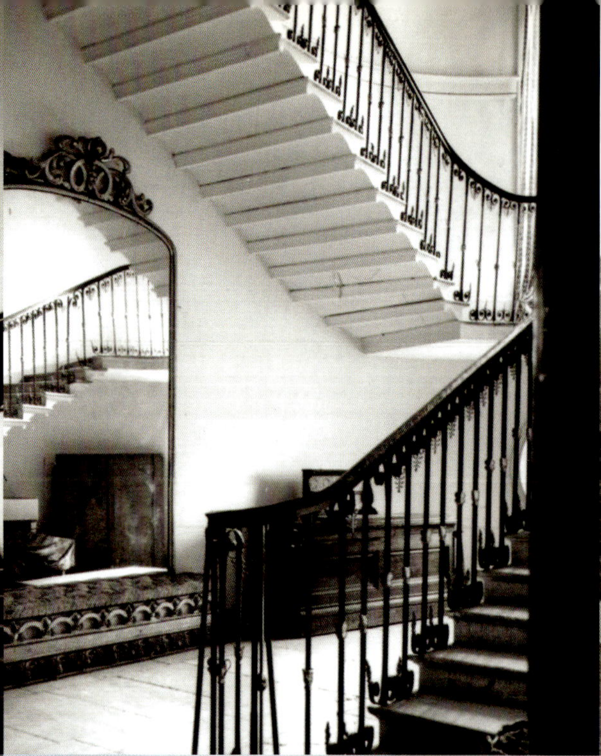
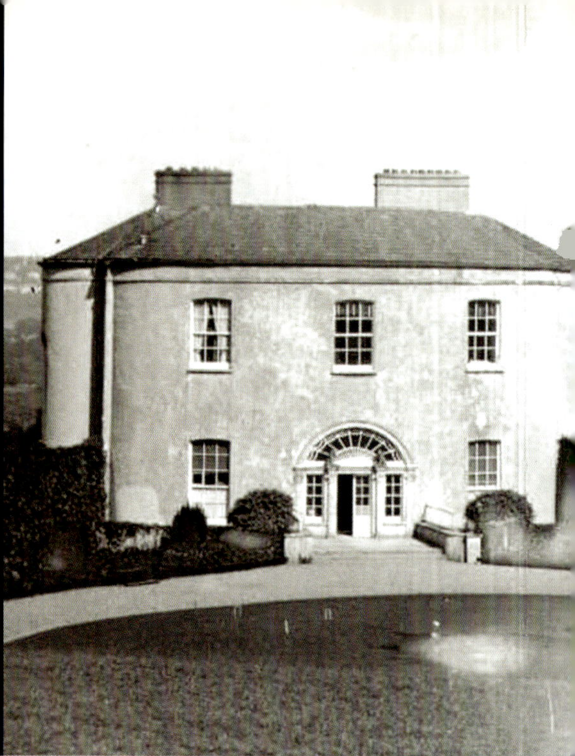
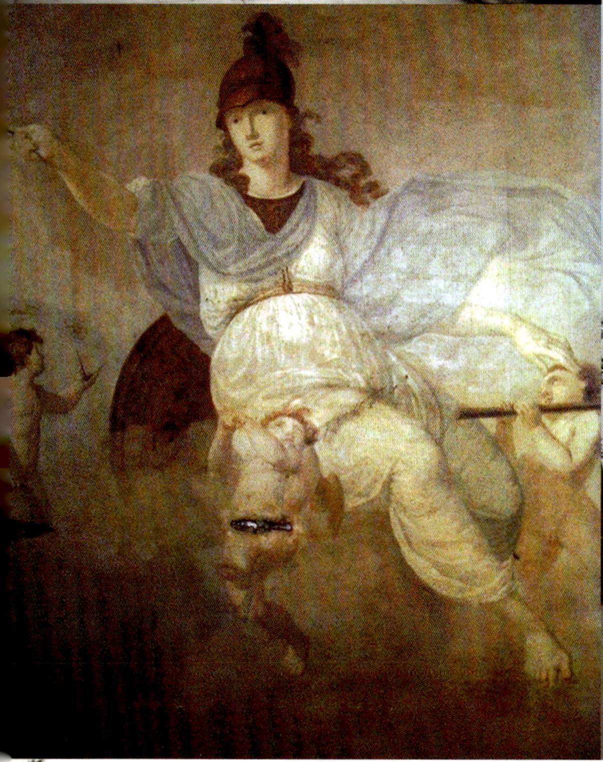
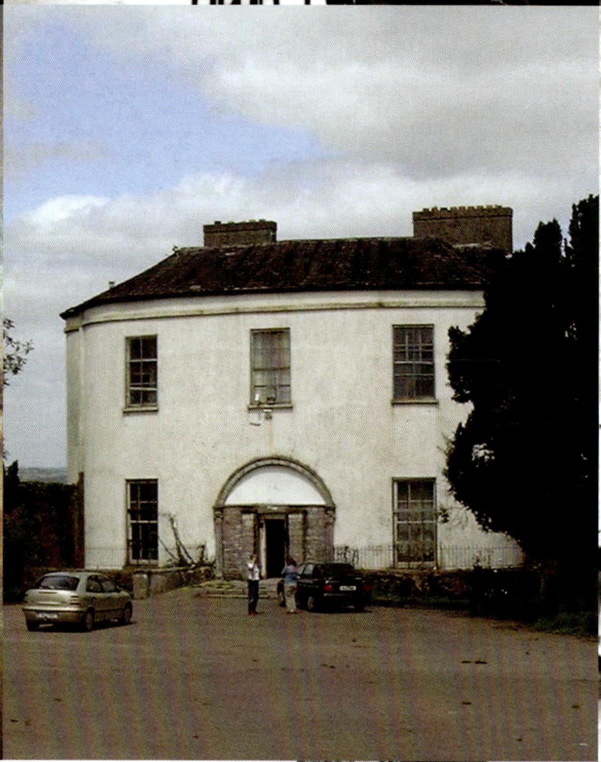
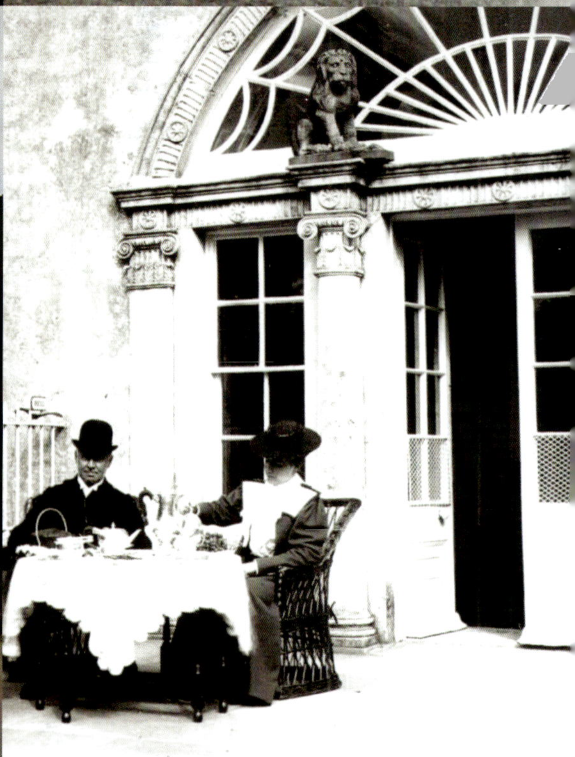
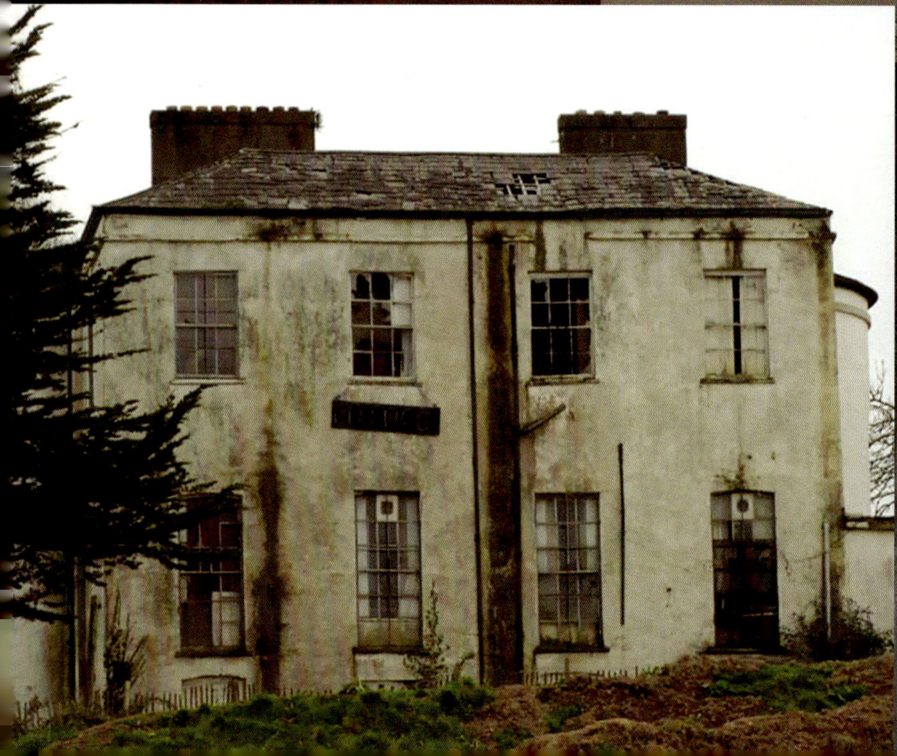
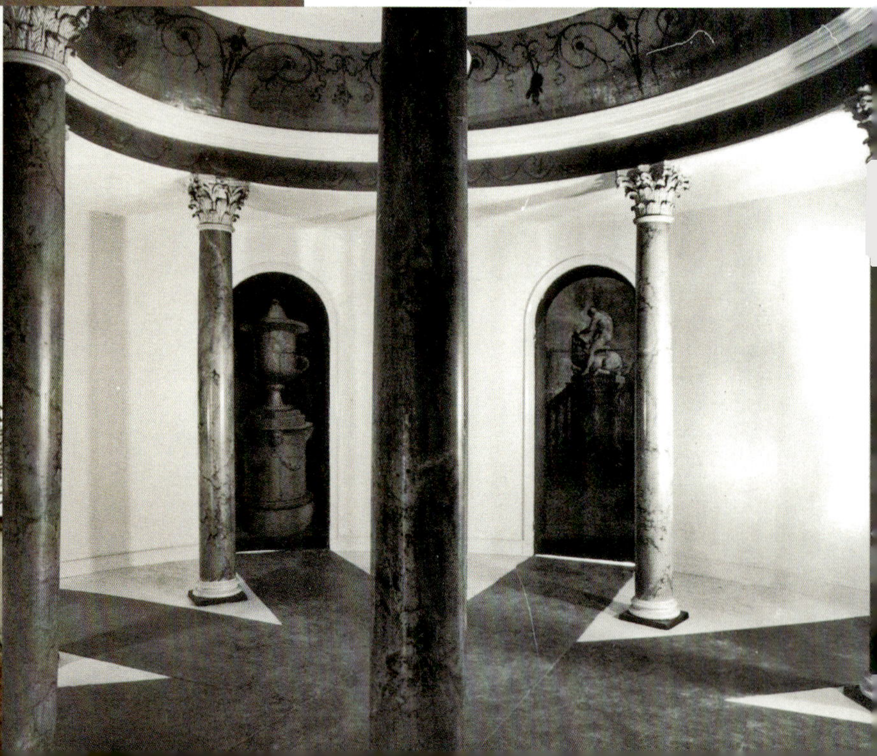

Vernon Mount, Co. Cork.

OPPOSITE:

Top left: Staircase hall with oval window.

Middle left: Ceiling detail: *Minerva Casting away the Spears of War*, Nathaniel Grogan, 1780s.

Bottom left: Rear view, 2007.

Top centre: Staircase.

Middle centre: Exterior view, 2007.

Top right: External front of Vernon Mount, with its drive and lawn, 1890.

Middle right: Entrance door, c.1910.

Bottom right: Vernon Mount, first-floor landing and marbled columns with neoclassical *trompe l'œil* painting by Nathanial Grogan.

ABOVE:

Vernon Mount, entrance front, c.1964.

SELECT BIBLIOGRAPHY

In addition to vast quantities of newspapers, magazines and other publications of the period covered (including all the Irish Georgian Society's *Bulletin*s, *Newsletter*s and miscellaneous printed material), the scrapbooks kept by Desmond Guinness from 1958–89 have been incredibly helpful. His disinclination to throw away anything means there is a vast archive at Leixlip Castle of documentation relating not just to the Irish Georgian Society but to the conservation and heritage movement in Ireland; enterprising students of architectural and social history could find enough primary source material here for several PhD theses.

There are, for example, boxes of papers relating solely to the Irish Georgian Society's proselytizing work in the United States that might one day form the basis for a fascinating book on Hiberno-American relations. For more recent years, the Society's own archives have proved extremely helpful, as have those kept by the Irish Architectural Archive and Dublin City Library and Archive (which holds complete sets of all national newspapers).

The following books have also been consulted:

Becker, Annette, John Olley and Wilfried Wang (eds.), *20th-Century Architecture, Ireland* (Munich: Prestel 1997).
Bence-Jones, Mark, *Burke's Guide to Country Houses, Vol. 1, Ireland* (London: Burke's Peerage 1978).
—, *Life in an Irish Country House* (London: Constable 1996).
—, *Twilight of the Ascendancy* (London: Constable 1987).
Bond, Valerie, *An Taisce, The First Fifty Years* (County Meath: The Hannon Press 2005).
Breffny, Brian de and Rosemary ffolliott, *The Houses of Ireland* (London: Thames & Hudson 1995).
Brown, Terence, *Ireland, A Social and Cultural History 1922–1985* (London: Fontana Press 1985).
Bryan, Mary et al., *The Georgian Squares of Dublin* (Dublin: Dublin City Council 2006).
Casey, Christine, *The Buildings of Ireland, Dublin* (London: Yale University Press 2005).
— and Alistair Rowan, *The Buildings of Ireland, North Leinster* (London: Penguin 1993).
Chambers, Anne, *At Arm's Length, Aristocrats in the Republic of Ireland* (Dublin: New Island 2004).
Coogan, Tim Pat, *Disillusioned Decades, Ireland 1966–1987* (Dublin: Gill & Macmillan 1987).
Craig, Maurice, *Classic Irish Houses of the Middle Size* (London: The Architectural Press 1976).
—, *Dublin 1660–1860* (London and Dublin 1952).
— and the Knight of Glin, *Ireland Observed* (Cork: Mercier Press 1970).
Dooley, Terence, *The Decline of the Big House in Ireland* (Dublin: Wolfhound Press 2001).

—, *The Land for the People, The Land Question in Independent Ireland* (Dublin: UCD Press 2004).

Fallon, Brian, *An Age of Innocence, Irish Culture 1930–1960* (Dublin: Gill & Macmillan 1999).

Georgian Society, The, *The Georgian Society Records of Eighteenth Century Domestic Architecture and Decoration in Dublin*, introduction by the Hon. Desmond Guinness (Shannon: Irish University Press 1969).

Guinness, the Hon. Desmond, *Georgian Dublin* (London: Batsford 1979).

— and William Ryan, *Irish Houses & Castles* (London: Thames & Hudson 1971).

— and Jacqueline O'Brien, *Great Irish Houses and Castles* (London: Weidenfeld and Nicolson 1992).

Harmon, Maurice (ed.), *The Dolmen Press: A Celebration* (Dublin: The Lilliput Press 2001).

Harrison, Wilmot, *Memorable Dublin Houses* (Dublin: S.R. Publishers Ltd 1971).

Kearns, Kevin Corrigan, *Georgian Dublin, Ireland's Imperilled Architectural Heritage* (London: David and Charles 1983).

Knight of Glin, David Griffin and Nicholas Robinson, *Vanishing Country Houses of Ireland* (Dublin: Irish Architectural Archive/Irish Georgian Society 1988).

— and James Peill, *Irish Furniture* (London: Yale University Press 2007).

Lucey, Conor, *The Stapleton Collection: Designs for the Irish Neoclassical Interior* (Dublin: Churchill House Press/National Library of Ireland 2007).

McDonald, Frank, *The Construction of Dublin* (County Cork: Gandon Editions 2000).

—, *The Destruction of Dublin* (Dublin: Gill & Macmillan 1985).

McParland, Edward, *Public Architecture in Ireland, 1680–1760* (New Haven: Yale University Press 2001).

Montgomery-Massingberd, Hugh and Christopher Simon Sykes, *Great Houses of Ireland* (London: Laurence King 1999).

Moraes, Henrietta, *Henrietta* (London: Hamish Hamilton 1994).

O'Dwyer, Frederick, *Lost Dublin* (Dublin: Gill & Macmillan 1981).

Pakenham, Valerie, *The Big House in Ireland* (London: Cassell & Co. 2000).

Pearson, Peter, *The Heart of Dublin* (Dublin: O'Brien Press 2000).

Peck, Carola, *Mariga and Her Friends* (Meath: The Hannon Press 1997).

Power, Con, *Under the Hammer, Property in Ireland – A History of the Irish Auctioneers & Valuers Institute, 1922–1997* (Dublin: Oak Tree Press 1997).

Somerville-Large, Peter, *The Irish Country House, A Social History* (London: Sinclair-Stevenson 1995).

Tobin, Fergal, *The Best of Decades, Ireland in the 1960s* (Dublin: Gill & Macmillan 1984).

APPENDIX I

Irish Georgian Society Board, Chapters, Committees and Staff

IGS BOARD MEMBERS
Galen Bales
Marion Cashman
Rose Mary Craig
Sir David Davies
Desmond FitzGerald, Knight of Glin (President)
David Griffin
Hon. Desmond Guinness (Founder)
Jerry Healy
Christopher Moore
Prof. Kevin B. Nowlan (Vice-president)
John Redmill (London Chapter Head)
Brian Redmond

IGS INC. BOARD MEMBERS
Carroll J. Cavanagh
Desmond FitzGerald, Knight of Glin
Paula Fogarty
Desmond Guinness
Judith P. Hadlock
William B. Hart
Pepper Jackson
Elizabeth King
Fred Krehbiel
Annette Lester
Gordon Mark
Michael J.C. Neagle
Sheila O'Malley Fuchs
Rose Marie O'Neill
Chantal O'Sullivan
Mary Agnes Quinn
Dr Stephen Seager
Tom Tormey
Brian D. White

IGS COMMITTEE
Victoria Browne
Marian Cashman
Rose Mary Craig
Desmond FitzGerald, Knight of Glin
Dr David Fleming
David Griffin
Hon. Desmond Guinness
John Holohan
Kevin Hurley
John Joyce
Chris Moore
Prof. Kevin B. Nowlan
John O'Brien

IRISH GEORGIAN SOCIETY IRISH CHAPTERS

Birr Chapter
Joe Breen
Gerry Bowne (Treasurer)
Caroline Cavanagh
Dereck Coulter
Sir David and Lady Davies (Chapter Patrons)
Theo Dillon
Clodagh Dowley (Secretary)
Roderick Downer
Clodagh Fay
Mary Graham
Margaret Hogan
John Joyce (Chairman)
Bill Larkin
Brendan Parsons, Earl of Rosse (Chapter Head)

Cork Chapter
Myrtle Allen (Chapter Patron)
Edmund Corrigan
Maura Currivan
Catherine FitzMaurice
Kevin Hurley (Chapter Head)
Geraldine O'Riordan
Alicia St Ledger

Limerick Chapter
Liam Clifford (Treasurer)
Desmond FitzGerald, Knight of Glin (Chapter Patron)
Dr David Fleming (Chapter Head)
Judith Hill
Liam Irwin
Clodagh Lynch (Secretary)
Mathew Shinnors

LONDON CHAPTER
Tim Bacon
Sir Adrian FitzGerald Bt, Knight of Kerry (Vice-chairman)
Miranda, Countess of Iveagh (Chapter Patron)
Robert Jennings (Events Secretary)
Andrew McKeon
Leela Meinetas
Rob van Mesdag (Hon. Treasurer)
Colm Owens
Michael Parsons
John Redmill (London Chapter Head)
Nabil Saidi
Nicholas Thompson
Hon. Mrs Janet Valentine
Jimmy Valentine (20 Ghost Club)

USA IGS INC CHAPTERS
Boston
Chicago
New York
Palm Beach
Washington, DC

IGS OFFICE STAFF
Donough Cahill (Director)
Cecily Cunningham (Office Administrator)
Emmeline Henderson (Conservation Research Manager and Assistant Director)
Aoife Kavanagh (Projects Administrator)
Doreen McNamara (Events and Membership Administrator)
Marjorie Malcolm (Accounts Administrator)

IGS INC. OFFICE
Maribeth Welsh (Executive Director)

APPENDIX II

Funding of Heritage and Conservation Activities

Apart from its advocacy of the cause of conservation and protection of Ireland's architectural heritage, the Society, since its inception, has played an active role in funding conservation and heritage activities. In the early years of its revived existence the Society's involvement took the form of a combination of physical effort on the part of its volunteers and direct financial assistance. In recent years these initiatives have evolved to the point where the Society now operates a scheme of systematic financial assistance. The scheme is funded from the Society's own resources and particularly through the generosity of its USA and UK supporters. Since the beginning of the millennium the Society had expended approximately €1.2m. in the provision of financial assistance for conservation and related projects.

The scheme embraces both research grants for scholarly work in the field of architectural heritage and related studies on the one hand, and direct financial assistance for conservation work on the other. The schedule below details properties, publications and other projects grant-aided since 2002. The publications and special projects listed give an indication of the wide span of scholarly and educational activity the Society has been able to facilitate by the provision of financial assistance. The schedule of building conservation grants extends from some of the grandest houses in the country to many more modest, but to the Society no less important, structures where the Society's grants have often been critical in securing the future of a heritage asset. In the period covered by the schedule, the largest grant was in the order of €65,000 and the smallest amounted to €500.

PROPERTIES

Annaghmore Schoolhouse, Collooney, Co. Sligo	General conservation
Annesbrook House, Duleek, Co. Meath	Repair of plasterwork and chimney piece
Ballinderry House, Carbury, Co. Kildare	Repair of front steps
Ballinderry, Kilconnell, Co. Galway	General conservation
Ballinlough Castle, Clonmellon, Co. Westmeath	Repair of cornices in various rooms
Barmeath Castle, Dunleer, Co. Louth	Repair of south tower roof
Bellevue Gate Lodges, Ballinasloe, Co. Galway	Window and door repairs
Bessmount Park, Co. Monaghan	General conservation
Birr Castle, Birr, Co. Offaly	Roof repairs
Borris House, Borris, Co. Carlow	Condition report for Borris Church
Brooklawn House, Blackrock, Co. Dublin	Window repairs
Browne Clayton Monument, Co. Wexford	General conservation
Carrowroe Park, Co. Roscommon	Stableyard roof
Castletown, Celbridge, Co. Kildare	Conservation work
Charles Lamb House, Carraroe, Co. Galway	Conservation report
Charleville Castle, Tullamore, Co. Offaly	Survey of stables
Church of St John the Evangelist, Dublin 4	General conservation
Clonalis, Castlerea, Co. Roscommon	General conservation
Cromwell Point Lightkeeper's house, Valentia Island, Co. Kerry	Window repairs
Crosshaven House, Crosshaven, Co. Cork	Staircase window repair
Curraghmore, Portlaw, Co. Waterford	Repairs of out-building roofs
The Deeps, Crossabeg, Co. Wexford	Window and roof repairs
20 Dominick Street Lower, Dublin 1	Repair of plasterwork
Dromoland Turret, Dromoland, Co. Clare	Repair of folly
Dun Laoi, 8 North Mall, Cork	Staircase gessowork
Ely House, 8 Ely Place, Dublin 2	Repair of Palladian window

APPENDIX II

Enniscoe House, Ballina, Co. Mayo	General conservation
25 Fitzwilliam Street Upper, Dublin 2	Repair of plasterwork
Geashill Old School, Geashill, Co. Offaly	Repairs to walls, ceilings and floors
Glebe House, Collooney, Co. Sligo	Window repairs
Hamwood, Dunboyne, Co. Meath	Conservation of sash windows
Harristown House, Brannockstown, Co. Kildare	Repair works to portico
Headfort House, Kells, Co. Meath	Rainwater pipes and conservation work in headmaster's study
Hilton Park, Clones, Co. Monaghan	Roof repairs
Holywell House, Ballyhaunis, Co. Mayo	Lime rendering
Kilballyowen Stables, Bruff, Co. Limerick	Roof repairs
Kilbixy Church, Ballynacarrgy, Co. Westmeath	Repair of pinnacles
Kildrought House, Celbridge, Co. Kildare	Roof repairs
Killadoon, Celbridge, Co. Kildare	Conservation of textiles
Killneer House, Drogheda, Co. Louth	Roof repairs
Kilrush House, Freshford, Co. Kilkenny	Roof repairs
Kilshannig, Rathcormac, Co. Cork	Repair of Lafrancini plasterwork and conservation of pavilions and cupolas
The Laundry, Mote Park, Roscommon	Repair of stone fireplace
Laurentinum House, Doneraile, Co. Cork	Window repairs and conservation of door
Ledwithstown House, Ballymahon, Co. Longford	Plasterwork repair and conservation of panelled rooms
Lime kiln, Nobber, Co. Meath	Conservation of lime kiln
Lurganboy Mill, Maudabawn, Cootehill, Co. Cavan	Conservation report
Magorban Parish Church, Fethard, Co. Tipperary	Window repairs and general repairs
Main Gate Lodge, Markree Estate, Collooney, Co. Sligo	Repair of parapets on telegraphic tower
Morgan's House, Askeaton, Co. Limerick	General conservation
Mount Ievers Court, Sixmilebridge, Co. Clare	Gutter repairs
54 Mountjoy Square, Dublin 1	Repair of portland stone flags and joinery in hall
Mucklagh Gateway, Charleville, Co. Offaly	Stabilization of towers
Mullane's Cottage, Kingtogher, Co. Sligo	Thatch repairs
38 North Great George's Street, Dublin 1	Roof repairs
50 North Great George's Street, Dublin 1	Repair of plasterwork in dining room
Obelisk at Killua Castle, Clonmellon, Co. Westmeath	General conservation
Old Kilbride Church & Howard Mausoleum, Arklow, Co. Wicklow	Conservation report
Oxmanton Hall, Birr, Co. Offaly	General conservation
4 Prior Park Terrace, Clonmel, Co. Tipperary	Window repairs
The Priory, Kells, Co. Meath	Roof repairs
Rossmore, Riverstown, Co. Sligo	Thatch repairs
Russborough, Co. Wicklow	Repair of parapet urns
Rustic temple lodge, Belline, Co. Kilkenny	Conservation report
St Fachtna's Cathedral, Rosscarbery, Co. Cork	Conservation of Gothic-style window
St James Church, Dingle, Co. Kerry	Window repairs
St John of God Trust, Lucena Clinic, Dunfillan House, Dublin 6	Ironwork repair on conservatory
St Mary's Church, Thomastown, Co. Kilkenny	Window repairs
St Paul's Church, Cahir, Co. Tipperary	Roof repairs
St Peters Church, Drogheda, Co. Louth	Repair works following an arson attack

Scregg House, Knockcroghery, Co. Roscommon	Roof repairs
Sooey Forge, Sooey, via Boyle, Co. Sligo	Thatch repairs
Springfield House, Daingean, Co. Offaly	Roof repairs
Summer Grove, Mountmellick, Co. Laois	Paint sample analysis
Tara Lodge, Rockingham, Co. Roscommon	Conservation of entrance gateway
The Thatch Public House, Cloneen, Co. Tipperary	Thatch repairs
Thomastown Church, Thomastown, Co. Kildare	Window repairs
Townley Hall, Drogheda, Co. Louth	Repairs to rotunda roof
The Warren, Culdaff, Inishowen, Co. Donegal	Window repairs
Whitewood House, Nobber, Co. Meath	Window repairs

PUBLICATIONS

Barnard, Toby, *The Grand Figure – Lives and Possessions in Ireland 1641–1770* (London: Yale University Press 2004).

Brantley, Robert S., *Life & Works of Henry Howard* (work in progress).

Butler, David, *The Quaker Meeting Houses of Ireland* (Dublin: Irish Friends Historical Committee 2004).

Casey, Christine, *The Buildings of Ireland – Dublin* (London: Yale University Press 2005).

Dean, J.A.K., *Gate Lodges of Ireland* (work in progress).

Gordon Bowe, Nicola, Photography for *Wilhelmina Geddes* (work in progress).

Harbison, Peter, *Beranger's Rambles in Ireland* (Dublin: Wordwell 2004).

Higgins, Jim, *Galway's Heritage in Stone; Catalogue of Late Medieval Sculpture down to the Late 17th Century in Galway City Museum*
(Galway: Galway City Council 2004).

Hill, Judith, Essay in *Limerick History and Society* (Dublin: Geography Publications, work in progress).

Laing, Alastair (ed.), *Clerics & Connoisseurs; An Irish Art Collection Through Three Centuries* (London: English Heritage & Azimutt Editions Ltd 2001).

Lawrence, David and Anne Wilson, *The Cathedral of Saint Fin Barre at Cork; William Burges in Ireland* (Dublin: Four Courts Press 2006).

Legg, Marie-Louise, *The Diary of Nicholas Peacock, 1740–51: The Worlds of a County Limerick Farmer And Agent* (Dublin: Four Courts Press 2005).

Malcolmson, Anthony, *Archbishop Charles Agar; Churchmanship and Politics in Ireland, 1760–1810* (Dublin: Four Courts Press 2002).

O'Kane, Finola, *Landscape Design in 18th Century Ireland* (Cork: Cork University Press, 2004).

Oram, Richard and Terence Reeves-Smyth (eds), *Avenues to the Past: Essays presented to Sir Charles Brett on his 75th year,* (Belfast: Ulster Architectural Heritage Society 2003).

Roden, Earl of, *Tollymore – The Story of an Irish Demesne* (Belfast: Ulster Architectural Heritage Society, 2005).

Rowe, David and Eithne Scallan, *Houses of Wexford* (Clare: Ballinakella Press, 2004).

APPENDIX II

SPECIAL PROJECTS

Centre for the Study of Historic Irish Houses & Estates, NUI Maynooth, Co. Kildare

Davison, David, photographic record of architectural artefacts in Peter Pearson's collection

Dublin Civic Trust, inventory of churches in Dublin city

Earth Horizon, TV series – *About the House*

Gothic Revival Conference to mark the retirement of Professor Michael McCarthy of UCD

Irish Architectural Archive, purchase of photos relating to the publication *Houses of Wexford* (Ballinakella Press, Co. Clare, 2004)

Irish Lime Producers, International Lime Forum

Limerick Civic Trust, conservation of three watercolour paintings and furniture

O'Boyle, Aidan, photographic report of Aldborough House, Portland Row, Dublin 1

Representative Church Body, Survey of Stained Glass in Church of Ireland Churches

RTÉ TV series – *About the House*

Video on *Skiddy's Almshouse,* Shandon, Co. Cork

INDEX

Note on the index

Buildings, houses and streets are in Dublin unless otherwise indicated.

Entries for Desmond and Mariga Guinness are limited, as one or other, or both, appear on almost every page. The same applies to the Knight of Glin.

Captions are not indexed.

Aall, Sally Sample 128, 159
Abbeyleix, Co. Laois 127, 222
Acton, Charles 78
Adam, Robert: work at Headfort 216
Adare Manor, Co. Limerick 153
Ahern, Bertie 212, 214
Aldborough House, Portland Row 184
Aldworth, Richard 160
Alfred Beit Foundation, the 81
Altamont, Lord 13, 146; *see also* Westport House
Amadeus Quartet 78
American interest and help 13, 19, 23, 27, 55, 59, 71, 98, 120 *sqq*
American Ireland Fund 129, 132
An Taisce *see* Taisce, An
Annamore, Co. Kerry 210
Antrim, Earl of 22
Apsley House, London 140
Áras an Uachtaráin 40
Ardgillan Castle, Co. Dublin 151
Arnold, Bruce 33
Arts Council, The 79, 86
Ash Hill Towers, Co. Limerick 182
Ashford, William 5
Ashlin and Coleman 148
Austin, John 124
Avery, Alice O'Neill 182
Avondale, Co. Wicklow 31

'Back Lane Parliament' 60
Baird, Kevin 215
Ballinlough Castle, Co. Westmeath 26
Ballyfin, Co. Laois 222
Ballynagall, Co. Westmeath 26, 148

Banotti, Mary 180
Bantry House, Co. Cork: open to visitors 62
Barmeath, Co. Laois 212
Barnard, Dr Toby 213
Barrow, Mr and Mrs Lennox 72
Barton, Anthony 186
Bassett, Arthur 124
Batchen, Mrs D. 13
Bayliss, Philippa 67, 78
Beit, Sir Alfred and Lady Clementine 7, 22, 35, 149
Belan, Co. Kildare 42, 105
Bell, Dorothy 152; *see also* Fota
Bellamont Forest, Co. Cavan 7
Bellinter, Co. Meath 148–9
Belvedere House, Co. Westmeath 26, 152
Belvedere Place, Dublin 128
Bence-Jones, Mark 3, 5, 7, 139; his *Burke's Guide to Irish Houses* reprinted 179
Benson, John 59
Benson & Forsyth 196
Berkeley, George, Bishop of Cloyne 80
Bernbaum, Glenn (Mortimer's Restaurant) 147
Bernelle, Agnes 32
Bert House, Co. Kildare 60, 111
Bessborough, Co. Kilkenny 37
Betjeman, John 22
Bhreathnach, Máire 22
Bianconi, Charles 107; *see also* O'Connell Bianconi-Watson
Biddesden, Wiltshire: visited 139
Birr Castle, Co. Offaly 7, 8, 134, 142
Birr Chapter: activity of 142
Blaney, Neil: signs death warrant for Lower Fitzwilliam Street 52
Blessington, Charles Gardiner, Earl of 102
Boland, Kevin: 'belted earl' onslaught in the Dáil 96
Bord Fáilte 37, 41, 66, 78, 109
Bord na Móna: threat to Upper Pembroke Street 86
Bord Pleanála 190, 191, 196
Borris House, Co. Carlow 25, 182
Bowen, Elizabeth 6
Bowen's Court, Co. Cork 6, 221

Boylan, Lena 66
Bradford, Sarah 74
Breteuil, Marquis de 186
Britcher, Rex 141
Brocket, Lord 7, 64, 152
Broderick, John 13
Brooking, Charles: map sold 164
Browne, Dr Jemmett, Bishop of Cork and Ross 40, 44
Browne's Hill, Carlow 26
Bruton, John 191
Bryan, Mary 178, 194, 222, 224
Bryson, Edwin 22
Bryson, John 33
Bulletin: superseded 25
Bunratty Castle, Co. Clare 182
Burnham, Bonnie 212
Busáras 48
Butler, Patrick and Aimée 71
Byrne, Kevin and Christa 93, 109, 110

Cabot, David 180
Caffrey, Dr Paul 184
Cafritz, Gwen 127
Cahill, Donough 205, 224, 226
Camerata String Orchestra 78
Canadian Chapter 126
Carew, John Edward 184
Carew, Lord of Castletown: 28; inherits it, sells it 81
Carlisle Building: replaced 48
Carton, Co. Kildare 7; tea parties at 10; obelisks 42, 152
Casey, Christine 148, 193; and Alistair Rowan 202
Casey, Michael: in Henrietta Street 100 *sqq*, 111
Cashel Palace, Co. Tipperary 64
Casino at Marino 86
Castle, Richard 6, 9, 24, 42, 105, 152
Castle Coole, Co. Fermanagh 33
Castle Forbes, Co. Longford 27
Castlelyons, Co. Cork: mausoleum 38
Castletown, Co. Kildare 8; balls in 82 *sqq*, 97, 162; history of 80 *sqq*; fire in East Wing 150

239

INDEX

Castletown Cox, Co. Kilkenny 222
Castletown Foundation, 81
Castletown Homes 75
Castleward, Co. Down 33
Cavanagh, Carroll 128
Cervin (Miskovitch), Nita-Carol 126
Chapters of the IGS 125 sqq, 189 sqq; see also Birr Chapter, Canadian Chapter, Limerick Chapter, London Chapter, New York
Charles, Sir William 86
Charleville Forest, Co. Offaly 38; sale of 5
Charleville, Co. Wicklow 26
Charlton, Hugh and Maureen 57
Château Latour 31
Château Mouton-Rothschild 31
Chieftains, the 111
Childers, Erskine 74–5
Cholmeley Cholmeley-Harrison, Major 74
Christie's: Kasbah Ball at 141
Church of Ireland Select Vestry and St Catherine's Church 57
Churchill, Tralee, Co. Kerry 133
Churchill House Press 222
Clements, Marcus 77
Clonalis, Co. Roscommon 134, 180–1
Clonfert Palace, Co. Galway 4
Clonmel Nationalist: article in 110
Cobbe, Tommy 27
Colegate, Isabel 179
collapse of buildings in Bolton Street and Fenian Street 47
Colley, George 89
Collins Barracks 194
Comerford, Máire 54
Comerford, Prof. Vincent 213
Connolly, Sybil 74, 128, 159
Conolly, Major Edward: dies (1956) 64
Conolly, John 133
Conolly, Katherine 64
Conolly, Thomas 81
Conolly, William (Speaker) 8, 80
Conolly Folly, the 34 sqq, 42, 64, 74
Coollattin, Co. Wicklow 153
Coolross, Roscrea, Co. Tipperary 210
Cooper, Patrice 127
Cork Civic Trust 195
Cork Corporation 195
Cornforth, John 16–17, 179
Corrigan, Edmund 143
Cosgrave Brothers: at George's Quay 197
Costin, John 37

Craig, Maurice 22, 24; his 1952 book 50; quotes 97–8, 110
Craig, Rose Mary 77, 78, 82, 117, 186
cricket matches 28 sqq; mixed impact of 97
Crom Castle, Co. Fermanagh 33
Crookshank, Prof. Anne 19, 23–4, 71, 125
Cross, Terry 186
cross-border encounters 33
Cuffesgrange, Co. Kilkenny 196
Cullen, Martin 214
Cunningham, George 115
Cunningham, Mary 125
Cunningham, Pauline 13
Curraghmore, Co. Waterford 7
Curran, Constantine P. 40, 44
Cusack-Smith, Lady Molly 83

Damer House, Roscrea, Co. Tipperary 112 sqq
Darley, Frederick 92
Dartrey, Co. Monaghan 5–6
Daunt, Miss Dorothea O'Neill 5
David, Mrs Patrick 54
Davies, Sir David 13, 127, 212–13
Davies, Donald and Mary 26
Davies, Mrs Kenneth 13
Davis, Meyer 127
Davison, Chris and Richard 93
Davitt, Maurice 166
Dawson, Richard, Earl of Dartrey 5
Dawson Mausoleum 6
de Burgh, Chris 93
de Lisle, Julian 65
de Valera, Síle 194
Deale, Edgar 22
Deane and Woodward 90
Debtors' Prison, Green Street 182
Deeps, The, Co. Wexford 117
Delahunty, Suzanne 124
Delany, Mrs, flower collages 164
Delville, Co. Dublin 5
destruction of 'Big Houses' 4 sqq
Dillon, Edward: move premises 90
Dillon, William 53
Dixon, Samuel, *Foreign and Domestick Birds* 164
Doherty, John 156
Dolmen Press *see* Miller, Liam
Dominick Street 9
Dominick Street, No. 20: grants to 190, 202 sqq
Doneraile Court, Co. Cork 117, 118, 148, 154–6; volunteers at 154; sale of 155; leased to Irish Georgian Society 155; *see also* St Legers
Doneraile, Lord 154; and Lady 154
Donleavy, J.P. 33
Dooley, John 40, 41, 43
Dooley, Dr Terence 4, 213
Douro, Marquis 140
Dr Steeven's Hospital: organ 71–2
Drenagh, Co. Derry 33
Dromana, Co. Waterford 37, 221
Dromore Castle, Co. Limerick 5
Dublin: decay and destruction in the 1950s and 60s 47 sqq
Dublin Castle: new building in Lower Castle Yard 85
Dublin Civic Group 88, 97–8, 178
Dublin Corporation 85, 90
Dublin Historical Record: quoted (1958) 46
Ducart, Davis 7; *see also* Kilshannig
Dugdale, Rose 149
Dunlavin courthouse, Co. Wicklow 106
Dunphy, Austin 56, 57, 95, 113, 159, 180
Dunsandle, Co. Galway 5
Dunsany, Lord 22
Dunsany Castle, Co. Meath 7, 8

Edinburgh, visit to 30
Edwards, Hilton 13
Electricity Supply Board, Lower Fitzwilliam Street 50; makes some amends on a crucial corner site 189; further amends 178
elitism, stigma of 96
Ely House, Ely Place 87
Emerson, Audrey 114, 117, 158, 177, 186
Emmet, Robert 89
Emo, Countess Marina 186
Emo, Villa 186
Emo Court, Co. Laois 104
Enniscoe House, Co. Mayo 182
Ensor, John 9
Europa Nostra 86; award to Desmond Guinness (2006) 211
Eustace Street 177
Ewart-Biggs, Christopher: assassinated 14

Fazel, Kami 82
Feeney, Laurence and Mary 158
Feeney family at Ledwithstown 157 sqq
Fenlon, Dr Jane 177, 193
Ferguson, Mrs F. 138

Ferrier Pollock & Co. 190
Festival of Music in Great Irish Houses 78 *sqq*
Fianna Fáil 193–4
Fiddown Chapel, Co. Kilkenny 37, 38, 117
Finian's Rainbow 123
FitzGerald, Adrian 138
Fitzgerald, Alison 184
FitzGerald, Desmond *see* Glin, Knight of
FitzGerald, Garret 88
FitzGerald, Lady Rosemary 13, 25
Fitzgibbon, Constantine 92
Fitzwilliam Street, Lower 50 *sqq*
Fitzwilliam Street, No. 29 189
Foley, James 114
Forenaughts, Co. Kildare 28
Foster, Roy 207
Foster, Sarah 184
Fota, Co. Cork 152, 216
Fownes Street: windows in 190
Frazier, Carol McGroarty 67
Frazier, Captain Samuel 67
French, R.B.D. 22
French Park, Co. Roscommon 5
Frick, Mrs R. Denison 59
Friends of the National Collections of Ireland 82
Furness, Co. Kildare 28, 41

Galilei, Alessandro 80, 118, 123
Gallagher, Matt and Patrick 90, 94, 103
Gannon, Cathal 112
Gardiner, Luke 103
Gardiner family 100, 102
Garner, William 67, 117, 158; a director of the Irish Georgian Foundation 163, 182; *see also* Bayliss, Phillipa
Garvan, Mabel Brady 128
Georgian Group (England): visit of 23
Georgian Society, the (old) 2, 10 *sqq*
Getty, J. Paul: gift to Castletown 184
Ghanian volunteers 117
Gibbs, Christopher 16
Gilfillan, Kathy 153
Gill Hall, Co. Down 39
Girouard, Mark 34
Givenchy: Le Clos Fiorentina 186
Glengall, Richard Butler, Earl of 159
Glin, Knight of 22, 23, 26, 123, 124, 129, 178, 181 thereafter *passim*; at Doneraile 157; a director of the Irish Georgian Foundation 163; and Glin Castle 222

Gloucester, Prince Richard, Duke of 138
golf: baleful effect of 207, 210
Goodman, Lord 138
Gore-Booth, Gabrielle 111
Gowrie, Lord ('Grey') 110
Graham, Richard 140
Granard, Lady: hospitality 27
Grand Canal 220; in Co. Kildare 104; threat to 85
Gray, Colonel Jim 156
Green, Elizabeth 138
Green Property Company 88, 89
Greevy, Bernadette 78
Guinness, Arthur 4
Guinness, Bryan (Lord Moyne) 4, 35, 139
Guinness, the Hon. Desmond 2, 7, 9 *sqq*, 13, 17; as an actor 77; as a director of the Irish Georgian Foundation (1982) 163; at Leixlip Castle 16 *sqq*; Europa Nostra award 211
Guinness, Mariga 2, 3, 7, 9, 27; at Leixlip Castle 16 *sqq*; between sandwich boards 54; death and burial 42, 172
Guinness, Marina 16
Guinness, the Hon. Murtogh and Anne 121, 123
Guinness, Patrick 17; at Furness 28; subscriber to Conolly Folly 37
Guinness, Penelope (Penny) 128
Guinness & Mahon, bankers 79
Guinness and Ryan: *Irish Houses and Castles* 147
Gwynn, Prof. Denis 7

Hall, Sheila: buys the Swiss Cottage 159
Hall, Terence 78
Hamwood, Co. Meath 134
handover of key properties 163
Hanly, Daithí 51, 54
Harris, Eileen 217
Harrison, Rex and Marcia 83
Hartley, L.P.: quoted 220
Hatfield, Hurd 127
hatred expressed by an anonymous correspondent 50; by a Lord Mayor 95; by others 113
Haughey, Charles 174; opens the Damer House 114
Hayes, Jarlath 14; and IGS *Bulletin* 14
Hazlewood, Co. Sligo 6
Headfort, Co. Meath 216 *sqq*; grant to 175
Heagney, John 95

Healy, Andrew 67
Healy, Robert 164
Hegarty, Paddy: at Doneraile 157
Henderson, Emmeline 211
Henrietta Street 24; No. 9 34; and Ian Lumley 210; Michael Casey in 100 *sqq*
Heritage Council 174
Heritage at Risk 148
Hickey, Des 84–5
high-rise threats 197
Hill, Derek 6
Hill, Judith 144
Historic Irish Tourist Houses Association 77
Hodges, Desmond 39
Holohan, John 187
Hope, Alan 187
Hornung, Mrs Robert ('Twinks') 126
Horst P. Horst 19
Howland, Dr Richard 120, 121, 127
Hughes, Frederick 128
Hume Street 87; battle of 88, 89
Humphries, Dermot 186
Hunt, John 182
Hurley, Kevin 143
Huston, Anjelica 180

Ileclash, Co. Cork 4
Irish Architectural Archive 148
Irish Architectural and Decorative Studies 25, 184, 221–2
Irish Country House, The 180
Irish Georgian Society: legal status 162 *sqq*; relations with Castletown 75 *sqq*
Irish Georgian Society Inc. (USA) 123
Irish Georgian Society Ltd: becomes Irish Georgian Foundation 163
Irish Heritage Trust: established (2006) 152, 215
Irish Historic Houses Association 223
Irish Houses and Landscapes exhibition 23
Irish Landmark Trust 177
Irish Times: quoted (1959) 46
India: tour in 31
Iveagh, Earl of 11
Iveagh, Miranda, Countess of 141

Johnston, Francis 38, 148, 190
Jolliffe, the Hon. John 30
Joyce, John 142
Jury, Peter 28

INDEX

Keane, Molly 25, 180; quoted 49
Kearns, Kevin Corrigan 49–50, 84, 93
Keating, Sean: as president of the Royal Hibernian Academy 51
Keelan, Edward 127
Kennan, Frank and Rosemary: bought Roundwood House 112
Kennedy, Edward 127
Kennedy, Jacqueline 67, 71–2
Kennedy, Susan 127
Kenure Park, Rush, Co. Dublin 147
Kilbixy Church, Co. Westmeath 26
Kilburn, William 132
Kilcascan Castle, Co. Cork 5
Kilcoleman, Co. Kerry 207
Kildare Place: houses, destruction of 8
Kilduff, Co. Offaly 182
Kilkenny Castle, Co. Kilkenny 195; deterioration of 206
Killua, Co. Westmeath 26, 211
Kilmacurragh, Co. Wicklow 225
Kilmainham, Royal Hospital (former): conference at (2002) 205
Kilshannig, Co. Cork 7, 212
Kindel Furniture Co. 132
King, A. 81
Kinsale courthouse, Co. Cork 34
Knickerbocker, Suzy (Aileen Mehle) 123
Knocklofty, Co. Tipperary: kidnap at 149; sold 150
Knockmaroon, Co. Dublin 4
Knocknamana, Co. Cork 59
Krehbiel, Fred 222, 228; and Kay 133
Kress Foundation 71 sqq, 156, 163

Lafranchini brothers 40, 44, 212
Laing, David 78
Land Commission, the 6–7, 154; sells Roundwood House to IGS 110
'Lapland Sauna': for fundraising 54
Lawford, Valentine 16
le Brocquy, Mrs Sybil 13
Leask, Mrs Ada 23, 25, 132, 182
Leask, Harold 23
LeClerc, Percy 12, 120
Ledwithstown, Co. Longford 116 sqq, 134, 141, 157 sqq
Lee, Ursula 13
Leigh, W. Colston 124
Leinster, Dukes of 42
Leinster Estates 90, 92, 94

Leixlip Castle, Co. Dublin 7–8, 16 sqq, 179
Lemass, Séan 48
Lenehan, John 41
Leningrad (formerly, and again, St Petersburg) 30
Lennox, Lady Emily (Duchess of Kildare) 81
Lennox, Lady Louisa (Conolly) 81
Leslie, Desmond 106
Leslie, Samantha 139
Leslie, Seymour 121
Leslie, Sir Shane 22
Liberties, the: used as set for bombed Berlin 84
Liberty Hall (the new) 48
Lichtenstein, Mrs Avery 142
Ligne, Prince de 186
Limerick: behind the times 193; Civic Trust and Pery Square 193
Limerick: Custom House, restoration of 194
Limerick, Earl of 141
Limerick, Patrick Pery, Earl of 144
Limerick Chapter 144, 193
Lisle House: staircase, recreated in 13 Henrietta Street 100
Lismore, Co. Cavan 5
London Chapter 135
Longfield, Co. Tipperary 107; sold in 1983 110
Lough Fea, Co. Monaghan 13
Lough Rynn, Co. Leitrim 33
Lucey, Conor 184
Lumley, Ian 100, 210
Luttrellstown, Co. Dublin 7, 153
Lyons, Co. Kildare 222, 224; gateway 26
Lysaght, Charles 32

Mac An Bheatha, Domnall 205
MacCabe, Gilbert and Helen 186
MacCarthy, Justine 83
McCarthy, Prof. Michael 183
McCrea, Patrick 95
McCullagh, James 190, 216
McDonald, Frank 97, 179
Mac Eoin, Uinseann 54
McGrath, Mary 158
McGrath, Raymond 40
McGroarty Frazier, Carol 93
Mac Liammóir, Micheál 13, 51, 67, 82
McNamara, Doreen 187
McNulty, Dottie 126

McNulty, Matt 151, 180
McParland, Edward 25; and the Irish Architectural Archive 147–8
McSweeney, Patricia 177
Mack, Robert 190
Magan, Dr Michael 22
Mahaffy, Revd John Pentland 10, 11
Mahon, Sir George 22
Malahide Castle, Co. Dublin 33; auction at 151
Maloney, Mr 125
Marino at Casino see Casino
Mark, Gordon St George 72, 133
Marshall, the Hon. Robert 202
Martyn, Edward 207
Mellon, Paul 128
membership survey (1994) 188
Merrion Square: No. 34 178; No. 42 178; No. 45 148; No. 63 148, 211; No. 74 168
Merry, Hugo and Elaine: at Kilshannig 212
Mespil House, Dublin 5
Mesta, Perle 127
Metternich, Graf and Grafeine Wolfe 186
Metternich family 31
Miller, Liam 14 sqq, 24
Milligan, Spike 98
Molesworth Street 89
Molloy, Brian 67, 106, 111, 114; at Doneraile 156; his life 118
Molloy, John and Anne 92–3
Moloney, Maurice 193
Monnington, Sir Thomas: as president of the Royal Academy 138
Montgomery, Arthur 156
Montgomery-Massingberd, Hugh 179, 181
Mooney, Francis 13
Moore, Christopher 83, 139
Morgan, Lady (Sydney Owenson) 89
Mosley, Lady Diana 4
Mount Charles, Earl of 139
Mount Ievers, Co. Clare 26
Mount Juliet, Co. Kilkenny: golf at 153
Mount Stewart, Co. Down 33
Mountjoy Estates Ltd 95
Mountjoy Square 89–92, 128; No. 50 92, 95, 123, 182; history of 102 sqq; rebuilding in the 1980s 95
Mountrath courthouse, Co. Laois 34
Moyne, Lord (Bryan Guinness) 4, 35, 139
Mulcahy, Jeremiah Hodges 23
Mulhuddart, Co. Dublin 94
Mumford, Lewis 98

Municipal Gallery, Charlemont House 120
Murphy, Frank 156
Murphy, Franklin B. 163
Murphy, Fr Patrick 106–7
Murray, Colm 223
Myers, Kevin 153

na gCopaleen, Myles 9
Nagle, Elmarie 184
Nairn, Ian 85
Nall-Cain, the Hon. David 42, 152
National Gallery: threat of new building 196
National Inventory of Architectural Heritage 222
National Monuments Advisory Council 35
National Trust (England): NI committee represented in HITHA 77
National Youth Federation: at 20 Dominick Street 190, 203
Neagle, Michael 125, 135
Neary, Christopher 53
Nelson's Pillar: bombed 85
New Hall, Co. Clare 26
New York: Chapter founded 134; headquarter of IGS Inc. 134
Newbridge, Co. Dublin 151
Newman House, St Stephen's Green 22
Nicholson, Felicity 138
Nicholson, Sara: box-model made by 138
North Great George's Street, No. 38 11, 100
Nowlan, Prof. Kevin B. 31, 54, 81, 88, 94, 95, 125, 157, 163, 172

O'Boyle, Aida 184
O'Carroll, Cormac 82, 118, 178; on Mariga 172
O'Connell, Daniel 107
O'Connell, John 152
O'Connell, Maurice 13
O'Connell Bianconi-Watson, Molly 107, 109
O'Connor, Brian and Consuelo 30, 31, 42
O'Connor, Cynthia 5, 25
O'Connor, Joan 193
O'Connor, Ulick 28, 31, 88, 124
O'Conor, Charles 181
O'Conor library, Clonalis, Co. Roscommon 134, 180–1
O'Conor Nash, Pyers 180
O'Faolain, Sean: quoted (1963) 46–7

office accommodation: pressure for 87
Office of Public Works ('Board of Works') 85, 87, 213; accepts Doneraile Court 157
O'Keefe, Cornelius 6
O'Kelly, Elizabeth 30
O'Kelly, Sean T. 40
Oldbridge House, Co. Louth 153
O'Leary, Declan 177, 178
O'Lochlainn, Dara 82
O'Mahony, Eoin ('the Pope') 22, 31, 120
O'Malley, Moira 126
O'Neill, Hugh 159
O'Neill, Rose Marie 133
O'Neill Flanagan, Don 37
opening of houses to the public 63 sqq, 76 sqq, 93; Castletown opened 66
O'Rourke, Miceal 186
O'Shea, Kevin 135
O'Toole, Fintan 190
Oxmantown Hall, Birr, Co. Offaly 142

Pakenham, Thomas 139, 153
Pakenham Hall, Co. Westmeath 26
Parke Bernet, New York 124
Pasteur, Louis: cures the coachman of rabies 160
Paxton, Betty 59
Pearce, Edward Lovett 5, 7, 80
Pearson, Peter 195
Pembroke, Earl of 51
Pembroke (Fitzwilliam) estate 193
Pery Square, Limerick 144, 193
Phipps, Sally 35
picnics 27
Plunket, the Hon. Mrs 7
Pole Bayer, Constance 126
Ponsonby family 37
Porter, Ronald 139
Potterton, Homan 139, 154
Power, Robin 190
Powerscourt, Co. Wicklow 190; fire at 150; sold to Slazengers 150
Powerscourt House, South William Street 190
Prager, Arthur 124, 128, 133
Praz, Mario: quoted 48–9
Prescott, Lydia 13
Provisional IRA 149
Provost's House, Trinity College 57, 120

'Quidnunc', Irish Times 12
Rainey and Sons 35

Ramelton, Co. Donegal 141
Randall, B. Carter 59
Redmill, John 139, 159
Reynolds, Albert 181
Reynolds, Michael 190
Rhatigan, Brian and Tony 75
Richardson, Sir Albert 52
Richter, Sviatoslav 78
Riley, Charles Reuben 81
Riley, Thomas 81
Riverstown House, Co. Cork 40–1, 44–5
Robertstown, Co. Kildare: Grand Canal Hotel, Festa at 106
Robinson, Nicholas 125, 148
Roche, Dick 215
Roche, Nessa: her book on windows 184
Roscrea, Damer House 112–13; still reviled in 1977 50
Roscrea Heritage Society 115
Rosse, Michael Parsons, late Earl of 22, 23
Rosse, Earl and Countess of 142
Rossmore, Lord 148
Roundwood House, Co. Laois 59, 110, 118
Rowan, Alistair 148, 222; and Christine Casey 148
Royal Institute of the Architects of Ireland 51
Royal Society of Antiquaries of Ireland 211
Ruane, Pat 143
Russborough, Co. Wicklow 7; burglary at (1974) 149
Russia: comparisons with 49; see also Leningrad
Ryan, Shirley 134
Ryan, William and Mary 147
Ryder, Thomas 81
Ryle, Joe 123

Sadleir, Thomas 24
St Ann's School and Hall 90
St Catherine's Church, Thomas Street 56 sqq, 58
St Legers, of Doneraile 160; Aldworth St Leger 160; death from rabies 160; Lieutenant Colonel Anthony and the St Leger races 160; Richard St John 154 sqq; withdrawal to USA 155
St Peter's Church, Drogheda, Co. Louth 40
St Petersburg (Leningrad) 30
St Stephen's Green 87
Salmon, Mrs Elizabeth H. 98
Salter, William 182

salvage: exhibition of 195; problems of 89
Scalamandré 132
scholarships 184
Scott, Michael 13, 94
Semple, George 216
Setanta Investments 89
Shanbally Castle, Co. Tipperary 7
Sheaff, Nicholas 224
Sheehan, David 184
Shortt, Desiree 10
Sigerson, Dr George 186
Simms, Dr George, Archbishop of Armagh 125
Skidmore Owings & Merrill 197
Skiddy's Almshouses, Cork 105–6
Skilling, Alice 134
Skinner, David 159
Sligo, Marquis of 24
Sligo, Methodist church in 280
Smith-Barry, of Fota 152; *see also* Fota, Co. Cork
Smithsonian Institution 121
Smyth, John 57
Spencer Dock 198
Stack, Jack 156
Stackallan, Co. Meath 222
Stacpoole, George 31
Standish Barry, Hilary 141
Stapleton, George 148
Stapleton, Michael 190
Stapleton Collection, The 184
Stephenson, Sam 47, 57, 86
Stephenson Gibney and Associates 57
Strokestown Park, Co. Roscommon 112
Stuart de Decies, Lord 37
Sully, Château de 186
Summerson, Sir John 52
Sweeney Todd: regularly presented 77
Swiss Cottage, the, Cahir, Co. Tipperary 159
Synnott, David 19, 27, 32, 92, 100, 111, 117
Synnott, Pierce 28, 41

Tailors' Hall, the 53 *sqq*, 59, 60 *sqq*, 127
Taisce, An 10, 60, 147–8; initiatives in 1976 147
Talbot, the Hon. Rose: offers Malahide Castle to the state 151; offer turned down 151; auction of contents 151
Talbot de Malahide, Lord 22, 64; death of 151
tax concessions 148

Taylour family, Earl of Bective and Marquises of Headfort 216
Templeton, Whitney 134
Tennessean, The 121
Terra, Daniel 59
Thompson, Nicholas 141
Timmons, Eugene 96
Tone, Theobald Wolfe 60
Tormey, John L. and Nell 126; buys Roundwood House 111
Tormey, Tom 126
Tortelier Trio 78
tourism: role of 62 *sqq*
tours: in Ireland, to Iran, Mexico, Cuba, South Africa, India (twice), Holland 186
Tracey, Noel 180, 212
traditional building skills: encouragement of 195
Trissino, Castello di 186
Troubles in the North 138
Tudenham, Co. Westmeath 5, 26
Tulira Castle, Co. Galway 207
Tully, James 86
Tullynally (Pakenham Hall), Co. Westmeath 26
Turvey, Donabate 147
20 Ghost Club 140
Tynte family, at Dunlavin 106
Tyrone House, Co. Galway 133–4; paintings from 72
Ulster Museum, Belfast 23
Underwood, Ivor 92

Valentine, Lady Freda 140
Vanishing Country Houses of Ireland exhibition 179
Verity, Peter 78, 111
Vernon Mount, Co. Cork 26; a desperate case 141, 231
Vicary, David 30
Villiers-Stuart family 37
Viney, Michael 180
Vogue, American 19
volunteer helpers/workers 38 *sqq*, 67, 114, 117 *sqq*

Walker, Barbara 125
Warhol, Andy 128, 186
Warren, Phelps 124
Washington World 121
Watkins, Kathleen 125
Watts, the Revd Robert 37

Welsh, Maribeth 134
wealth tax 146
West, Robert 190, 202
Westmeath County Council: buys Belvedere 152
Weston, Galen 72; and Hilary, target of a kidnap attempt 149
Westport House, Co. Mayo 24; grants to 175; opened 64; under threat 146
Wexford: Theatre Royal 34; Market House and Assembly Rooms 104
Whitaker, T.K. 48
White, Brian 134
White, Dr James 23
White House (Washington DC) 125
Whitney, Marylou Vanderbilt 83
Williams, Eric and June 156
Williams, Jeremy 27, 111
Willson, Major James 65
Windham, Lady Edith 5
Wingfield family 150, 190
Winter, Kathleen 126, 127
Wood, Richard 22–3, 26, 181; his collection of pictures 152
Wood Quay 47 *sqq*
Woodstown, Co. Waterford 73–4
Wyatt, James 24
Wylie, John 22
Wynne, Michael 25
Wyse Jackson, Dean Robert 22, 64

Yeats, W.B. 23, 220
York: visit to 27

Zalles, Rose Saul 42, 82, 127
Zlotover, Dr Melisande 28

Design of a Cieling for the Eating Parlor. for The Right

Scale